Introductory Business Statistics

Introductory Business Statistics

VOLUME 2

Melissa Cardon

Kruger Brentt
Publishers
2025

Kruger Brentt Publishers UK. LTD.
Company Number 9728962

Regd. Office: 68 St Margarets Road, Edgware, Middlesex HA8 9UU

ISBN: 978-1-78715-452-0 (Vol. 2)

For information on all our publications visit our website at http://krugerbrentt.com/

PREFACE

"Introductory Business Statistics" embarks on a foundational exploration of statistical concepts and techniques essential for making informed business decisions, offering readers a comprehensive understanding of the principles, methods, and applications of statistics in the business context. This book serves as an indispensable resource for students, professionals, and entrepreneurs seeking to harness the power of statistics to analyze data, draw meaningful insights, and drive evidence-based decision-making in business settings.

Statistics plays a crucial role in modern business operations by providing tools and techniques for summarizing, analyzing, and interpreting data to inform strategic planning, resource allocation, marketing strategies, financial forecasting, and performance evaluation. In an era characterized by big data and data-driven decision-making, statistical literacy has become an indispensable skill for success in various fields, including finance, marketing, operations management, and entrepreneurship.

The primary objective of this book is to provide readers with a comprehensive introduction to business statistics, covering key topics such as data collection and presentation, descriptive statistics, probability theory, statistical inference, hypothesis testing, regression analysis, and correlation analysis. Each chapter offers insights, theoretical frameworks, practical examples, and hands-on exercises to help readers develop proficiency in applying statistical methods to real-world business problems.

Contributions from leading experts in the field explore various aspects of business statistics, including techniques for analyzing categorical and numerical data, conducting market research, forecasting sales and demand, evaluating investment opportunities, and assessing risk and uncertainty. Special emphasis is placed on the use of statistical software packages such as Excel, SPSS, and R for data analysis and visualization, enabling readers to gain practical experience in using statistical tools to solve business problems.

As businesses increasingly rely on data-driven insights to gain a competitive edge in today's fast-paced and dynamic marketplaces, the ability to understand and interpret statistical information has become a critical skill for success. By mastering the principles and techniques of business statistics, individuals can make better-informed decisions, identify opportunities for growth and innovation, and drive sustainable business performance in an ever-changing world.

We extend our sincere gratitude to the contributors whose expertise and dedication have enriched this book. It is our hope that "Introductory Business Statistics" will serve as a valuable resource and reference guide for readers seeking to enhance their statistical literacy and analytical skills, empowering them to thrive in the modern business landscape.

Melissa Cardon

CONTENTS

VOLUME-2

8 Chapter

CONFIDENCE INTERVALS: TYPE OF ESTIMATE

Figure 8.1 Have you ever wondered what the average number of M&Ms in a bag at the grocery store is? You can use confidence intervals to answer this question. (credit: comedy_nose/flickr)

INTRODUCTION: AN OVERVIEW

Assume you are attempting to ascertain the average rent of a two-bedroom apartment in your locality. Consider examining the classified section of the newspaper, recording multiple rental listings, and calculating their average. You would have acquired a point estimate of the actual mean. To ascertain the shooting % in basketball, count the successful shots made and divide it by the total attempts. In this instance, you would have derived a point estimate for the true fraction of the parameter p in the binomial probability density function. We utilize sample data to extrapolate conclusions regarding an unidentified population. This segment of statistics is referred to as inferential statistics. The sample data assist in estimating a population parameter. We acknowledge that the point estimate is unlikely to represent the precise value of the population parameter, but is rather an approximation. Subsequent to calculating point estimates, we formulate interval estimates known as confidence intervals. Statistics offer more than a mere average or point estimate; they provide an estimate to which a probability of accuracy, referred to as a confidence level, can be assigned. We draw conclusions with a specified degree of probability. This chapter will teach you how to generate and interpret confidence intervals. You will also acquire knowledge of a novel distribution, the Student's-t, and its application with these intervals. It is essential to remember that the confidence interval constitutes a random variable throughout the chapter. The population parameter is constant. If you worked in the marketing department of an entertainment company, you might be interested in the mean number of songs a consumer downloads a month from iTunes. If so, you could conduct a survey and calculate the sample mean, $\overline{x}$, and the sample standard deviation, s. You would use $\overline{x}$ to estimate the population mean and s to estimate the population standard deviation. The sample mean, $\overline{x}$, is the point estimate for the population mean, μ. The sample standard deviation, s, is the point estimate for the population standard deviation, σ.

$\overline{x}$ and s are each called a statistic.

A confidence interval is another type of estimate but, instead of being just one number, it is an interval of numbers. The interval of numbers is a range of values calculated from a given set of sample data. The confidence interval is likely to include the unknown population parameter.

Suppose, for the iTunes example, we do not know the population mean μ, but we do know that the population standard deviation is $\sigma = 1$ and our sample size is 100. Then, by the central limit theorem, the standard deviation of the sampling distribution of the sample means is

$$\frac{\sigma}{\sqrt{n}} = \frac{1}{\sqrt{100}} = 0.1 .$$

The **Empirical Rule**, which applies to the normal distribution, says that in approximately 95% of the samples, the sample mean, $\overline{x}$, will be within two standard deviations of the population mean μ. For our iTunes example, two standard deviations is (2)(0.1) = 0.2. The sample mean $\overline{x}$ is likely to be within 0.2 units of μ.

Because $\overline{x}$ is within 0.2 units of μ, which is unknown, then μ is likely to be within 0.2 units of $\overline{x}$ with 95% probability. The population mean μ is contained in an interval whose lower number is calculated by taking the sample mean and subtracting two standard deviations (2)(0.1) and whose upper number is calculated by taking the sample mean and adding two standard deviations. In other words, μ is between $\bar{x}$ - 0.2 $\bar{x}$ - 0.2 and $\bar{x}$ + 0.2 $\bar{x}$ + 0.2 in 95% of all the samples.

For the iTunes example, suppose that a sample produced a sample mean x¯ = 2x¯ = 2. Then with 95% probability the unknown population mean μ is between

$$\bar{x} - 0.2 = 2 - 0.2 = 1.8 \text{ and } \bar{x} + 0.2 = 2 + 0.2 = 2.2$$

We say that we are 95% confident that the unknown population mean number of songs downloaded from iTunes per month is between 1.8 and 2.2. The 95% confidence interval is (1.8, 2.2). Please note that we talked in terms of 95% confidence using the empirical rule. The empirical rule for two standard deviations is only approximately 95% of the probability under the normal distribution. To be precise, two standard deviations under a normal distribution is actually 95.44% of the probability. To calculate the exact 95% confidence level we would use 1.96 standard deviations.

The 95% confidence interval implies two possibilities. Either the interval (1.8, 2.2) contains the true mean μ, or our sample produced an $\bar{x}$ that is not within 0.2 units of the true mean μ. The first possibility happens for 95% of well-chosen samples. It is important to remember that the second possibility happens for 5% of samples, even though correct procedures are followed.

Remember that a confidence interval is created for an unknown population parameter like the population mean, μ.

For the confidence interval for a mean the formula would be:

$$\mu = \bar{X} \pm Z_{\alpha} \frac{\sigma}{\sqrt{n}}$$

Or written another way as:

$$\bar{X} - Z_{\alpha} \frac{\sigma}{\sqrt{n}} \leq \mu \leq \bar{X} + Z_{\alpha} \frac{\sigma}{\sqrt{n}}$$

Where $\bar{X}$ is the sample mean. Z_{α} is determined by the level of confidence desired by the analyst, and $\frac{\sigma}{\sqrt{n}}$ is the standard deviation of the sampling distribution for means given to us by the Central Limit Theorem.

8.1 A CONFIDENCE INTERVAL FOR A POPULATION STANDARD

Deviation, Known or Large Sample Size

A confidence interval for a population mean, when the population standard deviation is known based on the conclusion of the Central Limit Theorem that the sampling distribution of the sample means follow an approximately normal distribution.

Calculating the Confidence Interval

Consider the standardizing formula for the sampling distribution developed in the discussion of the Central Limit Theorem:

$$Z_1 = \frac{\bar{X} - \mu_{\bar{X}}}{\sigma_{\bar{X}}} = \frac{\bar{X} - \mu}{\frac{\sigma}{\sqrt{n}}}$$

Notice that μ is substituted for $\mu_{\bar{x}}$ because we know that the expected value of $\mu_{\bar{x}}$ is μ from the Central Limit theorem and $\sigma_{\bar{x}}$ is replaced with $\frac{\sigma}{\sqrt{n}}$, also from the Central Limit Theorem.

In this formula we know $\bar{X}$, $\sigma_{\bar{x}}$ and n, the sample size. (In actuality we do not know the population standard deviation, but we do have a point estimate for it, s, from the sample we took. More on this later.) What we do not know is μ or Z_1. We can solve for either one of these in terms of the other. Solving for μ in terms of Z_1 gives:

$$\mu = \bar{X} \pm Z_1 \frac{\sigma}{\sqrt{n}}$$

Remembering that the Central Limit Theorem tells us that the distribution of the $\bar{X}$'s, the sampling distribution for means, is normal, and that the normal distribution is symmetrical, we can rearrange terms thus:

$$\bar{X} - Z_\alpha\left(\frac{\sigma}{\sqrt{n}}\right) \leq \mu \leq \bar{X} + Z_\alpha\left(\frac{\sigma}{\sqrt{n}}\right)$$

This is the formula for a confidence interval for the mean of a population.

Notice that Z_α has been substituted for Z_1 in this equation. This is where a choice must be made by the statistician. The analyst must decide the level of confidence they wish to impose on the confidence interval. α is the probability that the interval will not contain the true population mean. The confidence level is defined as (1-α). Z_α is the number of standard deviations X---X‾ lies from the mean with a certain probability. If we chose $Z_\alpha = 1.96$ we are asking for the 95% confidence interval because we are setting the probability that the true mean lies within the range at 0.95. If we set Z_α at 1.64 we are asking for the 90% confidence interval because we have set the probability at 0.90. These numbers can be verified by consulting the Standard Normal table. Divide either 0.95 or 0.90 in half and find that probability inside the body of the table. Then read on the top and left margins the number of standard deviations it takes to get this level of probability.

In reality, we can set whatever level of confidence we desire simply by changing the Z_α value in the formula. It is the analyst's choice. Common convention in

Economics and most social sciences sets confidence intervals at either 90, 95, or 99 percent levels. Levels less than 90% are considered of little value. The level of confidence of a particular interval estimate is called by (1-α).

A good way to see the development of a confidence interval is to graphically depict the solution to a problem requesting a confidence interval. This is presented in Figure 8.2 for the example in the introduction concerning the number of downloads from iTunes. That case was for a 95% confidence interval, but other levels of confidence could have just as easily been chosen depending on the need of the analyst. However, the level of confidence MUST be pre-set and not subject to revision as a result of the calculations.

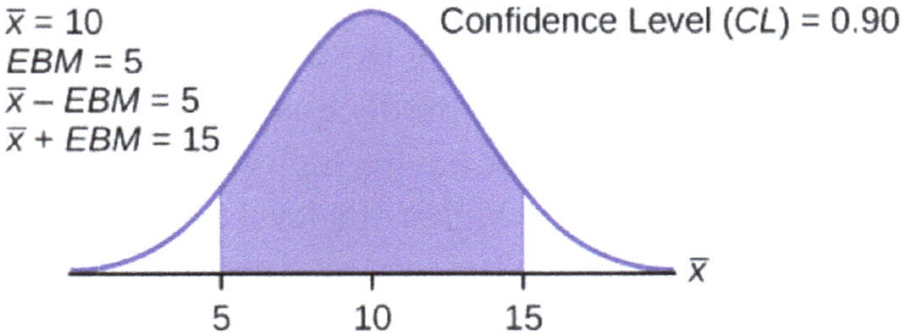

Figure 8.2

For this example, let's say we know that the actual population mean number of iTunes downloads is 2.1. The true population mean falls within the range of the 95% confidence interval. There is absolutely nothing to guarantee that this will happen. Further, if the true mean falls outside of the interval we will never know it. We must always remember that we will never ever know the true mean. Statistics simply allows us, with a given level of probability (confidence), to say that the true mean is within the range calculated. This is what was called in the introduction, the "level of ignorance admitted".

Changing the Confidence Level or Sample Size

Here again is the formula for a confidence interval for an unknown population mean assuming we know the population standard deviation:

$$\bar{X} - Z_\alpha\left(\frac{\sigma}{\sqrt{n}}\right) \leq \mu \leq \bar{X} + Z_\alpha\left(\frac{\sigma}{\sqrt{n}}\right)$$

It is clear that the confidence interval is driven by two things, the chosen level of confidence, Z_α, and the standard deviation of the sampling distribution. The Standard deviation of the sampling distribution is further affected by two things, the standard deviation of the population and the sample size we chose for our data. Here we wish to examine the effects of each of the choices we have made on the calculated confidence interval, the confidence level and the sample size.

For a moment we should ask just what we desire in a confidence interval. Our goal was to estimate the population mean from a sample. We have forsaken the hope that we will ever find the true population mean, and population standard deviation for that matter, for any case except where we have an extremely small population and the cost of gathering the data of interest is very small. In all other cases we must rely on samples. With the Central Limit Theorem we have the tools to provide a meaningful confidence interval with a given level of confidence, meaning a known probability of being wrong. By meaningful confidence interval we mean one that is useful. Imagine that you are asked for a confidence interval for the ages of your classmates. You have taken a sample and find a mean of 19.8 years. You wish to be very confident so you report an interval between 9.8 years and 29.8 years. This interval would certainly contain the true population mean and have a very high confidence level. However, it hardly qualifies as meaningful. The very best confidence interval is narrow while having high confidence. There is a natural tension between these two goals. The higher the level of confidence the wider the confidence interval as the case of the students' ages above. We can see this tension in the equation for the confidence interval.

$$\mu = \bar{x} \pm Z_{\alpha}\left(\frac{\sigma}{\sqrt{n}}\right)$$

The confidence interval will increase in width as Z_{α} increases, Z_{α} increases as the level of confidence increases. There is a tradeoff between the level of confidence and the width of the interval. Now let's look at the formula again and we see that the sample size also plays an important role in the width of the confidence interval. The sample size, nn, shows up in the denominator of the standard deviation of the sampling distribution. As the sample size increases, the standard deviation of the sampling distribution decreases and thus the width of the confidence interval, while holding constant the level of confidence. This relationship was demonstrated in [link]. Again we see the importance of having large samples for our analysis although we then face a second constraint, the cost of gathering data.

Calculating the Confidence Interval: An Alternative Approach

Another way to approach confidence intervals is through the use of something called the Error Bound. The Error Bound gets its name from the recognition that it provides the boundary of the interval derived from the standard error of the sampling distribution. In the equations above it is seen that the interval is simply the estimated mean, sample mean, plus or minus something. That something is the Error Bound and is driven by the probability we desire to maintain in our estimate, $Z\alpha Z\alpha$, times the standard deviation of the sampling distribution. The Error Bound for a mean is given the name, Error Bound Mean, or *EBM*.

To construct a confidence interval for a single unknown population mean μ, where the population standard deviation is known, we need $\bar{x}$ as an estimate for μ and we need the margin of error. Here, the margin of error (*EBM*) is called the error bound for a population mean (abbreviated EBM). The sample mean $\bar{x}$ is the **point estimate** of the unknown population mean μ.

The confidence interval estimate will have the form:

(point estimate - error bound, point estimate + error bound) or, in symbols $(\bar{x} - EBM, \bar{x} + EBM)$ The mathematical formula for this confidence interval is:

$$\bar{X} - Z_{\alpha}\left(\frac{\sigma}{\sqrt{n}}\right) \leq \mu \leq \bar{X} + Z_{\alpha}\left(\frac{\sigma}{\sqrt{n}}\right)$$

The margin of error (*EBM*) depends on the confidence level (abbreviated ***CL***). The confidence level is often considered the probability that the calculated confidence interval estimate will contain the true population parameter. However, it is more accurate to state that the confidence level is the percent of confidence intervals that contain the true population parameter when repeated samples are taken. Most often, it is the choice of the person constructing the confidence interval to choose a confidence level of 90% or higher because that person wants to be reasonably certain of his or her conclusions.

There is another probability called alpha (α). α is related to the confidence level, *CL*. α is the probability that the interval does not contain the unknown population parameter. Mathematically, $1 - \alpha = CL$.

A confidence interval for a population mean with a known standard deviation is based on the fact that the sampling distribution of the sample means follow an approximately normal distribution. Suppose that our sample has a mean of x−*x*- = 10, and we have constructed the 90% confidence interval (5, 15) where *EBM* = 5.

To get a 90% confidence interval, we must include the central 90% of the probability of the normal distribution. If we include the central 90%, we leave out a total of α = 10% in both tails, or 5% in each tail, of the normal distribution.

This is a normal distribution curve. The peak of the curve coincides with the point 10 on the horizontal axis. The points 5 and 15 are labeled on the axis. Vertical lines are drawn from these points to the curve, and the region between the lines is shaded. The shaded region has area equal to 0.90.

Figure 8.3

To capture the central 90%, we must go out 1.645 standard deviations on either side of the calculated sample mean. The value 1.645 is the *z*-score from a standard normal probability distribution that puts an area of 0.90 in the center, an area of 0.05 in the far left tail, and an area of 0.05 in the far right tail.

It is important that the standard deviation used must be appropriate for the parameter we are estimating, so in this section we need to use the standard deviation that applies to the sampling distribution for means which we studied with the Central Limit Theorem and is, $\frac{\sigma}{\sqrt{n}}$.

Calculating the Confidence Interval Using EBM

To construct a confidence interval estimate for an unknown population mean, we need data from a random sample. The steps to construct and interpret the confidence interval are:

- Calculate the sample mean $\bar{x}$ from the sample data. Remember, in this section we know the population standard deviation σ.
- Find the z-score from the standard normal table that corresponds to the confidence level desired.
- Calculate the error bound *EBM*.
- Construct the confidence interval.
- Write a sentence that interprets the estimate in the context of the situation in the problem.

We will first examine each step in more detail, and then illustrate the process with some examples.

Finding the *z*-score for the Stated Confidence Level

When we know the population standard deviation σ, we use a standard normal distribution to calculate the error bound EBM and construct the confidence interval. We need to find the value of *z* that puts an area equal to the confidence level (in decimal form) in the middle of the standard normal distribution $Z \sim N(0, 1)$.

The confidence level, *CL*, is the area in the middle of the standard normal distribution. $CL = 1 - \alpha$, so α is the area that is split equally between the two tails. Each of the tails contains an area equal to $\frac{\alpha}{2}$.

The z-score that has an area to the right of $\frac{\alpha}{2}$ is denoted by $Z_{\frac{\alpha}{2}}$.

For example, when $CL = 0.95$, $\alpha = 0.05$ and $\frac{\alpha}{2} = 0.025$; we write $Z_{\frac{\alpha}{2}} = Z_{0.025}$.

The area to the right of $Z_{0.025}$ is 0.025 and the area to the left of $Z_{0.025}$ is 1 – 0.025 = 0.975.

$Z_{\frac{\alpha}{2}} = Z_{0.025} = 1.96$, using a standard normal probability table. We will see later that we can use a different probability table, the Student's t-distribution, for finding the number of standard deviations of commonly used levels of confidence.

Calculating the Error Bound (*EBM*)

The error bound formula for an unknown population mean μ when the population standard deviation σ is known is

- $EBM = \left(Z_{\frac{\alpha}{2}}\right)\left(\frac{\sigma}{\sqrt{n}}\right)$

Constructing the Confidence Interval

- The confidence interval estimate has the format $(\bar{x} - EBM, \bar{x} + EBM)$ or the formula: $\bar{X} - Z_{\alpha}\left(\frac{\sigma}{\sqrt{n}}\right) \leq \mu \leq \bar{X} + Z_{\alpha}\left(\frac{\sigma}{\sqrt{n}}\right)$

The graph gives a picture of the entire situation.

$CL + \frac{\alpha}{2} + \frac{\alpha}{2} = CL + \alpha = 1.$

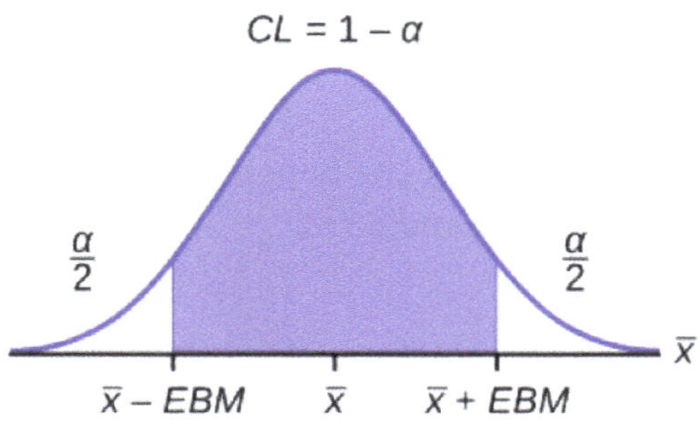

Figure 8.4

EXAMPLE 8.1

Suppose we are interested in the mean scores on an exam. A random sample of 36 scores is taken and gives a sample mean (sample mean score) of 68 ($\bar{X} = 68$). In this example we have the unusual knowledge that the population standard deviation is 3 points. Do not count on knowing the population parameters outside of textbook examples. Find a confidence interval estimate for the population mean exam score (the mean score on all exams).

Find a 90% confidence interval for the true (population) mean of statistics exam scores.

Solution 8.1

- The solution is shown step-by-step.

To find the confidence interval, you need the sample mean, $\bar{x}$, and the *EBM*.

$\bar{x} = 68$

$EBM = \left(Z_{\frac{\alpha}{2}}\right)\left(\frac{\sigma}{\sqrt{n}}\right)$

$\sigma = 3$; $n = 36$; The confidence level is 90% ($CL = 0.90$)

$CL = 0.90$ so $\alpha = 1 - CL = 1 - 0.90 = 0.10$

$\frac{\alpha}{2} = 0.05 \; Z_{\frac{\alpha}{2}} = z_{0.05}$

The area to the right of $Z_{0.05}$ is 0.05 and the area to the left of $Z_{0.05}$ is $1 - 0.05 = 0.95$.

This can be found using a computer, or using a probability table for the standard normal distribution. Because the common levels of confidence in the social sciences are 90%, 95% and 99% it will not be long until you become familiar with the numbers , 1.645, 1.96, and 2.56

$$EBM = (1.645)\left(\frac{3}{\sqrt{36}}\right) = 0.8225$$

$\bar{x}$ - EBM = 68 - 0.8225 = 67.1775

$\bar{x}$ + EBM = 68 + 0.8225 = 68.8225

The 90% confidence interval is (67.1775, 68.8225).

Interpretation

We estimate with 90% confidence that the true population mean exam score for all statistics students is between 67.18 and 68.82.

EXAMPLE 8.2

Suppose we change the original problem in Example 8.1 by using a 95% confidence level. Find a 95% confidence interval for the true (population) mean statistics exam score.

Solution 8.2

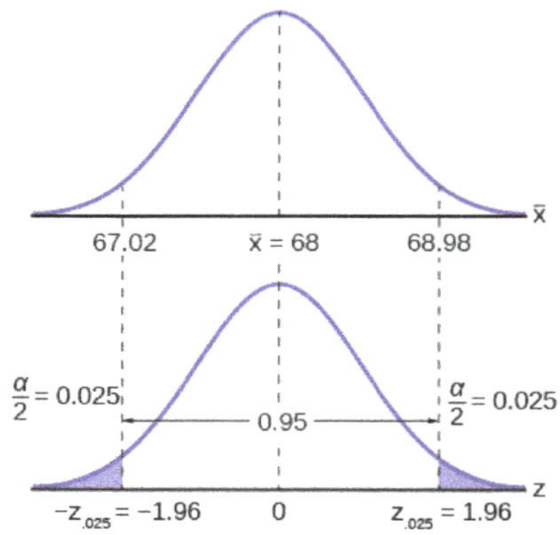

Figure 8.5

$$\mu = \bar{x} \pm Z_{\alpha}\left(\frac{\sigma}{\sqrt{n}}\right)$$

$$\mu = 68 \pm 1.96\left(\frac{3}{\sqrt{36}}\right)$$

$$67.02 \leq \mu \leq 68.98$$

$\sigma = 3$; $n = 36$; The confidence level is 95% ($CL = 0.95$).

$CL = 0.95$ so $\alpha = 1 - CL = 1 - 0.95 = 0.05$

$$Z_{\frac{\alpha}{2}} = Z_{0.025} = 1.96$$

Notice that the *EBM* is larger for a 95% confidence level in the original problem.

Comparing the results

The 90% confidence interval is (67.18, 68.82). The 95% confidence interval is (67.02, 68.98). The 95% confidence interval is wider. If you look at the graphs, because the area 0.95 is larger than the area 0.90, it makes sense that the 95% confidence interval is wider. To be more confident that the confidence interval actually does contain the true value of the population mean for all statistics exam scores, the confidence interval necessarily needs to be wider. This demonstrates a very important principle of confidence intervals. There is a trade off between the level of confidence and the width of the interval. Our desire is to have a narrow confidence interval, huge wide intervals provide little information that is useful. But we would also like to have a high level of confidence in our interval. This demonstrates that we cannot have both.

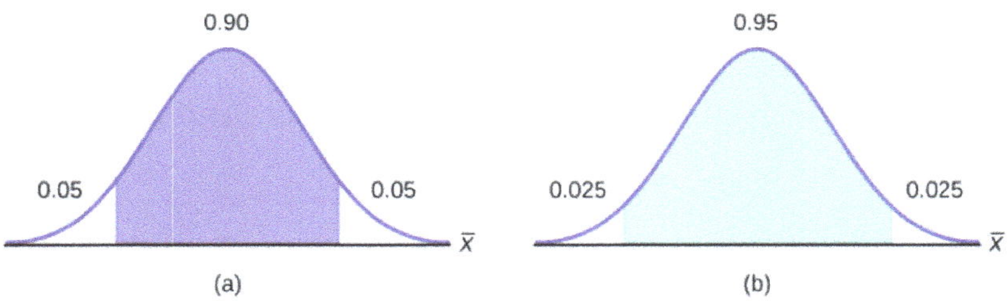

Figure 8.6

Summary: Effect of Changing the Confidence Level

- Increasing the confidence level makes the confidence interval wider.
- Decreasing the confidence level makes the confidence interval narrower.

And again here is the formula for a confidence interval for an unknown mean assuming we have the population standard deviation:

$$\bar{X} - Z_{\alpha}\left(\frac{\sigma}{\sqrt{n}}\right) \le \mu \le \bar{X} + Z_{\alpha}\left(\frac{\sigma}{\sqrt{n}}\right)$$

The standard deviation of the sampling distribution was provided by the Central Limit Theorem as $\frac{\sigma}{\sqrt{n}}$. While we infrequently get to choose the sample size it plays an important role in the confidence interval. Because the sample size is in the denominator of the equation, as *n* increases it causes the standard deviation of the sampling distribution to idecrease and thus the width of the confidence interval to decrease. We have met this before as we reviewed the effects of sample size on the Central Limit Theorem. There we saw that as *n* increases the sampling distribution narrows until in the limit it collapses on the true population mean.

EXAMPLE 8.3

Suppose we change the original problem in Example 8.1 to see what happens to the confidence interval if the sample size is changed.

Leave everything the same except the sample size. Use the original 90% confidence level. What happens to the confidence interval if we increase the sample size and use $n = 100$ instead of $n = 36$? What happens if we decrease the sample size to $n = 25$ instead of $n = 36$?

Solution 8.3

Solution A

$$\mu = \bar{x} \pm Z_{\alpha}\left(\frac{\sigma}{\sqrt{n}}\right)$$

$$\mu = 68 \pm 1.645\left(\frac{3}{\sqrt{100}}\right)$$

$$67.5065 \leq \mu \leq 68.4935$$

If we **increase** the sample size *n* to 100, we decrease the width of the confidence interval relative to the original sample size of 36 observations.

Solution 8.3

Solution B

$$\mu = \bar{x} \pm Z_{\alpha}\left(\frac{\sigma}{\sqrt{n}}\right)$$

$$\mu = 68 \pm 1.645\left(\frac{3}{\sqrt{25}}\right)$$

$$67.013 \leq \mu \leq 68.987$$

If we **decrease** the sample size *n* to 25, we increase the width of the confidence interval by comparison to the original sample size of 36 observations.

Summary: Effect of Changing the Sample Size

- Increasing the sample size makes the confidence interval narrower.
- Decreasing the sample size makes the confidence interval wider.

We have already seen this effect when we reviewed the effects of changing the size of the sample, *n*, on the Central Limit Theorem. See Figure 7.7 to see this effect. Before we saw that as the sample size increased the standard deviation of the sampling distribution decreases. This was why we choose the sample mean from a large sample as compared to a small sample, all other things held constant.

Thus far we assumed that we knew the population standard deviation. This will virtually never be the case. We will have the sample standard deviation, *s*, however. This is a point estimate for the population standard deviation and can be substituted into the formula for confidence intervals for a mean under certain circumstances. We just saw the effect the sample size has on the width of confidence interval and the impact on the sampling distribution for our discussion of the Central Limit Theorem. We can invoke this to substitute the point estimate for the standard deviation if the sample size is large "enough". Simulation studies indicate that 30 observations or more will be sufficient to eliminate any meaningful bias in the estimated confidence interval.

EXAMPLE 8.4

Spring break can be a very expensive holiday. A sample of 80 students is surveyed, and the average amount spent by students on travel and beverages is $593.84. The sample standard deviation is approximately $369.34.

Construct a 92% confidence interval for the population mean amount of money spent by spring breakers.

Solution 8.4

We begin with the confidence interval for a mean. We use the formula for a mean because the random variable is dollars spent and this is a continuous random variable. The point estimate for the population standard deviation, *s*, has been substituted for the true population standard deviation because with 80 observations there is no concern for bias in the estimate of the confidence interval.

$$\mu = \bar{x} \pm \left[Z_{(a/2)} \frac{s}{\sqrt{n}}\right]$$

Substituting the values into the formula, we have:

$$\mu = 593.84 \pm \left[1.75 \frac{369.34}{\sqrt{80}}\right]$$

$Z_{(a/2)}$ is found on the standard normal table by looking up 0.46 in the body of the table and finding the number of standard deviations on the side and top of the table; 1.75. The solution for the interval is thus:

$$\mu = 593.84 \pm 72.2636 = (521.57, 666.10)$$

$$\$\,521.58 \leq \mu \leq \$\,666.10$$

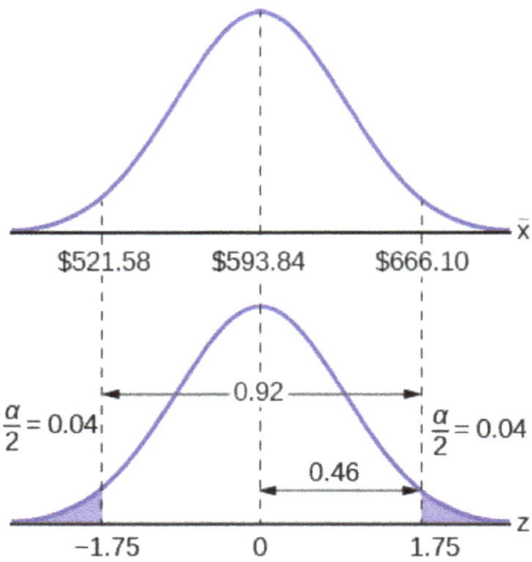

Figure 8.7

Formula Review

The general form for a confidence interval for a single population mean, known standard deviation, normal distribution is given by $\bar{X} - Z_{\alpha}\left(\frac{\sigma}{\sqrt{n}}\right) \leq \mu \leq \bar{X} + Z_{\alpha}\left(\frac{\sigma}{\sqrt{n}}\right)$ This formula is used when the population standard deviation is known.

CL = confidence level, or the proportion of confidence intervals created that are expected to contain the true population parameter

α = 1 – *CL* = the proportion of confidence intervals that will not contain the population parameter

zα2zα2 = the *z*-score with the property that the area to the right of the z-score is $\frac{\alpha}{2}$ this is the *z*-score used in the calculation of "*EBM* where α = 1 – *CL*.

8.2 A CONFIDENCE INTERVAL FOR A POPULATION STANDARD

Deviation Unknown, Small Sample Case

In practice, we rarely know the population standard deviation. In the past, when the sample size was large, this did not present a problem to statisticians. They used the sample standard deviation s as an estimate for σ and proceeded as before to calculate a confidence interval with close enough results. This is what we did in Example 8.4 above. The point estimate for the standard deviation, s, was substituted in the formula for the confidence interval for the population standard deviation. In this case there 80 observation well above the suggested 30 observations to eliminate any bias from a small sample. However, statisticians ran into problems when the sample size was small. A small sample size caused inaccuracies in the confidence interval.

William S. Goset (1876–1937) of the Guinness brewery in Dublin, Ireland ran into this problem. His experiments with hops and barley produced very few samples. Just replacing σ with s did not produce accurate results when he tried to calculate a confidence interval. He realized that he could not use a normal distribution for the calculation; he found that the actual distribution depends on the sample size. This problem led him to "discover" what is called the Student's t-distribution. The name comes from the fact that Gosset wrote under the pen name "A Student."

Up until the mid-1970s, some statisticians used the normal distribution approximation for large sample sizes and used the Student's t-distribution only for sample sizes of at most 30 observations.

If you draw a simple random sample of size n from a population with mean μ and unknown population standard deviation σ and calculate the t-score $t = \frac{\bar{x} - \mu}{\left(\frac{s}{\sqrt{n}}\right)}$, then the t-scores follow a Student's t-distribution with n – 1 degrees of freedom. The t-score has the same interpretation as the **z-score**. It measures how far in standard deviation units $\bar{x}$ is from its mean μ. For each sample size n, there is a different Student's t-distribution.

The degrees of freedom, n – 1, come from the calculation of the sample standard deviation **s**. Remember when we first calculated a sample standard deviation we divided the sum of the squared deviations by $n - 1$, but we used n deviations ($x - \bar{x}$ values) to calculate **s**. Because the sum of the deviations is zero, we can find the last deviation once we know the other n – 1 deviations. The other n – 1 deviations can change or vary freely. We call the number n – 1 the degrees of freedom (df) in recognition that one is lost in the calculations. The effect of losing a degree of freedom is that the t-value increases and the confidence interval increases in width.

Properties of the Student's t-Distribution

- The graph for the Student's t-distribution is similar to the standard normal curve and at infinite degrees of freedom it is the normal distribution. You can confirm this by reading the bottom line at infinite degrees of freedom for a familiar level of confidence, e.g. at column 0.05, 95% level of confidence, we find the t-value of 1.96 at infinite degrees of freedom.
- The mean for the Student's t-distribution is zero and the distribution is symmetric about zero, again like the standard normal distribution.
- The Student's t-distribution has more probability in its tails than the standard normal distribution because the spread of the t-distribution

is greater than the spread of the standard normal. So the graph of the Student's t-distribution will be thicker in the tails and shorter in the center than the graph of the standard normal distribution.

- The exact shape of the Student's t-distribution depends on the degrees of freedom. As the degrees of freedom increases, the graph of Student's t-distribution becomes more like the graph of the standard normal distribution.
- The underlying population of individual observations is assumed to be normally distributed with unknown population mean μ and unknown population standard deviation σ. This assumption comes from the Central Limit theorem because the individual observations in this case are the x¯$\bar{x}$s of the sampling distribution. The size of the underlying population is generally not relevant unless it is very small. If it is normal then the assumption is met and doesn't need discussion.

A probability table for the Student's t-distribution is used to calculate t-values at various commonly-used levels of confidence. The table gives t-scores that correspond to the confidence level (column) and degrees of freedom (row). When using a *t*-table, note that some tables are formatted to show the confidence level in the column headings, while the column headings in some tables may show only corresponding area in one or both tails. Notice that at the bottom the table will show the t-value for infinite degrees of freedom. Mathematically, as the degrees of freedom increase, the *t*-distribution approaches the standard normal distribution. You can find familiar Z-values by looking in the relevant alpha column and reading value in the last row.

A Student's t table (See Appendix A Statistical Tables) gives *t*-scores given the degrees of freedom and the right-tailed probability.

The Student's *t*-distribution has one of the most desirable properties of the normal: it is symmetrical. What the Student's *t*-distribution does is spread out the horizontal axis so it takes a larger number of standard deviations to capture the same amount of probability. In reality there are an infinite number of Student's *t*-distributions, one for each adjustment to the sample size. As the sample size increases, the Student's *t*-distribution become more and more like the normal distribution. When the sample size reaches 30 the normal distribution is usually substituted for the Student's t because they are so much alike. This relationship between the Student's *t*-distribution and the normal distribution is shown in Figure 8.8.

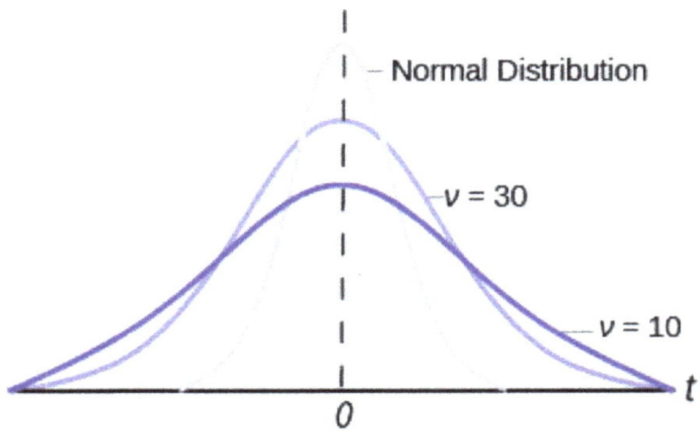

Figure 8.8

This is another example of one distribution limiting another one, in this case the normal distribution is the limiting distribution of the Student's t when the degrees of freedom in the Student's t approaches infinity. This conclusion comes directly from the derivation of the Student's *t*-distribution by Mr. Gosset. He recognized the problem as having few observations and no estimate of the population standard deviation. He was substituting the sample standard deviation and getting volatile results. He therefore created the Student's *t*-distribution as a ratio of the normal distribution and Chi squared distribution. The Chi squared distribution is itself a ratio of two variances, in this case the sample variance and the unknown population variance. The Student's *t*-distribution thus is tied to the normal distribution, but has degrees of freedom that come from those of the Chi squared distribution. The algebraic solution demonstrates this result.

Development of Student's t-distribution:

1. $$t = \frac{z}{\sqrt{\frac{\chi^2}{v}}}$$

where *z* is the standard normal variable and χ^2 is the chi-squared distribution with *v* degrees of freedom.

2. $$t = \frac{\frac{\left(\bar{x} - \mu\right)}{\sigma}}{\sqrt{\frac{\frac{s^2}{(n-1)}}{\frac{\sigma^2}{(n-1)}}}}$$

by substitution, and thus Student's with v=n−1 degree of freedom is:

3. $$t = \frac{\bar{x} - \mu}{\frac{s}{\sqrt{n}}}$$

Restating the formula for a confidence interval for the mean for cases when the sample size is smaller than 30 and we do not know the population standard deviation, σ:

$$\bar{x} - t_{v,\alpha}\left(\frac{s}{\sqrt{n}}\right) \leq \mu \leq \bar{x} + t_{v,\alpha}\left(\frac{s}{\sqrt{n}}\right)$$

Here the point estimate of the population standard deviation, s has been substituted for the population standard deviation, σ, and t_v,α has been substituted for Z_α. The Greek letter ν (pronounced nu) is placed in the general formula in recognition that there are many Student t_v distributions, one for each sample size. ν is the symbol for the degrees of freedom of the distribution and depends on the size of the sample. Often df is used to abbreviate degrees of freedom. **For this type of problem,** the degrees of freedom is ν = n-1, where n is the sample size. To look up a probability in the Student's t table we have to know the degrees of freedom in the problem.

EXAMPLE 8.5

The average earnings per share (EPS) for 10 industrial stocks randomly selected from those listed on the Dow-Jones Industrial Average was found to $\bar{X} = 1.85$ with a standard deviation of s=0.395. Calculate a 99% confidence interval for the average EPS of all the industrials listed on the DJIA.

$$\bar{x} - t_{v,\alpha}\left(\frac{s}{\sqrt{n}}\right) \leq \mu \leq \bar{x} + t_{v,\alpha}\left(\frac{s}{\sqrt{n}}\right)$$

Solution 8.5

To help visualize the process of calculating a confident interval we draw the appropriate distribution for the problem. In this case this is the Student's t because we do not know the population standard deviation and the sample is small, less than 30.

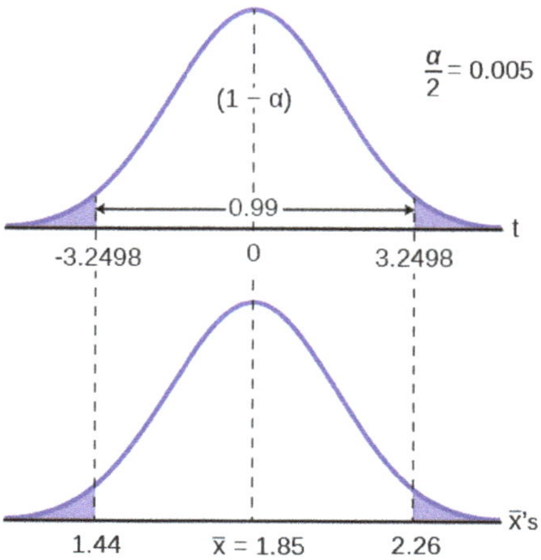

Figure 8.9

To find the appropriate t-value requires two pieces of information, the level of confidence desired and the degrees of freedom. The question asked for a 99% confidence level. On the graph this is shown where (1-α) , the level of confidence , is in the unshaded area. The tails, thus, have .005 probability each, α/2. The degrees of freedom for this type of problem is n-1= 9. From the Student's t table, at the row marked 9 and column marked .005, is the number of standard deviations to capture 99% of the probability, 3.2498. These are then placed on the graph remembering that the Student's t is symmetrical and so the t-value is both plus or minus on each side of the mean.

Inserting these values into the formula gives the result. These values can be placed on the graph to see the relationship between the distribution of the sample means, $\bar{X}$'s and the Student's t distribution.

$$\mu = \bar{X} \pm t_{\alpha/2,\text{df=n-1}} \frac{s}{\sqrt{n}} = 1.851 \pm 3.2498 \frac{0.395}{\sqrt{10}} = 1.8551 \pm 0.406$$

$$1.445 \leq \mu \leq 2.257$$

We state the formal conclusion as :

With 99% confidence level, the average EPS of all the industries listed at DJIA is from \$1.44 to \$2.26.

TRY IT 8.5

You do a study of hypnotherapy to determine how effective it is in increasing the number of hours of sleep subjects get each night. You measure hours of sleep for 12 subjects with the following results. Construct a 95% confidence interval for the mean number of hours slept for the population (assumed normal) from which you took the data.

8.2; 9.1; 7.7; 8.6; 6.9; 11.2; 10.1; 9.9; 8.9; 9.2; 7.5; 10.5

8.3 A CONFIDENCE INTERVAL FOR A POPULATION PROPORTION

During an election year, we see articles in the newspaper that state **confidence intervals** in terms of proportions or percentages. For example, a poll for a particular candidate running for president might show that the candidate has 40% of the vote within three percentage points (if the sample is large enough). Often, election polls are calculated with 95% confidence, so, the pollsters would be 95% confident that the true proportion of voters who favored the candidate would be between 0.37 and 0.43.

Investors in the stock market are interested in the true proportion of stocks that go up and down each week. Businesses that sell personal computers are interested in the proportion of households in the United States that own personal computers.

Confidence intervals can be calculated for the true proportion of stocks that go up or down each week and for the true proportion of households in the United States that own personal computers.

The procedure to find the confidence interval for a population proportion is similar to that for the population mean, but the formulas are a bit different although conceptually identical. While the formulas are different, they are based upon the same mathematical foundation given to us by the Central Limit Theorem. Because of this we will see the same basic format using the same three pieces of information: the sample value of the parameter in question, the standard deviation of the relevant sampling distribution, and the number of standard deviations we need to have the confidence in our estimate that we desire.

How do you know you are dealing with a proportion problem? First, the underlying distribution has a binary random variable and therefore is a binomial distribution. (There is no mention of a mean or average.) If X is a binomial random variable, then $X \sim B(n, p)$ where n is the number of trials and p is the probability of a success. To form a sample proportion, take X, the random variable for the number of successes and divide it by n, the number of trials (or the sample size). The random variable P' (read "P prime") is the sample proportion,

$$P' = \frac{X}{n}$$

(Sometimes the random variable is denoted as $\hat{P}$, read "P hat".)

p' = the estimated proportion of successes or sample proportion of successes (p' is a point estimate for p, the true population proportion, and thus q is the probability of a failure in any one trial.)

x = the number of successes in the sample

n = the size of the sample

The formula for the confidence interval for a population proportion follows the same format as that for an estimate of a population mean. Remembering the sampling distribution for the proportion from Chapter 7, the standard deviation was found to be:

$$\sigma_{p'} = \sqrt{\frac{p(1-p)}{n}}$$

The confidence interval for a population proportion, therefore, becomes:

$$p = p' \pm \left[Z_{\left(\frac{a}{2}\right)} \sqrt{\frac{p'(1-p')}{n}} \right]$$

$Z_{\left(\frac{a}{2}\right)}$ is set according to our desired degree of confidence and $\sqrt{\frac{p'(1-p')}{n}}$ is the standard deviation of the sampling distribution.

The sample proportions p' and q' are estimates of the unknown population proportions p and q. The estimated proportions p' and q' are used because p and q are not known.

Remember that as p moves further from 0.5 the binomial distribution becomes less symmetrical. Because we are estimating the binomial with the symmetrical normal distribution the further away from symmetrical the binomial becomes the less confidence we have in the estimate.

This conclusion can be demonstrated through the following analysis. Proportions are based upon the binomial probability distribution. The possible outcomes are binary, either "success" or "failure". This gives rise to a proportion, meaning the percentage of the outcomes that are "successes". It was shown that the binomial distribution could be fully understood if we knew only the probability of a success in any one trial, called p. The mean and the standard deviation of the binomial were found to be:

$$\mu = \mathrm{np}$$

$$\sigma = \sqrt{\mathrm{np}q}$$

It was also shown that the binomial could be estimated by the normal distribution if BOTH np AND nq were greater than 5. From the discussion above, it was found that the standardizing formula for the binomial distribution is:

$$Z = \frac{\mathrm{p}' - p}{\sqrt{\left(\frac{pq}{n}\right)}}$$

which is nothing more than a restatement of the general standardizing formula with appropriate substitutions for μ and σ from the binomial. We can use the standard normal distribution, the reason Z is in the equation, because the normal distribution is the limiting distribution of the binomial. This is another example of the Central Limit Theorem. We have already seen that the sampling distribution of means is normally distributed. Recall the extended discussion in Chapter 7 concerning the sampling distribution of proportions and the conclusions of the Central Limit Theorem.

We can now manipulate this formula in just the same way we did for finding the confidence intervals for a mean, but to find the confidence interval for the binomial population parameter, p.

$$p' - Z_{\alpha}\sqrt{\frac{p'q'}{n}} \leq p \leq p' + Z_{\alpha}\sqrt{\frac{p'q'}{n}}$$

Where p′ = x/n, the point estimate of p taken from the sample. Notice that p′ has replaced p in the formula. This is because we do not know p, indeed, this is just what we are trying to estimate.

Unfortunately, there is no correction factor for cases where the sample size is small so np′ and nq′ must always be greater than 5 to develop an interval estimate for p.

EXAMPLE 8.6

Suppose that a market research firm is hired to estimate the percent of adults living in a large city who have cell phones. Five hundred randomly selected adult residents in this city are surveyed to determine whether they have cell phones. Of the 500 people sampled, 421 responded yes - they own cell phones. Using a 95% confidence level, compute a confidence interval estimate for the true proportion of adult residents of this city who have cell phones.

Solution 8.6

- The solution step-by-step.

Let X = the number of people in the sample who have cell phones. X is binomial: the random variable is binary, people either have a cell phone or they do not.

To calculate the confidence interval, we must find p', q'.

$n = 500$

x = the number of successes in the sample = 421

$$p' = \frac{x}{n} = \frac{421}{500} = 0.842$$

$p' = 0.842$ is the sample proportion; this is the point estimate of the population proportion.

$q' = 1 - p' = 1 - 0.842 = 0.158$

Since the requested confidence level is $CL = 0.95$, then $\alpha = 1 - CL = 1 - 0.95 = 0.05$

$\left(\frac{\alpha}{2}\right) = 0.025.$

Then $z_{\frac{\alpha}{2}} = z_{0.025} = 1.96$

This can be found using the Standard Normal probability table in Appendix A. This can also be found in the students t table at the 0.025 column and infinity degrees of freedom because at infinite degrees of freedom the students t distribution becomes the standard normal distribution, Z.

The confidence interval for the true binomial population proportion is

$$p' - Z_{\alpha}\sqrt{\frac{p'q'}{n}} \leq p \leq p' + Z_{\alpha}\sqrt{\frac{p'q'}{n}}$$

Substituting in the values from above we find he confidence inte val is : $0.810 \leq p \leq 0.874$

Interpretation

We estimate with 95% confidence that between 81% and 87.4% of all adult residents of this city have cell phones.

Explanation of 95% Confidence Level

Ninety-five percent of the confidence intervals constructed in this way would contain the true value for the population proportion of all adult residents of this city who have cell phones.

TRY IT 8.6

Suppose 250 randomly selected people are surveyed to determine if they own a tablet. Of the 250 surveyed, 98 reported owning a tablet. Using a 95% confidence level, compute a confidence interval estimate for the true proportion of people who own tablets.

EXAMPLE 8.7

The Dundee Dog Training School has a larger than average proportion of clients who compete in competitive professional events. A confidence interval for the population proportion of dogs that compete in professional events from 150 different training schools is constructed. The lower limit is determined to be 0.08 and the upper limit is determined to be 0.16. Determine the level of confidence used to construct the interval of the population proportion of dogs that compete in professional events.

EXAMPLE 8.8

Problem

A financial officer for a company wants to estimate the percent of accounts receivable that are more than 30 days overdue. He surveys 500 accounts and finds that 300 are more than 30 days overdue. Compute a 90% confidence interval for the true percent of accounts receivable that are more than 30 days overdue, and interpret the confidence interval.

Solution 8.7

We begin with the formula for a confidence interval for a proportion because the random variable is binary; either the client competes in professional competitive dog events or they don't.

$$p = p' \pm \left[Z_{\left(\frac{a}{2}\right)} \sqrt{\frac{p'(1-p')}{n}} \right]$$

Next we find the sample proportion:

$$p' = \frac{0.08 + 0.16}{2} = 0.12$$

The ± that makes up the confidence interval is thus 0.04; 0.12 + 0.04 = 0.16 and 0.12 - 0.04 = 0.08, the boundaries of the confidence interval. Finally, we solve for Z.

$\left[Z \cdot \sqrt{\frac{0.12(1-0.12)}{150}} \right] = 0.04$, *therefore Z=1.51*

And then look up the probability for 1.51 standard deviations on the standard normal table.

$p(Z = 1.51) = 0.4345$, $p(Z) \cdot 2 = 0.8690$ **or** 86.90% .

Example 8.8

A financial officer for a company wants to estimate the percent of accounts receivable that are more than 30 days overdue. He surveys 500 accounts and finds that 300 are more than 30 days overdue. Compute a 90% confidence interval for the true percent of accounts receivable that are more than 30 days overdue, and interpret the confidence interval.

Solution 8.8

- The solution is step-by-step:

$x = 300$ and $n = 500$

$p' = \frac{x}{n} = \frac{300}{500} = 0.600$

$q' = 1 - p' = 1 - 0.600 = 0.400$

Since confidence level = 0.90, then α = 1 – confidence level $= (1 - 0.90) = 0.10 \left(\frac{\alpha}{2}\right) = 0.05$

$Z_{\frac{\alpha}{2}} = Z_{0.05} = 1.645$

This Z-value can be found using a standard normal probability table. The student's t-table can also be used by entering the table at the 0.05 column and reading at the line for infinite degrees of freedom. The t-distribution is the normal distribution at infinite degrees of freedom. This is a handy trick to remember in finding Z-values for commonly used levels of confidence. We use this formula for a confidence interval for a proportion:

$$p' - Z_\alpha\sqrt{\frac{p'q'}{n}} \leq p \leq p' + Z_\alpha\sqrt{\frac{p'q'}{n}}$$

Substituting in the values from above we find the confidence interval for the true binomial population proportion is $0.564 \leq p \leq 0.636$

Interpretation

- We estimate with 90% confidence that the true percent of all accounts receivable overdue 30 days is between 56.4% and 63.6%.
- Alternate Wording: We estimate with 90% confidence that between 56.4% and 63.6% of ALL accounts are overdue 30 days.

Explanation of 90% Confidence Level

Ninety percent of all confidence intervals constructed in this way contain the true value for the population percent of accounts receivable that are overdue 30 days.

TRY IT 8.8

A student polls his school to see if students in the school district are for or against the new legislation regarding school uniforms. She surveys 600 students and finds that 480 are against the new legislation.

a. Compute a 90% confidence interval for the true percent of students who are against the new legislation, and interpret the confidence interval.

b In a sample of 300 students, 68% said they own an iPod and a smart phone. Compute a 97% confidence interval for the true percent of students who own an iPod and a smartphone.

8.4 CALCULATING THE SAMPLE SIZE N: CONTINUOUS AND BINARY RANDOM VARIABLES

Continuous Random Variables

Usually we have no control over the sample size of a data set. However, if we are able to set the sample size, as in cases where we are taking a survey, it is very helpful to know just how large it should be to provide the most information. Sampling can be very costly in both time and product. Simple telephone surveys will cost approximately $30.00 each, for example, and some sampling requires the destruction of the product.

If we go back to our standardizing formula for the sampling distribution for means, we can see that it is possible to solve it for n. If we do this we have $(\bar{X} - \mu)$ in the denominator.

$$n = \frac{Z_{\alpha}^{2}\sigma^{2}}{(\bar{X} - \mu)^{2}} = \frac{Z_{\alpha}^{2}\sigma^{2}}{e^{2}}$$

Because we have not taken a sample yet we do not know any of the variables in the formula except that we can set Z_α to the level of confidence we desire just as we did when determining confidence intervals. If we set a predetermined acceptable error, or tolerance, for the difference between $\bar{X}$ and μ, called e in the formula, we are much further in solving for the sample size n. We still do not know the population standard deviation, σ. In practice, a pre-survey is usually done which allows for fine tuning the questionnaire and will give a sample standard deviation that can be used. In other cases, previous information from other surveys may be used for σ in the formula. While crude, this method of determining the sample size may help in reducing cost significantly. It will be the actual data gathered that determines the inferences about the population, so caution in the sample size is appropriate calling for high levels of confidence and small sampling errors.

Binary Random Variables

What was done in cases when looking for the mean of a distribution can also be done when sampling to determine the population parameter p for proportions. Manipulation of the standardizing formula for proportions gives:

$$n = \frac{Z_{\alpha}^{2}\text{pq}}{e^{2}}$$

where e = (p'-p), and is the acceptable sampling error, or tolerance, for this application. This will be measured in percentage points.

In this case the very object of our search is in the formula, p, and of course q because q =1-p. This result occurs because the binomial distribution is a one parameter distribution. If we know p then we know the mean and the standard deviation. Therefore, p shows up in the standard deviation of the sampling distribution which is where we got this formula. If, in an abundance of caution, we substitute 0.5 for p we will draw the largest required sample size that will provide the level of confidence specified by Zα and the tolerance we have selected. This is true because of all combinations of two fractions that add to one, the largest multiple is when each is 0.5. Without any other information concerning the population parameter p, this is the common practice. This may result in oversampling, but certainly not under sampling, thus, this is a cautious approach.

There is an interesting trade-off between the level of confidence and the sample size that shows up here when considering the cost of sampling. Table 8.1 shows the appropriate sample size at different levels of confidence and different level of the acceptable error, or tolerance.

Table 8.1

Required sample size (90%)	Required sample size (95%)	Tolerance level
1691	2401	2%
752	1067	3%
271	384	5%
68	96	10%

This table is designed to show the maximum sample size required at different levels of confidence given an assumed p= 0.5 and q=0.5 as discussed above.

The acceptable error, called tolerance in the table, is measured in plus or minus values from the actual proportion. For example, an acceptable error of 5% means that if the sample proportion was found to be 26 percent, the conclusion would be that the actual population proportion is between 21 and 31 percent with a 90 percent level of confidence if a sample of 271 had been taken. Likewise, if the acceptable error was set at 2%, then the population proportion would be between 24 and 28 percent with a 90 percent level of confidence, but would require that the sample size be increased from 271 to 1,691. If we wished a higher level of confidence, we would require a larger sample size. Moving from a 90 percent level of confidence to a 95 percent level at a plus or minus 5% tolerance requires changing the sample size from 271 to 384. A very common sample size often seen reported in political surveys is 384. With the survey results it is frequently stated that the results are good to a plus or minus 5% level of "accuracy".

EXAMPLE 8.9

Suppose a mobile phone company wants to determine the current percentage of customers aged 50+ who use text messaging on their cell phones. How many customers aged 50+ should the company survey in order to be 90% confident that the estimated (sample) proportion is within three percentage points of the true population proportion of customers aged 50+ who use text messaging on their cell phones.

Solution 8.9

From the problem, we know that the acceptable error, *e*, is 0.03 (3%=0.03) and $z_{\frac{\alpha}{2}}$ $z_{0.05} = 1.645$ because the confidence level is 90%. The acceptable error, *e*, is the difference between the actual population proportion *p*, and the sample proportion we expect to get from the sample.

However, in order to find *n*, we need to know the estimated (sample) proportion *p'*. Remember that *q'* = 1 – *p'*. But, we do not know *p'* yet. Since we multiply *p'* and *q'* together, we make them both equal to 0.5 because *p'q'* = (0.5)(0.5) = 0.25 results in the largest possible product. (Try other products: (0.6)(0.4) = 0.24; (0.3)(0.7) = 0.21; (0.2)(0.8) = 0.16 and so on). The largest possible product gives us the largest *n*. This gives us a large enough sample so that we can be 90% confident that we are within three percentage points of the true population proportion. To calculate the sample size *n*, use the formula and make the substitutions.

$$n = \frac{z^2 p' q'}{e^2} \text{ gives } n = \frac{1.645^2(0.5)(0.5)}{0.03^2} = 751.7$$

Round the answer to the next higher value. The sample size should be 752 cell phone customers aged 50+ in order to be 90% confident that the estimated (sample) proportion is within three percentage points of the true population proportion of all customers aged 50+ who use text messaging on their cell phones.

TRY IT 8.9

Suppose an internet marketing company wants to determine the current percentage of customers who click on ads on their smartphones. How many customers should the company survey in order to be 90% confident that the estimated proportion is within five percentage points of the true population proportion of customers who click on ads on their smartphones?

Terminolgy

Binomial Distribution a discrete random variable (RV) which arises from Bernoulli trials; there are a fixed number, *n*, of independent trials. "Independent" means that the result of any trial (for example, trial 1) does not affect the results of the following trials, and all trials are conducted under the same conditions. Under these circumstances the binomial RV *X* is defined as the number of successes in *n* trials. The notation is: *X*~*B*(n,p). The mean is $\mu = np$ and the standard deviation is $\sigma = \sqrt{npq}$. The probability of exactly *x* successes in *n* trials is $P(X = x) = \binom{n}{x} p^x q^{n-x}$

Confidence Interval (CI) an interval estimate for an unknown population parameter. This depends on:

- the desired confidence level,

- information that is known about the distribution (for example, known standard deviation),
- the sample and its size.

Confidence Level (CL) the percent expression for the probability that the confidence interval contains the true population parameter; for example, if the CL = 90%, then in 90 out of 100 samples the interval estimate will enclose the true population parameter.

Degrees of Freedom (*df*) the number of objects in a sample that are free to vary

Error Bound for a Population Mean (*EBM*) the margin of error; depends on the confidence level, sample size, and known or estimated population standard deviation.

Error Bound for a Population Proportion (EBP) the margin of error; depends on the confidence level, the sample size, and the estimated (from the sample) proportion of successes.

Inferential Statistics also called statistical inference or inductive statistics; this facet of statistics deals with estimating a population parameter based on a sample statistic. For example, if four out of the 100 calculators sampled are defective we might infer that four percent of the production is defective.

Normal Distribution a continuous random variable (RV) with pdf $f(x) = \frac{1}{\sigma\sqrt{2\pi}}e^{-(x-\mu)^2/2\sigma^2}$, where μ is the mean of the distribution and σ is the standard deviation, notation: $X \sim N(\mu,\sigma)$. If $\mu = 0$ and $\sigma = 1$, the RV is called the standard normal distribution.

Parameter a numerical characteristic of a population

Point Estimate a single number computed from a sample and used to estimate a population parameter

Standard Deviation a number that is equal to the square root of the variance and measures how far data values are from their mean; notation: s for sample standard deviation and σ for population standard deviation

Student's t-Distribution investigated and reported by William S. Gossett in 1908 and published under the pseudonym Student; the major characteristics of this random variable (RV) are:

- It is continuous and assumes any real values.
- The pdf is symmetrical about its mean of zero.
- It approaches the standard normal distribution as n get larger.
- There is a "family" of t–distributions: each representative of the family

is completely defined by the number of degrees of freedom, which depends upon the application for which the t is being used.

CHAPTER REVIEW

8.2 A Confidence Interval for a Population Standard Deviation Unknown, Small Sample Case

In many cases, the researcher does not know the population standard deviation, σ, of the measure being studied. In these cases, it is common to use the sample standard deviation, s, as an estimate of σ. The normal distribution creates accurate confidence intervals when σ is known, but it is not as accurate when s is used as an estimate. In this case, the Student's t-distribution is much better. Define a t-score using the following formula:

$$t = \frac{\bar{x} - \mu}{\frac{s}{\sqrt{n}}}$$

The t-score follows the Student's t-distribution with n – 1 degrees of freedom. The confidence interval under this distribution is calculated with $\bar{x} \pm \left(t_{\frac{\alpha}{2}}\right)\frac{s}{\sqrt{n}}$ where $t_{\frac{\alpha}{2}}$ is the t-score with area to the right equal to $\frac{\alpha}{2}$, s is the sample standard deviation, and n is the sample size. Use a table, calculator, or computer to find $t_{\frac{\alpha}{2}}$ for a given α.

8.3 A Confidence Interval for A Population Proportion

Some statistical measures, like many survey questions, measure qualitative rather than quantitative data. In this case, the population parameter being estimated is a proportion. It is possible to create a confidence interval for the true population proportion following procedures similar to those used in creating confidence intervals for population means. The formulas are slightly different, but they follow the same reasoning.

Let p' represent the sample proportion, x/n, where x represents the number of successes and n represents the sample size. Let $q' = 1 - p'$. Then the confidence interval for a population proportion is given by the following formula:

$$p' - Z_{\alpha}\sqrt{\frac{p'q'}{n}} \leq p \leq p' + Z_{\alpha}\sqrt{\frac{p'q'}{n}}$$

8.4 Calculating the Sample Size n: Continuous and Binary Random Variables

Sometimes researchers know in advance that they want to estimate a population mean within a specific margin of error for a given level of confidence. In that case, solve the relevant confidence interval formula for n to discover the size of the sample that is needed to achieve this goal:

$$n = \frac{Z_{\alpha}^2 \sigma^2}{(\bar{x} - \mu)^2}$$

If the random variable is binary then the formula for the appropriate sample size to maintain a particular level of confidence with a specific tolerance level is given by

$$n = \frac{Z_{\alpha}^2 \mathrm{pq}}{e^2}$$

FORMULA REVIEW

8.2 A Confidence Interval for a Population Standard Deviation Unknown, Small Sample Case

s = the standard deviation of sample values.

$t = \frac{\bar{x} - \mu}{\frac{s}{\sqrt{n}}}$ is the formula for the t-score which measures how far away a measure is from the population mean in the Student's t-distribution

$df = n - 1$; the degrees of freedom for a Student's t-distribution where n represents the size of the sample

$T \sim t_{df}$ the random variable, T, has a Student's t-distribution with df degrees of freedom

The general form for a confidence interval for a single mean, population standard deviation unknown, and sample size less than 30 Student's t is given by: $\bar{x} - t_{v,\alpha}\left(\frac{s}{\sqrt{n}}\right) \leq \mu \leq \bar{x} + t_{v,\alpha}\left(\frac{s}{\sqrt{n}}\right)$

8.3 A Confidence Interval for A Population Proportion

$p' = \frac{x}{n}$ where x represents the number of successes in a sample and n represents the sample size. The variable p' is the sample proportion and serves as the point estimate for the true population proportion.

$q' = 1 - p'$

The variable p' has a binomial distribution that can be approximated with the normal distribution shown here. The confidence interval for the true population proportion is given by the formula:

$$p' - Z_{\alpha}\sqrt{\frac{p'q'}{n}} \leq p \leq p' + Z_{\alpha}\sqrt{\frac{p'q'}{n}}$$

$n = \frac{Z_{\frac{\alpha}{2}}^{2} p' q'}{e^{2}}$ provides the number of observations needed to sample to estimate the population proportion, *p*, with confidence 1 - *α* and margin of error *e*. Where *e* = the acceptable difference between the actual population proportion and the sample proportion.

8.4 Calculating the Sample Size n: Continuous and Binary Random Variables

$n = \frac{Z^2 \sigma^2}{(\bar{x} - \mu)^2}$ = the formula used to determine the sample size (*n*) needed to achieve a desired margin of error at a given level of confidence for a continuous random variable

$n = \frac{Z_{\alpha}^{2} pq}{e^{2}}$ = the formula used to determine the sample size if the random variable is binary

PRACTICE

8.2 A Confidence Interval for a Population Standard Deviation Unknown, Small Sample Case

Use the following information to answer the next five exercises. A hospital is trying to cut down on emergency room wait times. It is interested in the amount of time patients must wait before being called back to be examined. An investigation committee randomly surveyed 70 patients. The sample mean was 1.5 hours with a sample standard deviation of 0.5 hours.

1. Identify the following:
   a. $\bar{x}$ =_______
   b. s_x =_______
   c. n =_______
   d. $n - 1$ =_______
2. Define the random variables *X* and X–*X*- in words.
3. Which distribution should you use for this problem?
4. Construct a 95% confidence interval for the population mean time spent waiting. State the confidence interval, sketch the graph, and calculate the error bound.
5. Explain in complete sentences what the confidence interval means.

Use the following information to answer the next six exercises: One hundred eight Americans were surveyed to determine the number of hours they spend watching television each month. It was revealed that they watched an average of 151 hours each month with a standard deviation of 32 hours. Assume that the underlying population distribution is normal.

6. Identify the following:
   a. $\bar{x}$ - =_______
   b. s_x =_______
   c. n =_______
   d. n – 1 =_______
7. Define the random variable X in words.
8. Define the random variable $\bar{X}$ in words.
9. Which distribution should you use for this problem?
10. Construct a 99% confidence interval for the population mean hours spent watching television per month. (a) State the confidence interval, (b) sketch the graph, and (c) calculate the error bound.
11. Why would the error bound change if the confidence level were lowered to 95%?

Use the following information to answer the next 13 exercises: The data in Table 8.2 are the result of a random survey of 39 national flags (with replacement between picks) from various countries. We are interested in finding a confidence interval for the true mean number of colors on a national flag. Let *X* = the number of colors on a national flag.

Table 8.2

X	Freq.
1	1
2	7
3	18
4	7
5	6

12. Calculate the following:
   a. $\bar{x}$ =______
   b. s_x =______
   c. n =______
13. Define the random variable $\bar{X}$ in words.
14. What is $\bar{x}$ estimating?
15. Is σ_x known?
16. As a result of your answer to Exercise 8.15, state the exact distribution to use when calculating the confidence interval.

Construct a 95% confidence interval for the true mean number of colors on national flags.

17. How much area is in both tails (combined)?
18. How much area is in each tail?
19. Calculate the following:
    a. lower limit
    b. upper limit
    c. error bound
20. The 95% confidence interval is_____.
21. Fill in the blanks on the graph with the areas, the upper and lower limits of the Confidence Interval and the sample mean.

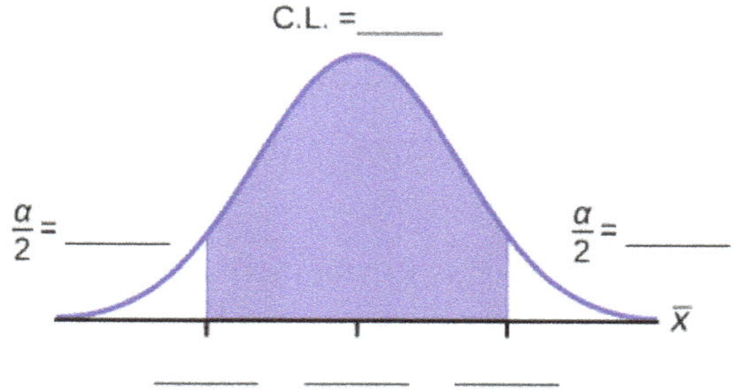

Figure 8.10

22. In one complete sentence, explain what the interval means.
23. Using the same $\bar{x}$, s_x , and level of confidence, suppose that n were 69 instead of 39. Would the error bound become larger or smaller? How do you know?
24. Using the same $\bar{x}$, s_x , and n = 39, how would the error bound change if the confidence level were reduced to 90%? Why?

8.3 A Confidence Interval for A Population Proportion

Use the following information to answer the next two exercises: Marketing companies are interested in knowing the population percent of women who make the majority of household purchasing decisions.

25. When designing a study to determine this population proportion, what is the minimum number you would need to survey to be 90% confident that the population proportion is estimated to within 0.05?
26. If it were later determined that it was important to be more than 90% confident and a new survey were commissioned, how would it affect the minimum number you need to survey? Why?

Use the following information to answer the next five exercises: Suppose the marketing company did do a survey. They randomly surveyed 200 households and found that in 120 of them, the woman made the majority of the purchasing decisions. We are interested in the population proportion of households where women make the majority of the purchasing decisions.

27. Identify the following:

a. $x =$ ______
b. $n =$ ______
c. $p' =$ ______

28. Define the random variables X and P′ in words.

29. Which distribution should you use for this problem?

30. Construct a 95% confidence interval for the population proportion of households where the women make the majority of the purchasing decisions. State the confidence interval, sketch the graph, and calculate the error bound.

31. List two difficulties the company might have in obtaining random results, if this survey were done by email.

Use the following information to answer the next five exercises: Of 1,050 randomly selected adults, 360 identified themselves as manual laborers, 280 identified themselves as non-manual wage earners, 250 identified themselves as mid-level managers, and 160 identified themselves as executives. In the survey, 82% of manual laborers preferred trucks, 62% of non-manual wage earners preferred trucks, 54% of mid-level managers preferred trucks, and 26% of executives preferred trucks.

32. We are interested in finding the 95% confidence interval for the percent of executives who prefer trucks. Define random variables X and P′ in words.

33. Which distribution should you use for this problem?

34. Construct a 95% confidence interval. State the confidence interval, sketch the graph, and calculate the error bound.

35. Suppose we want to lower the sampling error. What is one way to accomplish that?

36. The sampling error given in the survey is ±2%. Explain what the ±2% means.

Use the following information to answer the next five exercises: A poll of 1,200 voters asked what the most significant issue was in the upcoming election. Sixty-five percent answered the economy. We are interested in the population proportion of voters who feel the economy is the most important.

37. Define the random variable X in words.

38. Define the random variable P′ in words.

39. Which distribution should you use for this problem?

40. Construct a 90% confidence interval, and state the confidence interval and the error bound.

41. What would happen to the confidence interval if the level of confidence were 95%?

Use the following information to answer the next 16 exercises: The Ice Chalet offers dozens of different beginning ice-skating classes. All of the class names are put into a bucket. The 5 P.M., Monday night, ages 8 to 12, beginning ice-skating class was picked. In that class were 64 girls and 16 boys. Suppose that we are interested in the true proportion of girls, ages 8 to 12, in all beginning ice-skating classes at the Ice Chalet. Assume that the children in the selected class are a random sample of the population.

42. What is being counted?

43. In words, define the random variable X.

44. Calculate the following:

a. x = _______
b. n = _______
c. p′ = _______

45. State the estimated distribution of X. X~________

46. Define a new random variable P′. What is p′ estimating?

47. In words, define the random variable P′.

48. State the estimated distribution of P′. Construct a 92% Confidence Interval for the true proportion of girls in the ages 8 to 12 beginning ice-skating classes at the Ice Chalet.

49. How much area is in both tails (combined)?

50. How much area is in each tail?

51. Calculate the following:

a. lower limit
b. upper limit
c. error bound

52. The 92% confidence interval is _______.

53. Fill in the blanks on the graph with the areas, upper and lower limits of the confidence interval, and the sample proportion.

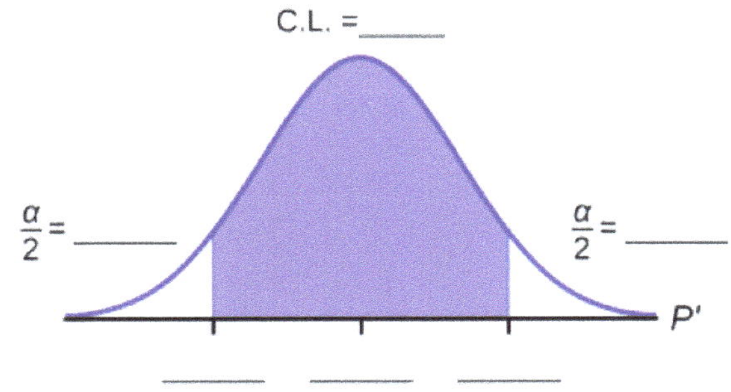

Figure 8.11

54. In one complete sentence, explain what the interval means.

55. Using the same p′ and level of confidence, suppose that n were increased to 100. Would the error bound become larger or smaller? How do you know?

56. Using the same p′ and n = 80, how would the error bound change if the confidence level were increased to 98%? Why?

57. If you decreased the allowable error bound, why would the minimum sample size increase (keeping the same level of confidence)?

8.4 Calculating the Sample Size n: Continuous and Binary Random Variables

Use the following information to answer the next five exercises: The standard deviation of the weights of elephants is known to be approximately 15 pounds. We wish to construct a 95% confidence interval for the mean weight of newborn elephant calves. Fifty newborn elephants are weighed. The sample mean is 244 pounds. The sample standard deviation is 11 pounds.

58. Identify the following:

a. $\bar{x}$ = _____

b. σ = _____

c. n = _____

59. In words, define the random variables X and $\bar{X}$.

60. Which distribution should you use for this problem?

61. Construct a 95% confidence interval for the population mean weight of newborn elephants. State the confidence interval, sketch the graph, and calculate the error bound.

62. What will happen to the confidence interval obtained, if 500 newborn elephants are weighed instead of 50? Why?

Use the following information to answer the next seven exercises: The U.S. Census Bureau conducts a study to determine the time needed to complete the short form. The

Bureau surveys 200 people. The sample mean is 8.2 minutes. There is a known standard deviation of 2.2 minutes. The population distribution is assumed to be normal.

63. Identify the following:

a. $\bar{x}$ = _____

b. σ = _____

c. n = _____

64. In words, define the random variables X and $\bar{X}$

65. Which distribution should you use for this problem?

66. Construct a 90% confidence interval for the population mean time to complete the forms. State the confidence interval, sketch the graph, and calculate the error bound.

67. If the Census wants to increase its level of confidence and keep the error bound the same by taking another survey, what changes should it make?

68. If the Census did another survey, kept the error bound the same, and surveyed only 50 people instead of 200, what would happen to the level of confidence? Why?

69. Suppose the Census needed to be 98% confident of the population mean length of time. Would the Census have to survey more people? Why or why not?

Use the following information to answer the next ten exercises: A sample of 20 heads of lettuce was selected. Assume that the population distribution of head weight is normal. The weight of each head of lettuce was then recorded. The mean weight was 2.2 pounds with a standard deviation of 0.1 pounds. The population standard deviation is known to be 0.2 pounds.

70. Identify the following:

a. $\bar{x}$ = ______

b. σ = ______

c. n = ______

71. In words, define the random variable X.

72. In words, define the random variable $\bar{X}$.

73. Which distribution should you use for this problem?

74. Construct a 90% confidence interval for the population mean weight of the heads of lettuce. State the confidence interval, sketch the graph, and calculate the error bound.

75. Construct a 95% confidence interval for the population mean weight of the heads of lettuce. State the confidence interval, sketch the graph, and calculate the error bound.

76. In complete sentences, explain why the confidence interval in **Exercise 8.74** is larger than in Exercise 8.75.

77. In complete sentences, give an interpretation of what the interval in **Exercise 8.75** means.

78. What would happen if 40 heads of lettuce were sampled instead of 20, and the error bound remained the same?

79. What would happen if 40 heads of lettuce were sampled instead of 20, and the confidence level remained the same?

Use the following information to answer the next 14 exercises: The mean age for all Foothill College students for a recent Fall term was 33.2. The population standard deviation has been pretty consistent at 15. Suppose that twenty-five Winter students were randomly selected. The mean age for the sample was 30.4. We are interested in the true mean age for Winter Foothill College students. Let X = the age of a Winter Foothill College student.

80. $\bar{x}$ = _____

81. n = _____

82. ________ = 15

83. In words, define the random variable $\bar{X}$.

84. What is x-x- estimating?

85. Is σxσx known?

86. As a result of your answer to **Exercise 8.83**, state the exact distribution to use when calculating the confidence interval.

Construct a 95% Confidence Interval for the true mean age of Winter Foothill College students by working out then answering the next seven exercises.

87. How much area is in both tails (combined)? α =_______

88. How much area is in each tail? α2$\alpha 2$ =_______

89. Identify the following specifications:

a. lower limit
b. upper limit
c. error bound

90. The 95% confidence interval is:_________________.

91. Fill in the blanks on the graph with the areas, upper and lower limits of the confidence interval, and the sample mean.

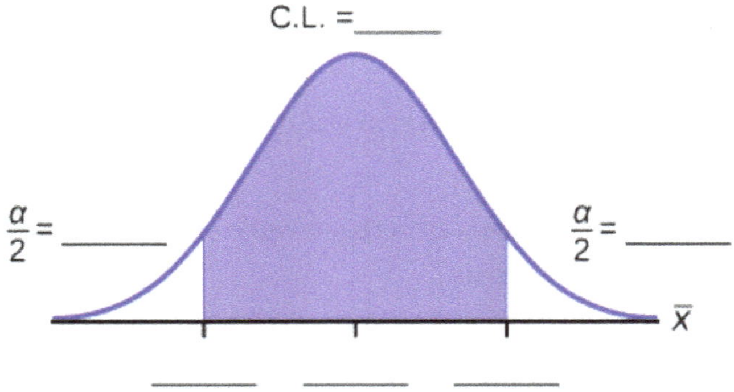

Figure 8.12

92. In one complete sentence, explain what the interval means.

93. Using the same mean, standard deviation, and level of confidence, suppose that n were 69 instead of 25. Would the error bound become larger or smaller? How do you know?

94. Using the same mean, standard deviation, and sample size, how would the error bound change if the confidence level were reduced to 90%? Why?

95. Find the value of the sample size needed to be 90% confident that the sample proportion and the population proportion are within 4% of each other. The sample proportion is 0.60. Note: Round all fractions up for n.

96. Find the value of the sample size needed to be 95% confident that the sample proportion and the population proportion are within 2% of each other. The sample proportion is 0.650. Note: Round all fractions up for n.

97. Find the value of the sample size needed to be 96% confident that the sample proportion and the population proportion are within 5% of each other. The sample proportion is 0.70. Note: Round all fractions up for n.

98. Find the value of the sample size needed to be 90% confident that the sample proportion and the population proportion are within 1% of each other. The sample proportion is 0.50. Note: Round all fractions up for n.

99. Find the value of the sample size needed to be 94% confident that the sample proportion and the population proportion are within 2% of each other. The sample proportion is 0.65. Note: Round all fractions up for n.

100. Find the value of the sample size needed to be 95% confident that the sample proportion and the population proportion are within 4% of each other. The sample proportion is 0.45. Note: Round all fractions up for n.

101. Find the value of the sample size needed to be 90% confident that the sample proportion and the population proportion are within 2% of each other. The sample proportion is 0.3. Note: Round all fractions up for n.

HOMEWORK

8.2 A Confidence Interval for a Population Standard Deviation Unknown, Small Sample Case

102. In six packages of "The Flintstones® Real Fruit Snacks" there were five Bam-Bam snack pieces. The total number of snack pieces in the six bags was 68. We wish to calculate a 96% confidence interval for the population proportion of Bam-Bam snack pieces.

a. Define the random variables X and P' in words.

b. Which distribution should you use for this problem? Explain your choice

c. Calculate p'.

d. Construct a 96% confidence interval for the population proportion of Bam-Bam snack pieces per bag.

  i. State the confidence interval.

  ii. Sketch the graph.

  iii. Calculate the error bound.

e. Do you think that six packages of fruit snacks yield enough data to give accurate results? Why or why not?

103. A random survey of enrollment at 35 community colleges across the United States yielded the following figures: 6,414; 1,550; 2,109; 9,350; 21,828; 4,300; 5,944; 5,722; 2,825; 2,044; 5,481; 5,200; 5,853; 2,750; 10,012; 6,357; 27,000; 9,414; 7,681; 3,200; 17,500; 9,200; 7,380; 18,314; 6,557; 13,713; 17,768; 7,493; 2,771; 2,861; 1,263; 7,285; 28,165; 5,080; 11,622. Assume the underlying population is normal.

a.

  i. $\bar{x}$ = __________

  ii. s_x = __________

  iii. n = __________

  iv. $n - 1$ = __________

b. Define the random variables X and $\bar{X}$ in words.

c. Which distribution should you use for this problem? Explain your choice.

d. Construct a 95% confidence interval for the population mean enrollment at community colleges in the United States.

  i. State the confidence interval.

  ii. Sketch the graph.

a. What will happen to the error bound and confidence interval if 500 community colleges were surveyed? Why?

104. Suppose that a committee is studying whether or not there is waste of time in our judicial system. It is interested in the mean amount of time individuals waste at the courthouse waiting to be called for jury duty. The committee randomly surveyed 81 people who recently served as jurors. The sample mean wait time was eight hours with a sample standard deviation of four hours.

a.
   i. $\bar{x}$ = __________
   ii. s_x = __________
   iii. n = __________
   iv. $n - 1$ = __________

b. Define the random variables XX and X−X- in words.

c. Which distribution should you use for this problem? Explain your choice.

d. Construct a 95% confidence interval for the population mean time wasted.
   i. State the confidence interval.
   ii. Sketch the graph.

e. Explain in a complete sentence what the confidence interval means.

105. A pharmaceutical company makes tranquilizers. It is assumed that the distribution for the length of time they last is approximately normal. Researchers in a hospital used the drug on a random sample of nine patients. The effective period of the tranquilizer for each patient (in hours) was as follows: 2.7; 2.8; 3.0; 2.3; 2.3; 2.2; 2.8; 2.1; and 2.4.

a.
   i. $\bar{x}$ = __________
   ii. s_x = __________
   iii. n = __________
   iv. $n - 1$ = __________

b. Define the random variable X in words.

c. Define the random variable $\bar{X}$ in words.

d. Which distribution should you use for this problem? Explain your choice.

e. Construct a 95% confidence interval for the population mean length of time.
   i. State the confidence interval.
   ii. Sketch the graph.

f. What does it mean to be "95% confident" in this problem?

106. Suppose that 14 children, who were learning to ride two-wheel bikes, were surveyed to determine how long they had to use training wheels. It was revealed that they used them an average of six months with a sample standard deviation of three months. Assume that the underlying population distribution is normal.

a.

i. $\bar{x}$ = __________

ii. s_x = __________

iii. n = __________

iv. $n - 1$ = __________

b. Define the random variable X in words.

c. Define the random variable $\bar{X}$ in words.

d. Which distribution should you use for this problem? Explain your choice.

e. Construct a 99% confidence interval for the population mean length of time using training wheels.

i. State the confidence interval.

ii. Sketch the graph.

f. Why would the error bound change if the confidence level were lowered to 90%?

107. The Federal Election Commission (FEC) collects information about campaign contributions and disbursements for candidates and political committees each election cycle. A political action committee (PAC) is a committee formed to raise money for candidates and campaigns. A Leadership PAC is a PAC formed by a federal politician (senator or representative) to raise money to help other candidates' campaigns.

The FEC has reported financial information for 556 Leadership PACs that operating during the 2011–2012 election cycle. The following table shows the total receipts during this cycle for a random selection of 30 Leadership PACs.

Table 8.3

$46,500.00	$0	$40,966.50	$105,887.20	$5,175.00
$29,050.00	$19,500.00	$181,557.20	$31,500.00	$149,970.80
$2,555,363.20	$12,025.00	$409,000.00	$60,521.70	$18,000.00
$61,810.20	$76,530.80	$119,459.20	$0	$63,520.00
$6,500.00	$502,578.00	$705,061.10	$708,258.90	$135,810.00
$2,000.00	$2,000.00	$0	$1,287,933.80	$219,148.30

$\bar{x}$ = \$251, 854.23

s = \$521, 130.41

Use this sample data to construct a 95% confidence interval for the mean amount of money raised by all Leadership PACs during the 2011–2012 election cycle. Use the Student's t-distribution.

108. *Forbes* magazine published data on the best small firms in 2012. These were firms that had been publicly traded for at least a year, have a stock price of at least $5 per share, and have reported annual revenue between $5 million and $1 billion. The Table 8.4 shows the ages of the corporate CEOs for a random sample of these firms.

Table 8.4

48	58	51	61	56
59	74	63	53	50
59	60	60	57	46
55	63	57	47	55
57	43	61	62	49
67	67	55	55	49

Use this sample data to construct a 90% confidence interval for the mean age of CEO's for these top small firms. Use the Student's t-distribution.

109. Unoccupied seats on flights cause airlines to lose revenue. Suppose a large airline wants to estimate its mean number of unoccupied seats per flight over the past year. To accomplish this, the records of 225 flights are randomly selected and the number of unoccupied seats is noted for each of the sampled flights. The sample mean is 11.6 seats and the sample standard deviation is 4.1 seats.

a.
   i. $\bar{x}$ = __________
   ii. s_x = __________
   iii. n = __________
   iv. n-1 = __________

b. Define the random variables X and $\bar{X}$ in words.

c. Which distribution should you use for this problem? Explain your choice.

d. Construct a 92% confidence interval for the population mean number of unoccupied seats per flight.
   i. State the confidence interval.
   ii Sketch the graph.

110. In a recent sample of 84 used car sales costs, the sample mean was $6,425 with a standard deviation of $3,156. Assume the underlying distribution is approximately normal.

a. Which distribution should you use for this problem? Explain your choice.

b. Define the random variable X–X- in words.

c. Construct a 95% confidence interval for the population mean cost of a used car.

  i. State the confidence interval.

  ii. Sketch the graph.

d. Explain what a "95% confidence interval" means for this study.

111. Six different national brands of chocolate chip cookies were randomly selected at the supermarket. The grams of fat per serving are as follows: 8; 8; 10; 7; 9; 9. Assume the underlying distribution is approximately normal.

a. Construct a 90% confidence interval for the population mean grams of fat per serving of chocolate chip cookies sold in supermarkets.

  i. State the confidence interval.

  ii. Sketch the graph.

b. If you wanted a smaller error bound while keeping the same level of confidence, what should have been changed in the study before it was done?

c. Go to the store and record the grams of fat per serving of six brands of chocolate chip cookies.

d. Calculate the mean.

e. Is the mean within the interval you calculated in part a? Did you expect it to be? Why or why not?

112. A survey of the mean number of cents off that coupons give was conducted by randomly surveying one coupon per page from the coupon sections of a recent San Jose Mercury News. The following data were collected: 20¢; 75¢; 50¢; 65¢; 30¢; 55¢; 40¢; 40¢; 30¢; 55¢; $1.50; 40¢; 65¢; 40¢. Assume the underlying distribution is approximately normal.

a.

  i. $\bar{x}$ = __________

  ii. s_x = __________

  iii. n = __________

  iv. n-1 = __________

b. Define the random variables X and $\bar{X}$ in words.

c. Which distribution should you use for this problem? Explain your choice.

d. Construct a 95% confidence interval for the population mean worth of coupons.

  i State the confidence interval.

  ii. Sketch the graph.

e. If many random samples were taken of size 14, what percent of the confidence intervals constructed should contain the population mean worth of coupons? Explain why.

Use the following information to answer the next two exercises: A quality control specialist for a restaurant chain takes a random sample of size 12 to check the amount of soda served in the 16 oz. serving size. The sample mean is 13.30 with a sample standard deviation of 1.55. Assume the underlying population is normally distributed.

113. Find the 95% Confidence Interval for the true population mean for the amount of soda served.

a. (12.42, 14.18)
b. (12.32, 14.29)
c. (12.50, 14.10)
d. Impossible to determine

8.3 A Confidence Interval for A Population Proportion

114. Insurance companies are interested in knowing the population percent of drivers who always buckle up before riding in a car.

a. When designing a study to determine this population proportion, what is the minimum number you would need to survey to be 95% confident that the population proportion is estimated to within 0.03?
b. If it were later determined that it was important to be more than 95% confident and a new survey was commissioned, how would that affect the minimum number you would need to survey? Why?

115. Suppose that the insurance companies did do a survey. They randomly surveyed 400 drivers and found that 320 claimed they always buckle up. We are interested in the population proportion of drivers who claim they always buckle up.

a.
   i. x = __________
   ii. n = __________
   iii. p' = __________
b. Define the random variables X and P', in words.
c. Which distribution should you use for this problem? Explain your choice.
d. Construct a 95% confidence interval for the population proportion who claim they always buckle up.
   i. State the confidence interval.
   ii. Sketch the graph.
e. If this survey were done by telephone, list three difficulties the companies might have in obtaining random results.

116. According to a recent survey of 1,200 people, 61% feel that the president is doing an acceptable job. We are interested in the population proportion of people who feel the president is doing an acceptable job.

a. Define the random variables *X* and *P′* in words.

b. Which distribution should you use for this problem? Explain your choice.

c. Construct a 90% confidence interval for the population proportion of people who feel the president is doing an acceptable job.

  i. State the confidence interval.

  ii. Sketch the graph.

117. An article regarding interracial dating and marriage recently appeared in the Washington Post. Of the 1,709 randomly selected adults, 315 identified themselves as Latino, 323 identified themselves as Black, 254 identified themselves as Asian, and 779 identified themselves as White. In this survey, 86% of Blacks said that they would welcome a White person into their families. Among Asians, 77% would welcome a White person into their families, 71% would welcome a Latino, and 66% would welcome a Black person.

a. We are interested in finding the 95% confidence interval for the percent of all Black adults who would welcome a White person into their families. Define the random variables *X* and *P*', in words.

b. Which distribution should you use for this problem? Explain your choice.

c. Construct a 95% confidence interval.

  i. State the confidence interval.

  ii. Sketch the graph.

118. Refer to the information in Exercise 8.117.

a. Construct three 95% confidence intervals.

  i. percent of all Asians who would welcome a White person into their families.

  ii. percent of all Asians who would welcome a Latino into their families.

  iii. percent of all Asians who would welcome a Black person into their families.

b. Even though the three point estimates are different, do any of the confidence intervals overlap? Which?

c. For any intervals that do overlap, in words, what does this imply about the significance of the differences in the true proportions?

d. For any intervals that do not overlap, in words, what does this imply about the significance of the differences in the true proportions?

119. Stanford University conducted a study of whether running is healthy for men and women over age 50. During the first eight years of the study, 1.5%

of the 451 members of the 50-Plus Fitness Association died. We are interested in the proportion of people over 50 who ran and died in the same eight-year period.

a. Define the random variables X and P' in words.
b. Which distribution should you use for this problem? Explain your choice.
c. Construct a 97% confidence interval for the population proportion of people over 50 who ran and died in the same eight–year period.
    i. State the confidence interval.
    ii. Sketch the graph.
d. Explain what a "97% confidence interval" means for this study.

120. A telephone poll of 1,000 adult Americans was reported in an issue of Time Magazine. One of the questions asked was "What is the main problem facing the country?" Twenty percent answered "crime." We are interested in the population proportion of adult Americans who feel that crime is the main problem.

a. Define the random variables X and P' in words.
b. Which distribution should you use for this problem? Explain your choice.
c. Construct a 95% confidence interval for the population proportion of adult Americans who feel that crime is the main problem.
    i. State the confidence interval.
    ii. Sketch the graph.
d. Suppose we want to lower the sampling error. What is one way to accomplish that?
e. The sampling error given by Yankelovich Partners, Inc. (which conducted the poll) is ±3%. In one to three complete sentences, explain what the ±3% represents.

121. Refer to Exercise 8.120. Another question in the poll was "[How much are] you worried about the quality of education in our schools?" Sixty-three percent responded "a lot". We are interested in the population proportion of adult Americans who are worried a lot about the quality of education in our schools.

a. Define the random variables X and P' in words.
b. Which distribution should you use for this problem? Explain your choice.
c. Construct a 95% confidence interval for the population proportion of adult Americans who are worried a lot about the quality of education in our schools.
    i. State the confidence interval.
    ii. Sketch the graph.

d. The sampling error given by Yankelovich Partners, Inc. (which conducted the poll) is ±3%. In one to three complete sentences, explain what the ±3% represents.

Use the following information to answer the next three exercises: According to a Field Poll, 79% of California adults (actual results are 400 out of 506 surveyed) feel that "education and our schools" is one of the top issues facing California. We wish to construct a 90% confidence interval for the true proportion of California adults who feel that education and the schools is one of the top issues facing California.

122. A point estimate for the true population proportion is:

a. 0.90
b. 1.27
c. 0.79
d. 400

123. A 90% confidence interval for the population proportion is _______.

a. (0.761, 0.820)
b. (0.125, 0.188)
c. (0.755, 0.826)
d. (0.130, 0.183)

Use the following information to answer the next two exercises: Five hundred and eleven (511) homes in a certain southern California community are randomly surveyed to determine if they meet minimal earthquake preparedness recommendations. One hundred seventy-three (173) of the homes surveyed met the minimum recommendations for earthquake preparedness, and 338 did not.

124. Find the confidence interval at the 90% Confidence Level for the true population proportion of southern California community homes meeting at least the minimum recommendations for earthquake preparedness.

a. (0.2975, 0.3796)
b. (0.6270, 0.6959)
c. (0.3041, 0.3730)
d. (0.6204, 0.7025)

125. The point estimate for the population proportion of homes that do not meet the minimum recommendations for earthquake preparedness is ______.

a. 0.6614
b. 0.3386
c. 173
d. 338

126. On May 23, 2013, Gallup reported that of the 1,005 people surveyed, 76% of U.S. workers believe that they will continue working past retirement age. The confidence level for this study was reported at 95% with a ±3% margin of error.

a. Determine the estimated proportion from the sample.
b. Determine the sample size.
c. Identify CL and α.
d. Calculate the error bound based on the information provided.
e. Compare the error bound in part d to the margin of error reported by Gallup. Explain any differences between the values.

f. Create a confidence interval for the results of this study.

g. A reporter is covering the release of this study for a local news station. How should she explain the confidence interval to her audience?

127. A national survey of 1,000 adults was conducted on May 13, 2013 by Rasmussen Reports. It concluded with 95% confidence that 49% to 55% of Americans believe that big-time college sports programs corrupt the process of higher education.

a. Find the point estimate and the error bound for this confidence interval.

b. Can we (with 95% confidence) conclude that more than half of all American adults believe this?

c. Use the point estimate from part a and n = 1,000 to calculate a 75% confidence interval for the proportion of American adults that believe that major college sports programs corrupt higher education.

d. Can we (with 75% confidence) conclude that at least half of all American adults believe this?

128. Public Policy Polling recently conducted a survey asking adults across the U.S. about music preferences. When asked, 80 of the 571 participants admitted that they have illegally downloaded music.

a. Create a 99% confidence interval for the true proportion of American adults who have illegally downloaded music.

b. This survey was conducted through automated telephone interviews on May 6 and 7, 2013. The error bound of the survey compensates for sampling error, or natural variability among samples. List some factors that could affect the survey's outcome that are not covered by the margin of error.

c. Without performing any calculations, describe how the confidence interval would change if the confidence level changed from 99% to 90%.

129. You plan to conduct a survey on your college campus to learn about the political awareness of students. You want to estimate the true proportion of college students on your campus who voted in the 2012 presidential election with 95% confidence and a margin of error no greater than five percent. How many students must you interview?

8.4 Calculating the Sample Size n: Continuous and Binary Random Variables

130. Among various ethnic groups, the standard deviation of heights is known to be approximately three inches. We wish to construct a 95% confidence interval for the mean height of male Swedes. Forty-eight male Swedes are surveyed. The sample mean is 71 inches. The sample standard deviation is 2.8 inches.

a.
   i. $\bar{x}$ =________
   ii. σ =________
   iii. n =________
b. In words, define the random variables X and $\bar{X}$.
c. Which distribution should you use for this problem? Explain your choice.
d. Construct a 95% confidence interval for the population mean height of male Swedes.
   i. State the confidence interval.
   ii. Sketch the graph.
e. What will happen to the level of confidence obtained if 1,000 male Swedes are surveyed instead of 48? Why?

131. Announcements for 84 upcoming engineering conferences were randomly picked from a stack of IEEE Spectrum magazines. The mean length of the conferences was 3.94 days, with a standard deviation of 1.28 days. Assume the underlying population is normal.

a. In words, define the random variables X and $\bar{X}$.
b. Which distribution should you use for this problem? Explain your choice.
c. Construct a 95% confidence interval for the population mean length of engineering conferences.
   i. State the confidence interval.
   ii. Sketch the graph.

132. Suppose that an accounting firm does a study to determine the time needed to complete one person's tax forms. It randomly surveys 100 people. The sample mean is 23.6 hours. There is a known standard deviation of 7.0 hours. The population distribution is assumed to be normal.

a.
   i. $\bar{x}$ =________
   ii. σ =________
   iii. n =________
b. In words, define the random variables X and $\bar{X}$.
c. Which distribution should you use for this problem? Explain your choice.
d. Construct a 90% confidence interval for the population mean time to complete the tax forms.
   i. State the confidence interval.
   ii. Sketch the graph.

e. If the firm wished to increase its level of confidence and keep the error bound the same by taking another survey, what changes should it make?

f. If the firm did another survey, kept the error bound the same, and only surveyed 49 people, what would happen to the level of confidence? Why?

g. Suppose that the firm decided that it needed to be at least 96% confident of the population mean length of time to within one hour. How would the number of people the firm surveys change? Why?

133. A sample of 16 small bags of the same brand of candies was selected. Assume that the population distribution of bag weights is normal. The weight of each bag was then recorded. The mean weight was two ounces with a standard deviation of 0.12 ounces. The population standard deviation is known to be 0.1 ounce.

a.

i. $\bar{x}$ =________

ii. σ =________

ii. s_x =________

b. In words, define the random variable *X*.

c. In words, define the random variable $\bar{X}$.

d. Which distribution should you use for this problem? Explain your choice.

d. Construct a 90% confidence interval for the population mean weight of the candies.

i. State the confidence interval.

ii. Sketch the graph.

e. Construct a 98% confidence interval for the population mean weight of the candies.

i. State the confidence interval.

ii. Sketch the graph.

iii. Calculate the error bound.

f. In complete sentences, explain why the confidence interval in part f is larger than the confidence interval in part e.

g. In complete sentences, give an interpretation of what the interval in part f means.

134. A camp director is interested in the mean number of letters each child sends during his or her camp session. The population standard deviation is known to be 2.5. A survey of 20 campers is taken. The mean from the sample is 7.9 with a sample standard deviation of 2.8.

a.

i. $\bar{x}$ =________

ii. σ =________
iii. n =________

b. Define the random variables X and $\bar{X}$ in words.
c. Which distribution should you use for this problem? Explain your choice.
d. Construct a 90% confidence interval for the population mean number of letters campers send home.
   i. State the confidence interval.
   ii. Sketch the graph.
e. What will happen to the error bound and confidence interval if 500 campers are surveyed? Why?

135. What is meant by the term "90% confident" when constructing a confidence interval for a mean?
a. If we took repeated samples, approximately 90% of the samples would produce the same confidence interval.
b. If we took repeated samples, approximately 90% of the confidence intervals calculated from those samples would contain the sample mean.
c. If we took repeated samples, approximately 90% of the confidence intervals calculated from those samples would contain the true value of the population mean.
d. If we took repeated samples, the sample mean would equal the population mean in approximately 90% of the samples.

136. The Federal Election Commission collects information about campaign contributions and disbursements for candidates and political committees each election cycle. During the 2012 campaign season, there were 1,619 candidates for the House of Representatives across the United States who received contributions from individuals. Table 8.5 shows the total receipts from individuals for a random selection of 40 House candidates rounded to the nearest \$100. The standard deviation for this data to the nearest hundred is σ = \$909,200.

Table 8.5

\$3,600	\$1,243,900	\$10,900	\$385,200	\$581,500
\$7,400	\$2,900	\$400	\$3,714,500	\$632,500
\$391,000	\$467,400	\$56,800	\$5,800	\$405,200
\$733,200	\$8,000	\$468,700	\$75,200	\$41,000
\$13,300	\$9,500	\$953,800	\$1,113,500	\$1,109,300
\$353,900	\$986,100	\$88,600	\$378,200	\$13,200
\$3,800	\$745,100	\$5,800	\$3,072,100	\$1,626,700
\$512,900	\$2,309,200	\$6,600	\$202,400	\$15,800

a. Find the point estimate for the population mean.

b. Using 95% confidence, calculate the error bound.

c. Create a 95% confidence interval for the mean total individual contributions.

d. Interpret the confidence interval in the context of the problem.

137. The American Community Survey (ACS), part of the United States Census Bureau, conducts a yearly census similar to the one taken every ten years, but with a smaller percentage of participants. The most recent survey estimates with 90% confidence that the mean household income in the U.S. falls between \$69,720 and \$69,922. Find the point estimate for mean U.S. household income and the error bound for mean U.S. household income.

138. The average height of young adult males has a normal distribution with standard deviation of 2.5 inches. You want to estimate the mean height of students at your college or university to within one inch with 93% confidence. How many male students must you measure?

139. If the confidence interval is change to a higher probability, would this cause a lower, or a higher, minimum sample size?

140. If the tolerance is reduced by half, how would this affect the minimum sample size?

141. If the value of p is reduced, would this necessarily reduce the sample size needed?

142. Is it acceptable to use a higher sample size than the one calculated by $\frac{z^2 pq}{e^2}$?

143. A company has been running an assembly line with 97.42%% of the products made being acceptable. Then, a critical piece broke down. After the repairs the decision was made to see if the number of defective products made was still close enough to the long standing production quality. Samples of 500 pieces were selected at random, and the defective rate was found to be 0.025%.

a. Is this sample size adequate to claim the company is checking within the 90% confidence interval?

b. The 95% confidence interval?

REFERENCES

8.1 A Confidence Interval for a Population Standard Deviation, Known or Large Sample Size

"American Fact Finder." U.S. Census Bureau. Available online at http://factfinder2.census.gov/faces/nav/jsf/pages/searchresults.xhtml?refresh=t (accessed July 2, 2013).

"Disclosure Data Catalog: Candidate Summary Report 2012." U.S. Federal Election Commission. Available online at http://www.fec.gov/data/index.jsp (accessed July 2, 2013).

"Headcount Enrollment Trends by Student Demographics Ten-Year Fall Trends to Most Recently Completed Fall." Foothill De Anza Community College District. Available online at http://research.fhda.edu/factbook/FH_Demo_Trends/FoothillDemographicTrends.htm (accessed September 30,2013).

Kuczmarski, Robert J., Cynthia L. Ogden, Shumei S. Guo, Laurence M. Grummer-Strawn, Katherine M. Flegal, Zuguo Mei, Rong Wei, Lester R. Curtin, Alex F. Roche, Clifford L. Johnson. "2000 CDC Growth Charts for the United States: Methods and Development." Centers for Disease Control and Prevention. Available online at http://www.cdc.gov/growthcharts/2000growthchart-us.pdf (accessed July 2, 2013).

La, Lynn, Kent German. "Cell Phone Radiation Levels." c|net part of CBX Interactive Inc. Available online at http://reviews.cnet.com/cell-phone-radiation-levels/ (accessed July 2, 2013).

"Mean Income in the Past 12 Months (in 2011 Inflation-Adjusted Dollars): 2011 American Community Survey 1-Year Estimates." American Fact Finder, U.S. Census Bureau. Available online at http://factfinder2.census.gov/faces/tableservices/jsf/pages/productview.xhtml?pid=ACS_11_1YR_S1902&prodType=table (accessed July 2, 2013).

"Metadata Description of Candidate Summary File." U.S. Federal Election Commission. Available online at http://www.fec.gov/finance/disclosure/metadata/metadataforcandidatesummary.shtml (accessed July 2, 2013).

"National Health and Nutrition Examination Survey." Centers for Disease Control and Prevention. Available online at http://www.cdc.gov/nchs/nhanes.htm (accessed July 2, 2013).

8.2 A Confidence Interval for a Population Standard Deviation Unknown, Small Sample Case

"America's Best Small Companies." Forbes, 2013. Available online at http://www.forbes.com/best-small-companies/list/ (accessed July 2, 2013).

Data from *Microsoft Bookshelf.*

Data from http://www.businessweek.com/.

Data from http://www.forbes.com/.

"Disclosure Data Catalog: Leadership PAC and Sponsors Report, 2012." Federal Election Commission. Available online at http://www.fec.gov/data/index.jsp (accessed July 2,2013).

"Human Toxome Project: Mapping the Pollution in People." Environmental Working Group. Available online at http://www.ewg.org/sites/humantoxome/participants/participant-group.php?group=in+utero%2Fnewborn (accessed July 2, 2013).

"Metadata Description of Leadership PAC List." Federal Election Commission. Available online at http://www.fec.gov/finance/disclosure/metadata/metadataLeadershipPacList.shtml (accessed July 2, 2013).

8.3 A Confidence Interval for A Population Proportion

Jensen, Tom. "Democrats, Republicans Divided on Opinion of Music Icons." Public Policy Polling. Available online at http://www.publicpolicypolling.com/Day2MusicPoll.pdf (accessed July 2, 2013).

Madden, Mary, Amanda Lenhart, Sandra Coresi, Urs Gasser, Maeve Duggan, Aaron Smith, and Meredith Beaton. "Teens, Social Media, and Privacy." PewInternet, 2013. Available online at http://www.pewinternet.org/Reports/2013/Teens-Social-Media-And-Privacy.aspx (accessed July 2, 2013).

Prince Survey Research Associates International. "2013 Teen and Privacy Management Survey." Pew Research Center: Internet and American Life Project. Available online at http://www.pewinternet.org/~/media//Files/Questionnaire/2013/Methods%20and%20Questions_Teens%20and%20Social%20Media.pdf (accessed July 2, 2013).

Saad, Lydia. "Three in Four U.S. Workers Plan to Work Pas Retirement Age: Slightly more say they will do this by choice rather than necessity." Gallup® Economy, 2013. Available online at http://www.gallup.com/poll/162758/three-four-workers-plan-work-past-retirement-age.aspx (accessed July 2, 2013).

The Field Poll. Available online at http://field.com/fieldpollonline/subscribers/ (accessed July 2, 2013).

Zogby. "New SUNYIT/Zogby Analytics Poll: Few Americans Worry about Emergency Situations Occurring in Their Community; Only one in three have an Emergency Plan; 70% Support Infrastructure 'Investment' for National Security." Zogby Analytics, 2013. Available online at http://www.zogbyanalytics.com/news/299-americans-neither-worried-nor-prepared-in-case-of-a-disaster-sunyit-zogby-analytics-poll (accessed July 2, 2013).

"52% Say Big-Time College Athletics Corrupt Education Process." Rasmussen Reports, 2013. Available online at http://www.rasmussenreports.com/public_content/lifestyle/sports/may_2013/52_say_big_time_college_athletics_corrupt_education_process (accessed July 2, 2013).

SOLUTIONS

2. X is the number of hours a patient waits in the emergency room before being called back to be examined. X-X- is the mean wait time of 70 patients in the emergency room.

4. CI: (1.3808, 1.6192)

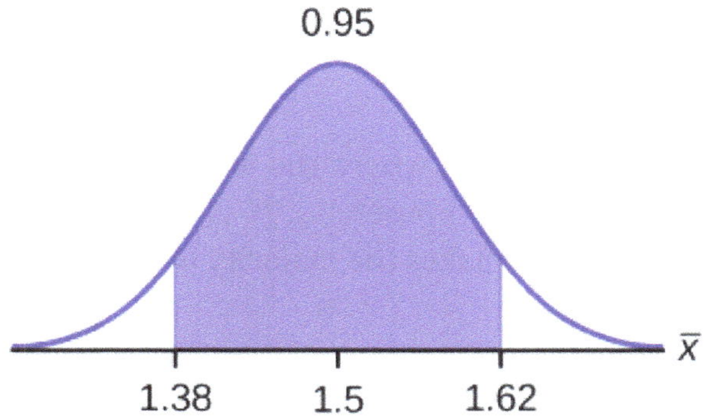

Figure 8.13

$EBM = 0.12$

6. a. $\bar{x} = 151$b. $s_x = 32$

c. $n = 108$ d. $n - 1 = 107$

8. $\bar{X}$ is the mean number of hours spent watching television per month from a sample of 108 Americans.

10. CI: (142.92, 159.08)

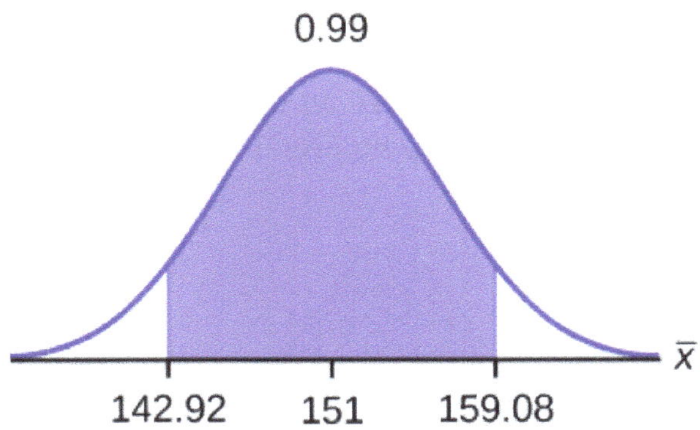

Figure 8.14

$EBM = 8.08$

12. a. 3.26 b. 1.02 c. 39

14. μ

16. t_{38}

18. 0.025

20. (2.93, 3.59)

22. We are 95% confident that the true mean number of colors for national flags is between 2.93 colors and 3.59 colors.

23. The error bound would become EBM = 0.245. This error bound decreases because as sample sizes increase, variability decreases and we need less interval length to capture the true mean.

26. The sample size needed would increase. As the confidence level increases, αα decreases and z(a2)z(a2) increases. To maintain the same error bound, the size of the sample needs to increase.

28. *X* is the number of "successes" where the woman makes the majority of the purchasing decisions for the household. *P'* is the percentage of households sampled where the woman makes the majority of the purchasing decisions for the household.

30. CI: (0.5321, 0.6679)

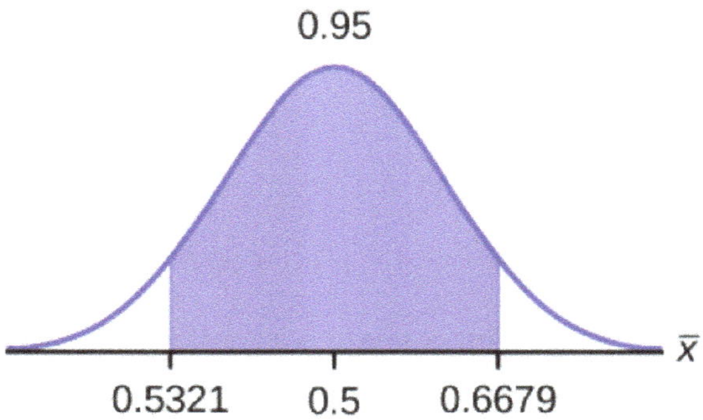

Figure 8.15

EBM: 0.0679

32. *X* is the number of "successes" where an executive prefers a truck. *P'* is the percentage of executives sampled who prefer a truck.

34. CI: (0.19432, 0.33068)

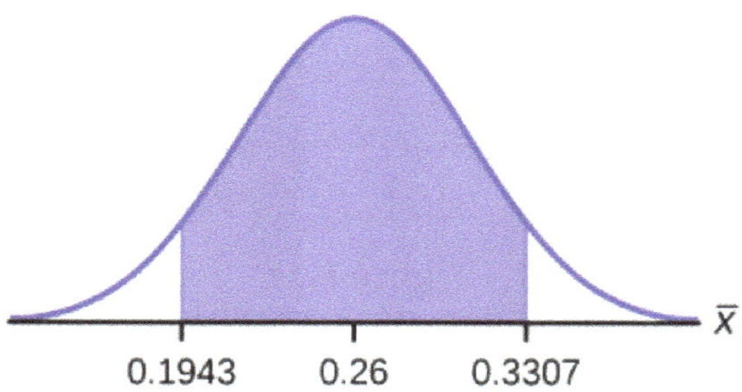

Figure 8.16

36. The sampling error means that the true mean can be 2% above or below the sample mean.

38. P' is the proportion of voters sampled who said the economy is the most important issue in the upcoming election.

40. CI: (0.62735, 0.67265)

EBM: 0.02265

42. The number of girls, ages 8 to 12, in the 5 P.M. Monday night beginning ice-skating class.

44. a. $x = 64$
b. $n = 80$
c. $p' = 0.8$

46. p

48. $P' \sim N\left(0.8, \sqrt{\frac{(0.8)(0.2)}{80}}\right)$. (0.72171, 0.87829).

50. 0.04

52. (0.72; 0.88)

54. With 92% confidence, we estimate the proportion of girls, ages 8 to 12, in a beginning ice-skating class at the Ice Chalet to be between 72% and 88%.

56. The error bound would increase. Assuming all other variables are kept constant, as the confidence level increases, the area under the curve corresponding to the confidence level becomes larger, which creates a wider interval and thus a larger error.

58. a. 244
b. 15
c. 50

60. $N\left(244, \frac{15}{\sqrt{50}}\right)$

62. As the sample size increases, there will be less variability in the mean, so the interval size decreases.

64. X is the time in minutes it takes to complete the U.S. Census short form. X–X- is the mean time it took a sample of 200 people to complete the U.S. Census short form.

66. CI: (7.9441, 8.4559)

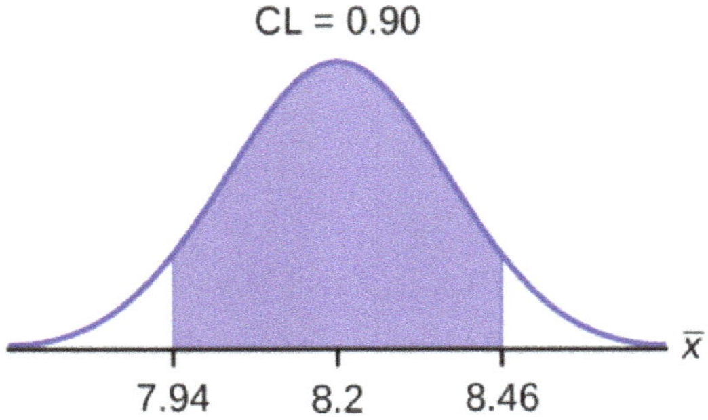

Figure 8.17

68. The level of confidence would decrease because decreasing *n* makes the confidence interval wider, so at the same error bound, the confidence level decreases.

70. a. x‑x‑ = 2.2

b. $\sigma = 0.2$

c. $n = 20$

72. $\bar{X}$ is the mean weight of a sample of 20 heads of lettuce.

74. $EBM = 0.07$

CI: (2.1264, 2.2736)

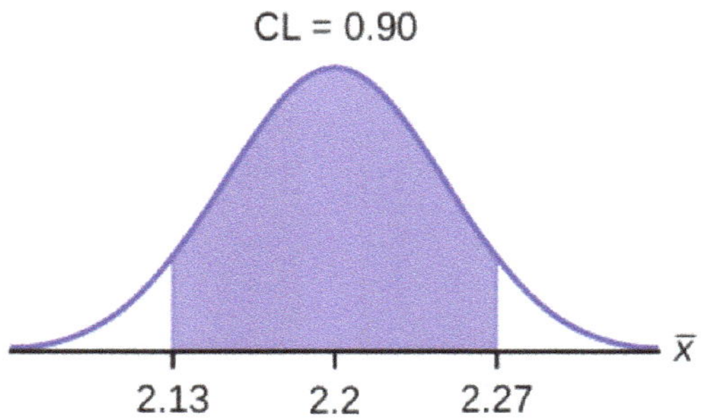

Figure 8.18

76. The interval is greater because the level of confidence increased. If the only change made in the analysis is a change in confidence level, then all we are doing is changing how much area is being calculated for the normal distribution. Therefore, a larger confidence level results in larger areas and larger intervals.

78. The confidence level would increase.

80. 30.4

82. σ

84. μ

86. normal

88. 0.025

90. (24.52,36.28)

92. We are 95% confident that the true mean age for Winger Foothill College students is between 24.52 and 36.28.

94. The error bound for the mean would decrease because as the CL decreases, you need less area under the normal curve (which translates into a smaller interval) to capture the true population mean.

96 2,185

98. 6,765

100. 595

103.

a.
   i. 8629
   ii. 6944
   iii. 35
   iv. 34

b. t_{34}

c.
   i. CI: (6244, 11,014)
   ii.

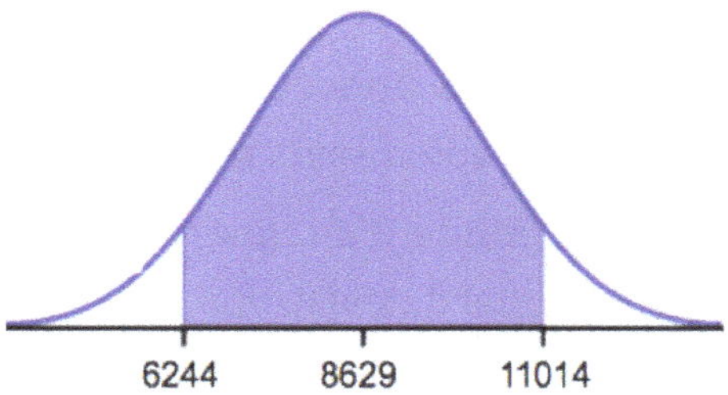

Figure 8.19

d. It will become smaller

105. a.
   i. $\bar{x} = 2.51$
   ii. $s_x = 0.318$
   iii. $n = 9$
   iv. $n - 1 = 8$

b. the effective length of time for a tranquilizer

c. the mean effective length of time of tranquilizers from a sample of nine patients

d. We need to use a Student's-t distribution, because we do not know the population standard deviation.

e.

i. CI: (2.27, 2.76)

ii. Check student's solution.

f. If we were to sample many groups of nine patients, 95% of the samples would contain the true population mean length of time.

107. $\bar{x}$=$251,854.23 s= $521,130.41 Note that we are not given the population standard deviation, only the standard deviation of the sample. There are 30 measures in the sample, so n = 30, and $df = 30 - 1 = 29$ $CL = 0.96$, so $\alpha = 1 - CL = 1 - 0.96 = 0.04$ $\frac{\alpha}{2} = 0.02 t_{\frac{\alpha}{2}} = t_{0.02} = 2.150$ $EBM = t_{\frac{\alpha}{2}}\left(\frac{s}{\sqrt{n}}\right) = 2.150\left(\frac{521,130.41}{\sqrt{30}}\right) \sim \$204,561.66$ $\bar{x} - EBM = \$251,854.23 - \$204,561.66 = \$47,292.57$ $\bar{x} + EBM = \$251,854.23 + \$204,561.66 = \$456,415.89$

We estimate with 96% confidence that the mean amount of money raised by all Leadership PACs during the 2011–2012 election cycle lies between $47,292.57 and $456,415.89.

109. a.

i. $\bar{x} = 11.6$

ii. $s_x = 4.1$

iii. $n = 225$

iv. $n - 1 = 224$

b. X is the number of unoccupied seats on a single flight $\bar{X}$ is the mean number of unoccupied seats from a sample of 225 flights.

c. We will use a Student's-t distribution, because we do not know the population standard deviation.

d.

i. CI: (11.12 , 12.08)

ii. Check student's solution.

111. a.

i. CI: (7.64 , 9.36)

ii.

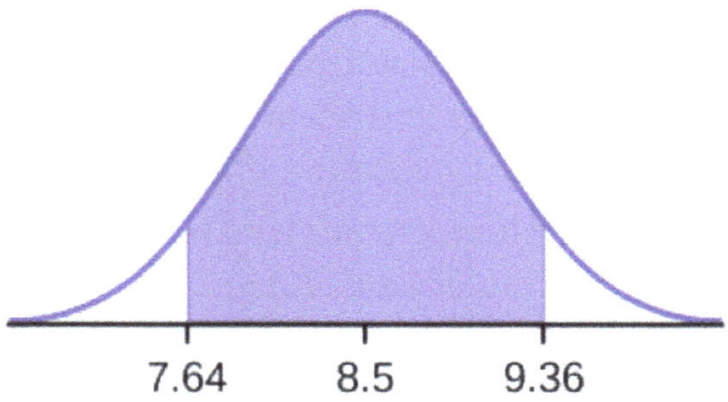

Figure 8.20

a. The sample should have been increased.
b. Answers will vary.
c. Answers will vary.
d. Answers will vary.

113. b

114. a. 1,068
b. The sample size would need to be increased since the critical value increases as the confidence level increases.

116. a. X = the number of people who feel that the president is doing an acceptable job;
P' = the proportion of people in a sample who feel that the president is doing an acceptable job.

$$N\left(0.61, \sqrt{\frac{(0.61)(0.39)}{1200}}\right)$$

b.
i. CI: (0.59, 0.63)
ii. Check student's solution

118. a.
i. (0.72, 0.82)
ii. (0.65, 0.76)
iii (0.60, 0.72)

b. Yes, the intervals (0.72, 0.82) and (0.65, 0.76) overlap, and the intervals (0.65, 0.76) and (0.60, 0.72) overlap.
c. We can say that there does not appear to be a significant difference between the proportion of Asian adults who say that their families would welcome a White person into their families and the proportion of Asian adults who say that their families would welcome a Latino person into their families.

d. We can say that there is a significant difference between the proportion of Asian adults who say that their families would welcome a White person into their families and the proportion of Asian adults who say that their families would welcome a Black person into their families.

120. a. X = the number of adult Americans who feel that crime is the main problem; P' = the proportion of adult Americans who feel that crime is the main problem

b. Since we are estimating a proportion, given P' = 0.2 and n = 1000, the distribution we should use is $N\left(0.2, \sqrt{\frac{(0.2)(0.8)}{1000}}\right)$.

c. i. CI: (0.18, 0.22)

ii. Check student's solution.

d. One way to lower the sampling error is to increase the sample size.

e. The stated "± 3%" represents the maximum error bound. This means that those doing the study are reporting a maximum error of 3%. Thus, they estimate the percentage of adult Americans who feel that crime is the main problem to be between 18% and 22%.

122. c

125. a

127. a. $p' = \frac{(0.55 + 0.49)}{2} = 0.52; EBP = 0.55 - 0.52 = 0.03$

b. No, the confidence interval includes values less than or equal to 0.50. It is possible that less than half of the population believe this.

c. $CL = 0.75$, so $\alpha = 1 - 0.75 = 0.25$ and $\frac{\alpha}{2} = 0.125$ $z_{\frac{\alpha}{2}} = 1.150$. (The area to the right of this z is 0.125, so the area to the left is 1 – 0.125 = 0.875.)

$$EBP = (1.150)\sqrt{\frac{0.52(0.48)}{1,000}} \approx 0.018$$

$$(p' - EBP, p' + EBP) = (0.52 - 0.018, 0.52 + 0.018) = (0.502, 0.538)$$

d. Yes – this interval does not fall less than 0.50 so we can conclude that at least half of all American adults believe that major sports programs corrupt education – but we do so with only 75% confidence.

130. a.

i. 71

ii. 2.8

iii 48

b. X is the height of a male Swede, and $\bar{x}$ is the mean height from a sample of 48 male Swedes.

c. Normal. We know the standard deviation for the population, and the sample size is greater than 30.

i. CI: (70.151, 71.85)

ii.

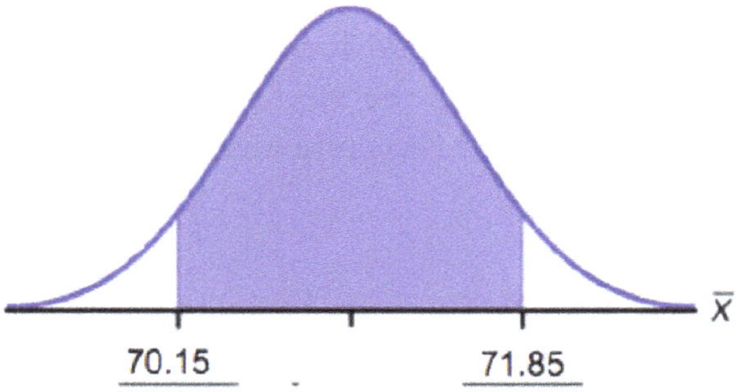

Figure 8.21

e. The confidence interval will decrease in size, because the sample size increased. Recall, when all factors remain unchanged, an increase in sample size decreases variability. Thus, we do not need as large an interval to capture the true population mean.

132. a.

i. $\bar{x}$ = 23.6

ii. σ = 7

iii. n = 100

b. X is the time needed to complete an individual tax form. $\bar{X}$ is the mean time to complete tax forms from a sample of 100 customers.

c. $N\left(23.6, \frac{7}{\sqrt{100}}\right)$ because we know sigma.

d.

i. (22.228, 24.972)

ii.

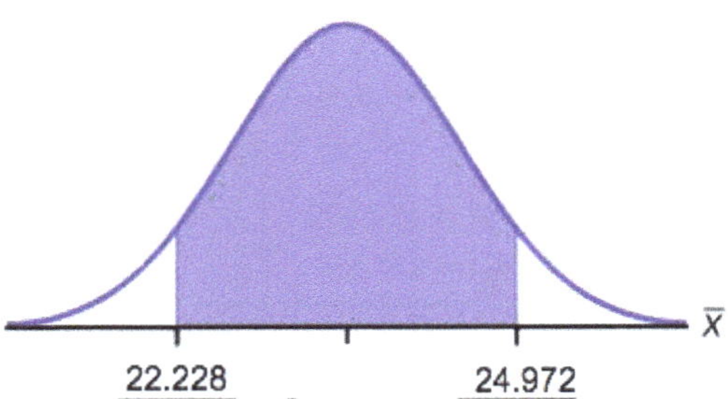

Figure 8.22

e. It will need to change the sample size. The firm needs to determine what the confidence level should be, then apply the error bound formula to determine the necessary sample size.

f. The confidence level would increase as a result of a larger interval. Smaller sample sizes result in more variability. To capture the true population mean, we need to have a larger interval.

g. According to the error bound formula, the firm needs to survey 206 people. Since we increase the confidence level, we need to increase either our error bound or the sample size.

134. a.

i. 7.9

ii. 2.5

iii. 20

b. X is the number of letters a single camper will send home. $\bar{X}$ is the mean number of letters sent home from a sample of 20 campers.

$N\ 7.9\left(\frac{2.5}{\sqrt{20}}\right)$

c.

i. CI: (6.98, 8.82)

ii.

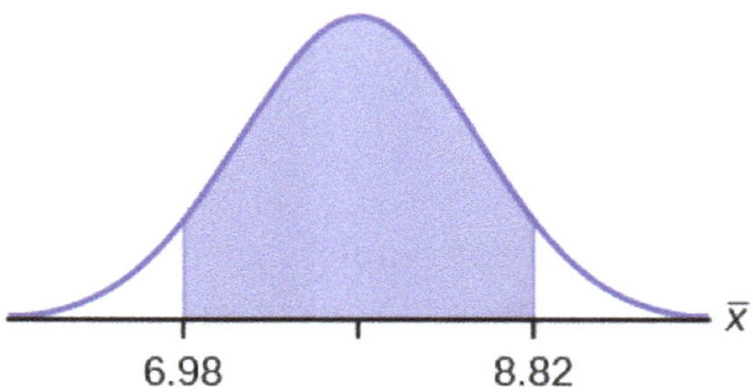

Figure 8.23

d. The error bound and confidence interval will decrease.

136. a. $\bar{x} = \$568{,}873$

$CL = 0.95\ \alpha = 1 - 0.95 = 0.05\ z_{\frac{\alpha}{2}} = 1.96$

b. $EBM = z_{0.025}\frac{\sigma}{\sqrt{n}} = 1.96\frac{909200}{\sqrt{40}} = \$281{,}764$

c. $\bar{x} - EBM = 568{,}873 - 281{,}764 = 287{,}109$

$\bar{x} + EBM = 568{,}873 + 281{,}764 = 850{,}637$

d. We estimate with 95% confidence that the mean amount of contributions received from all individuals by House candidates is between $287,109 and $850,637.

139. Higher

140. It would increase to four times the prior value.

141. No, It could have no affect if it were to change to 1 – p, for example. If it gets closer to 0.5 the minimum sample size would increase.

142. Yes

143.

a. No

b. No

9 Chapter

ONE-SAMPLE HYPOTHESIS TESTING

Figure 9.1 You can use a hypothesis test to decide if a dog breeder's claim that every Dalmatian has 35 spots is statistically sound. (Credit: Robert Neff)

INTRODUCTION: AN OVERVIEW

We are now engaged in the fundamental tasks of the statistician: formulating and evaluating hypotheses. It is essential to situate this content within a broader framework to ensure a comprehensive understanding of the hypothesis formation procedure. Utilizing textbook examples frequently obscures the authentic origin of statistical theories. Statistical testing constitutes a component of the broader process referred to as the scientific method. This method was established over two centuries ago as the recognized means of generating new knowledge. Until then, and regrettably even now, among certain individuals, "knowledge" may be established only by an authority asserting its veracity, ipso dictum. Superstition and conspiracy theories were accepted without serious examination. The scientific method posits that only by a meticulous and defined procedure can a claim be incorporated into the established corpus of knowledge. The process commences with a series of assumptions upon which a hypothesis, also referred to as a model, is constructed. This theory, if valid, will yield predictions, referred to as hypotheses. In Microeconomics, the idea of consumer choice is predicated on specific assumptions regarding human behavior. Based on these assumptions, a theory emerges on consumer choice utilizing indifference curves and the budget constraint. This hypothesis led to a significant prediction: an inverse relationship exists between price and quantity required. This relationship is referred to as the demand curve. The negative slope of the demand curve is only a forecast or hypothesis that may be empirically tested using statistical methods. Had numerous statistical studies of this theory not substantiated this link, the so-called Law of Demand would have been abandoned years ago. The role of statistics is to evaluate the assumptions of diverse theories to ascertain their validity for inclusion in the acknowledged corpus of knowledge; this shapes our understanding of the world. Once accepted, they may subsequently be rejected if alternative theories emerge that offer superior predictions. Recently, two scientists asserted that they could extract more energy from a process than was inputted. This caused a significant commotion for evident reasons. They graced the cover of Time and received substantial offers to transfer their findings to private sector and various universities. Their effort was soon submitted to the stringent evaluations of the scientific method and deemed a failure. No other laboratory was able to reproduce their results. As a result, they have fallen into obscurity and their hypothesis has been abandoned. It may reemerge when an individual can satisfy the hypotheses mandated by the scientific method; nevertheless, until that point, it remains merely a curiosity. Numerous instances of pure fraud have occurred over time, although the majority have been exposed by the application of the scientific method. This discourse aims to elucidate the position of statistics within this process. Statistics and statisticians mostly engage in the evaluation of existing theories rather than the formulation of new ones. Hypotheses originate from these theories grounded in a clear set of assumptions and robust reasoning. The hypothesis precedes the collection of any data. Data do not produce hypotheses; they are employed to evaluate them. Considering this as we examine this part will elucidate the process of hypothesis formation and testing. A statistician's role involves drawing statistical inferences about populations from samples derived from those communities. Confidence intervals serve as a method for estimating a population parameter. Another method for making a statistical inference involves determining the value of a certain parameter. For example, an automobile dealership promotes that its new compact vehicle achieves an average fuel efficiency of 35 miles per gallon. A tutoring organization asserts that their instructional style enables 90% of its students to get an A or B grade. A corporation reports that female managers inside the organization earn an average annual salary of $60,000. A statistician will evaluate these assertions. This procedure is referred to as "hypothesis testing." A hypothesis test entails gathering data from a sample and assessing the findings. The statistician determines if there is adequate evidence, based on data analysis, to reject the null hypothesis. This chapter will focus on doing hypothesis testing for single means and single proportions. You will also acquire knowledge on the faults linked to these tests.

9.1 NULL AND ALTERNATIVE HYPOTHESES

The actual test begins by considering two hypotheses. They are called the null hypothesis and the alternative hypothesis. These hypotheses contain opposing viewpoints.

H_0: **The null hypothesis:** It is a statement of no difference between the variables– they are not related. This can often be considered the status quo and as a result if you cannot accept the null it requires some action.

H_a: **The alternative hypothesis:** It is a claim about the population that is contradictory to H_0 and what we conclude when we cannot accept H_0. This is usually what the researcher is trying to prove. The alternative hypothesis is the contender and must win with significant evidence to overthrow the status quo. This concept is sometimes referred to the tyranny of the status quo because as we will see later, to overthrow the null hypothesis takes usually 90 or greater confidence that this is the proper decision.

Since the null and alternative hypotheses are contradictory, you must examine evidence to decide if you have enough evidence to reject the null hypothesis or not. The evidence is in the form of sample data.

After you have determined which hypothesis the sample supports, you make a decision. There are two options for a decision. They are "cannot accept H_0" if the sample information favors the alternative hypothesis or "do not reject H_0" or "decline to reject H_0" if the sample information is insufficient to reject the null hypothesis. These conclusions are all based upon a level of probability, a significance level, that is set my the analyst.

Table 9.1 presents the various hypotheses in the relevant pairs. For example, if the null hypothesis is equal to some value, the alternative has to be not equal to that value.

Table 9.1

H0	Ha
equal (=)	not equal (≠)
greater than or equal to (≥)	less than (<)
less than or equal to (≤)	more than (>)

NOTE

As a mathematical convention H_0 always has a symbol with an equal in it. H_a never has a symbol with an equal in it. The choice of symbol depends on the wording of the hypothesis test.

EXAMPLE 9.1

H_0: No more than 30% of the registered voters in Santa Clara County voted in the primary election. $p \leq .30$

H_a: More than 30% of the registered voters in Santa Clara County voted in the primary election. $p > 30$

EXAMPLE 9.2

We want to test whether the mean GPA of students in American colleges is different from 2.0 (out of 4.0). The null and alternative hypotheses are: H_0: $\mu = 2.0$

H_a: $\mu \neq 2.0$

EXAMPLE 9.3

We want to test if college students take less than five years to graduate from college, on the average. The null and alternative hypotheses are: H_0: $\mu \geq 5$

H_a: $\mu < 5$

9.2 OUTCOMES AND THE TYPE I AND TYPE II ERRORS

When you perform a hypothesis test, there are four possible outcomes depending on the actual truth (or falseness) of the null hypothesis H_0 and the decision to reject or not. The outcomes are summarized in the following table:

Table 9.2

Statistical Decision	H0 is actually...	
	True	False
Cannot reject *H0*	Correct outcome	Type II error
Cannot accept *H0*	Type I error	Correct outcome

The four possible outcomes in the table are:

1. The decision is cannot reject H_0 when H_0 is true (correct decision).
2. The decision is cannot accept H_0 when H_0 is true (incorrect decision known as a Type I error). This case is described as "rejecting a good null". As we will see later, it is this type of error that we will guard against by setting the probability of making such an error. The goal is to NOT take an action that is an error.
3. The decision is cannot reject H_0 when, in fact, H_0 is false (incorrect decision known as a Type II error). This is called "accepting a false null". In this situation you have allowed the status quo to remain in force when it should be overturned. As we will see, the null hypothesis has the advantage in competition with the alternative.
4. The decision is cannot accept H_0 when H_0 is false (correct decision).

Each of the errors occurs with a particular probability. The Greek letters α and β represent the probabilities.

α = probability of a Type I error = P(Type I error) = probability of rejecting the null hypothesis when the null hypothesis is true: rejecting a good null.

β = probability of a Type II error = P**(Type II error)** = probability of not rejecting the null hypothesis when the null hypothesis is false. $(1 - \beta)$ is called the Power of the Test.

α and β should be as small as possible because they are probabilities of errors.

Statistics allows us to set the probability that we are making a Type I error. The probability of making a Type I error is α. Recall that the confidence intervals in the last unit were set by choosing a value called Z_α (or t_α) and the alpha value determined the confidence level of the estimate because it was the probability of the interval failing to capture the true mean (or proportion parameter p). This alpha and that one are the same.

The easiest way to see the relationship between the alpha error and the level of confidence is with the following figure.

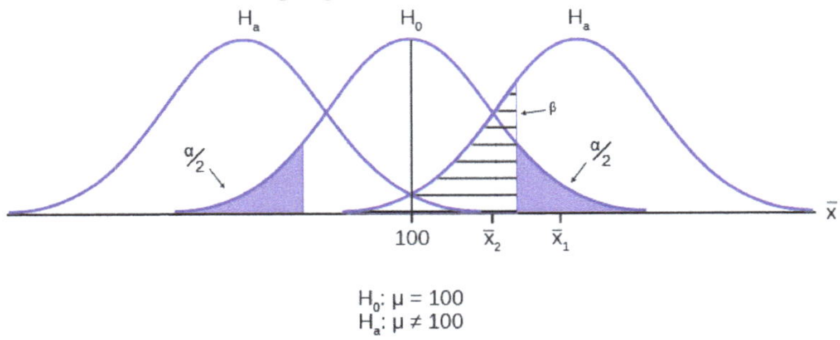

Figure 9.2

In the center of Figure 9.2 is a normally distributed sampling distribution marked H_0. This is a sampling distribution of $\bar{X}$ and by the Central Limit Theorem it is normally distributed. The distribution in the center is marked H_0 and represents the distribution for the null hypotheses H_0: μ = 100. This is the value that is being tested. The formal statements of the null and alternative hypotheses are listed below the figure.

The distributions on either side of the H_0 distribution represent distributions that would be true if H_0 is false, under the alternative hypothesis listed as H_a. We do not know which is true, and will never know. There are, in fact, an infinite number of distributions from which the data could have been drawn if H_a is true, but only two of them are on Figure 9.2 representing all of the others.

To test a hypothesis we take a sample from the population and determine if it could have come from the hypothesized distribution with an acceptable level of significance. This level of significance is the alpha error and is marked on Figure 9.2 as the shaded areas in each tail of the H_0 distribution. (Each area is actually $\alpha/2$ because the distribution is symmetrical and the alternative hypothesis allows for the possibility for the value to be either greater than or less than the hypothesized value--called a two-tailed test).

If the sample mean marked as $\bar{X}_1$ is in the tail of the distribution of H_0, we conclude that the probability that it could have come from the H_0 distribution is less than alpha. We consequently state, "the null hypothesis cannot be accepted with (α) level of significance". The truth may be that this $\bar{X}_1$ did come from the H_0 distribution, but from out in the tail. If this is so then we have falsely rejected a true null hypothesis and have made a Type I error. What statistics has done is provide an estimate about what we know, and what we control, and that is the probability of us being wrong, α.

We can also see in Figure 9.2 that the sample mean could be really from an H_a distribution, but within the boundary set by the alpha level. Such a case is marked as $\bar{X}_2$. There is a probability that $\bar{X}_2$ actually came from H_a but shows up in the range of H_0 between the two tails. This probability is the beta error, the probability of accepting a false null.

Our problem is that we can only set the alpha error because there are an infinite number of alternative distributions from which the mean could have come that are not equal to H_0. As a result, the statistician places the burden of proof on the alternative hypothesis. That is, we will not reject a null hypothesis unless there is a greater than 90, or 95, or even 99 percent probability that the null is false: the burden of proof lies with the alternative hypothesis. This is why we called this the tyranny of the status quo earlier.

By way of example, the American judicial system begins with the concept that a defendant is "presumed innocent". This is the status quo and is the null hypothesis. The judge will tell the jury that they cannot find the defendant guilty unless the evidence indicates guilt beyond a "reasonable doubt" which is usually defined in criminal cases as 95% certainty of guilt. If the jury cannot accept the null, innocent, then action will be taken, jail time. The burden of proof always lies with the alternative hypothesis. (In civil cases, the jury needs only to be more than 50% certain of wrongdoing to find culpability, called "a preponderance of the evidence").

The example above was for a test of a mean, but the same logic applies to tests of hypotheses for all statistical parameters one may wish to test.

The following are examples of Type I and Type II errors.

EXAMPLE 9.4

Suppose the null hypothesis, H_0, is: Frank's rock climbing equipment is safe.

Type I error: Frank thinks that his rock climbing equipment may not be safe when, in fact, it really is safe.

Type II error: Frank thinks that his rock climbing equipment may be safe when, in fact, it is not safe.

α = probability that Frank thinks his rock climbing equipment may not be safe when, in fact, it really is safe. β = probability that Frank thinks his rock climbing equipment may be safe when, in fact, it is not safe.

Notice that, in this case, the error with the greater consequence is the Type II error. (If Frank thinks his rock climbing equipment is safe, he will go ahead and use it.)

This is a situation described as "accepting a false null".

EXAMPLE 9.5

Suppose the null hypothesis, H_0, is: The victim of an automobile accident is alive when he arrives at the emergency room of a hospital. This is the status quo and requires no action if it is true. If the null hypothesis cannot be accepted then action is required and the hospital will begin appropriate procedures.

Type I error: The emergency crew thinks that the victim is dead when, in fact, the victim is alive. Type II error: The emergency crew does not know if the victim is alive when, in fact, the victim is dead.

α = probability that the emergency crew thinks the victim is dead when, in fact, he is really alive = P(Type I error). β = probability that the emergency crew does not know if the victim is alive when, in fact, the victim is dead = *P*(Type II error).

The error with the greater consequence is the Type I error. (If the emergency crew thinks the victim is dead, they will not treat him.)

TRY IT 9.5

Suppose the null hypothesis, H_0, is: a patient is not sick. Which type of error has the greater consequence, Type I or Type II?

EXAMPLE 9.6

It's a Boy Genetic Labs claim to be able to increase the likelihood that a pregnancy will result in a boy being born. Statisticians want to test the claim. Suppose that the null hypothesis, H_0, is: It's a Boy Genetic Labs has no effect on gender outcome. The status quo is that the claim is false. The burden of proof always falls to the person making the claim, in this case the Genetics Lab.

Type I error: This results when a true null hypothesis is rejected. In the context of this scenario, we would state that we believe that It's a Boy Genetic Labs influences the gender outcome, when in fact it has no effect. The probability of this error occurring is denoted by the Greek letter alpha, α.

Type II error: This results when we fail to reject a false null hypothesis. In context, we would state that It's a Boy Genetic Labs does not influence the gender outcome of a pregnancy when, in fact, it does. The probability of this error occurring is denoted by the Greek letter beta, β.

The error of greater consequence would be the Type I error since couples would use the It's a Boy Genetic Labs product in hopes of increasing the chances of having a boy.

TRY IT 9.6

"Red tide" is a bloom of poison-producing algae–a few different species of a class of plankton called dinoflagellates. When the weather and water conditions cause these blooms, shellfish such as clams living in the area develop dangerous levels of a paralysis-inducing toxin. In Massachusetts, the Division of Marine Fisheries (DMF) monitors levels of the toxin in shellfish by regular sampling of shellfish along the coastline. If the mean level of toxin in clams exceeds 800 μg (micrograms) of toxin per kg of clam meat in any area, clam harvesting is banned there until the bloom is over and levels of toxin in clams subside. Describe both a Type I and a Type II error in this context, and state which error has the greater consequence.

EXAMPLE 9.7

A certain experimental drug claims a cure rate of at least 75% for males with prostate cancer. Describe both the Type I and Type II errors in context. Which error is the more serious?

Type I: A cancer patient believes the cure rate for the drug is less than 75% when it actually is at least 75%.

Type II: A cancer patient believes the experimental drug has at least a 75% cure rate when it has a cure rate that is less than 75%.

In this scenario, the Type II error contains the more severe consequence. If a patient believes the drug works at least 75% of the time, this most likely will influence the patient's (and doctor's) choice about whether to use the drug as a treatment option.

9.3 DISTRIBUTION NEEDED FOR HYPOTHESIS TESTING

Earlier, we discussed sampling distributions. Particular distributions are associated with hypothesis testing.We will perform hypotheses tests of a population mean using a normal distribution or a Student's *t*-distribution. (Remember, use a Student's *t*-distribution when the population standard deviation is unknown and the sample size is small, where small is considered to be less than 30 observations.) We perform tests of a population proportion using a normal distribution when we can assume that the distribution is normally distributed. We consider this to be true if the sample proportion, *p*', times the sample size is greater than 5 and 1-*p*' times the sample size is also greater than 5. This is the same rule of thumb we used when developing the formula for the confidence interval for a population proportion.

Hypothesis Test for the Mean

Going back to the standardizing formula we can derive the test statistic for testing hypotheses concerning means.

$$Z_c = \frac{\bar{x} - \mu_0}{\sigma / \sqrt{n}}$$

The standardizing formula cannot be solved as it is because we do not have μ, the population mean. However, if we substitute in the hypothesized value of the mean, μ_0 in the formula as above, we can compute a Z value. This is the test statistic for a test of hypothesis for a mean and is presented in Figure 9.3. We interpret this Z value as the associated probability that a sample with a sample mean of $\bar{X}$ could have come from a distribution with a population mean of H_0 and we call this Z value Z_c for "calculated". Figure 9.3 and Figure 9.4 show this process.

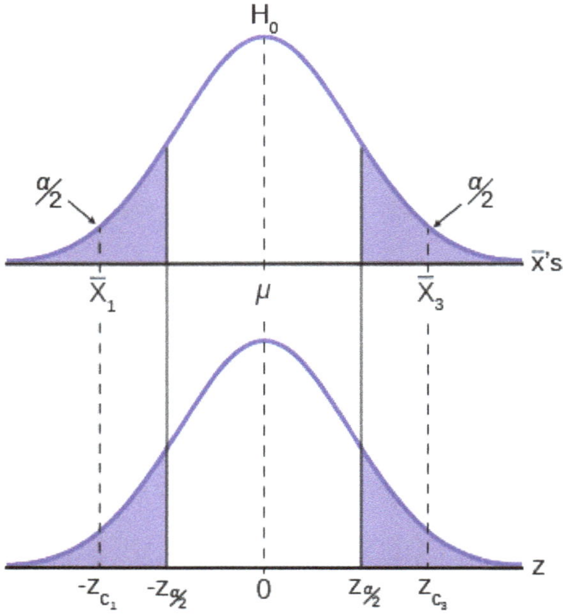

Figure 9.3

In Figure 9.3 two of the three possible outcomes are presented. $\bar{X}_1$ and $\bar{X}_3$ are in the tails of the hypothesized distribution of H_0. Notice that the horizontal axis in the top panel is labeled $\bar{X}$'s. This is the same theoretical distribution of $\bar{X}$'s, the sampling distribution, that the Central Limit Theorem tells us is normally distributed. This is why we can draw it with this shape. The horizontal axis of the bottom panel is labeled Z and is the standard normal distribution. $Z_{\frac{\alpha}{2}}$ and $-Z_{\frac{\alpha}{2}}$, called the **critical values**, are marked on the bottom panel as the Z values associated with the probability the analyst has set as the level of significance in the test, (α). The probabilities in the tails of both panels are, therefore, the same.

Notice that for each $\bar{X}$ there is an associated Z_c, called the calculated Z, that comes from solving the equation above. This calculated Z is nothing more than the number of standard deviations that the hypothesized mean is from the sample mean. If the sample mean falls "too many" standard deviations from the hypothesized mean we conclude that the sample mean could not have come from the distribution with the hypothesized mean, given our pre-set required level of significance. It could have come from H_0, but it is deemed just too unlikely. In Figure 9.3 both $\bar{X}_1$ and $\bar{X}_3$ are in the tails of the distribution. They are deemed "too far" from the hypothesized value of the mean given the chosen level of alpha. If in fact this sample mean it did come from H_0, but from in the tail, we have made a Type I error: we have rejected a good null. Our only real comfort is that we know the probability of making such an error, α, and we can control the size of α.

Figure 9.4 shows the third possibility for the location of the sample mean, $\overline{x}$. Here the sample mean is within the two critical values. That is, within the probability of (1-α) and we cannot reject the null hypothesis.

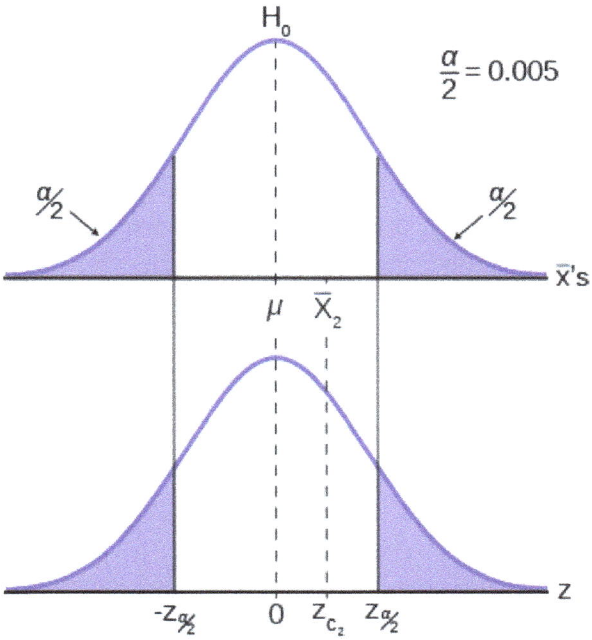

Figure 9.4

This gives us the decision rule for testing a hypothesis for a two-tailed test:

Table 9.3

Decision rule: two-tail test
If $Z_c < \left\|Z_{\frac{\alpha}{2}}\right\|$: then do not REJECT *H0*
If $Z_c > \left\|Z_{\frac{\alpha}{2}}\right\|$: then REJECT *H0*

This rule will always be the same no matter what hypothesis we are testing or what formulas we are using to make the test. The only change will be to change the Z_c to the appropriate symbol for the test statistic for the parameter being tested. Stating the decision rule another way: if the sample mean is unlikely to have come from the distribution with the hypothesized mean we cannot accept the null hypothesis. Here we define "unlikely" as having a probability less than alpha of occurring.

P-Value Approach

An alternative decision rule can be developed by calculating the probability that a sample mean could be found that would give a test statistic larger than the test statistic found from the current sample data assuming that the null hypothesis is true. Here the notion of "likely" and "unlikely" is defined by the probability of drawing a sample with a mean from a population with the hypothesized mean that is either larger or smaller than that found in the sample data. Simply stated, the p-value approach compares the desired significance level, α, to the p-value which is the probability of drawing a sample mean further from the hypothesized value than the actual sample mean. A large *p*-value calculated from the data indicates that we should not reject the **null hypothesis.** The smaller the *p*-value, the more unlikely the outcome, and the stronger the evidence is against the null hypothesis. We would reject the null hypothesis if the evidence is strongly against it. The relationship between the decision rule of comparing the calculated test statistics, Z_c, and the Critical Value, Z_α , and using the *p*-value can be seen in Figure 9.5.

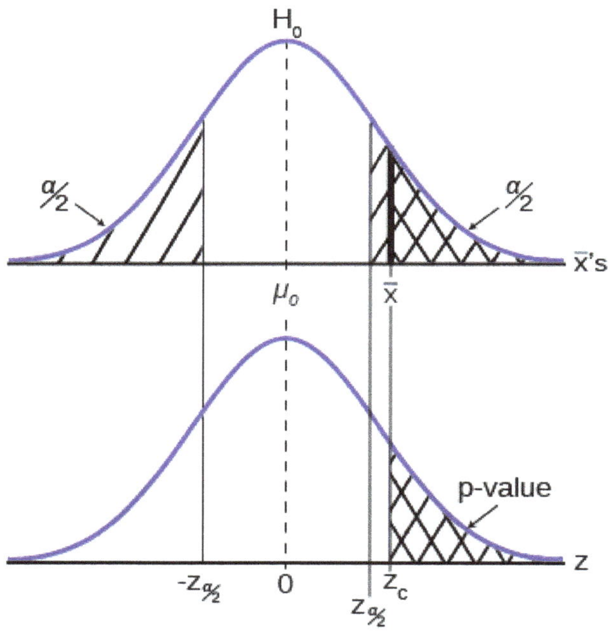

Figure 9.5

The calculated value of the test statistic is Z_c in this example and is marked on the bottom graph of the standard normal distribution because it is a Z value. In this case the calculated value is in the tail and thus we cannot accept the null hypothesis, the associated $\bar{X}$ is just too unusually large to believe that it came from the distribution with a mean of μ_0 with a significance level of α.

If we use the *p*-value decision rule we need one more step. We need to find in the standard normal table the probability associated with the calculated test statistic, Z_c. We then compare that to the α associated with our selected level of confidence. In Figure 9.5 we see that the *p*-value is less than α and therefore we cannot accept the null. We know that the *p*-value is less than α because the area under the p-value is smaller than α/2. It is important to note that two researchers drawing randomly from the same population may find two different P-values from their samples. This occurs because the P-value is calculated as the probability in the tail beyond the sample mean assuming that the null hypothesis is correct. Because the sample means will in all likelihood be different this will create two different P-values. Nevertheless, the conclusions as to the null hypothesis should be different with only the level of probability of α.

Here is a systematic way to make a decision of whether you cannot accept or cannot reject a null hypothesis if using the *p*-value and a preset or preconceived α (the "significance level"). A preset α is the probability of a Type I error (rejecting the null hypothesis when the null hypothesis is true). It may or may not be given to you at the beginning of the problem. In any case, the value of α is the decision of the analyst. When you make a decision to reject or not reject H_0, do as follows:

- If $\alpha > p$-value, cannot accept H_0. The results of the sample data are significant. There is sufficient evidence to conclude that H_0 is an incorrect belief and that the alternative hypothesis, H_a, may be correct.
- If $\alpha \leq p$-value, cannot reject H_0. The results of the sample data are not significant. There is not sufficient evidence to conclude that the alternative hypothesis, H_a, may be correct. In this case the status quo stands.
- When you "cannot reject H_0", it does not mean that you should believe that H_0 is true. It simply means that the sample data have failed to provide sufficient evidence to cast serious doubt about the truthfulness of H_0. Remember that the null is the status quo and it takes high probability to overthrow the status quo. This bias in favor of the null hypothesis is what gives rise to the statement "tyranny of the status quo" when discussing hypothesis testing and the scientific method.

Both decision rules will result in the same decision and it is a matter of preference which one is used.

One and Two-tailed Tests

The discussion of Figure 9.3-Figure 9.5 was based on the null and alternative hypothesis presented in Figure 9.3. This was called a two-tailed test because the alternative hypothesis allowed that the mean could have come from a population which was either larger or smaller than the hypothesized mean in the null hypothesis. This could be seen by the statement of the alternative hypothesis as $\mu \neq 100$, in this example.

It may be that the analyst has no concern about the value being "too" high or "too" low from the hypothesized value. If this is the case, it becomes a one-tailed test and all of the alpha probability is placed in just one tail and not split into α/2 as in the above case of a two-tailed test. Any test of a claim will be a one-tailed test. For example, a car manufacturer claims that their Model 17B provides gas mileage of greater than 25 miles per gallon. The null and alternative hypothesis would be:

- H_0: $\mu \le 25$
- H_a: $\mu > 25$

The claim would be in the alternative hypothesis. The burden of proof in hypothesis testing is carried in the alternative. This is because failing to reject the null, the status quo, must be accomplished with 90 or 95 percent confidence that it cannot be maintained. Said another way, we want to have only a 5 or 10 percent probability of making a Type I error, rejecting a good null; overthrowing the status quo.

This is a one-tailed test and all of the alpha probability is placed in just one tail and not split into α/2 as in the above case of a two-tailed test.

Figure 9.6 shows the two possible cases and the form of the null and alternative hypothesis that give rise to them.

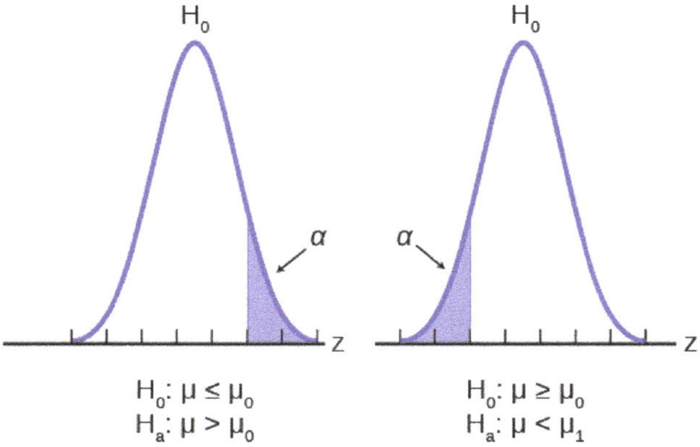

Figure 9.6

where μ_0 is the hypothesized value of the population mean.

Table 9.4 Test Statistics for Test of Means, Varying Sample Size, Population Standard Deviation Known or Unknown

Sample size	Test statistic
< 30 (σ unknown)	$t_c = \frac{\bar{X} - \mu_0}{s / \sqrt{n}}$
< 30 (σ known)	$Z_c = \frac{\bar{X} - \mu_0}{\sigma / \sqrt{n}}$
> 30 (σ unknown)	$Z_c = \frac{\bar{X} - \mu_0}{s / \sqrt{n}}$
> 30 (σ known)	$Z_c = \frac{\bar{X} - \mu_0}{\sigma / \sqrt{n}}$

Effects of Sample Size on Test Statistic

In developing the confidence intervals for the mean from a sample, we found that most often we would not have the population standard deviation, σ. If the sample size were less than 30, we could simply substitute the point estimate for σ, the sample standard deviation, s, and use the student's *t*-distribution to correct for this lack of information.

When testing hypotheses we are faced with this same problem and the solution is exactly the same. Namely: If the population standard deviation is unknown, and the sample size is less than 30, substitute s, the point estimate for the population standard deviation, σ, in the formula for the test statistic and use the student's *t*-distribution. All the formulas and figures above are unchanged except for this substitution and changing the Z distribution to the student's *t*-distribution on the graph. Remember that the student's *t*-distribution can only be computed knowing the proper degrees of freedom for the problem. In this case, the degrees of freedom is computed as before with confidence intervals: df = (n-1). The calculated t-value is compared to the t-value associated with the pre-set level of confidence required in the test, $t_{\alpha, df}$ found in the student's t tables. If we do not know σ, but the sample size is 30 or more, we simply substitute s for σ and use the normal distribution.

Table 9.4 summarizes these rules.

A Systematic Approach for Testing A Hypothesis

A systematic approach to hypothesis testing follows the following steps and in this order. This template will work for all hypotheses that you will ever test.

- Set up the null and alternative hypothesis. This is typically the hardest part of the process. Here the question being asked is reviewed. What parameter is being tested, a mean, a proportion, differences in means, etc. Is this a one-tailed test or two-tailed test?

- Decide the level of significance required for this particular case and determine the critical value. These can be found in the appropriate statistical table. The levels of confidence typical for businesses are 80, 90, 95, 98, and 99. However, the level of significance is a policy decision and should be based upon the risk of making a Type I error, rejecting a good null. Consider the consequences of making a Type I error.

  Next, on the basis of the hypotheses and sample size, select the appropriate test statistic and find the relevant critical value: Z_α, t_α, etc. Drawing the relevant probability distribution and marking the critical value is always big help. Be sure to match the graph with the hypothesis, especially if it is a one-tailed test.

- Take a sample(s) and calculate the relevant parameters: sample mean, standard deviation, or proportion. Using the formula for the test statistic from above in step 2, now calculate the test statistic for this particular case using the parameters you have just calculated.
- Compare the calculated test statistic and the critical value. Marking these on the graph will give a good visual picture of the situation. There are now only two situations:
    a. The test statistic is in the tail: Cannot Accept the null, the probability that this sample mean (proportion) came from the hypothesized distribution is too small to believe that it is the real home of these sample data.
    b. The test statistic is not in the tail: Cannot Reject the null, the sample data are compatible with the hypothesized population parameter.
- Reach a conclusion. It is best to articulate the conclusion two different ways. First a formal statistical conclusion such as "With a 5 % level of significance we cannot accept the null hypotheses that the population mean is equal to XX (units of measurement)". The second statement of the conclusion is less formal and states the action, or lack of action, required. If the formal conclusion was that above, then the informal one might be, "The machine is broken and we need to shut it down and call for repairs".

All hypotheses tested will go through this same process. The only changes are the relevant formulas and those are determined by the hypothesis required to answer the original question.

9.4 FULL HYPOTHESIS TEST EXAMPLES

Tests on Means

EXAMPLE 9.8

Jeffrey, as an eight-year old, established a mean time of 16.43 seconds for swimming the 25-yard freestyle, with a standard deviation of 0.8 seconds. His dad, Frank, thought that Jeffrey could swim the 25-yard freestyle faster using goggles. Frank bought Jeffrey a new pair of expensive goggles and timed Jeffrey for 15 25-yard freestyle swims. For the 15 swims, Jeffrey's mean time was 16 seconds. Frank thought that the goggles helped Jeffrey to swim faster than the 16.43 seconds. Conduct a hypothesis test using a preset $\alpha = 0.05$.

Solution 9.8

Set up the Hypothesis Test:

Since the problem is about a mean, this is a test of a single population mean.

Set the null and alternative hypothesis:

In this case there is an implied challenge or claim. This is that the goggles will reduce the swimming time. The effect of this is to set the hypothesis as a one-tailed test. The claim will always be in the alternative hypothesis because the burden of proof always lies with the alternative. Remember that the status quo must be defeated with a high degree of confidence, in this case 95 % confidence. The null and alternative hypotheses are thus:

$H_0: \mu \geq 16.43 \qquad H_a: \mu < 16.43$

For Jeffrey to swim faster, his time will be less than 16.43 seconds. The "<" tells you this is left-tailed.

Determine the distribution needed:

Random variable: $\bar{X}$ = the mean time to swim the 25-yard freestyle.

Distribution for the test statistic:

The sample size is less than 30 and we do not know the population standard deviation so this is a t-test. and the proper formula is: $t_c = \frac{\bar{X} - \mu_0}{\sigma / \sqrt{n}}$

$\mu0$ = 16.43 comes from *H0* and not the data. $\bar{x}$ = 16. *s* = 0.8, and *n* = 15.

Our step 2, setting the level of significance, has already been determined by the problem, .05 for a 95 % significance level. It is worth thinking about the meaning of this choice. The Type I error is to conclude that Jeffrey swims the 25-yard freestyle, on average, in less than 16.43 seconds when, in fact, he actually swims the 25-yard freestyle, on average, in 16.43 seconds. (Reject the null hypothesis when the null hypothesis is true.) For this case the only concern with a Type I error would seem to be that Jeffery's dad may fail to bet on his son's victory because he does not have appropriate confidence in the effect of the goggles.

To find the critical value we need to select the appropriate test statistic. We have concluded that this is a t-test on the basis of the sample size and that we are interested in a population mean. We can now draw the graph of the t-distribution and mark the critical value. For this problem the degrees of freedom are n-1, or 14. Looking up 14 degrees of freedom at the 0.05 column of the t-table we find 1.761. This is the critical value and we can put this on our graph.

Step 3 is the calculation of the test statistic using the formula we have selected. We find that the calculated test statistic is 2.08, meaning that the sample mean is 2.08 standard deviations away from the hypothesized mean of 16.43.

$$t_c = \frac{\bar{x} - \mu_0}{\frac{s}{\sqrt{n}}} = \frac{16 - 16.43}{\frac{.8}{\sqrt{15}}} = -2.08$$

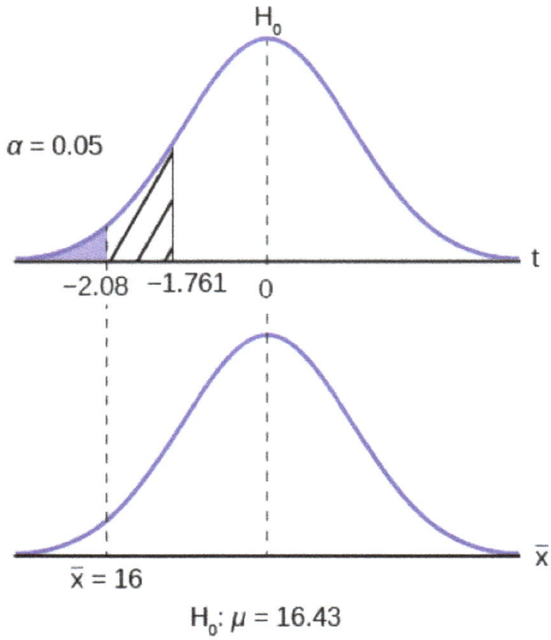

Figure 9.7

Step 4 has us compare the test statistic and the critical value and mark these on the graph. We see that the test statistic is in the tail and thus we move to step 4 and reach a conclusion. The probability that an average time of 16 minutes could come from a distribution with a population mean of 16.43 minutes is too unlikely for us to accept the null hypothesis. We cannot accept the null.

Step 5 has us state our conclusions first formally and then less formally. A formal conclusion would be stated as: "With a 95% level of significance we cannot accept the null hypothesis that the swimming time with goggles comes from a distribution with a population mean time of 16.43 minutes." Less formally, "With 95% significance we believe that the goggles improves swimming speed"

If we wished to use the p-value system of reaching a conclusion we would calculate the statistic and take the additional step to find the probability of being 2.08 standard deviations from the mean on a t-distribution. This value is .0187. Comparing this to the α-level of .05 we see that we cannot accept the null. The p-value has been put on the graph as the shaded area beyond -2.08 and it shows that it is smaller than the hatched area which is the alpha level of 0.05. Both methods reach the same conclusion that we cannot accept the null hypothesis.

TRY IT 9.8

The mean throwing distance of a football for Marco, a high school freshman quarterback, is 40 yards, with a standard deviation of two yards. The team coach tells Marco to adjust his grip to get more distance. The coach records the distances for 20 throws. For the 20 throws, Marco's mean distance was 45 yards. The coach thought the different grip helped Marco throw farther than 40 yards. Conduct a hypothesis test using a preset $\alpha = 0.05$. Assume the throw distances for footballs are normal.

First, determine what type of test this is, set up the hypothesis test, find the *p*-value, sketch the graph, and state your conclusion.

EXAMPLE 9.9

Jane has just begun her new job as on the sales force of a very competitive company. In a sample of 16 sales calls it was found that she closed the contract for an average value of 108 dollars with a standard deviation of 12 dollars. Test at 5% significance that the population mean is at least 100 dollars against the alternative that it is less than 100 dollars. Company policy requires that new members of the sales force must exceed an average of $100 per contract during the trial employment period. Can we conclude that Jane has met this requirement at the significance level of 95%?

Solution 9.9

1. $H_0: \mu \leq 100$

   $H_a: \mu > 100$

The null and alternative hypothesis are for the parameter μ because the number of dollars of the contracts is a continuous random variable. Also, this is a one-tailed test because the company has only an interested if the number of dollars per contact is below a particular number not "too high" a number. This can be thought of as making a claim that the requirement is being met and thus the claim is in the alternative hypothesis.

2. Test statistic: $t_c = \frac{\bar{x} - \mu_0}{\frac{s}{\sqrt{n}}} = \frac{108 - 100}{\left(\frac{12}{\sqrt{16}}\right)} = 2.67$

3. Critical value: $t_a = 1.753$ with n-1 degrees of freedom= 15

The test statistic is a Student's t because the sample size is below 30; therefore, we cannot use the normal distribution. Comparing the calculated value of the test statistic and the critical value of t (t_a) at a 5% significance level, we see that the calculated value is in the tail of the distribution. Thus, we conclude that 108 dollars per contract is significantly larger than the hypothesized value of 100 and thus we cannot accept the null hypothesis. There is evidence that supports Jane's performance meets company standards.

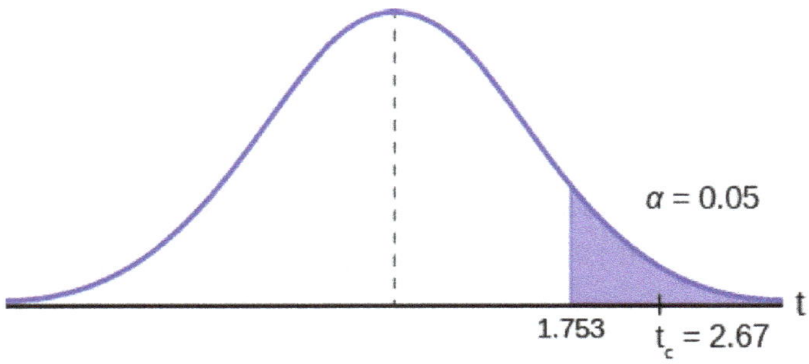

Figure 9.8

TRY IT 9.9

It is believed that a stock price for a particular company will grow at a rate of \$5 per week with a standard deviation of \$1. An investor believes the stock won't grow as quickly. The changes in stock price is recorded for ten weeks and are as follows: \$4, \$3, \$2, \$3, \$1, \$7, \$2, \$1, \$1, \$2. Perform a hypothesis test using a 5% level of significance. State the null and alternative hypotheses, state your conclusion, and identify the Type I errors.

EXAMPLE 9.10

A manufacturer of salad dressings uses machines to dispense liquid ingredients into bottles that move along a filling line. The machine that dispenses salad dressings is working properly when 8 ounces are dispensed. Suppose that the average amount dispensed in a particular sample of 35 bottles is 7.91 ounces with a variance of 0.03 ounces squared, s^2. Is there evidence that the machine should be stopped and production wait for repairs? The lost production from a shutdown is potentially so great that management feels that the level of significance in the analysis should be 99%.

Again we will follow the steps in our analysis of this problem.

Solution 9.10

Step 1: Set the Null and Alternative Hypothesis. The random variable is the quantity of fluid placed in the bottles. This is a continuous random variable and the parameter we are interested in is the mean. Our hypothesis therefore is about the mean. In this case we are concerned that the machine is not filling properly. From what we are told it does not matter if the machine is over-filling or under-filling, both seem to be an equally bad error. This tells us that this is a two-tailed test: if the machine is malfunctioning it will be shutdown regardless if it is from over-filling or under-filling. The null and alternative hypotheses are thus:

$$H_0 : \mu = 8$$
$$H_a : \mu \neq 8$$

Step 2: Decide the level of significance and draw the graph showing the critical value.

This problem has already set the level of significance at 99%. The decision seems an appropriate one and shows the thought process when setting the significance level. Management wants to be very certain, as certain as probability will allow, that they are not shutting down a machine that is not in need of repair. To draw the distribution and the critical value, we need to know which distribution to use. Because this is a continuous random variable and we are interested in the mean, and the sample size is greater than 30, the appropriate distribution is the normal distribution and the relevant critical value is 2.575 from the normal table or the t-table at 0.005 column and infinite degrees of freedom. We draw the graph and mark these points.

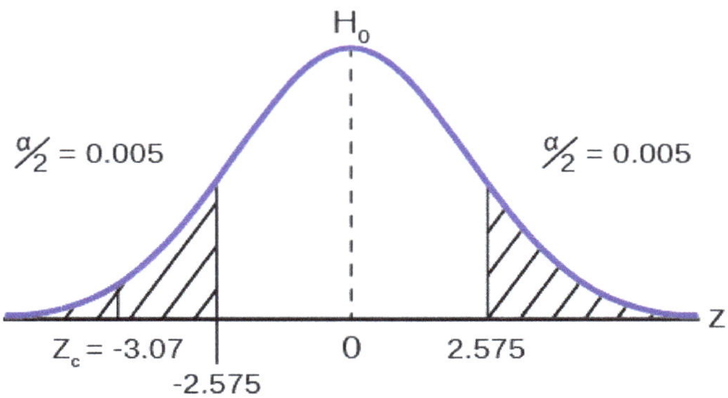

Figure 9.9

Step 3: Calculate sample parameters and the test statistic. The sample parameters are provided, the sample mean is 7.91 and the sample variance is .03 and the sample size is 35. We need to note that the sample variance was provided not the sample standard deviation, which is what we need for the formula. Remembering that the standard deviation is simply the square root of the variance, we therefore know the sample standard deviation, s, is 0.173. With this information we calculate the test statistic as -3.07, and mark it on the graph.

$$Z_c = \frac{\bar{x} - \mu_0}{\frac{s}{\sqrt{n}}} = \frac{7.91 - 8}{\frac{.173}{\sqrt{35}}} = -3.07$$

Step 4: Compare test statistic and the critical values Now we compare the test statistic and the critical value by placing the test statistic on the graph. We see that the test statistic is in the tail, decidedly greater than the critical value of 2.575. We note that even the very small difference between the hypothesized value and the sample value is still a large number of standard deviations. The sample mean is only 0.08 ounces different from the required level of 8 ounces, but it is 3 plus standard deviations away and thus we cannot accept the null hypothesis.

STEP 5: Reach a Conclusion

Three standard deviations of a test statistic will guarantee that the test will fail. The probability that anything is within three standard deviations is almost zero. Actually it is 0.0026 on the normal distribution, which is certainly almost zero in a practical sense. Our formal conclusion would be " At a 99% level of significance we cannot accept the hypothesis that the sample mean came from a distribution with a mean of 8 ounces" Or less formally, and getting to the point, "At a 99% level of significance we conclude that the machine is under filling the bottles and is in need of repair".

Hypothesis Test for Proportions

Just as there were confidence intervals for proportions, or more formally, the population parameter *p* of the binomial distribution, there is the ability to test hypotheses concerning *p*.

The population parameter for the binomial is *p*. The estimated value (point estimate) for *p* is *p′* where *p′* = *x*/*n*, *x* is the number of successes in the sample and *n* is the sample size.

When you perform a hypothesis test of a population proportion *p*, you take a simple random sample from the population. The conditions for a **binomial distribution** must be met, which are: there are a certain number *n* of independent trials meaning random sampling, the outcomes of any trial are binary, success or failure, and each trial has the same probability of a success *p*. The shape of the binomial distribution needs to be similar to the shape of the normal distribution. To ensure this, the quantities *np′* and *nq′* must both be greater than five ($np' > 5$ and $nq' > 5$). In this case the binomial distribution of a sample (estimated) proportion can be approximated by the normal distribution with μ=np and $\sigma = \sqrt{npq}$. Remember that q=1−*p*. There is no distribution that can correct for this small sample bias and thus if these conditions are not met we simply cannot test the hypothesis with the data available at that time. We met this condition when we first were estimating confidence intervals for *p*.

Again, we begin with the standardizing formula modified because this is the distribution of a binomial.

$$Z = \frac{p' - p}{\sqrt{\frac{pq}{n}}}$$

Substituting p_0, the hypothesized value of *p*, we have:

$$Z_c = \frac{p' - p_0}{\sqrt{\frac{p_0 q_0}{n}}}$$

This is the test statistic for testing hypothesized values of *p*, where the null and alternative hypotheses take one of the following forms:

Table 9.5

Two-tailed test	One-tailed test	One-tailed test
H0: p = p0	H0: p ≤ p0	H0: p ≥ p0
Ha: p ≠ p0	Ha: p > p0	Ha: p < p0

The decision rule stated above applies here also: if the calculated value of Z_c shows that the sample proportion is "too many" standard deviations from the hypothesized proportion, the null hypothesis cannot be accepted. The decision as to what is "too many" is pre-determined by the analyst depending on the level of significance required in the test.

EXAMPLE 9.11

The mortgage department of a large bank is interested in the nature of loans of first-time borrowers. This information will be used to tailor their marketing strategy. They believe that 50% of first-time borrowers take out smaller loans than other borrowers. They perform a hypothesis test to determine if the percentage is **the same or different from 50%.** They sample **100 first-time borrowers** and find **53** of these loans are smaller that the other borrowers. For the hypothesis test, they choose a 5% level of significance.

Solution 9.11

Step 1: Set the null and alternative hypothesis.

H_0: $p = 0.50$ $\qquad$ H_a: $p \neq 0.50$

The words "is the same or different from" tell you this is a two-tailed test. The Type I and Type II errors are as follows: The Type I error is to conclude that the proportion of borrowers is different from 50% when, in fact, the proportion is actually 50%. (Reject the null hypothesis when the null hypothesis is true). The Type II error is there is not enough evidence to conclude that the proportion of first time borrowers differs from 50% when, in fact, the proportion does differ from 50%. (You fail to reject the null hypothesis when the null hypothesis is false.)

Step 2: Decide the level of significance and draw the graph showing the critical value

The level of significance has been set by the problem at the 95% level. Because this is two-tailed test one-half of the alpha value will be in the upper tail and one-half in the lower tail as shown on the graph. The critical value for the normal distribution at the 95% level of confidence is 1.96. This can easily be found on the student's t-table at the very bottom at infinite degrees of freedom remembering that at infinity the t-distribution is the normal distribution. Of course the value can also be found on the normal table but you have go looking for one-half of 95 (0.475) inside the body of the table and then read out to the sides and top for the number of standard deviations.

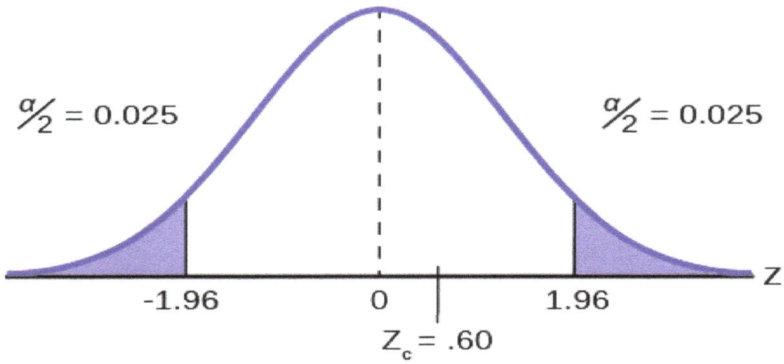

Figure 9.10

Step 3: Calculate the sample parameters and critical value of the test statistic.

The test statistic is a normal distribution, Z, for testing proportions and is:

$$Z = \frac{p' - p_0}{\sqrt{\frac{p_0 q_0}{n}}} = \frac{.53 - .50}{\sqrt{\frac{.5(.5)}{100}}} = 0.60$$

For this case, the sample of 100 found 53 first-time borrowers were different from other borrowers. The sample proportion, p' = 53/100= 0.53 The test question, therefore, is : "Is 0.53 significantly different from .50?" Putting these values into the formula for the test statistic we find that 0.53 is only 0.60 standard deviations away from .50. This is barely off of the mean of the standard normal distribution of zero. There is virtually no difference from

the sample proportion and the hypothesized proportion in terms of standard deviations.

Step 4: Compare the test statistic and the critical value.

The calculated value is well within the critical values of ± 1.96 standard deviations and thus we cannot reject the null hypothesis. To reject the null hypothesis we need significant evident of difference between the hypothesized value and the sample value. In this case the sample value is very nearly the same as the hypothesized value measured in terms of standard deviations.

Step 5: Reach a conclusion

The formal conclusion would be "At a 95% level of significance we cannot reject the null hypothesis that 50% of first-time borrowers have the same size loans as other borrowers". Less formally we would say that "There is no evidence that one-half of first-time borrowers are significantly different in loan size from other borrowers". Notice the length to which the conclusion goes to include all of the conditions that are attached to the conclusion. Statisticians for all the criticism they receive, are careful to be very specific even when this seems trivial. Statisticians cannot say more than they know and the data constrain the conclusion to be within the metes and bounds of the data.

TRY IT 9.11

A teacher believes that 85% of students in the class will want to go on a field trip to the local zoo. She performs a hypothesis test to determine if the percentage is the same or different from 85%. The teacher samples 50 students and 39 reply that they would want to go to the zoo. For the hypothesis test, use a 1% level of significance.

EXAMPLE 9.12

Suppose a consumer group suspects that the proportion of households that have three or more cell phones is 30%. A cell phone company has reason to believe that the proportion is not 30%. Before they start a big advertising campaign, they conduct a hypothesis test. Their marketing people survey 150 households with the result that 43 of the households have three or more cell phones.

Solution 9.12

Here is an abbreviate version of the system to solve hypothesis tests applied to a test on a proportions.

$$H_0 : p = 0.3$$

$$H_a : p \neq 0.3$$

$$n = 150$$

$$\mathrm{p'} = \frac{x}{n} = \frac{43}{150} = 0.287$$

$$Z_c = \frac{\mathrm{p'} - p_0}{\sqrt{\frac{p_0 q_0}{n}}} = \frac{0.287 - 0.3}{\sqrt{\frac{.3(.7)}{150}}} = 0.347$$

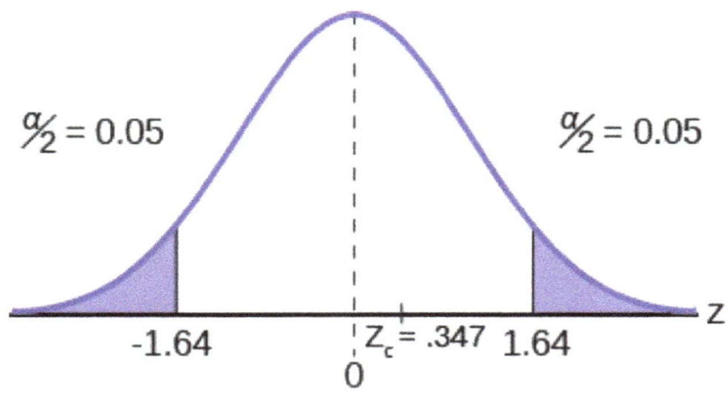

At a significance level of 90%
we cannot reject H_0:
the consumer group is correct.

Figure 9.11

EXAMPLE 9.13

The National Institute of Standards and Technology provides exact data on conductivity properties of materials. Following are conductivity measurements for 11 randomly selected pieces of a particular type of glass.

1.11; 1.07; 1.11; 1.07; 1.12; 1.08; .98; .98 1.02; .95; .95

Is there convincing evidence that the average conductivity of this type of glass is greater than one? Use a significance level of 0.05.

Solution 9.13

Let's follow a four-step process to answer this statistical question.

1. **State the Question**: We need to determine if, at a 0.05 significance level, the average conductivity of the selected glass is greater than one. Our hypotheses will be
   a. $H0: \mu \leq 1$
   b. $Ha: \mu > 1$
2. **Plan:** We are testing a sample mean without a known population standard deviation with less than 30 observations. Therefore, we need to use a Student's-t distribution. Assume the underlying population is normal.
3. **Do the calculations and draw the graph.**
4. **State the Conclusions**: We cannot accept the null hypothesis. It is reasonable to state that the data supports the claim that the average conductivity level is greater than one.

EXAMPLE 9.14

In a study of 420,019 cell phone users, 172 of the subjects developed brain cancer. Test the claim that cell phone users developed brain cancer at a greater rate than that for non-cell phone users (the rate of brain cancer for non-cell phone users is 0.0340%). Since this is a critical issue, use a 0.005 significance level. Explain why the significance level should be so low in terms of a Type I error.

Solution 9.14

1. We need to conduct a hypothesis test on the claimed cancer rate. Our hypotheses will be
   a. H_0: $p \leq 0.00034$
   b. H_a: $p > 0.00034$

If we commit a Type I error, we are essentially accepting a false claim. Since the claim describes cancercausing environments, we want to minimize the chances of incorrectly identifying causes of cancer.

2. We will be testing a sample proportion with x = 172 and n = 420,019. The sample is sufficiently large because we have np' = 420,019(0.00034) = 142.8, nq' = 420,019(0.99966) = 419,876.2, two independent outcomes, and a fixed probability of success p' = 0.00034. Thus we will be able to generalize our results to the population.

Key Terms

Binomial Distribution a discrete random variable (RV) that arises from Bernoulli trials. There are a fixed number, n, of independent trials. "Independent" means that the result of any trial (for example, trial 1) does not affect the results of the following trials, and all trials are conducted under the same conditions. Under these circumstances the binomial RV X is defined as the number of successes in n trials. The notation is: $X \sim B(n, p)$ $\mu = np$ and the standard deviation is $\sigma = \sqrt{npq}$. The probability of exactly x successes in n trials is $P(X = x) = \binom{n}{x} p^x q^{n-x}$.

Central Limit Theorem Given a random variable (RV) with known mean $\mu\mu$ and known standard deviation σ. We are sampling with size n and we are interested in two new RVs - the sample mean, $\bar{X}$. If the size n of the sample is sufficiently large, then $\bar{X} \sim N\left(\mu, \frac{\sigma}{\sqrt{n}}\right)$. If the size n of the sample is sufficiently large, then the distribution of the sample means will approximate a normal distribution regardless of the shape of the population. The expected value of the mean of the sample means will equal the population mean. The standard deviation of the distribution of the sample means, $\frac{\sigma}{\sqrt{n}}$, is called the standard error of the mean.

Confidence Interval (CI) an interval estimate for an unknown population parameter. This depends on:

- The desired confidence level.
- Information that is known about the distribution (for example, known standard deviation).
- The sample and its size.

Critical Value The t or Z value set by the researcher that measures the probability of a Type I error, α.

Hypothesis a statement about the value of a population parameter, in case of two hypotheses, the statement assumed to be true is called the null hypothesis (notation H_0) and the contradictory statement is called the alternative hypothesis (notation H_a).

Hypothesis Testing Based on sample evidence, a procedure for determining whether the hypothesis stated is a reasonable statement and should not be rejected, or is unreasonable and should be rejected.

Normal Distribution a continuous random variable (RV) with pdf $f(x) = \frac{1}{\sigma\sqrt{2\pi}}e^{\frac{-(x-\mu)^2}{2\sigma^2}}$, where μ is the mean of the distribution, and σ is the standard deviation, notation: $X \sim N(\mu, \sigma)$. If $\mu = 0$ and $\sigma = 1$, the RV is called **the standard normal distribution.**

Standard Deviation a number that is equal to the square root of the variance and measures how far data values are from their mean; notation: s for sample standard deviation and σ for population standard deviation.

Student's *t*-Distribution investigated and reported by William S. Gossett in 1908 and published under the pseudonym Student. The major characteristics of the random variable (RV) are:

- It is continuous and assumes any real values.
- The pdf is symmetrical about its mean of zero. However, it is more spread out and flatter at the apex than the normal distribution.
- It approaches the standard normal distribution as n gets larger.
- There is a "family" of t-distributions: every representative of the family is completely defined by the number of degrees of freedom which is one less than the number of data items.

Test Statistic The formula that counts the number of standard deviations on the relevant distribution that estimated parameter is away from the hypothesized value.

Type I Error The decision is to reject the null hypothesis when, in fact, the null hypothesis is true.

Type II Error The decision is not to reject the null hypothesis when, in fact, the null hypothesis is false.

CHAPTER REVIEW

9.1 Null and Alternative Hypotheses

In a **hypothesis test**, sample data is evaluated in order to arrive at a decision about some type of claim. If certain conditions about the sample are satisfied, then the claim can be evaluated for a population. In a hypothesis test, we:

1. Evaluate the **null hypothesis**, typically denoted with H_0. The null is not rejected unless the hypothesis test shows otherwise. The null statement must always contain some form of equality (=, ≤ or ≥)
2. Always write the **alternative hypothesis**, typically denoted with H_a or H_1, using not equal, less than or greater than symbols, i.e., (≠, <, or >).
3. If we reject the null hypothesis, then we can assume there is enough evidence to support the alternative hypothesis.
4. Never state that a claim is proven true or false. Keep in mind the underlying fact that hypothesis testing is based on probability laws; therefore, we can talk only in terms of non-absolute certainties.

9.2 Outcomes and the Type I and Type II Errors

In every hypothesis test, the outcomes are dependent on a correct interpretation of the data. Incorrect calculations or misunderstood summary statistics can yield errors that affect the results. A **Type I** error occurs when a true null hypothesis is rejected. A **Type II error** occurs when a false null hypothesis is not rejected.

The probabilities of these errors are denoted by the Greek letters α and β, for a Type I and a Type II error respectively. The power of the test, $1 - \beta$, quantifies the likelihood that a test will yield the correct result of a true alternative hypothesis being accepted. A high power is desirable.

9.3 Distribution Needed for Hypothesis Testing

In order for a hypothesis test's results to be generalized to a population, certain requirements must be satisfied.

When testing for a single population mean:

1. A Student's *t*-test should be used if the data come from a simple, random sample and the population is approximately normally distributed, or the sample size is large, with an unknown standard deviation.
2. The normal test will work if the data come from a simple, random sample and the population is approximately normally distributed, or the sample size is large.

When testing a single population proportion use a normal test for a single population proportion if the data comes from a simple, random sample, fill the requirements for a binomial distribution, and the mean number of success and the mean number of failures satisfy the conditions: $np > 5$ and $nq > 5$ where n is the sample size, p is the probability of a success, and q is the probability of a failure.

9.4 Full Hypothesis Test Examples

The **hypothesis test** itself has an established process. This can be summarized as follows:

1. Determine H_0 and H_a. Remember, they are contradictory.
2. Determine the random variable.
3. Determine the distribution for the test.
4. Draw a graph and calculate the test statistic.
5. Compare the calculated test statistic with the Z critical value determined by the level of significance required by the test and make a decision (cannot reject H_0 or cannot accept H_0), and write a clear conclusion using English sentences.

Formula Review

9.3 Distribution Needed for Hypothesis Testing

Table 9.6 Test Statistics for Test of Means, Varying Sample Size, Population Known or Unknown

Sample size	Test statistic
< 30 (σ unknown)	$t_c = \frac{\bar{X} - \mu_0}{s / \sqrt{n}}$
< 30 (σ known)	$Z_c = \frac{\bar{X} - \mu_0}{\sigma / \sqrt{n}}$
> 30 (σ unknown)	$Z_c = \frac{\bar{X} - \mu_0}{s / \sqrt{n}}$
> 30 (σ known)	$Z_c = \frac{\bar{X} - \mu_0}{\sigma / \sqrt{n}}$

Practice

9.1 Null and Alternative Hypotheses

1. You are testing that the mean speed of your cable Internet connection is more than three Megabits per second. What is the random variable? Describe in words.

2. You are testing that the mean speed of your cable Internet connection is more than three Megabits per second. State the null and alternative hypotheses.
3. The American family has an average of two children. What is the random variable? Describe in words.
4. The mean entry level salary of an employee at a company is $58,000. You believe it is higher for IT professionals in the company. State the null and alternative hypotheses.
5. A sociologist claims the probability that a person picked at random in Times Square in New York City is visiting the area is 0.83. You want to test to see if the proportion is actually less. What is the random variable? Describe in words.
6. A sociologist claims the probability that a person picked at random in Times Square in New York City is visiting the area is 0.83. You want to test to see if the claim is correct. State the null and alternative hypotheses.
7. In a population of fish, approximately 42% are female. A test is conducted to see if, in fact, the proportion is less. State the null and alternative hypotheses.
8. Suppose that a recent article stated that the mean time spent in jail by a first–time convicted burglar is 2.5 years. A study was then done to see if the mean time has increased in the new century. A random sample of 26 first-time convicted burglars in a recent year was picked. The mean length of time in jail from the survey was 3 years with a standard deviation of 1.8 years. Suppose that it is somehow known that the population standard deviation is 1.5. If you were conducting a hypothesis test to determine if the mean length of jail time has increased, what would the null and alternative hypotheses be? The distribution of the population is normal.
   a. H_0: ________
   b. H_a: ________
9. A random survey of 75 death row inmates revealed that the mean length of time on death row is 17.4 years with a standard deviation of 6.3 years. If you were conducting a hypothesis test to determine if the population mean time on death row could likely be 15 years, what would the null and alternative hypotheses be?
   a. H_0: __________
   b. H_a: __________
10. The National Institute of Mental Health published an article stating that in any one-year period, approximately 9.5 percent of American adults suffer from depression or a depressive illness. Suppose that in a survey of 100 people in a certain town, seven of them suffered from depression or a depressive illness.

If you were conducting a hypothesis test to determine if the true proportion of people in that town suffering from depression or a depressive illness is lower than the percent in the general adult American population, what would the null and alternative hypotheses be?

a. H_0: ________
b. H_a: ________

9.2 Outcomes and the Type I and Type II Errors

11. The mean price of mid-sized cars in a region is $32,000. A test is conducted to see if the claim is true. State the Type I and Type II errors in complete sentences.

12. A sleeping bag is tested to withstand temperatures of –15 °F. You think the bag cannot stand temperatures that low. State the Type I and Type II errors in complete sentences.

13. For **Exercise 9.12**, what are α and β in words?

14. In words, describe $1 - \beta$ For **Exercise 9.12**.

15. A group of doctors is deciding whether or not to perform an operation. Suppose the null hypothesis, H_0, is: the surgical procedure will go well. State the Type I and Type II errors in complete sentences.

16. A group of doctors is deciding whether or not to perform an operation. Suppose the null hypothesis, H_0, is: the surgical procedure will go well. Which is the error with the greater consequence?

17. The power of a test is 0.981. What is the probability of a Type II error?

18. A group of divers is exploring an old sunken ship. Suppose the null hypothesis, H_0, is: the sunken ship does not contain buried treasure. State the Type I and Type II errors in complete sentences.

19. A microbiologist is testing a water sample for E-coli. Suppose the null hypothesis, H_0, is: the sample does not contain E-coli. The probability that the sample does not contain E-coli, but the microbiologist thinks it does is 0.012. The probability that the sample does contain E-coli, but the microbiologist thinks it does not is 0.002. What is the power of this test?

20. A microbiologist is testing a water sample for E-coli. Suppose the null hypothesis, H_0, is: the sample contains E-coli. Which is the error with the greater consequence?

9.3 Distribution Needed for Hypothesis Testing

21. Which two distributions can you use for hypothesis testing for this chapter?

22. Which distribution do you use when you are testing a population mean and the population standard deviation is known? Assume sample size is large. Assume a normal distribution with $n \geq 30$.

23. Which distribution do you use when the standard deviation is not known and you are testing one population mean? Assume a normal distribution, with $n \geq 30$.

24. A population mean is 13. The sample mean is 12.8, and the sample standard deviation is two. The sample size is 20. What distribution should you use to perform a hypothesis test? Assume the underlying population is normal.

25. A population has a mean is 25 and a standard deviation of five. The sample mean is 24, and the sample size is 108. What distribution should you use to perform a hypothesis test?

26. It is thought that 42% of respondents in a taste test would prefer Brand *A*. In a particular test of 100 people, 39% preferred Brand *A*. What distribution should you use to perform a hypothesis test?

27. You are performing a hypothesis test of a single population mean using a Student's *t*-distribution. What must you assume about the distribution of the data?

28. You are performing a hypothesis test of a single population mean using a Student's *t*-distribution. The data are not from a simple random sample. Can you accurately perform the hypothesis test?

29. You are performing a hypothesis test of a single population proportion. What must be true about the quantities of *np* and *nq*?

30. You are performing a hypothesis test of a single population proportion. You find out that *np* is less than five. What must you do to be able to perform a valid hypothesis test?

31. You are performing a hypothesis test of a single population proportion. The data come from which distribution?

9.4 Full Hypothesis Test Examples

32. Assume H_0: $\mu = 9$ and H_a: $\mu < 9$. Is this a left-tailed, right-tailed, or two-tailed test?

33. Assume H_0: $\mu \leq 6$ and H_a: $\mu > 6$. Is this a left-tailed, right-tailed, or two-tailed test?

34. Assume H_0: $p = 0.25$ and H_a: $p \neq 0.25$. Is this a left-tailed, right-tailed, or two-tailed test?

35. Draw the general graph of a left-tailed test.

36. Draw the graph of a two-tailed test.
37. A bottle of water is labeled as containing 16 fluid ounces of water. You believe it is less than that. What type of test would you use?
38. Your friend claims that his mean golf score is 63. You want to show that it is higher than that. What type of test would you use?
39. A bathroom scale claims to be able to identify correctly any weight within a pound. You think that it cannot be that accurate. What type of test would you use?
40. You flip a coin and record whether it shows heads or tails. You know the probability of getting heads is 50%, but you think it is less for this particular coin. What type of test would you use?
41. If the alternative hypothesis has a not equals (≠) symbol, you know to use which type of test?
42. Assume the null hypothesis states that the mean is at least 18. Is this a left-tailed, right-tailed, or two-tailed test?
43. Assume the null hypothesis states that the mean is at most 12. Is this a left-tailed, right-tailed, or two-tailed test?
44. Assume the null hypothesis states that the mean is equal to 88. The alternative hypothesis states that the mean is not equal to 88. Is this a left-tailed, right-tailed, or two-tailed test?

HOMEWORK

9.1 Null and Alternative Hypotheses

45. Some of the following statements refer to the null hypothesis, some to the alternate hypothesis.

    State the null hypothesis, H_0, and the alternative hypothesis. H_a, in terms of the appropriate parameter (μ or p).

    a. The mean number of years Americans work before retiring is 34.
    b. At most 60% of Americans vote in presidential elections.
    c. The mean starting salary for San Jose State University graduates is at least \$100,000 per year.
    d. Twenty-nine percent of high school seniors get drunk each month.
    e. Fewer than 5% of adults ride the bus to work in Los Angeles.
    f. The mean number of cars a person owns in her lifetime is not more than ten.
    g. About half of Americans prefer to live away from cities, given the choice.

h. Europeans have a mean paid vacation each year of six weeks.
i. The chance of developing breast cancer is under 11% for women.
j. Private universities' mean tuition cost is more than $20,000 per year.

46. Over the past few decades, public health officials have examined the link between weight concerns and teen girls' smoking. Researchers surveyed a group of 273 randomly selected teen girls living in Massachusetts (between 12 and 15 years old). After four years the girls were surveyed again. Sixty-three said they smoked to stay thin. Is there good evidence that more than thirty percent of the teen girls smoke to stay thin? The alternative hypothesis is:

a. $p < 0.30$
b. $p \leq 0.30$
c. $p \geq 0.30$
d. $p > 0.30$

47. A statistics instructor believes that fewer than 20% of Evergreen Valley College (EVC) students attended the opening night midnight showing of the latest Harry Potter movie. She surveys 84 of her students and finds that 11 attended the midnight showing. An appropriate alternative hypothesis is:

a. $p = 0.20$
b. $p > 0.20$
c. $p < 0.20$
d. $p \leq 0.20$

48. Previously, an organization reported that teenagers spent 4.5 hours per week, on average, on the phone. The organization thinks that, currently, the mean is higher. Fifteen randomly chosen teenagers were asked how many hours per week they spend on the phone. The sample mean was 4.75 hours with a sample standard deviation of 2.0. Conduct a hypothesis test. The null and alternative hypotheses are:

a. H_o: x¯$\bar{x}$ = 4.5, H_a : x¯$\bar{x}$ > 4.5
b. $H_o: \mu \geq 4.5, H_a: \mu < 4.5$
c. $H_o: \mu = 4.75, H_a: \mu > 4.75$
d. $H_o: \mu = 4.5, H_a: \mu > 4.5$

9.2 Outcomes and the Type I and Type II Errors

49. State the Type I and Type II errors in complete sentences given the following statements.

a. The mean number of years Americans work before retiring is 34.
b. At most 60% of Americans vote in presidential elections.
c. The mean starting salary for San Jose State University graduates is at least $100,000 per year.
d. Twenty-nine percent of high school seniors get drunk each month.
e. Fewer than 5% of adults ride the bus to work in Los Angeles.
f. The mean number of cars a person owns in his or her lifetime is not more than ten.

g. About half of Americans prefer to live away from cities, given the choice.
h. Europeans have a mean paid vacation each year of six weeks.
i. The chance of developing breast cancer is under 11% for women.
j. Private universities mean tuition cost is more than $20,000 per year.

50. For statements a-j in **Exercise 9.109**, answer the following in complete sentences.

a. State a consequence of committing a Type I error.
b. State a consequence of committing a Type II error.

51. When a new drug is created, the pharmaceutical company must subject it to testing before receiving the necessary permission from the Food and Drug Administration (FDA) to market the drug. Suppose the null hypothesis is "the drug is unsafe." What is the Type II Error?

a. To conclude the drug is safe when in, fact, it is unsafe.
b. Not to conclude the drug is safe when, in fact, it is safe.
c. To conclude the drug is safe when, in fact, it is safe.
d. Not to conclude the drug is unsafe when, in fact, it is unsafe.

52. A statistics instructor believes that fewer than 20% of Evergreen Valley College (EVC) students attended the opening midnight showing of the latest Harry Potter movie. She surveys 84 of her students and finds that 11 of them attended the midnight showing. The Type I error is to conclude that the percent of EVC students who attended is ________.

a. at least 20%, when in fact, it is less than 20%.
b. 20%, when in fact, it is 20%.
c. less than 20%, when in fact, it is at least 20%.
d. less than 20%, when in fact, it is less than 20%.

53. It is believed that Lake Tahoe Community College (LTCC) Intermediate Algebra students get less than seven hours of sleep per night, on average. A survey of 22 LTCC Intermediate Algebra students generated a mean of 7.24 hours with a standard deviation of 1.93 hours. At a level of significance of 5%, do LTCC Intermediate Algebra students get less than seven hours of sleep per night, on average?

The Type II error is not to reject that the mean number of hours of sleep LTCC students get per night is at least seven when, in fact, the mean number of hours

a. is more than seven hours.
b. is at most seven hours.
c. is at least seven hours.
d. is less than seven hours.

54. Previously, an organization reported that teenagers spent 4.5 hours per week, on average, on the phone. The organization thinks that, currently, the mean is higher. Fifteen randomly chosen teenagers were asked how many hours per week they spend on the phone. The sample mean was 4.75 hours with a sample standard deviation of 2.0. Conduct a hypothesis test, the Type I error is:

a. to conclude that the current mean hours per week is higher than 4.5, when in fact, it is higher
b. to conclude that the current mean hours per week is higher than 4.5, when in fact, it is the same
c. to conclude that the mean hours per week currently is 4.5, when in fact, it is higher
d. to conclude that the mean hours per week currently is no higher than 4.5, when in fact, it is not higher

9.3 Distribution Needed for Hypothesis Testing

55. It is believed that Lake Tahoe Community College (LTCC) Intermediate Algebra students get less than seven hours of sleep per night, on average. A survey of 22 LTCC Intermediate Algebra students generated a mean of 7.24 hours with a standard deviation of 1.93 hours. At a level of significance of 5%, do LTCC Intermediate Algebra students get less than seven hours of sleep per night, on average? The distribution to be used for this test $\bar{X} \sim$ _______________

a. $N(7.24, \frac{1.93}{\sqrt{22}})$
b. $N(7.24, 1.93)$
c. t_{22}
d. t_{21}

9.4 Full Hypothesis Test Examples

56. A particular brand of tires claims that its deluxe tire averages at least 50,000 miles before it needs to be replaced. From past studies of this tire, the standard deviation is known to be 8,000. A survey of owners of that tire design is conducted. From the 28 tires surveyed, the mean lifespan was 46,500 miles with a standard deviation of 9,800 miles. Using alpha = 0.05, is the data highly inconsistent with the claim?

57. From generation to generation, the mean age when smokers first start to smoke varies. However, the standard deviation of that age remains constant of around 2.1 years. A survey of 40 smokers of this generation was done to see if the mean starting age is at least 19. The sample mean was 18.1 with a sample standard deviation of 1.3. Do the data support the claim at the 5% level?

58. The cost of a daily newspaper varies from city to city. However, the variation among prices remains steady with a standard deviation of 20¢. A study was done to test the claim that the mean cost of a daily newspaper is $1.00. Twelve costs yield a mean cost of 95¢ with a standard deviation of 18¢. Do the data support the claim at the 1% level?

59. An article in the *San Jose Mercury News* stated that students in the California state university system take 4.5 years, on average, to finish their undergraduate degrees. Suppose you believe that the mean time is longer. You conduct a survey of 49 students and obtain a sample mean of 5.1 with a sample standard deviation of 1.2. Do the data support your claim at the 1% level?

60. The mean number of sick days an employee takes per year is believed to be about ten. Members of a personnel department do not believe this figure. They randomly survey eight employees. The number of sick days they took for the past year are as follows: 12; 4; 15; 3; 11; 8; 6; 8. Let x = the number of sick days they took for the past year. Should the personnel team believe that the mean number is ten?

61. In 1955, *Life Magazine* reported that the 25 year-old mother of three worked, on average, an 80 hour week. Recently, many groups have been studying whether or not the women's movement has, in fact, resulted in an increase in the average work week for women (combining employment and at-home work). Suppose a study was done to determine if the mean work week has increased. 81 women were surveyed with the following results. The sample mean was 83; the sample standard deviation was ten. Does it appear that the mean work week has increased for women at the 5% level?

62. Your statistics instructor claims that 60 percent of the students who take her Elementary Statistics class go through life feeling more enriched. For some reason that she can't quite figure out, most people don't believe her. You decide to check this out on your own. You randomly survey 64 of her past Elementary Statistics students and find that 34 feel more enriched as a result of her class. Now, what do you think?

63. A Nissan Motor Corporation advertisement read, "The average man's I.Q. is 107. The average brown trout's I.Q. is 4. So why can't man catch brown trout?" Suppose you believe that the brown trout's mean I.Q. is greater than four. You catch 12 brown trout. A fish psychologist determines the I.Q.s as follows: 5; 4; 7; 3; 6; 4; 5; 3; 6; 3; 8; 5. Conduct a hypothesis test of your belief.

64. Refer to Exercise 9.119. Conduct a hypothesis test to see if your decision and conclusion would change if your belief were that the brown trout's mean I.Q. is not four.

65. According to an article in *Newsweek*, the natural ratio of girls to boys is 100:105. In China, the birth ratio is 100: 114 (46.7% girls). Suppose you don't believe the reported figures of the percent of girls born in China. You conduct a study. In this study, you count the number of girls and boys born in 150 randomly chosen recent births. There are 60 girls and 90 boys born of the 150. Based on your study, do you believe that the percent of girls born in China is 46.7?

66. A poll done for *Newsweek* found that 13% of Americans have seen or sensed the presence of an angel. A contingent doubts that the percent is really that high. It conducts its own survey. Out of 76 Americans surveyed, only two had seen or sensed the presence of an angel. As a result of the contingent's survey, would you agree with the *Newsweek* poll? In complete sentences, also give three reasons why the two polls might give different results.

67. The mean work week for engineers in a start-up company is believed to be about 60 hours. A newly hired engineer hopes that it's shorter. She asks ten engineering friends in start-ups for the lengths of their mean work weeks. Based on the results that follow, should she count on the mean work week to be shorter than 60 hours?

    Data (length of mean work week): 70; 45; 55; 60; 65; 55; 55; 60; 50; 55.

68. Sixty-eight percent of online courses taught at community colleges nationwide were taught by full-time faculty. To test if 68% also represents California's percent for full-time faculty teaching the online classes, Long Beach City College (LBCC) in California, was randomly selected for comparison. In the same year, 34 of the 44 online courses LBCC offered were taught by full-time faculty. Conduct a hypothesis test to determine if 68% represents California. NOTE: For more accurate results, use more California community colleges and this past year's data.

69. According to an article in *Bloomberg Businessweek*, New York City's most recent adult smoking rate is 14%. Suppose that a survey is conducted to determine this year's rate. Nine out of 70 randomly chosen N.Y. City residents reply that they smoke. Conduct a hypothesis test to determine if the rate is still 14% or if it has decreased.

70. The mean age of De Anza College students in a previous term was 26.6 years old. An instructor thinks the mean age for online students is older than 26.6. She randomly surveys 56 online students and finds that the sample mean is 29.4 with a standard deviation of 2.1. Conduct a hypothesis test.

71. Registered nurses earned an average annual salary of $69,110. For that same year, a survey was conducted of 41 California registered nurses to determine if the annual salary is higher than $69,110 for California nurses. The sample

average was $71,121 with a sample standard deviation of $7,489. Conduct a hypothesis test.

72. La Leche League International reports that the mean age of weaning a child from breastfeeding is age four to five worldwide. In America, most nursing mothers wean their children much earlier. Suppose a random survey is conducted of 21 U.S. mothers who recently weaned their children. The mean weaning age was nine months (3/4 year) with a standard deviation of 4 months. Conduct a hypothesis test to determine if the mean weaning age in the U.S. is less than four years old.

73. Over the past few decades, public health officials have examined the link between weight concerns and teen girls' smoking. Researchers surveyed a group of 273 randomly selected teen girls living in Massachusetts (between 12 and 15 years old). After four years the girls were surveyed again. Sixty-three said they smoked to stay thin. Is there good evidence that more than thirty percent of the teen girls smoke to stay thin?

After conducting the test, your decision and conclusion are

a. Reject H_0: There is sufficient evidence to conclude that more than 30% of teen girls smoke to stay thin.
b. Do not reject H_0: There is not sufficient evidence to conclude that less than 30% of teen girls smoke to stay thin.
c. Do not reject H_0: There is not sufficient evidence to conclude that more than 30% of teen girls smoke to stay thin.
d. Reject H_0: There is sufficient evidence to conclude that less than 30% of teen girls smoke to stay thin.

74. A statistics instructor believes that fewer than 20% of Evergreen Valley College (EVC) students attended the opening night midnight showing of the latest Harry Potter movie. She surveys 84 of her students and finds that 11 of them attended the midnight showing.

At a 1% level of significance, an appropriate conclusion is:

a. There is insufficient evidence to conclude that the percent of EVC students who attended the midnight showing of Harry Potter is less than 20%.
b. There is sufficient evidence to conclude that the percent of EVC students who attended the midnight showing of Harry Potter is more than 20%.
c. There is sufficient evidence to conclude that the percent of EVC students who attended the midnight showing of Harry Potter is less than 20%.
d. There is insufficient evidence to conclude that the percent of EVC students who attended the midnight showing of Harry Potter is at least 20%.

75. Previously, an organization reported that teenagers spent 4.5 hours per week, on average, on the phone. The organization thinks that, currently, the mean is higher. Fifteen randomly chosen teenagers were asked how many hours per week they spend on the phone. The sample mean was 4.75 hours with a sample standard deviation of 2.0. Conduct a hypothesis test.

At a significance level of $\alpha = 0.05$, what is the correct conclusion?

a. There is enough evidence to conclude that the mean number of hours is more than 4.75
b. There is enough evidence to conclude that the mean number of hours is more than 4.5
c. There is not enough evidence to conclude that the mean number of hours is more than 4.5
d. There is not enough evidence to conclude that the mean number of hours is more than 4.75

Instructions: For the following ten exercises,

Hypothesis testing: For the following ten exercises, answer each question.

a. State the null and alternate hypothesis.
b. State the *p*-value.
c. State alpha.
d. What is your decision?
e. Write a conclusion.

Answer any other questions asked in the problem.

76. According to the Center for Disease Control website, in 2011 at least 18% of high school students have smoked a cigarette. An Introduction to Statistics class in Davies County, KY conducted a hypothesis test at the local high school (a medium sized–approximately 1,200 students–small city demographic) to determine if the local high school's percentage was lower. One hundred fifty students were chosen at random and surveyed. Of the 150 students surveyed, 82 have smoked. Use a significance level of 0.05 and using appropriate statistical evidence, conduct a hypothesis test and state the conclusions.

77. A recent survey in the *N.Y. Times Almanac* indicated that 48.8% of families own stock. A broker wanted to determine if this survey could be valid. He surveyed a random sample of 250 families and found that 142 owned some type of stock. At the 0.05 significance level, can the survey be considered to be accurate?

78. Driver error can be listed as the cause of approximately 54% of all fatal auto accidents, according to the American Automobile Association. Thirty randomly selected fatal accidents are examined, and it is determined that 14 were caused by driver error. Using $\alpha = 0.05$, is the AAA proportion accurate?

79. The US Department of Energy reported that 51.7% of homes were heated by natural gas. A random sample of 221 homes in Kentucky found that 115 were heated by natural gas. Does the evidence support the claim for Kentucky at the $\alpha = 0.05$ level in Kentucky? Are the results applicable across the country? Why?

80. For Americans using library services, the American Library Association claims that at most 67% of patrons borrow books. The library director in Owensboro, Kentucky feels this is not true, so she asked a local college statistic class to conduct a survey. The class randomly selected 100 patrons and found that 82 borrowed books. Did the class demonstrate that the percentage was higher in Owensboro, KY? Use $\alpha = 0.01$ level of significance. What is the possible proportion of patrons that do borrow books from the Owensboro Library?

81. The Weather Underground reported that the mean amount of summer rainfall for the northeastern US is at least 11.52 inches. Ten cities in the northeast are randomly selected and the mean rainfall amount is calculated to be 7.42 inches with a standard deviation of 1.3 inches. At the $\alpha = 0.05$ level, can it be concluded that the mean rainfall was below the reported average? What if $\alpha = 0.01$? Assume the amount of summer rainfall follows a normal distribution.

82. A survey in the *N.Y. Times Almanac* finds the mean commute time (one way) is 25.4 minutes for the 15 largest US cities. The Austin, TX chamber of commerce feels that Austin's commute time is less and wants to publicize this fact. The mean for 25 randomly selected commuters is 22.1 minutes with a standard deviation of 5.3 minutes. At the $\alpha = 0.10$ level, is the Austin, TX commute significantly less than the mean commute time for the 15 largest US cities?

83. A report by the Gallup Poll found that a woman visits her doctor, on average, at most 5.8 times each year. A random sample of 20 women results in these yearly visit totals

3; 2; 1; 3; 7; 2; 9; 4; 6; 6; 8; 0; 5; 6; 4; 2; 1; 3; 4; 1

At the $\alpha = 0.05$ level can it be concluded that the sample mean is higher than 5.8 visits per year?

84. According to the *N.Y. Times Almanac* the mean family size in the U.S. is 3.18. A sample of a college math class resulted in the following family sizes:

5; 4; 5; 4; 4; 3; 6; 4; 3; 3; 5; 5; 6; 3; 3; 2; 7; 4; 5; 2; 2; 2; 3; 2

At $\alpha = 0.05$ level, is the class' mean family size greater than the national average? Does the Almanac result remain valid? Why?

85. The student academic group on a college campus claims that freshman students study at least 2.5 hours per day, on average. One Introduction to Statistics class was skeptical. The class took a random sample of 30 freshman students and found a mean study time of 137 minutes with a standard deviation of 45 minutes. At $\alpha = 0.01$ level, is the student academic group's claim correct?

REFERENCES

9.1 Null and Alternative Hypotheses

Data from the National Institute of Mental Health. Available online at http://www.nimh.nih.gov/publicat/depression.cfm.

9.4 Full Hypothesis Test Examples

Data from Amit Schitai. Director of Instructional Technology and Distance Learning. LBCC.

Data from Bloomberg Businessweek. Available online at http://www.businessweek.com/news/2011- 09-15/nyc-smoking-rate-falls-to-record-low-of-14-bloomberg-says.html.

Data from energy.gov. Available online at http://energy.gov (accessed June 27. 2013).

Data from Gallup®. Available online at www.gallup.com (accessed June 27, 2013).

Data from Growing by Degrees by Allen and Seaman.

Data from La Leche League International. Available online at http://www.lalecheleague.org/Law/BAFeb01.html.

Data from the American Automobile Association. Available online at www.aaa.com (accessed June 27, 2013).

Data from the American Library Association. Available online at www.ala.org (accessed June 27, 2013).

Data from the Bureau of Labor Statistics. Available online at http://www.bls.gov/oes/current/oes291111.htm.

Data from the Centers for Disease Control and Prevention. Available online at www.cdc.gov (accessed June 27, 2013)

Data from the U.S. Census Bureau, available online at http://quickfacts.census.gov/qfd/states/00000.html (accessed June 27, 2013).

Data from the United States Census Bureau. Available online at http://www.census.gov/hhes/socdemo/language/.

Data from Toastmasters International. Available online at http://toastmasters.org/artisan/detail.asp?CategoryID=1&SubCategoryID=10&ArticleID=429&Page=1.

Data from Weather Underground. Available online at www.wunderground.com (accessed June 27, 2013).

Federal Bureau of Investigations. "Uniform Crime Reports and Index of Crime in Daviess in the State of Kentucky enforced by Daviess County from 1985 to 2005." Available online at http://www.disastercenter.com/kentucky/crime/3868.htm (accessed June 27, 2013).

"Foothill-De Anza Community College District." De Anza College, Winter 2006. Available online at http://research.fhda.edu/factbook/DAdemofs/Fact_sheet_da_2006w.pdf.

Johansen, C., J. Boice, Jr., J. McLaughlin, J. Olsen. "Cellular Telephones and Cancer—a Nationwide Cohort Study in Denmark." Institute of Cancer Epidemiology and the Danish Cancer Society, 93(3):203-7. Available online at http://www.ncbi.nlm.nih.gov/pubmed/11158188 (accessed June 27, 2013).

Rape, Abuse & Incest National Network. "How often does sexual assault occur?" RAINN, 2009. Available online at http://www.rainn.org/get-information/statistics/frequency-of-sexual-assault (accessed June 27, 2013).

SOLUTIONS

1. The random variable is the mean Internet speed in Megabits per second.

3. The random variable is the mean number of children an American family has.

5. The random variable is the proportion of people picked at random in Times Square visiting the city.

7.

a. $H_0: p = 0.42$
b. $H_a: p < 0.42$

9.

a. $H_0: \mu = 15$
b. $H_a: \mu \neq 15$

11. Type I: The mean price of mid-sized cars is $32,000, but we conclude that it is not $32,000.

Type II: The mean price of mid-sized cars is not $32,000, but we conclude that it is $32,000.

13. α = the probability that you think the bag cannot withstand -15 degrees F, when in fact it can β = the probability that you think the bag can withstand -15 degrees F, when in fact it cannot

15. Type I: The procedure will go well, but the doctors think it will not. Type II: The procedure will not go well, but the doctors think it will.

17. 0.019

19. 0.998

21. A normal distribution or a Student's *t*-distribution

23. Use a Student's *t*-distribution

25. a normal distribution for a single population mean

27. It must be approximately normally distributed.

29. They must both be greater than five.

31. binomial distribution

32. This is a left-tailed test.

34. This is a two-tailed test.

36.

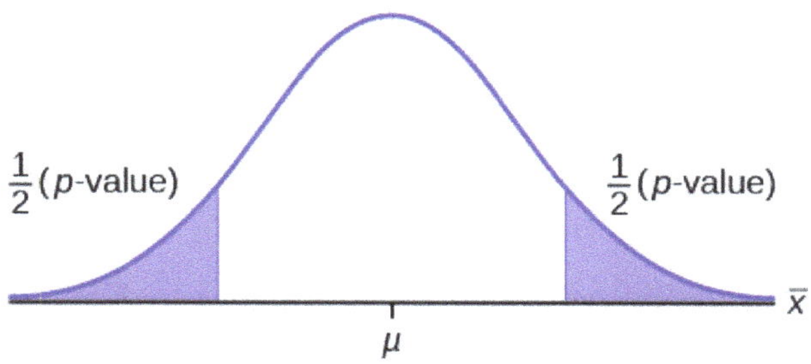

Figure 9.12

38. a right-tailed test

40. a left-tailed test

42. This is a left-tailed test.

44. This is a two-tailed test.

45.

a. H_0: $\mu = 34$; H_a: $\mu \neq 34$
b. H_0: $p \leq 0.60$; H_a: $p > 0.60$
c. H_0: $\mu \geq 100{,}000$; H_a: $\mu < 100{,}000$
d. H_0: $p = 0.29$; H_a: $p \neq 0.29$
e. H_0: $p = 0.05$; H_a: $p < 0.05$
f. H_0: $\mu \leq 10$; H_a: $\mu > 10$
g. H_0: $p = 0.50$; H_a: $p \neq 0.50$
h. H_0: $\mu = 6$; H_a: $\mu \neq 6$
i. H_0: $p \geq 0.11$; H_a: $p < 0.11$
j. H_0: $\mu \leq 20{,}000$; H_a: $\mu > 20{,}000$

47. c

49. a. Type I error: We conclude that the mean is not 34 years, when it really is 34 years. Type II error: We conclude that the mean is 34 years, when in fact it really is not 34 years.

b. Type I error: We conclude that more than 60% of Americans vote in presidential elections, when the actual percentage is at most 60%.Type II error: We conclude that at most 60% of Americans vote in presidential elections when, in fact, more than 60% do.

c. Type I error: We conclude that the mean starting salary is less than $100,000, when it really is at least $100,000. Type II error: We conclude that the mean starting salary is at least $100,000 when, in fact, it is less than $100,000.

d. Type I error: We conclude that the proportion of high school seniors who get drunk each month is not 29%, when it really is 29%. Type II error: We conclude that the proportion of high school seniors who get drunk each month is 29% when, in fact, it is not 29%.

e. Type I error: We conclude that fewer than 5% of adults ride the bus to work in Los Angeles, when the percentage that do is really 5% or more. Type II error: We conclude that 5% or more adults ride the bus to work in Los Angeles when, in fact, fewer that 5% do.

f. Type I error: We conclude that the mean number of cars a person owns in his or her lifetime is more than 10, when in reality it is not more than 10. Type II error: We conclude that the mean number of cars a person owns in his or her lifetime is not more than 10 when, in fact, it is more than 10.

g. Type I error: We conclude that the proportion of Americans who prefer to live away from cities is not about half, though the actual proportion is about half. Type II error: We conclude that the proportion of Americans who prefer to live away from cities is half when, in fact, it is not half.

h. Type I error: We conclude that the duration of paid vacations each year for Europeans is not six weeks, when in fact it is six weeks. Type II error: We conclude that the duration of paid vacations each year for Europeans is six weeks when, in fact, it is not.

i. Type I error: We conclude that the proportion is less than 11%, when it is really at least 11%. Type II error: We conclude that the proportion of women who develop breast cancer is at least 11%, when in fact it is less than 11%.

j. Type I error: We conclude that the average tuition cost at private universities is more than $20,000, though in reality it is at most $20,000. Type II error: We conclude that the average tuition cost at private universities is at most $20,000 when, in fact, it is more than $20,000.

51. b

53. d

55. d

56. a. H_0: $\mu \geq 50,000$
b. H_a: $\mu < 50,000$
c. Let $\bar{X}$ = the average lifespan of a brand of tires.
d. normal distribution
e. $z = -2.315$
f. p-value = 0.0103
g. Check student's solution.
h.
i. alpha: 0.05
ii. Decision: Reject the null hypothesis.
iii. Reason for decision: The p-value is less than 0.05.
iv. Conclusion: There is sufficient evidence to conclude that the mean lifespan of the tires is less than 50,000 miles.
i. (43,537, 49,463)

58. a. H_0: μ = \$1.00
b. H_a: $\mu \neq$ \$1.00
c. Let $\bar{X}$ = the average cost of a daily newspaper.
d. normal distribution
e. $z = -0.866$
f. p-value = 0.3865
g. Check student's solution.
h.
i. Alpha: 0.01
ii. Decision: Do not reject the null hypothesis.
iii. Reason for decision: The p-value is greater than 0.01.
iv. Conclusion: There is sufficient evidence to support the claim that the mean cost of daily papers is \$1. The mean cost could be \$1.
i. (\$0.84, \$1.06)

60. a. H_0: $\mu = 10$
b. H_a: $\mu \neq 10$
c. Let $\bar{X}$ the mean number of sick days an employee takes per year.
d. Student's t-distribution
e. $t = -1.12$
f. p-value = 0.300

g. Check student's solution.
h.
   i. Alpha: 0.05
   ii. Decision: Do not reject the null hypothesis.
   iii. Reason for decision: The p-value is greater than 0.05.
   iv. Conclusion: At the 5% significance level, there is insufficient evidence to conclude that the mean number of sick days is not ten.
i. (4.9443, 11.806)

62. a. $H_0: p \geq 0.6$
b. $H_a: p < 0.6$
c. Let P' = the proportion of students who feel more enriched as a result of taking Elementary Statistics.
d. normal for a single proportion
e. 1.12
f. p-value = 0.1308
g. Check student's solution.
h.
   i. Alpha: 0.05
   ii. Decision: Do not reject the null hypothesis.
   iii. Reason for decision: The p-value is greater than 0.05.
   iv. Conclusion: There is insufficient evidence to conclude that less than 60 percent of her students feel more enriched.
i. Confidence Interval: (0.409, 0.654)
The "plus-4s" confidence interval is (0.411, 0.648)

64. *a.* $H_0: \mu = 4$
b. $H_a: \mu \neq 4$
c. Let $\bar{X}$ the average I.Q. of a set of brown trout.
d. two-tailed Student's t-test
e. $t = 1.95$
f. p-value = 0.076
g. Check student's solution.
h.
   i. Alpha: 0.05
   ii. Decision: Reject the null hypothesis.
   iii. Reason for decision: The p-value is greater than 0.05
   iv Conclusion: There is insufficient evidence to conclude that the average IQ of brown trout is not four.
i. (3.8865,5.9468)

66. a. $H_0: p \geq 0.13$
   b. $H_a: p < 0.13$
   c. Let P' = the proportion of Americans who have seen or sensed angels
   d. normal for a single proportion
   e. −2.688
   f. p-value = 0.0036
   g. Check student's solution.
   h.
      i. alpha: 0.05
      ii. Decision: Reject the null hypothesis.
      iii. Reason for decision: The p-value is less than 0.05.
      iv. Conclusion: There is sufficient evidence to conclude that the percentage of Americans who have seen or sensed an angel is less than 13%.
   i. (0, 0.0623).
   The"plus-4s" confidence interval is (0.0022, 0.0978)

69. *a.* $H_0: p = 0.14$
   b. $H_a: p < 0.14$
   c. Let P' = the proportion of NYC residents that smoke.
   d. normal for a single proportion
   e. −0.2756
   f. p-value = 0.3914
   g. Check student's solution.
   h.
      i. alpha: 0.05
      ii. Decision: Do not reject the null hypothesis.
      iii. Reason for decision: The p-value is greater than 0.05.
      iv. At the 5% significance level, there is insufficient evidence to conclude that the proportion of NYC residents who smoke is less than 0.14.
   i. Confidence Interval: (0.0502, 0.2070): The "plus-4s" confidence interval (see chapter 8) is (0.0676, 0.2297).

71. a. $H_0: \mu = 69{,}110$
   b. $H_a: \mu > 69{,}110$
   c. Let $\bar{X}$ = the mean salary in dollars for California registered nurses.
   d. Student's t-distribution
   e. $t = 1.719$
   f. p-value: 0.0466

g. Check student's solution.
h.
   i. Alpha: 0.05
   ii. Decision: Reject the null hypothesis.
   iii. Reason for decision: The p-value is less than 0.05.
   iv. Conclusion: At the 5% significance level, there is sufficient evidence to conclude that the mean salary of California registered nurses exceeds \$69,110.

i. (\$68,757, \$73,485)

73. c

75. c

77. a. H_0: $p = 0.488$ H_a: $p \neq 0.488$
b. p-value = 0.0114
c. alpha = 0.05
d. Reject the null hypothesis.
e. At the 5% level of significance, there is enough evidence to conclude that 48.8% of families own stocks.
f. The survey does not appear to be accurate.

79. a. H_0: $p = 0.517$ H_a: $p \neq 0.517$
b. p-value = 0.9203.
c. alpha = 0.05.
d. Do not reject the null hypothesis.
e. At the 5% significance level, there is not enough evidence to conclude that the proportion of homes in Kentucky that are heated by natural gas is 0.517.
f. However, we cannot generalize this result to the entire nation. First, the sample's population is only the state of Kentucky. Second, it is reasonable to assume that homes in the extreme north and south will have extreme high usage and low usage, respectively. We would need to expand our sample base to include these possibilities if we wanted to generalize this claim to the entire nation.

81. *a.* H_0: $\mu \geq 11.52$ H_a: $\mu < 11.52$
b. p-value = 0.000002 which is almost 0.
c. alpha = 0.05.
d. Reject the null hypothesis.
e. At the 5% significance level, there is enough evidence to conclude that the mean amount of summer rain in the northeaster US is less than 11.52 inches, on average.

f. We would make the same conclusion if alpha was 1% because the *p*-value is almost 0.

83. a. $H_0: \mu \leq 5.8$ $H_a: \mu > 5.8$

b. *p*-value = 0.9987

c. alpha = 0.05

d. Do not reject the null hypothesis.

e. At the 5% level of significance, there is not enough evidence to conclude that a woman visits her doctor, on average, more than 5.8 times a year.

85. a. $H_0: \mu \geq 150$ $H_a: \mu < 150$

b. *p*-value = 0.0622

c. alpha = 0.01

d. Do not reject the null hypothesis.

e. At the 1% significance level, there is not enough evidence to conclude that freshmen students study less than 2.5 hours per day, on average.

f. The student academic group's claim appears to be correct.

10 Chapter HYPOTHESIS TESTING WITH TWO SAMPLES

Figure 10.1 If you want to test a claim that involves two groups (the types of breakfasts eaten east and west of the Mississippi River) you can use a slightly different technique when conducting a hypothesis test. (credit: Chloe Lim)

INTRODUCTION: AN OVERVIEW

Research frequently contrasts two cohorts. Researchers are investigating the impact of aspirin on the prevention of heart attacks. In recent years, newspapers and magazines have published numerous research on aspirin including two cohorts. Generally, one cohort receives aspirin while the other cohort is administered a placebo. The incidence of heart attacks is analyzed over multiple years. There are further scenarios that involve the comparison of two groups. For instance, research evaluates different dietary and exercise regimens. Politicians analyze the percentage of individuals from various income classes who are likely to vote for them. Students are curious about the efficacy of SAT or GRE preparatory courses in improving their results. Numerous business applications necessitate the comparison of two groups. It could be to the investment yields of two distinct strategies or the variances in production efficiency attributable to differing management styles. To compare two means or two proportions, one analyzes two groups. The groups are categorized as either independent or matched pairs. Independent groups comprise two samples that are unrelated; specifically, sample values drawn from one population bear no connection to sample values drawn from the other population. Matched pairs comprise two interdependent samples. The parameter evaluated with matched pairings is the population mean. The metrics evaluated with independent groups are either the population means or the population proportions of each group.

10.1 COMPARING TWO INDEPENDENT POPULATION MEANS

The comparison of two independent population means is very common and provides a way to test the hypothesis that the two groups differ from each other. Is the night shift less productive than the day shift, are the rates of return from fixed asset investments different from those from common stock investments, and so on? An observed difference between two sample means depends on both the means and the sample standard deviations. Very different means can occur by chance if there is great variation among the individual samples. The test statistic will have to account for this fact. The test comparing two independent population means with unknown and possibly unequal population standard deviations is called the Aspin-Welch t-test. The degrees of freedom formula we will see later was developed by Aspin-Welch.

When we developed the hypothesis test for the mean and proportions we began with the Central Limit Theorem. We recognized that a sample mean came from a distribution of sample means, and sample proportions came from the sampling distribution of sample proportions. This made our sample parameters, the sample means and sample proportions, into random variables. It was important for us to know the distribution that these random variables came from. The Central Limit Theorem gave us the answer: the normal distribution. Our Z and t statistics came from this theorem. This provided us with the solution to our question of how to measure the probability that a sample mean came from a distribution with a particular hypothesized value of the mean or proportion. In both cases that was the question: what is the probability that the mean (or proportion) from our sample data came from a population distribution with the hypothesized value we are interested in?

Now we are interested in whether or not two samples have the same mean. Our question has not changed: Do these two samples come from the same population distribution? To approach this problem we create a new random variable. We recognize that we have two sample means, one from each set of data, and thus we have two random variables coming from two unknown distributions. To solve the problem we create a new random variable, the difference between the sample means. This new random variable also has a distribution and, again, the Central Limit Theorem tells us that this new distribution is normally distributed, regardless of the underlying distributions of the original data. A graph may help to understand this concept.

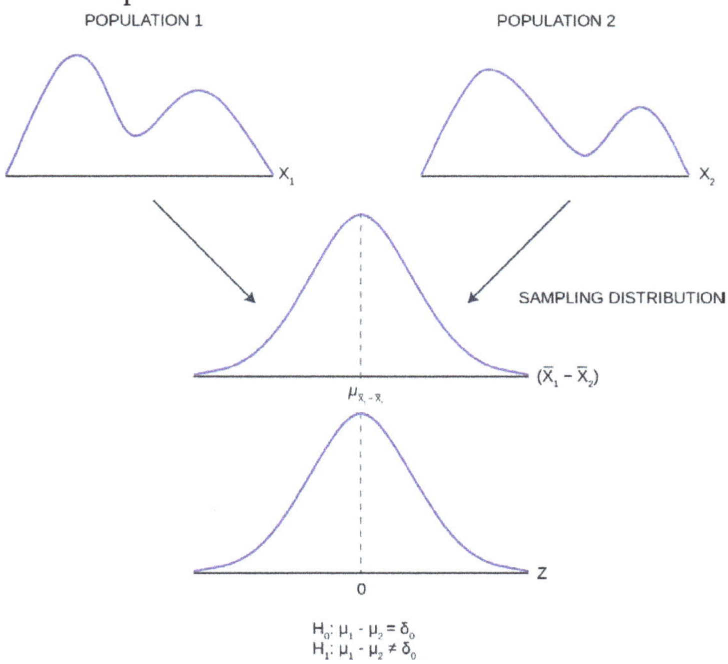

Figure 10.2

Pictured are two distributions of data, X_1 and X_2, with unknown means and standard deviations. The second panel shows the sampling distribution of the newly created random variable $(\bar{X}_1 - \bar{X}_2)$. This distribution is the theoretical distribution of many sample means from population 1 minus sample means from population 2. The Central Limit Theorem tells us that this theoretical sampling distribution of differences in sample means is normally distributed, regardless of the distribution of the actual population data shown in the top panel. Because the sampling distribution is normally distributed, we can develop a standardizing formula and calculate probabilities from the standard normal distribution in the bottom panel, the Z distribution. We have seen this same analysis before in Chapter 7 Figure 7.2 .

The Central Limit Theorem, as before, provides us with the standard deviation of the sampling distribution, and further, that the expected value of the mean of the distribution of differences in sample means is equal to the differences in the population means. Mathematically this can be stated:

$$E\left(\mu_{\bar{x}_1} - \mu_{\bar{x}_2}\right) = \mu_1 - \mu_2$$

Because we do not know the population standard deviations, we estimate them using the two sample standard deviations from our independent samples. For the hypothesis test, we calculate the estimated standard deviation, or standard error, of the difference in sample means, $\bar{X}_1 - \bar{X}_2$.

The standard error is:

$$\sqrt{\frac{(s_1)^2}{n_1} + \frac{(s_2)^2}{n_2}}$$

We remember that substituting the sample variance for the population variance when we did not have the population variance was the technique we used when building the confidence interval and the test statistic for the test of hypothesis for a single mean back in Confidence Intervals and Hypothesis Testing with One Sample. The test statistic (**t**-score) is calculated as follows:

$$t_c = \frac{(\bar{x}_1 - \bar{x}_2) - \delta_0}{\sqrt{\frac{(s_1)^2}{n_1} + \frac{(s_2)^2}{n_2}}}$$

where:

- s_1 and s_2, the sample standard deviations, are estimates of σ_1 and σ_2, respectively and
- σ_1 and σ_2 are the unknown population standard deviations.
- $\bar{x}_1$ and $\bar{x}_2$ are the sample means. μ_1 and μ_2 are the unknown population means.

The number of degrees of freedom (*df*) requires a somewhat complicated calculation. The *df* are not always a whole number. The test statistic above is approximated by the Student's *t*-distribution with *df* as follows:

Degrees of freedom

$$df = \frac{\left(\frac{(s_1)^2}{n_1} + \frac{(s_2)^2}{n_2}\right)^2}{\left(\frac{1}{n_1 - 1}\right)\left(\frac{(s_1)^2}{n_1}\right)^2 + \left(\frac{1}{n_2 - 1}\right)\left(\frac{(s_2)^2}{n_2}\right)^2}$$

When both sample sizes n_1 and n_2 are 30 or larger, the Student's *t* approximation is very good. If each sample has more than 30 observations then the degrees of freedom can be calculated as n1 + n2 - 2.

The format of the sampling distribution, differences in sample means, specifies that the format of the null and alternative hypothesis is:

$$H_0 : \mu_1 - \mu_2 = \delta_0$$
$$H_a : \mu_1 - \mu_2 \neq \delta_0$$

where δ_0 is the hypothesized difference between the two means. If the question is simply "is there any difference between the means?" then $\delta_0 = 0$ and the null and alternative hypotheses becomes:

$$H_0 : \mu_1 = \mu_2$$
$$H_a : \mu_1 \neq \mu_2$$

An example of when δ_0 might not be zero is when the comparison of the two groups requires a specific difference for the decision to be meaningful. Imagine that you are making a capital investment. You are considering changing from your current model machine to another. You measure the productivity of your machines by the speed they produce the product. It may be that a contender to replace the old model is faster in terms of product throughput, but is also more expensive. The second machine may also have more maintenance costs, setup costs, etc. The null hypothesis would be set up so that the new machine would have to be better than the old one by enough to cover these extra costs in terms of speed and cost of production. This form of the null and alternative hypothesis shows how valuable this particular hypothesis test can be. For most of our work we will be testing simple hypotheses asking if there is any difference between the two distribution means.

EXAMPLE 10.1

Independent groups

The Kona Iki Corporation produces coconut milk. They take coconuts and extract the milk inside by drilling a hole and pouring the milk into a vat for processing. They have both a day shift (called the B shift) and a night shift (called the G shift) to do this part of the process. They would like to know if the day shift and the night shift are equally efficient in processing the coconuts. A study is done sampling 9 shifts of the G shift and 16 shifts of the B shift. The results of the number of hours required to process 100 pounds of coconuts is presented in Table 10.1. A study is done and data are collected, resulting in the data in Table 10.1.

Table 10.1

	Sample Size	Average Number of Hours to Process 100 Pounds of Coconuts	Sample Standard Deviation
G Shift	9	2	0.8660.866
B Shift	16	3.2	1.00

Is there a difference in the mean amount of time for each shift to process 100 pounds of coconuts? Test at the 5% level of significance.

Solution 10.1

The population standard deviations are not known and cannot be assumed to equal each other. Let g be the subscript for the G Shift and b be the subscript for the B Shift. Then, μg is the population mean for G Shift and μb is the population mean for B Shift. This is a test of two independent groups, two population means.

Random variable: $\bar{X}_g - \bar{X}_b$ = difference in the sample mean amount of time between the G Shift and the B Shift takes to process the coconuts.

H_0: $\mu_g = \mu_b$ $\quad$ H_0: $\mu_g - \mu_b = 0$

H_a: $\mu_g \neq \mu_b$ $\quad$ H_a: $\mu_g - \mu_b \neq 0$

The words "the same" tell you *H0* has an "=". Since there are no other words to indicate *Ha*, is either faster or slower. This is a two tailed test.

Distribution for the test: Use t_{df} where *df* is calculated using the *df* formula for independent groups, two population means above. Using a calculator, *df* is approximately 18.8462.

Graph:

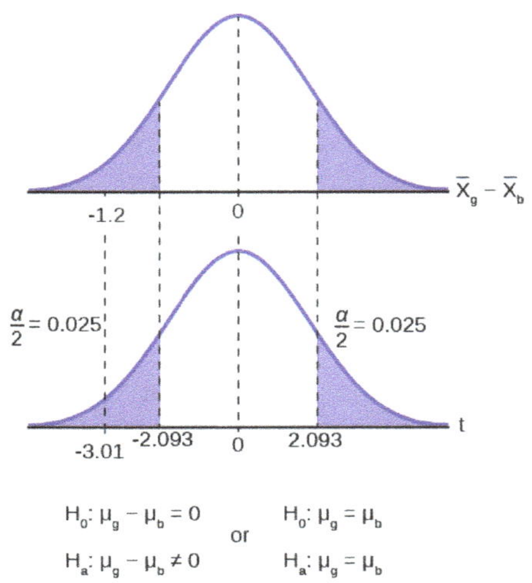

Figure 10.3

$$t_c = \frac{(\bar{X}_1 - \bar{X}_2) - \delta_0}{\sqrt{\frac{s_1^2}{n_1} + \frac{s_2^2}{n_2}}} = -3.01$$

We next find the critical value on the t-table using the degrees of freedom from above. The critical value, 2.093, is found in the .025 column, this is $\alpha/2$, at 19 degrees of freedom. (The convention is to round up the degrees of freedom to make the conclusion more conservative.) Next we calculate the test statistic and mark this on the t-distribution graph.

Make a decision: Since the calculated t-value is in the tail we cannot accept the null hypothesis that there is no difference between the two groups. The means are different.

The graph has included the sampling distribution of the differences in the sample means to show how the t-distribution aligns with the sampling distribution data. We see in the top panel that the calculated difference in the two means is -1.2 and the bottom panel shows that this is 3.01 standard deviations from the mean. Typically we do not need to show the sampling distribution graph and can rely on the graph of the test statistic, the t-distribution in this case, to reach our conclusion.

Conclusion: At the 5% level of significance, the sample data show there is sufficient evidence to conclude that the mean number of hours that the G Shift takes to process 100 pounds of coconuts is different from the B Shift (mean number of hours for the B Shift is greater than the mean number of hours for the G Shift).

NOTE

When the sum of the sample sizes is larger than 30 ($n_1 + n_2 > 30$) you can use the normal distribution to approximate the Student's *t*.

EXAMPLE 10.2

A study is done to determine if Company A retains its workers longer than Company B. It is believed that Company A has a higher retention than Company B. The study finds that in a sample of 11 workers at Company A their average time with the company is four years with a standard deviation of 1.5 years. A sample of 9 workers at Company B finds that the average time with the company was 3.5 years with a standard deviation of 1 year. Test this proposition at the 1% level of significance.

a. Is this a test of two means or two proportions?

Problem

b. Are the populations standard deviations known or unknown?

Solution 10.2

a. two means because time is a continuous random variable.

b. Are the populations standard deviations known or unknown?

Solution 10.2

b. unknown

c. Which distribution do you use to perform the test?

Solution 10.2

c. Student's *t*

d. What is the random variable?

Solution 10.2

d. $\bar{X}_A - \bar{X}_B$

e. What are the null and alternate hypotheses?

Solution 10.2

e.

- $H_o: \mu_A \leq \mu_B$
- $H_a: \mu_A > \mu_B$

f. Is this test right-, left-, or two-tailed?

Solution 10.2

f. right one-tailed test

g. What is the value of the test statistic?

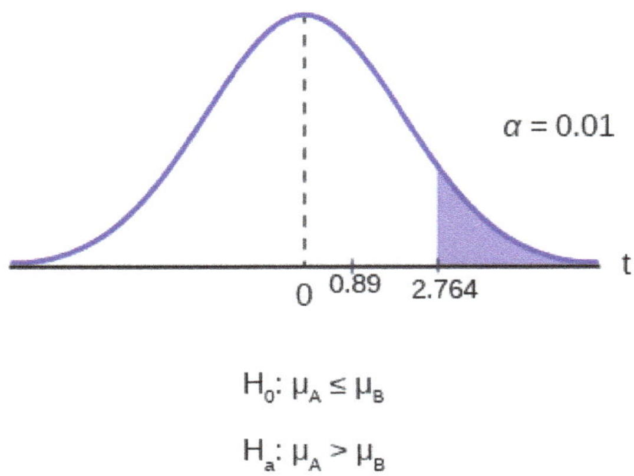

Figure 10.4

Solution 10.2

$$t_c = \frac{(\bar{X}_1 - \bar{X}_2) - \delta_0}{\sqrt{\frac{S_1^2}{n_1} + \frac{S_2^2}{n_2}}} = 0.89$$

h. Can you accept/reject the null hypothesis?

Solution 10.2

h. Cannot reject the null hypothesis that there is no difference between the two groups. Test statistic is not in the tail. The critical value of the t distribution is 2.764 with 10 degrees of freedom. This example shows how difficult it is to reject a null hypothesis with a very small sample. The critical values require very large test statistics to reach the tail.

i. **Conclusion:**

Solution 10.2

i. At the 1% level of significance, from the sample data, there is not sufficient evidence to conclude that the retention of workers at Company A is longer than Company B, on average.

EXAMPLE 10.3

Problem

An interesting research question is the effect, if any, that different types of teaching formats have on the grade outcomes of students. To investigate this issue one sample of students' grades was taken from a hybrid class and another sample taken from a standard lecture format class. Both classes were for the same subject. The mean course grade in percent for the 35 hybrid students is 74 with a standard deviation of 16. The mean grades of the 40 students form the standard lecture class was 76 percent with a standard deviation of 9. Test at 5% to see if there is any significant difference in the population mean grades between standard lecture course and hybrid class.

Solution 10.3

We begin by noting that we have two groups, students from a hybrid class and students from a standard lecture format class. We also note that the random variable, what we are interested in, is students' grades, a continuous random variable. We could have asked the research question in a different way and had a binary random variable. For example, we could have studied the percentage of students with a failing grade, or with an A grade. Both of these would be binary and thus a test of proportions and not a test of means as is the case here. Finally, there is no presumption as to which format might lead to higher grades so the hypothesis is stated as a two-tailed test.

$H_0: \mu_1 = \mu_2$
$H_a: \mu_1 \neq \mu_2$

As would virtually always be the case, we do not know the population variances of the two distributions and thus our test statistic is:

$$t_c = \frac{(\bar{x}_1 - \bar{x}_2) - \delta_0}{\sqrt{\frac{s^2}{n_1} + \frac{s^2}{n_2}}} = \frac{(74 - 76) - 0}{\sqrt{\frac{16^2}{35} + \frac{9^2}{40}}} = -0.65$$

To determine the critical value of the Student's t we need the degrees of freedom. For this case we use: df = n1 + n2 - 2 = 35 + 40 -2 = 73. This is large enough to consider it the normal distribution thus $t_{a/2} = 1.96$. Again as always we determine if the calculated value is in the tail determined by the critical value. In this case we do not even need to look up the critical value: the calculated value of the difference in these two average grades is not even one standard deviation apart. Certainly not in the tail.

Conclusion: Cannot reject the null at α=5%. Therefore, evidence does not exist to prove that the grades in hybrid and standard classes differ.

10.2 COHEN'S STANDARDS FOR SMALL, MEDIUM, AND LARGE EFFECT SIZES

Cohen's *d* is a measure of "effect size" based on the differences between two means. Cohen's *d*, named for United States statistician Jacob Cohen, measures the relative strength of the differences between the means of two populations based on sample data. The calculated value of effect size is then compared to Cohen's standards of small, medium, and large effect sizes.

Table 10.2 Cohen's Standard Effect Sizes

Size of effect	d
Small	0.2
Medium	0.5
Large	0.8

Cohen's *d* is the measure of the difference between two means divided by the pooled standard deviation: $d = \frac{\bar{x}_1 - \bar{x}_2}{s_{pooled}}$ where $s_{pooled} = \sqrt{\frac{(n_1 - 1)s_1^2 + (n_2 - 1)s_2^2}{n_1 + n_2 - 2}}$

It is important to note that Cohen's d does not provide a level of confidence as to the magnitude of the size of the effect comparable to the other tests of hypothesis we have studied. The sizes of the effects are simply indicative.

Example 10.4

Calculate Cohen's *d* for example 10.2. Is the size of the effect small, medium, or large? Explain what the size of the effect means for this problem.

Solution 10.4

$\bar{x}_1 = 4$ $s_1 = 1.5$ $n_1 = 11$

$\bar{x}_2 = 3.5$ $s_2 = 1$ $n_2 = 9$

$d = 0.384$

The effect is small because 0.384 is between Cohen's value of 0.2 for small effect size and 0.5 for medium effect size. The size of the differences of the means for the two companies is small indicating that there is not a significant difference between them.

10.3 TEST FOR DIFFERENCES IN MEANS: ASSUMING EQUAL

Population Variances

Typically we can never expect to know any of the population parameters, mean, proportion, or standard deviation. When testing hypotheses concerning differences in means we are faced with the difficulty of two unknown variances that play a critical role in the test statistic. We have been substituting the sample variances just as we did when testing hypotheses for a single mean. And as we did before, we used a Student's t to compensate for this lack of information on the population variance. There may be situations, however, when we do not know the population variances, but we can assume that the two populations have the same variance. If this is true then the pooled sample variance will be smaller than the individual sample variances. This will give more precise estimates and reduce the probability of discarding a good null. The null and alternative hypotheses remain the same, but the test statistic changes to:

$$t_c = \frac{\left(\bar{x}_1 - \bar{x}_2\right) - \delta_0}{\sqrt{Sp^2\left(\frac{1}{n_1} + \frac{1}{n_2}\right)}}$$

where Sp^2 is the pooled variance given by the formula:

$$Sp^2 = \frac{\left(n_1 - 1\right)s_1^2 + \left(n_2 - 1\right)s_2^2}{n_1 + n_2 - 2}$$

EXAMPLE 10.5

A drug trial is attempted using a real drug and a pill made of just sugar. 18 people are given the real drug in hopes of increasing the production of endorphins. The increase in endorphins is found to be on average 8 micrograms per person, and the sample standard deviation is 5.4 micrograms. 11 people are given the sugar pill, and their average endorphin increase is 4 micrograms with a standard deviation of 2.4. From previous research on endorphins it is determined that it can be assumed that the variances within the two samples can be assumed to be the same. Test at 5% to see if the population mean for the real drug had a significantly greater impact on the endorphins than the population mean with the sugar pill.

Solution 10.5

First we begin by designating one of the two groups Group 1 and the other Group 2. This will be needed to keep track of the null and alternative hypotheses. Let's set Group 1 as those who received the actual new medicine being tested and therefore Group 2 is those who received the sugar pill. We can now set up the null and alternative hypothesis as:

$H_0: \mu_1 \leq \mu_2$
$H_1: \mu_1 > \mu_2$

This is set up as a one-tailed test with the claim in the alternative hypothesis that the medicine will produce more endorphins than the sugar pill. We now calculate the test statistic which requires us to calculate the pooled variance, S_p^2 using the formula above.

$$t_c = \frac{\left(\bar{x}_1 - \bar{x}_2\right) - \delta_0}{\sqrt{S_p^2\left(\frac{1}{n_1} + \frac{1}{n_2}\right)}} = \frac{(8-4)-0}{\sqrt{20.4933\left(\frac{1}{18} + \frac{1}{11}\right)}} = 2.31$$

t_α, allows us to compare the test statistic and the critical value.

$$t_\alpha = 1.703 \text{ at } df = n_1 + n_2 - 2 = 18 + 11 - 2 = 27$$

The test statistic is clearly in the tail, 2.31 is larger than the critical value of 1.703, and therefore we cannot maintain the null hypothesis. Thus, we conclude that there is significant evidence at the 95% level of confidence that the new medicine produces the effect desired.

10.4 COMPARING TWO INDEPENDENT POPULATION PROPORTIONS

When conducting a hypothesis test that compares two independent population proportions, the following characteristics should be present:

1. The two independent samples are random samples that are independent.
2. The number of successes is at least five, and the number of failures is at least five, for each of the samples.
3. Growing literature states that the population must be at least ten or even perhaps 20 times the size of the sample. This keeps each population from being over-sampled and causing biased results.

Comparing two proportions, like comparing two means, is common. If two estimated proportions are different, it may be due to a difference in the populations or it may be due to chance in the sampling. A hypothesis test can help determine if a difference in the estimated proportions reflects a difference in the two population proportions.

Like the case of differences in sample means, we construct a sampling distribution for differences in sample proportions: $(p'_A - p'_B)$ where $p'_A = \frac{X_A}{n_A}$ and $p'_B = \frac{X_B}{n_B}$ are the sample proportions for the two sets of data in question. X_A and X_B are the number of successes in each sample group respectively, and n_A and n_B are the respective sample sizes from the two groups. Again we go the Central Limit theorem to find the distribution of this sampling distribution for the differences in sample proportions. And again we find that this sampling distribution, like the ones past, are normally distributed as proved by the Central Limit Theorem, as seen in Figure 10.5 .

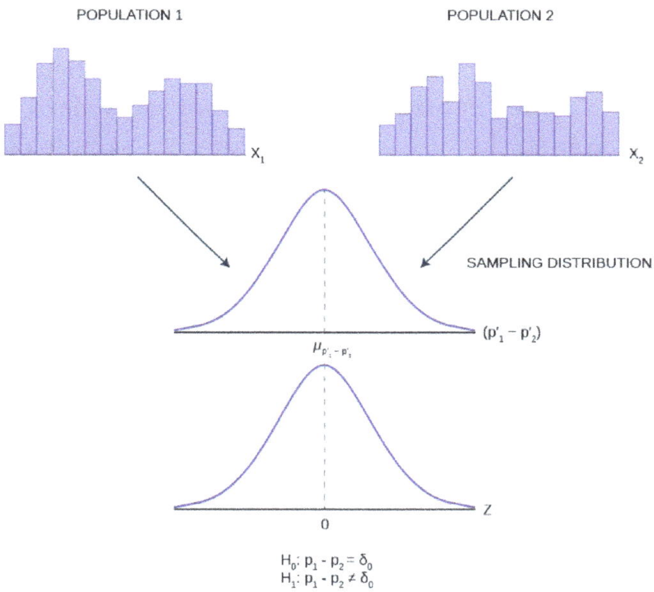

Figure 10.5

Generally, the null hypothesis allows for the test of a difference of a particular value, δ_0, just as we did for the case of differences in means.

$$H_0 : p_1 - p_2 = \delta_0$$
$$H_1 : p_1 - p_2 \neq \delta_0$$

Most common, however, is the test that the two proportions are the same. That is,

$$H_0 : p_A = p_B$$
$$H_a : p_A \neq p_B$$

To conduct the test, we use a pooled proportion, p_c.

The pooled proportion is calculated as follows:

$$p_c = \frac{x_A + x_B}{n_A + n_B}$$

The test statistic (z-score) is:

$$Z_c = \frac{(p'_A - p'_B) - \delta_0}{\sqrt{p_c(1 - p_c)(\frac{1}{n_A} + \frac{1}{n_B})}}$$

where δ_0 is the hypothesized differences between the two proportions and p_c is the pooled variance from the formula above.

EXAMPLE 10.6

A bank has recently acquired a new branch and thus has customers in this new territory. They are interested in the default rate in their new territory. They wish to test the hypothesis that the default rate is different from their current customer base. They sample 200 files in area A, their current customers, and find that 20 have defaulted. In area B, the new customers, another sample of 200 files shows 12 have defaulted on their loans. At a 10% level of significance can we say that the default rates are the same or different?

Solution 10.6

This is a test of proportions. We know this because the underlying random variable is binary, default or not default. Further, we know it is a test of differences in proportions because we have two sample groups, the current customer base and the newly acquired customer base. Let A and B be the subscripts for the two customer groups. Then p_A and p_B are the two population proportions we wish to test.

Random Variable:

P′A – P′B = difference in the proportions of customers who defaulted in the two groups.

$H_0 : p_A = p_B$
$H_a : p_A \neq p_B$

The words "is a difference" tell you the test is two-tailed.

Distribution for the test: Since this is a test of two binomial population proportions, the distribution is normal:

$$p_c = \frac{x_A + x_B}{n_A + n_B} = \frac{20 + 12}{200 + 200} = 0.08 \quad 1 - p_c = 0.92$$

$(p'A - p'B) = 0.04$ follows an approximate normal distribution.

Estimated proportion for group A: $p'_A = \frac{x_A}{n_A} = \frac{20}{200} = 0.1$

Estimated proportion for group B: $p'_B = \frac{x_B}{n_B} = \frac{12}{200} = 0.06$

The estimated difference between the two groups is : $p'A - p'B = 0.1 - 0.06 = 0.04$.

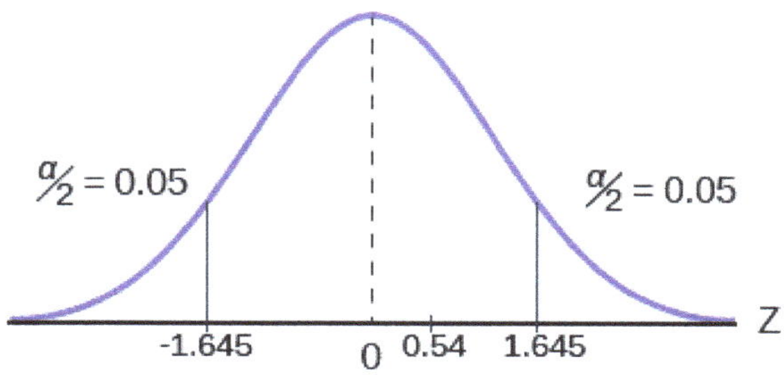

$H_0: P_A = P_B$

$H_a: P_A \neq P_B$

Figure 10.6

$$Z_c = \frac{(P'_A - P'_B) - \delta_0}{P_c(1 - P_c)\left(\frac{1}{n_A} + \frac{1}{n_B}\right)} = 0.54$$

The calculated test statistic is .54 and is not in the tail of the distribution.
Make a decision: Since the calculate test statistic is not in the tail of the distribution we cannot reject *H0*.

Conclusion: At a 1% level of significance, from the sample data, there is not sufficient evidence to conclude that there is a difference between the proportions of customers who defaulted in the two groups.

TRY IT 10.6

Two types of valves are being tested to determine if there is a difference in pressure tolerances. Fifteen out of a random sample of 100 of Valve *A* cracked under 4,500 psi. Six out of a random sample of 100 of Valve *B* cracked under 4,500 psi. Test at a 5% level of significance.

10.5 TWO POPULATION MEANS WITH KNOWN STANDARD DEVIATIONS

Even though this situation is not likely (knowing the population standard deviations is very unlikely), the following example illustrates hypothesis testing for independent means with known population standard deviations. The sampling distribution for the difference between the means is normal in accordance with the central limit theorem. The random variable is $\bar{X}_1 - \bar{X}_2$. The normal distribution has the following format:

The standard deviation is:

$$\sqrt{\frac{(\sigma_1)^2}{n_1} + \frac{(\sigma_2)^2}{n_2}}$$

The test statistic (*z*-score) is:

$$Z_c = \frac{(\overline{x}_1 - \overline{x}_2) - \delta_0}{\sqrt{\frac{(\sigma_1)^2}{n_1} + \frac{(\sigma_2)^2}{n_2}}}$$

Example 10.7

Independent groups, population standard deviations known: The mean lasting time of two competing floor waxes is to be compared. Twenty floors are randomly assigned to test each wax. Both populations have a normal distributions. The data are recorded in Table 10.3.

Table 10.3

Wax	Sample mean number of months floor wax lasts	Population standard deviation
1	3	0.33
2	2.9	0.36

Does the data indicate that **wax 1 is more effective than wax 2**? Test at a 5% level of significance.

Solution 10.7

This is a test of two independent groups, two population means, population standard deviations known.

Random Variable: $\overline{X}_1 - \overline{X}_2$ = difference in the mean number of months the competing floor waxes last.

$H_0 : \mu_1 \leq \mu_2$
$H_a : \mu_1 > \mu_2$

The words "is more effective" says that wax 1 lasts longer than wax 2, on average. "Longer" is a ">" symbol and goes into *Ha*. Therefore, this is a right-tailed test.

Distribution for the test: The population standard deviations are known so the distribution is normal. Using the formula for the test statistic we find the calculated value for the problem.

$$Z_c = \frac{(\mu_1 - \mu_2) - \delta_0}{\sqrt{\frac{\sigma_1^2}{n_1} + \frac{\sigma_2^2}{n_2}}} = 0.1$$

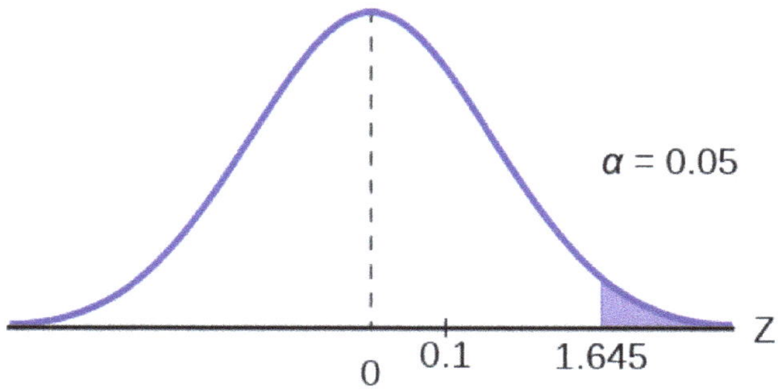

$H_0: \mu_1 \leq \mu_2$

$H_a: \mu_1 > \mu_2$

Figure 10.7

The estimated difference between he two means is : $\bar{X}_1 - \bar{X}_2 = 3 - 2.9 = 0.1$

Compare calculated value and critical value and Zα: We mark the calculated value on the graph and find the the calculate value is not in the tail therefore we cannot reject the null hypothesis.

Make a decision: the calculated value of the test statistic is not in the tail, therefore you cannot reject H_0.

Conclusion: At the 5% level of significance, from the sample data, there is not sufficient evidence to conclude that the mean time wax 1 lasts is longer (wax 1 is more effective) than the mean time wax 2 lasts.

TRY IT 10.7

The means of the number of revolutions per minute of two competing engines are to be compared. Thirty engines of each type are randomly assigned to be tested. Both populations have normal distributions. Table 10.4 shows the result. Do the data indicate that Engine 2 has higher RPM than Engine 1? Test at a 5% level of significance.

Table 10.4

Engine	Sample mean number of RPM	Population standard deviation
1	1,500	50
2	1,600	60

EXAMPLE 10.8

An interested citizen wanted to know if Democratic U. S. senators are older than Republican U.S. senators, on average. On May 26 2013, the mean age of 30 randomly selected Republican Senators was 61 years 247 days old (61.675 years) with a standard deviation of 10.17 years. The mean age of 30 randomly selected Democratic senators was 61 years 257 days old (61.704 years) with a standard deviation of 9.55 years.

Do the data indicate that Democratic senators are older than Republican senators, on average? Test at a 5% level of significance.

Solution 10.8

This is a test of two independent groups, two population means. The population standard deviations are unknown, but the sum of the sample sizes is 30 + 30 = 60, which is greater than 30, so we can use the normal approximation to the Student's-t distribution. Subscripts: 1: Democratic senators 2: Republican senators

Random variable: $\overline{X}_1 - \overline{X}_2$ = difference in the mean age of Democratic and Republican U.S. senators.

$H_0: \mu_1 \leq \mu_2$ $H_0: \mu_1 - \mu_2 \leq 0$

$H_a: \mu_1 > \mu_2$ $H_a: \mu_1 - \mu_2 > 0$

The words "older than" translates as a ">" symbol and goes into H_a. Therefore, this is a right-tailed test.

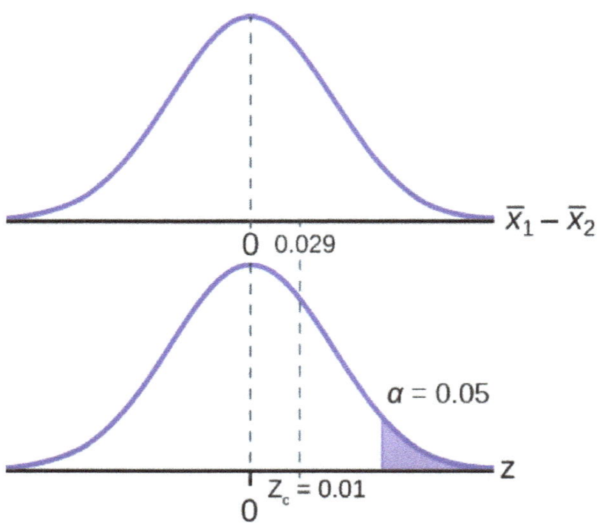

Figure 10.8

Make a decision: The p-value is larger than 5%, therefore we cannot reject the null hypothesis. By calculating the test statistic we would find that the test statistic does not fall in the tail, therefore we cannot reject the null hypothesis. We reach the same conclusion using either method of a making this statistical decision.

Conclusion: At the 5% level of significance, from the sample data, there is not sufficient evidence to conclude that the mean age of Democratic senators is greater than the mean age of the Republican senators.

10.6 MATCHED OR PAIRED SAMPLES

In most cases of economic or business data we have little or no control over the process of how the data are gathered. In this sense the data are not the result of a planned controlled experiment. In some cases, however, we can develop data that are part of a controlled experiment. This situation occurs frequently in quality control situations. Imagine that the production rates of two machines built to the same design, but at different manufacturing plants, are being tested for differences in some production metric such as speed of output or meeting some production specification such as strength of the product. The test is the same in format to what we have been testing, but here we can have matched pairs for which we can test if differences exist. Each observation has its matched pair against which differences are calculated. First, the differences in the metric to be tested between the two lists of observations must be calculated, and this is typically labelled with the letter "d." Then, the average of these matched differences, X_d is calculated as is its standard deviation, S_d. We expect that the standard deviation of the differences of the matched pairs will be smaller than unmatched pairs because presumably fewer differences should exist because of the correlation between the two groups.

When using a hypothesis test for matched or paired samples, the following characteristics may be present:

1. Simple random sampling is used.
2. Sample sizes are often small.
3. Two measurements (samples) are drawn from the same pair of individuals or objects.
4. Differences are calculated from the matched or paired samples.
5. The differences form the sample that is used for the hypothesis test.
6. Either the matched pairs have differences that come from a population that is normal or the number of differences is sufficiently large so that distribution of the sample mean of differences is approximately normal.

In a hypothesis test for matched or paired samples, subjects are matched in pairs and differences are calculated. The differences are the data. The population mean for the differences, μ_d, is then tested using a Student's-t test for a single population mean with $n - 1$ degrees of freedom, where n is the number of differences, that is, the number of pairs not the number of observations.

The null and alternative hypotheses for this test are:

$$H_0 : \mu_d = 0$$
$$H_a : \mu_d \neq 0$$

The test statistic is:

$$t_c = \frac{\overline{x}_d - \mu_d}{\left(\frac{s_d}{\sqrt{n}}\right)}$$

EXAMPLE 10.9

Problem

A company has developed a training program for its entering employees because they have become concerned with the results of the six-month employee review. They hope that the training program can result in better six-month reviews. Each trainee constitutes a "pair", the entering score the employee received when first entering the firm and the score given at the six-month review. The difference in the two scores were calculated for each employee and the means for before and after the training program was calculated. The sample mean before the training program was 20.4 and the sample mean after the training program was 23.9. The standard deviation of the differences in the two scores across the 20 employees was 3.8 points. Test at the 10% significance level the null hypothesis that the two population means are equal against the alternative that the training program helps improve the employees' scores.

Solution 10.9

The first step is to identify this as a two sample case: before the training and after the training. This differentiates this problem from simple one sample issues. Second, we determine that the two samples are "paired." Each observation in the first sample has a paired observation in the second sample. This information tells us that the null and alternative hypotheses should be:

$$H_0 : \mu_d \leq 0$$
$$H_a : \mu_d > 0$$

This form reflects the implied claim that the training course improves scores; the test is one-tailed and the claim is in the alternative hypothesis. Because the experiment was conducted as a matched paired sample rather than simply taking scores from people who took the training course those who didn't, we use the matched pair test statistic:

$$\text{Test Statistic: } t_c = \frac{\bar{X}_d - \mu_d}{\frac{s_d}{\sqrt{n}}} = \frac{(23.9 - 20.4) - 0}{\left(\frac{3.8}{\sqrt{20}}\right)} = 4.12$$

In order to solve this equation, the individual scores, pre-training course and post-training course need to be used to calculate the individual differences. These scores are then averaged and the average difference is calculated:

$$\bar{X}_d = \bar{x}_1 - \bar{x}_2$$

From these differences we can calculate the standard deviation across the individual differences:

$$S_d = \frac{\Sigma\left(d_i - \bar{X}_d\right)^2}{n - 1} \text{ where } d_i = x_{1i} - x_{2i}$$

We can now compare the calculated value of the test statistic, 4.12, with the critical value. The critical value is a Student's t with degrees of freedom equal to the number of pairs, not observations, minus 1. In this case 20 pairs and at 90% confidence level $t_{a/2} = \pm 1.729$ at $df = 20 - 1 = 19$. The calculated test statistic is most certainly in the tail of the distribution and thus we cannot accept the null hypothesis that there is no difference from the training program. Evidence seems indicate that the training aids employees in gaining higher scores.

EXAMPLE 10.10

A study was conducted to investigate the effectiveness of hypnotism in reducing pain. Results for randomly selected subjects are shown in Table 10.5. A lower score indicates less pain. The "before" value is matched to an "after" value and the differences are calculated. Are the sensory measurements, on average, lower after hypnotism? Test at a 5% significance level.

Table 10.5

Subject:	A	B	C	D	E	F	G	H
Before	6.6	6.5	9.0	10.3	11.3	8.1	6.3	11.6
After	6.8	2.4	7.4	8.5	8.1	6.1	3.4	2.0

Solution 10.10

Corresponding "before" and "after" values form matched pairs. (Calculate "after" – "before.")

Table 10.6

After data	Before data	Difference
6.8	6.6	0.2
2.4	6.5	-4.1
7.4	9	-1.6
8.5	10.3	-1.8
8.1	11.3	-3.2
6.1	8.1	-2
3.4	6.3	-2.9
2	11.6	-9.6

The data **for the test** are the differences: {0.2, –4.1, –1.6, –1.8, –3.2, –2, –2.9, –9.6}

The sample mean and sample standard deviation of the differences are: $\bar{x}_d = -3.13$ and s_d=2.91 Verify these values.

Let μd be the population mean for the differences. We use the subscript dd to denote "differences."

Random variable: $\bar{X}_d$ = the mean difference of the sensory measurements

$H_0: \mu_d \geq 0$

The null hypothesis is zero or positive, meaning that there is the same or more pain felt after hypnotism. That means the subject shows no improvement. μ_d is the population mean of the differences.)

$H_a: \mu_d < 0$

The alternative hypothesis is negative, meaning there is less pain felt after hypnotism. That means the subject shows improvement. The score should be lower after hypnotism, so the difference ought to be negative to indicate improvement.

Distribution for the test: The distribution is a Student's t with $df = n - 1 = 8 - 1 = 7$. Use t_7. (Notice that the test is for a single population mean.)

Calculate the test statistic and look up the critical value using the Student's-t distribution: The calculated value of the test statistic is 3.06 and the critical value of the t-distribution with 7 degrees of freedom at the 5% level of confidence is 1.895 with a one-tailed test.

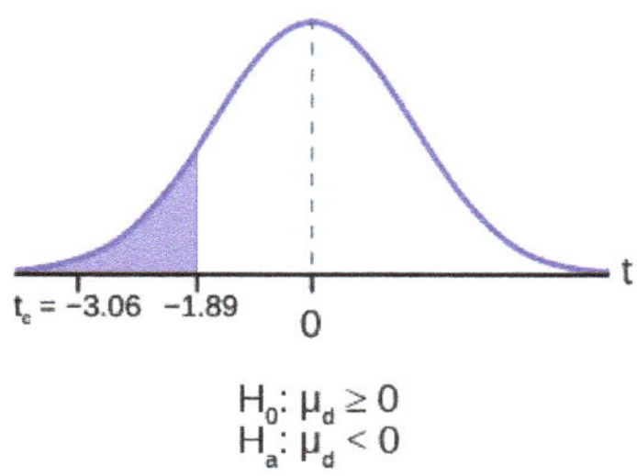

Figure 10.9

$\overline{X}_d$ is the random variable for the differences.

The sample mean and sample standard deviation of the differences are:

$\overline{x}_d = -3.13$

$\overline{s}_d = 2.91$

Compare the critical value for alpha against the calculated test statistic.

The conclusion from using the comparison of the calculated test statistic and the critical value will gives us the result. In this question the calculated test statistic is 3.06 and the critical value is 1.895. The test statistic is clearly in the tail and thus we cannot accept the null hypotheses that there is no difference between the two situations, hypnotized and not hypnotized.

Make a decision: Cannot accept the null hypothesis, H_0. This means that $\mu_d < 0$ and there is a statistically significant improvement.

Conclusion: At a 5% level of significance, from the sample data, there is sufficient evidence to conclude that the sensory measurements, on average, are lower after hypnotism. Hypnotism appears to be effective in reducing pain.

Example 10.11

A college football coach was interested in whether the college's strength development class increased his players' maximum lift (in pounds) on the bench press exercise. He asked four of his players to participate in a study. The amount of weight they could each lift was recorded before they took the strength development class. After completing the class, the amount of weight they could each lift was again measured. The data are as follows:

Table 10.7

Weight (in pounds)	Player 1	Player 2	Player 3	Player 4
Amount of weight lifted prior to the class	205	241	338	368
Amount of weight lifted after the class	295	252	330	360

The coach wants to know if the strength development class makes his players stronger, on average.

Record the differences data. Calculate the differences by subtracting the amount of weight lifted prior to the class from the weight lifted after completing the class. The data for the differences are: {90, 11, -8, -8}.

$\overline{x}_d = 21.3$, $s_d = 46.7$

Using the difference data, this becomes a test of a single mean.

Define the random variable: $\bar{X}_d$ mean difference in the maximum lift per player.

The distribution for the hypothesis test is a student's t with 3 degrees of freedom.

H_0: $\mu_d \leq 0$, H_a: $\mu_d > 0$

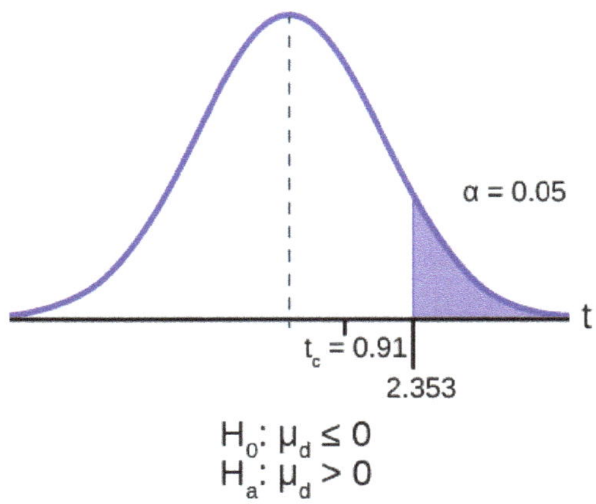

Figure 10.10

Calculate the test statistic look up the critical value: Critical value of the test statistic is 0.91. The critical value of the student's t at 5% level of significance and 3 degrees of freedom is 2.353.

Decision: If the level of significance is 5%, we cannot reject the null hypothesis, because the calculated value of the test statistic is not in the tail.

What is the conclusion?

At a 5% level of significance, from the sample data, there is not sufficient evidence to conclude that the strength development class helped to make the players stronger, on average.

Key Terms

Cohen's *d* a measure of effect size based on the differences between two means. If *d* is between 0 and 0.2 then the effect is small. If *d* approaches is 0.5, then the effect is medium, and if *d* approaches 0.8, then it is a large effect.

Independent Groups two samples that are selected from two populations, and the values from one population are not related in any way to the values from the other population.

Matched Pairs two samples that are dependent. Differences between a before and after scenario are tested by testing one population mean of differences.

Pooled Variance a weighted average of two variances that can then be used when calculating standard error.

CHAPTER REVIEW

10.1 Comparing Two Independent Population Means

Two population means from independent samples where the population standard deviations are not known

- Random Variable: $\bar{X}_1 - \bar{X}_2$= the difference of the sampling means
- Distribution: Student's *t*-distribution with degrees of freedom (variances not pooled)

10.2 Cohen's Standards for Small, Medium, and Large Effect Sizes

Cohen's *d* is a measure of "effect size" based on the differences between two means.

It is important to note that Cohen's *d* does not provide a level of confidence as to the magnitude of the size of the effect comparable to the other tests of hypothesis we have studied. The sizes of the effects are simply indicative.

10.3 Test for Differences in Means: Assuming Equal Population Variances

In situations when we do not know the population variances but assume the variances are the same, the pooled sample variance will be smaller than the individual sample variances.

This will give more precise estimates and reduce the probability of discarding a good null.

10.4 Comparing Two Independent Population Proportions

Test of two population proportions from independent samples.

- Random variable: $=p'_A-p'_B=$ difference between the two estimated proportions
- Distribution: normal distribution

10.5 Two Population Means with Known Standard Deviations

A hypothesis test of two population means from independent samples where the population standard deviations are known will have these characteristics:

- Random variable: $\bar{X}_1 - \bar{X}_2$ = the difference of the means
- Distribution: normal distribution

10.6 Matched or Paired Samples

A hypothesis test for matched or paired samples (t-test) has these characteristics:

- Test the differences by subtracting one measurement from the other measurement

- Random Variable: $\bar{x}_d$ = mean of the differences
- Distribution: Student's-t distribution with $n - 1$ degrees of freedom
- If the number of differences is small (less than 30), the differences must follow a normal distribution.
- Two samples are drawn from the same set of objects.
- Samples are dependent.

FORMULA REVIEW

10.1 Comparing Two Independent Population Means

Standard error: $SE = \sqrt{\frac{(s_1)^2}{n_1} + \frac{(s_2)^2}{n_2}}$

Test statistic (t-score): $t_c = \frac{(\bar{x}_1 - \bar{x}_2) - \delta_0}{\sqrt{\frac{(s_1)^2}{n_1} + \frac{(s_2)^2}{n_2}}}$

Degrees of freedom:

$$df = \frac{\left(\frac{(s_1)^2}{n_1} + \frac{(s_2)^2}{n_2}\right)^2}{\left(\frac{1}{n_1 - 1}\right)\left(\frac{(s_1)^2}{n_1}\right)^2 + \left(\frac{1}{n_2 - 1}\right)\left(\frac{(s_2)^2}{n_2}\right)^2}$$

where:

s_1 and s_2 are the sample standard deviations, and n_1 and n_2 are the sample sizes.
$\bar{x}_1$ and $\bar{x}_2$ are the sample means.

10.2 Cohen's Standards for Small, Medium, and Large Effect Sizes

Cohen's d is the measure of effect size:

$$d = \frac{\bar{x}_1 - \bar{x}_2}{s_{pooled}}$$

where $s_{pooled} = \sqrt{\frac{(n_1 - 1)s_1^2 + (n_2 - 1)s_2^2}{n_1 + n_2 - 2}}$

10.3 Test for Differences in Means: Assuming Equal Population Variances

$$t_c = \frac{\left(\bar{x}_1 - \bar{x}_2\right) - \delta_0}{\sqrt{Sp^2\left(\frac{1}{n_1} + \frac{1}{n_2}\right)}}$$

where Sp^2 is the pooled variance given by the formula:

$$Sp^2 = \frac{(n_1 - 1)s_2^1 + (n_2 - 1)s_2^2}{n_1 + n_2 - 2}$$

10.4 Comparing Two Independent Population Proportions

Pooled Proportion: $p_c = \frac{x_A + x_B}{n_A + n_B}$

Test Statistic (z-score): $Z_c = \frac{(p'_A - p'_B)}{\sqrt{p_c(1 - p_c)\left(\frac{1}{n_A} + \frac{1}{n_B}\right)}}$

where

p'_A and p'_B are the sample proportions, p_A and p_B are the population proportions, P_c is the pooled proportion, and n_A and n_B are the sample sizes.

10.5 Two Population Means with Known Standard Deviations

Test Statistic (z-score):

$$Z_c = \frac{(\bar{x}_1 - \bar{x}_2) - \delta_0}{\sqrt{\frac{(\sigma_1)^2}{n_1} + \frac{(\sigma_2)^2}{n_2}}}$$

where:

σ_1 and σ_2 are the known population standard deviations. n_1 and n_2 are the sample sizes. $\bar{x}_1$ and $\bar{x}_2$ are the sample means. μ_1 and μ_2 are the population means.

10.6 Matched or Paired Samples

Test Statistic (*t*-score): $t_c = \frac{\bar{x}_d - \mu_d}{\left(\frac{s_d}{\sqrt{n}}\right)}$

where:

$\bar{x}_d$ is the mean of the sample differences. μ_d is the mean of the population differences. s_d is the sample standard deviation of the differences. n is the sample size.

PRACTICE

10.1 Comparing Two Independent Population Means

Use the following information to answer the next 15 exercises: Indicate if the hypothesis test is for

a. independent group means, population standard deviations, and/or variances known
b. independent group means, population standard deviations, and/or variances unknown
c. matched or paired samples
d. single mean
e. two proportions
f. single proportion

1. It is believed that 70% of males pass their drivers test in the first attempt, while 65% of females pass the test in the first attempt. Of interest is whether the proportions are in fact equal.

2. A new laundry detergent is tested on consumers. Of interest is the proportion of consumers who prefer the new brand over the leading competitor. A study is done to test this.

3. A new windshield treatment claims to repel water more effectively. Ten windshields are tested by simulating rain without the new treatment. The same windshields are then treated, and the experiment is run again. A hypothesis test is conducted.

4. The known standard deviation in salary for all mid-level professionals in the financial industry is $11,000. Company A and Company B are in the financial industry. Suppose samples are taken of mid-level professionals from Company A and from Company B. The sample mean salary for mid-level professionals in Company A is $80,000. The sample mean salary for mid-level professionals in Company B is $96,000. Company A and Company B management want to know if their mid-level professionals are paid differently, on average.

5. The average worker in Germany gets eight weeks of paid vacation.

6. According to a television commercial, 80% of dentists agree that Ultrafresh toothpaste is the best on the market.

7. It is believed that the average grade on an English essay in a particular school system for females is higher than for males. A random sample of 31 females had a mean score of 82 with a standard deviation of three, and a random sample of 25 males had a mean score of 76 with a standard deviation of four.

8. The league mean batting average is 0.280 with a known standard deviation of 0.06. The Rattlers and the Vikings belong to the league. The mean batting average for a sample of eight Rattlers is 0.210, and the mean batting average for a sample of eight Vikings is 0.260. There are 24 players on the Rattlers and 19 players on the Vikings. Are the batting averages of the Rattlers and Vikings statistically different?

9. In a random sample of 100 forests in the United States, 56 were coniferous or contained conifers. In a random sample of 80 forests in Mexico, 40 were coniferous or contained conifers. Is the proportion of conifers in the United States statistically more than the proportion of conifers in Mexico?

10. A new medicine is said to help improve sleep. Eight subjects are picked at random and given the medicine. The means hours slept for each person were recorded before starting the medication and after.

11. It is thought that teenagers sleep more than adults on average. A study is done to verify this. A sample of 16 teenagers has a mean of 8.9 hours slept and a standard deviation of 1.2. A sample of 12 adults has a mean of 6.9 hours slept and a standard deviation of 0.6.

12. Varsity athletes practice five times a week, on average.

13. A sample of 12 in-state graduate school programs at school A has a mean tuition of \$64,000 with a standard deviation of \$8,000. At school B, a sample of 16 in-state graduate programs has a mean of \$80,000 with a standard deviation of \$6,000. On average, are the mean tuitions different?

14. A new WiFi range booster is being offered to consumers. A researcher tests the native range of 12 different routers under the same conditions. The ranges are recorded. Then the researcher uses the new WiFi range booster and records the new ranges. Does the new WiFi range booster do a better job?

15. A high school principal claims that 30% of student athletes drive themselves to school, while 4% of non-athletes drive themselves to school. In a sample of 20 student athletes, 45% drive themselves to school. In a sample of 35 non-athlete students, 6% drive themselves to school. Is the percent of student athletes who drive themselves to school more than the percent of nonathletes?

Use the following information to answer the next three exercises: A study is done to determine which of two soft drinks has more sugar. There are 13 cans of Beverage A in a sample and six cans of Beverage B. The mean amount of sugar in Beverage A is 36 grams with a standard deviation of 0.6 grams. The mean amount of sugar in Beverage B is 38 grams with a standard deviation of 0.8 grams. The researchers believe that Beverage B has more sugar than Beverage A, on average. Both populations have normal distributions.

16. Are standard deviations known or unknown?

17. What is the random variable?

18. Is this a one-tailed or two-tailed test?

Use the following information to answer the next 12 exercises: The U.S. Center for Disease Control reports that the mean life expectancy was 47.6 years for White people born in 1900 and 33.0 years for non-White people. Suppose that you randomly survey death records for people born in 1900 in a certain county. Of the 124 White people, the mean life span was 45.3 years with a standard deviation of 12.7 years. Of the 82 non-White people, the mean life span was 34.1 years with a standard deviation of 15.6 years. Conduct a hypothesis test to see if the mean life spans in the county were the same for White and non-White people.

19. Is this a test of means or proportions?

20. State the null and alternative hypotheses.

a. H_0: __________
b. H_a: __________

21. Is this a right-tailed, left-tailed, or two-tailed test?

22. In symbols, what is the random variable of interest for this test?

23. In words, define the random variable of interest for this test.

24. Which distribution (normal or Student's t) would you use for this hypothesis test?

25. Explain why you chose the distribution you did for **Exercise 10.24.**

26. Calculate the test statistic.

27. Sketch a graph of the situation. Label the horizontal axis. Mark the hypothesized difference and the sample difference. Shade the area corresponding to the p-value.

28. At a pre-conceived $\alpha = 0.05$, what is your:

a, Decision:
b. Reason for the decision:
c. Conclusion (write out in a complete sentence):

29. Does it appear that the means are the same? Why or why not?

10.4 Comparing Two Independent Population Proportions

Use the following information for the next five exercises. Two types of phone operating system are being tested to determine if there is a difference in the proportions of system failures (crashes). Fifteen out of a random sample of 150 phones with OS_1 had system failures within the first eight hours of operation. Nine out of another random sample of 150 phones with OS_2 had system failures within the first eight hours of operation. OS_2 is believed to be more stable (have fewer crashes) than OS_1.

30. Is this a test of means or proportions?

31. What is the random variable?

32. State the null and alternative hypotheses.

33. What can you conclude about the two operating systems?

Use the following information to answer the next twelve exercises. In the recent Census, three percent of the U.S. population reported being of two or more races. However, the percent varies tremendously from state to state. Suppose that two random surveys are conducted. In the first random survey, out of 1,000 North Dakotans, only nine people reported being of two or more races. In the second random survey, out of 500 Nevadans, 17 people reported being of two or more races. Conduct a hypothesis test to determine if the population percents are the same for the two states or if the percent for Nevada is statistically higher than for North Dakota.

34. Is this a test of means or proportions?

35. State the null and alternative hypotheses.

a. H_0: _________
b. H_a: _________

36. Is this a right-tailed, left-tailed, or two-tailed test? How do you know?

37. What is the random variable of interest for this test?

38. In words, define the random variable for this test.

39. Which distribution (normal or Student's t) would you use for this hypothesis test?

40. Explain why you chose the distribution you did for the **Exercise 10.56.**

41. Calculate the test statistic.

42. At a pre-conceived $\alpha = 0.05$, what is your:

a. Decision:
b. Reason for the decision:
c. Conclusion (write out in a complete sentence):

43. Does it appear that the proportion of Nevadans who are two or more races is higher than the proportion of North Dakotans? Why or why not?

10.5 Two Population Means with Known Standard Deviations

Use the following information to answer the next five exercises. The mean speeds of fastball pitches from two different baseball pitchers are to be compared. A sample of 14 fastball pitches is measured from each pitcher. The populations have normal distributions. Table 10.8 shows the result. Scouters believe that Rodriguez pitches a speedier fastball.

Table 10.8

Pitcher	Sample mean speed of pitches (mph)	Population standard deviation
Wesley	86	3
Rodriguez	91	7

44. What is the random variable?

45. State the null and alternative hypotheses.

46. What is the test statistic?

47. At the 1% significance level, what is your conclusion?

Use the following information to answer the next five exercises. A researcher is testing the effects of plant food on plant growth. Nine plants have been given the plant food. Another nine plants have not been given the plant food. The heights of the plants are recorded after eight weeks. The populations have normal distributions. The following table is the result. The researcher thinks the food makes the plants grow taller.

Table 10.9

Plant group	Sample mean height of plants (inches)	Population standard deviation
Food	16	2.5
No food	14	1.5

48. Is the population standard deviation known or unknown?

49. State the null and alternative hypotheses.

50. At the 1% significance level, what is your conclusion?

Use the following information to answer the next five exercises. Two metal alloys are being considered as material for ball bearings. The mean melting point of the two alloys is to be compared. 15 pieces of each metal are being tested. Both populations have normal distributions. The following table is the result. It is believed that Alloy Zeta has a different melting point.

Table 10.10

	Sample mean melting temperatures (°F)	Population standard deviation
Alloy Gamma	800	95
Alloy Zeta	900	105

51. State the null and alternative hypotheses.

52. Is this a right-, left-, or two-tailed test?

53. At the 1% significance level, what is your conclusion?

10.6 Matched or Paired Samples

Use the following information to answer the next five exercises. A study was conducted to test the effectiveness of a software patch in reducing system failures over a six-month period. Results for randomly selected installations are shown in Table 10.11. The "before" value is matched to an "after" value, and the differences are calculated. The differences have a normal distribution. Test at the 1% significance level.

Table 10.11

Installation	A	B	C	D	E	F	G	H
Before	3	6	4	2	5	8	2	6
After	1	5	2	0	1	0	2	2

54. What is the random variable?

55. State the null and alternative hypotheses.

56. What conclusion can you draw about the software patch?

Use the following information to answer next five exercises. A study was conducted to test the effectiveness of a juggling class. Before the class started, six subjects juggled as many balls as they could at once. After the class, the same six subjects juggled as many balls as they could. The differences in the number of balls are calculated. The differences have a normal distribution. Test at the 1% significance level.

Table 10.12

Subject	A	B	C	D	E	F
Before	3	4	3	2	4	5
After	4	5	6	4	5	7

57. State the null and alternative hypotheses.

58. What is the sample mean difference?

59. What conclusion can you draw about the juggling class?

Use the following information to answer the next five exercises. A doctor wants to know if a blood pressure medication is effective. Six subjects have their blood pressures recorded. After twelve weeks on the medication, the same six subjects have their blood pressure recorded again. For this test, only systolic pressure is of concern. Test at the 1% significance level.

Table 10.13

Patient	A	B	C	D	E	F
Before	161	162	165	162	166	171
After	158	159	166	160	167	169

60. State the null and alternative hypotheses.

61. What is the test statistic?

62. What is the sample mean difference?

63. What is the conclusion?

HOMEWORK

10.1 Comparing Two Independent Population Means

64. The mean number of English courses taken in a two–year time period by male and female college students is believed to be about the same. An experiment is conducted and data are collected from 29 males and 16 females. The males took an average of three English courses with a standard deviation of 0.8. The females took an average of four English courses with a standard deviation of 1.0. Are the means statistically the same?

65. A student at a four-year college claims that mean enrollment at four–year colleges is higher than at two–year colleges in the United States. Two surveys are conducted. Of the 35 two–year colleges surveyed, the mean enrollment was 5,068 with a standard deviation of 4,777. Of the 35 four-year colleges surveyed, the mean enrollment was 5,466 with a standard deviation of 8,191.

66. At Rachel's 11th birthday party, eight girls were timed to see how long (in seconds) they could hold their breath in a relaxed position. After a two-minute rest, they timed themselves while jumping. The girls thought that the mean difference between their jumping and relaxed times would be zero. Test their hypothesis.

Table 10.14

Relaxed time (seconds)	Jumping time (seconds)
26	21
47	40
30	28
22	21
23	25
45	43
37	35
29	32

67. Mean entry-level salaries for college graduates with mechanical engineering degrees and electrical engineering degrees are believed to be approximately the same. A recruiting office thinks that the mean mechanical engineering salary is actually lower than the mean electrical engineering salary. The recruiting office randomly surveys 50 entry level mechanical engineers and 60 entry level electrical engineers. Their mean salaries were $46,100 and $46,700, respectively. Their standard deviations were $3,450 and $4,210, respectively. Conduct a hypothesis test to determine if you agree that the mean entry-level mechanical engineering salary is lower than the mean entry-level electrical engineering salary.

68. Marketing companies have collected data implying that teenage girls use more ring tones on their cellular phones than teenage boys do. In one particular study of 40 randomly chosen teenage girls and boys (20 of each) with cellular phones, the mean number of ring tones for the girls was 3.2 with a standard deviation of 1.5. The mean for the boys was 1.7 with a standard deviation of 0.8. Conduct a hypothesis test to determine if the means are approximately the same or if the girls' mean is higher than the boys' mean.

Use the information from Data Sets in *Appendix A: Statistical Tables* to answer the next four exercises.

69. Using the data from Lap 1 only, conduct a hypothesis test to determine if the mean time for completing a lap in races is the same as it is in practices.

70. Repeat the test in **Exercise 10.69**, but use Lap 5 data this time.

71. Repeat the test in **Exercise 10.69**, but this time combine the data from Laps 1 and 5.

72. In two to three complete sentences, explain in detail how you might use Terri Vogel's data to answer the following question. "Does Terri Vogel drive faster in races than she does in practices?"

Use the following information to answer the next two exercises. The Eastern and Western Major League Soccer conferences have a new Reserve Division that allows new players to develop their skills. Data for a randomly picked date showed the following annual goals.

Table 10.15

Western	Eastern
Los Angeles 9	D.C. United 9
FC Dallas 3	Chicago 8
Chivas USA 4	Columbus 7
Real Salt Lake 3	New England 6
Colorado 4	MetroStars 5
San Jose 4	Kansas City 3

Conduct a hypothesis test to answer the next two exercises.

73. The exact distribution for the hypothesis test is:

a. the normal distribution
b. the Student's t-distribution
c. the uniform distribution
d. the exponential distribution

74. If the level of significance is 0.05, the conclusion is:

a. There is sufficient evidence to conclude that the W Division teams score fewer goals, on average, than the E teams
b. There is insufficient evidence to conclude that the W Division teams score more goals, on average, than the E teams.
c. There is insufficient evidence to conclude that the W teams score fewer goals, on average, than the E teams score.
d. Unable to determine

75. Suppose a statistics instructor believes that there is no significant difference between the mean class scores of statistics day students on Exam 2 and statistics night students on Exam 2. She takes random samples from each of the populations. The mean and standard deviation for 35 statistics day students were 75.86 and 16.91. The mean and standard deviation for 37 statistics night students were 75.41 and 19.73. The "day" subscript refers to the statistics day students. The "night" subscript refers to the statistics night students. A concluding statement is:

a. There is sufficient evidence to conclude that statistics night students' mean on Exam 2 is better than the statistics day students' mean on Exam 2.
b. There is insufficient evidence to conclude that the statistics day students' mean on Exam 2 is better than the statistics night students' mean on Exam 2.
c. There is insufficient evidence to conclude that there is a significant difference between the means of the statistics day students and night students on Exam 2.
d. There is sufficient evidence to conclude that there is a significant difference between the means of the statistics day students and night students on Exam 2.

76. Elijah wants to know whether textbook costs are different for different courses of study. He selects a random sample of 33 sociology textbooks offered on a popular online site. The mean price of his sample is $74.64 with a standard deviation of $49.36. He then selects a random sample of 33 math and science textbooks from the same site. The mean price of this sample is $111.56 with a standard deviation of $66.90. Is the mean price of a sociology textbook lower than the mean price of a math or science textbook? Test at a 1% significance level.

77. A powder diet is tested on 49 people, and a liquid diet is tested on 36 different people. Of interest is whether the liquid diet yields a higher mean weight loss than the powder diet. The powder diet group had a mean weight loss of 42 pounds with a standard deviation of 12 pounds. The liquid diet group had a mean weight loss of 45 pounds with a standard deviation of 14 pounds.

78. Suppose a statistics instructor believes that there is no significant difference between the mean class scores of statistics day students on Exam 2 and statistics night students on Exam 2. She takes random samples from each of the populations. The mean and standard deviation for 35 statistics day students were 75.86 and 16.91, respectively. The mean and standard deviation for 37 statistics night students were 75.41 and 19.73. The "day" subscript refers to the statistics day students. The "night" subscript refers to the statistics night students. An appropriate alternative hypothesis for the hypothesis test is:

a. $\mu_{day} > \mu_{night}$
b. $\mu_{day} < \mu_{night}$
c. $\mu_{day} = \mu_{night}$
d. $\mu_{day} \neq \mu_{night}$

10.4 Comparing Two Independent Population Proportions

79. A recent drug survey showed an increase in the use of drugs and alcohol among local high school seniors as compared to the national percent. Suppose that a survey of 100 local seniors and 100 national seniors is conducted to see if the proportion of drug and alcohol use is higher locally than nationally. Locally, 65 seniors reported using drugs or alcohol within the past month, while 60 national seniors reported using them.

80. We are interested in whether the proportions of female suicide victims for ages 15 to 24 are the same for White and the Black people in the United States. We randomly pick one year, 1992, to compare the races. The number of suicides estimated in the United States in 1992 for White females is 4,930. Five hundred eighty were aged 15 to 24. The estimate for Black females is 330. Forty were aged 15 to 24. We will let female suicide victims be our population.

81. Elizabeth Mjelde, an art history professor, was interested in whether the value from the Golden Ratio formula, $\left(\frac{\text{larger + smaller dimension}}{\text{larger dimension}}\right)$ was the same in the Whitney Exhibit for works from 1900 to 1919 as for works from 1920 to 1942. Thirty-seven early works were sampled, averaging 1.74 with a standard deviation of 0.11. Sixty-five of the later works were sampled, averaging 1.746 with a standard deviation of 0.1064. Do you think that there is a significant difference in the Golden Ratio calculation?

82. A recent year was randomly picked from 1985 to the present. In that year, there were 2,051 Hispanic students at Cabrillo College out of a total of 12,328 students. At Lake Tahoe College, there were 321 Hispanic students out of a total of 2,441 students. In general, do you think that the percent of Hispanic students at the two colleges is basically the same or different?

Use the following information to answer the next three exercises. Neuroinvasive West Nile virus is a severe disease that affects a person's nervous system . It is spread by the Culex species of mosquito. In the United States in 2010 there were 629 reported cases of neuroinvasive West Nile virus out of a total of 1,021 reported cases and there were 486 neuroinvasive reported cases out of a total of 712 cases reported in 2011. Is the 2011 proportion of neuroinvasive West Nile virus cases more than the 2010 proportion of neuroinvasive West Nile virus cases? Using a 1% level of significance, conduct an appropriate hypothesis test.

- "2011" subscript: 2011 group.
- "2010" subscript: 2010 group

83. This is:

a. a test of two proportions
b. a test of two independent means
c. a test of a single mean
d. a test of matched pairs.

84. An appropriate null hypothesis is:

a. $p_{2011} \leq p_{2010}$
b. $p_{2011} \geq p_{2010}$
c. $\mu_{2011} \leq \mu_{2010}$
d. $p_{2011} > p_{2010}$

85. Researchers conducted a study to find out if there is a difference in the use of eReaders by different age groups. Randomly selected participants were divided into two age groups. In the 16- to 29-year-old group, 7% of the 628 surveyed use eReaders, while 11% of the 2,309 participants 30 years old and older use eReaders.

86. Adults aged 18 years old and older were randomly selected for a survey on obesity. Adults are considered obese if their body mass index (BMI) is at least 30. The researchers wanted to determine if the proportion of women who are obese in the south is less than the proportion of southern men who are obese. The results are shown in **Table 10.16.** Test at the 1% level of significance.

Table 10.16

	Number who are obese	Sample size
Men	42,769	155,525
Women	67,169	248,775

87. Two computer users were discussing tablet computers. A higher proportion of people ages 16 to 29 use tablets than the proportion of people age 30 and older. **Table 10.17** details the number of tablet owners for each age group. Test at the 1% level of significance.

Table 10.17

	16–29 year olds	30 years old and older
Own a tablet	69	231
Sample size	628	2,309

88. A group of friends debated whether more men use smartphones than women. They consulted a research study of smartphone use among adults. The results of the survey indicate that of the 973 men randomly sampled, 379 use smartphones. For women, 404 of the 1,304 who were randomly sampled use smartphones. Test at the 5% level of significance.

89. While her husband spent 2½ hours picking out new speakers, a statistician decided to determine whether the percent of men who enjoy shopping for electronic equipment is higher than the percent of women who enjoy shopping for electronic equipment. The population was Saturday afternoon shoppers. Out of 67 men, 24 said they enjoyed the activity. Eight of the 24 women surveyed claimed to enjoy the activity. Interpret the results of the survey.

90. We are interested in whether children's educational computer software costs less, on average, than children's entertainment software. Thirty-six educational software titles were randomly picked from a catalog. The mean cost was $31.14 with a standard deviation of $4.69. Thirty-five entertainment software titles were randomly picked from the same catalog. The mean cost was $33.86 with a standard deviation of $10.87. Decide whether children's educational software costs less, on average, than children's entertainment software.

91. Joan Nguyen recently claimed that the proportion of college-age males with at least one pierced ear is as high as the proportion of college-age females. She conducted a survey in her classes. Out of 107 males, 20 had at least one pierced ear. Out of 92 females, 47 had at least one pierced ear. Do you believe that the proportion of males has reached the proportion of females?

92. "To Breakfast or Not to Breakfast?" by Richard Ayore

In the American society, birthdays are one of those days that everyone looks forward to. People of different ages and peer groups gather to mark the 18th, 20th, ..., birthdays. During this time, one looks back to see what he or she has achieved for the past year and also focuses ahead for more to come.

If, by any chance, I am invited to one of these parties, my experience is always different. Instead of dancing around with my friends while the music is booming, I get carried away by memories of my family back home in Kenya. I remember the good times I had with my brothers and sister while we did our daily routine.

Every morning, I remember we went to the shamba (garden) to weed our crops. I remember one day arguing with my brother as to why he always remained behind just to join us an hour later. In his defense, he said that he preferred waiting for breakfast before he came to weed. He said, "This is why I always work more hours than you guys!"

And so, to prove him wrong or right, we decided to give it a try. One day we went to work as usual without breakfast, and recorded the time we could work before getting tired and stopping. On the next day, we all ate breakfast before going to work. We recorded how long we worked again before getting tired and stopping. Of interest was our mean increase in work time. Though not sure, my brother insisted that it was more than two hours. Using the data in Table 10.18, solve our problem.

Table 10.18

Work hours with breakfast	Work hours without breakfast
8	6
7	5
9	5
5	4
9	7
8	7
10	7
7	5
6	6
9	5

10.5 Two Population Means with Known Standard Deviations

NOTE

If you are using a Student's *t*-distribution for one of the following homework problems, including for paired data, you may assume that the underlying population is normally distributed. (When using these tests in a real situation, you must first prove that assumption, however.)

93. A study is done to determine if students in the California state university system take longer to graduate, on average, than students enrolled in private universities. One hundred students from both the California state university system and private universities are surveyed. Suppose that from years of research, it is known that the population standard deviations are 1.5811 years and 1 year, respectively. The following data are collected. The California state university system students took on average 4.5 years with a standard deviation of 0.8. The private university students took on average 4.1 years with a standard deviation of 0.3.

94. Parents of teenage boys often complain that auto insurance costs more, on average, for teenage boys than for teenage girls. A group of concerned parents examines a random sample of insurance bills. The mean annual cost for 36 teenage boys was $679. For 23 teenage girls, it was $559. From past years, it is known that the population standard deviation for each group is $180. Determine whether or not you believe that the mean cost for auto insurance for teenage boys is greater than that for teenage girls.

95. A group of transfer bound students wondered if they will spend the same mean amount on texts and supplies each year at their four-year university as they have at their community college. They conducted a random survey of 54 students at their community college and 66 students at their local four-year university. The sample means were $947 and $1,011, respectively. The population standard deviations are known to be $254 and $87, respectively. Conduct a hypothesis test to determine if the means are statistically the same.

96. Some manufacturers claim that non-hybrid sedan cars have a lower mean miles-per-gallon (mpg) than hybrid ones. Suppose that consumers test 21 hybrid sedans and get a mean of 31 mpg with a standard deviation of seven mpg. Thirty-one non-hybrid sedans get a mean of 22 mpg with a standard deviation of four mpg. Suppose that the population standard deviations are known to be six and three, respectively. Conduct a hypothesis test to evaluate the manufacturers claim.

97. A baseball fan wanted to know if there is a difference between the number of games played in a World Series when the American League won the series versus when the National League won the series. From 1922 to 2012, the population standard deviation of games won by the American League was 1.14, and the population standard deviation of games won by the National League was 1.11. Of 19 randomly selected World Series games won by the American League, the mean number of games won was 5.76. The mean number of 17 randomly selected games won by the National League was 5.42. Conduct a hypothesis test.

98. One of the questions in a study of marital satisfaction of dual-career couples was to rate the statement "I'm pleased with the way we divide the responsibilities for childcare." The ratings went from one (strongly agree) to five (strongly disagree). **Table 10.19** contains ten of the paired responses for husbands and wives. Conduct a hypothesis test to see if the mean difference in the husband's versus the wife's satisfaction level is negative (meaning that, within the partnership, the husband is happier than the wife).

Table 10.19

Wife's score	2	2	3	3	4	2	1	1	2	4
Husband's score	2	2	1	3	2	1	1	1	2	4

10.6 Matched or Paired Samples

99. Ten individuals went on a low-fat diet for 12 weeks to lower their cholesterol. The data are recorded in **Table 10.20**. Do you think that their cholesterol levels were significantly lowered?

Table 10.20

Starting cholesterol level	Ending cholesterol level
140	140
220	230
110	120
240	220
200	190
180	150
190	200
360	300
280	300
260	240

Use the following information to answer the next two exercises. A new AIDS prevention drug was tried on a group of 224 HIV positive patients. Forty-five patients developed AIDS after four years. In a control group of 224 HIV positive patients, 68 developed AIDS after four years. We want to test whether the method of treatment reduces the proportion of patients that develop AIDS after four years or if the proportions of the treated group and the untreated group stay the same.

Let the subscript t = treated patient and ut = untreated patient.

100. The appropriate hypotheses are:

a. H_0: $p_t < p_{ut}$ and H_a: $p_t \geq p_{ut}$

b. H_0: $p_t \leq p_{ut}$ and H_a: $p_t > p_{ut}$

c. H_0: $p_t = p_{ut}$ and H_a: $p_t \neq p_{ut}$

d. H_0: $p_t = p_{ut}$ and H_a: $p_t < p_{ut}$

Use the following information to answer the next two exercises. An experiment is conducted to show that blood pressure can be consciously reduced in people trained in a "biofeedback exercise program." Six subjects were randomly selected and blood pressure measurements were recorded before and after the training. The difference between blood pressures was calculated (after - before) producing the following results: $x{-}dx{-}d = -10.2$ $s_d = 8.4$. Using the data, test the hypothesis that the blood pressure has decreased after the training.

101. The distribution for the test is:

a. t_5
b. t_6
c. $N(-10.2, 8.4)$
d. $N(-10.2, \frac{8.4}{\sqrt{6}})$

102. A golf instructor is interested in determining if her new technique for improving players' golf scores is effective. She takes four new students. She records their 18-hole scores before learning the technique and then after having taken her class. She conducts a hypothesis test. The data are as follows.

Table 10.21

	Player 1	Player 2	Player 3	Player 4
Mean score before class	83	78	93	87
Mean score after class	80	80	86	86

The correct decision is:

a. Reject H_0.
b. Do not reject the H_0.

103. A local cancer support group believes that the estimate for new female breast cancer cases in the south is higher in 2013 than in 2012. The group compared the estimates of new female breast cancer cases by southern state in 2012 and in 2013. The results are in **Table 10.22.**

Table 10.22

Southern states	2012	2013
Alabama	3,450	3,720
Arkansas	2,150	2,280
Florida	15,540	15,710
Georgia	6,970	7,310
Kentucky	3,160	3,300
Louisiana	3,320	3,630
Mississippi	1,990	2,080
North Carolina	7,090	7,430
Oklahoma	2,630	2,690
South Carolina	3,570	3,580
Tennessee	4,680	5,070
Texas	15,050	14,980
Virginia	6,190	6,280

104. A traveler wanted to know if the prices of hotels are different in the ten cities that he visits the most often. The list of the cities with the corresponding hotel prices for his two favorite hotel chains is in **Table 10.23**. Test at the 1% level of significance.

Table 10.23

Cities	Hyatt Regency prices in dollars	Hilton prices in dollars
Atlanta	107	169
Boston	358	289
Chicago	209	299
Dallas	209	198
Denver	167	169
Indianapolis	179	214
Los Angeles	179	169
New York City	625	459
Philadelphia	179	159
Washington, DC	245	239

105. A politician asked his staff to determine whether the underemployment rate in the northeast decreased from 2011 to 2012. The results are in Table 10.24.

Table 10.24

Northeastern states	2011	2012
Connecticut	17.3	16.4
Delaware	17.4	13.7
Maine	19.3	16.1
Maryland	16.0	15.5
Massachusetts	17.6	18.2
New Hampshire	15.4	13.5
New Jersey	19.2	18.7
New York	18.5	18.7
Ohio	18.2	18.8
Pennsylvania	16.5	16.9
Rhode Island	20.7	22.4
Vermont	14.7	12.3
West Virginia	15.5	17.3

Bringing It Together: Homework

Use the following information to answer the next ten exercises. indicate which of the following choices best identifies the hypothesis test.

a. independent group means, population standard deviations and/or variances known

b. independent group means, population standard deviations and/or variances unknown
c. matched or paired samples
d. single mean
e. two proportions
f. single proportion

106. A powder diet is tested on 49 people, and a liquid diet is tested on 36 different people. The population standard deviations are two pounds and three pounds, respectively. Of interest is whether the liquid diet yields a higher mean weight loss than the powder diet.

107. A new chocolate bar is taste-tested on consumers. Of interest is whether the proportion of children who like the new chocolate bar is greater than the proportion of adults who like it.

108. The mean number of English courses taken in a two–year time period by male and female college students is believed to be about the same. An experiment is conducted and data are collected from nine males and 16 females.

109. A football league reported that the mean number of touchdowns per game was five. A study is done to determine if the mean number of touchdowns has decreased.

110. A study is done to determine if students in the California state university system take longer to graduate than students enrolled in private universities. One hundred students from both the California state university system and private universities are surveyed. From years of research, it is known that the population standard deviations are 1.5811 years and one year, respectively.

111. According to a YWCA Rape Crisis Center newsletter, 75% of rape victims know their attackers. A study is done to verify this.

112. According to a recent study, U.S. companies have a mean maternity-leave of six weeks.

113. A recent drug survey showed an increase in use of drugs and alcohol among local high school students as compared to the national percent. Suppose that a survey of 100 local youths and 100 national youths is conducted to see if the proportion of drug and alcohol use is higher locally than nationally.

114. A new SAT study course is tested on 12 individuals. Pre-course and post-course scores are recorded. Of interest is the mean increase in SAT scores. The following data are collected:

Table 10.25

Pre-course score	Post-course score
1	300
960	920
1010	1100
840	880
1100	1070
1250	1320
860	860
1330	1370
790	770
990	1040
1110	1200
740	850

115. University of Michigan researchers reported in the *Journal of the National Cancer Institute* that quitting smoking is especially beneficial for those under age 49. In this American Cancer Society study, the risk (probability) of dying of lung cancer was about the same as for those who had never smoked.

116. Lesley E. Tan investigated the relationship between left-handedness vs. right-handedness and motor competence in preschool children. Random samples of 41 left-handed preschool children and 41 right-handed preschool children were given several tests of motor skills to determine if there is evidence of a difference between the children based on this experiment. The experiment produced the means and standard deviations shown **Table 10.26.** Determine the appropriate test and best distribution to use for that test.

Table 10.26

	Left-handed	Right-handed
Sample size	41	41
Sample mean	97.5	98.1
Sample standard deviation	17.5	19.2

a. Two independent means, normal distribution

b. Two independent means, Student's-t distribution

c. Matched or paired samples, Student's-t distribution

d. Two population proportions, normal distribution

117. A golf instructor is interested in determining if her new technique for improving players' golf scores is effective. She takes four (4) new students. She records their 18-hole scores before learning the technique and then after having taken her class. She conducts a hypothesis test. The data are as **Table 10.27.**

Table 10.27

	Player 1	Player 2	Player 3	Player 4
Mean score before class	83	78	93	87
Mean score after class	80	80	86	86

This is:

a. a test of two independent means.
b. a test of two proportions.
c. a test of a single mean.
d. a test of a single proportion.

REFERENCES

10.1 Comparing Two Independent Population Means

Data from Graduating Engineer + Computer Careers. Available online at http://www.graduatingengineer.com

Data from *Microsoft Bookshelf.*

Data from the United States Senate website, available online at www.Senate.gov (accessed June 17, 2013).

"List of current United States Senators by Age." Wikipedia. Available online at http://en.wikipedia.org/wiki/List_of_current_United_States_Senators_by_age (accessed June 17, 2013).

"Sectoring by Industry Groups." Nasdaq. Available online at http://www.nasdaq.com/markets/barchart-sectors.aspx?page=sectors&base=industry (accessed June 17, 2013).

"Strip Clubs: Where Prostitution and Trafficking Happen." Prostitution Research and Education, 2013. Available online at www.prostitutionresearch.com/ProsViolPosttrauStress.html (accessed June 17, 2013).

"World Series History." Baseball-Almanac, 2013. Available online at http://www.baseball-almanac.com/ws/wsmenu.shtml (accessed June 17, 2013).

10.4 Comparing Two Independent Population Proportions

Data from *Educational Resources*, December catalog.

Data from Hilton Hotels. Available online at http://www.hilton.com (accessed June 17, 2013).

Data from Hyatt Hotels. Available online at http://hyatt.com (accessed June 17, 2013).

Data from Statistics, United States Department of Health and Human Services.

Data from Whitney Exhibit on loan to San Jose Museum of Art.

Data from the American Cancer Society. Available online at http://www.cancer.org/index (accessed June 17, 2013).

Data from the Chancellor's Office, California Community Colleges, November 1994.

"State of the States." Gallup, 2013. Available online at http://www.gallup.com/poll/125066/State-States.aspx?ref=interactive (accessed June 17, 2013).

"West Nile Virus." Centers for Disease Control and Prevention. Available online at http://www.cdc.gov/ncidod/dvbid/westnile/index.htm (accessed June 17, 2013).

10.5 Two Population Means with Known Standard Deviations

Data from the United States Census Bureau. Available online at http://www.census.gov/prod/cen2010/briefs/c2010br-02.pdf

Hinduja, Sameer. "Sexting Research and Gender Differences." Cyberbullying Research Center, 2013. Available online at http://cyberbullying.us/blog/sexting-research-and-gender-differences/ (accessed June 17, 2013).

"Smart Phone Users, By the Numbers." Visually, 2013. Available online at http://visual.ly/smart-phone-users-numbers (accessed June 17, 2013).

Smith, Aaron. "35% of American adults own a Smartphone." Pew Internet, 2013. Available online at http://www.pewinternet.org/~/media/Files/Reports/2011/PIP_Smartphones.pdf (accessed June 17, 2013).

"State-Specific Prevalence of Obesity AmongAduls—Unites States, 2007." MMWR, CDC. Available online at http://www.cdc.gov/mmwr/preview/mmwrhtml/mm5728a1.htm (accessed June 17, 2013).

"Texas Crime Rates 1960–1012." FBI, Uniform Crime Reports, 2013. Available online at: http://www.disastercenter.com/crime/txcrime.htm (accessed June 17, 2013).

Solutions

1. two proportions

3. matched or paired samples

5. single mean
7. independent group means, population standard deviations and/or variances unknown
9. two proportions
11. independent group means, population standard deviations and/or variances unknown
13. independent group means, population standard deviations and/or variances unknown
15. two proportions
17. The random variable is the difference between the mean amounts of sugar in the two soft drinks.
19. means
21. two-tailed
23. the difference between the mean life spans of White and non-White people
25. This is a comparison of two population means with unknown population standard deviations.
27. Check student's solution.
28. a. Cannot accept the null hypothesis
    b. p-value < 0.05
    c. There is not enough evidence at the 5% level of significance to support the claim that life expectancy in the 1900s is different between White and non-White people.
31. $P'_{OS1} - P'_{OS2}$ = difference in the proportions of phones that had system failures within the first eight hours of operation with OS_1 and OS_2.
34. proportions
36. right-tailed
38. The random variable is the difference in proportions (percents) of the populations that are of two or more races in Nevada and North Dakota.
40. Our sample sizes are much greater than five each, so we use the normal for two proportions distribution for this hypothesis test.
42. a. Cannot accept the null hypothesis.
    b. p-value < alpha
    c. At the 5% significance level, there is sufficient evidence to conclude that the proportion (percent) of the population that is of two or more races in Nevada is statistically higher than that in North Dakota.

44. The difference in mean speeds of the fastball pitches of the two pitchers

46. −2.46

47. At the 1% significance level, we can reject the null hypothesis. There is sufficient data to conclude that the mean speed of Rodriguez's fastball is faster than Wesley's.

49. Subscripts: 1 = Food, 2 = No Food

$H_0: \mu_1 \leq \mu_2$

$H_a: \mu_1 > \mu_2$

51. Subscripts: 1 = Gamma, 2 = Zeta

$H_0: \mu_1 = \mu_2$

$H_a: \mu_1 \neq \mu_2$

53. There is sufficient evidence so we cannot accept the null hypothesis. The data support that the melting point for Alloy Zeta is different from the melting point of Alloy Gamma.

54. the mean difference of the system failures

56. With a *p*-value 0.0067, we can cannot accept the null hypothesis. There is enough evidence to support that the software patch is effective in reducing the number of system failures.

60. $H_0: \mu_d \geq 0$ $H_a: \mu_d < 0$

63. We decline to reject the null hypothesis. There is not sufficient evidence to support that the medication is effective.

65. Subscripts: 1: two-year colleges; 2: four-year colleges

a. $H_0: \mu_1 \geq \mu_2$
b. $H_a: \mu_1 < \mu_2$
c. $\bar{X}_1 - \bar{X}_2$ is the difference between the mean enrollments of the two-year colleges and the four-year colleges.
d. Student's-*t*
e. test statistic: -0.2480
f. *p*-value: 0.4019
g. Check student's solution.
h
  i. Alpha: 0.05
  ii. Decision: Cannot reject
  iii. Reason for Decision: *p*-value > alpha
  iv. Conclusion: At the 5% significance level, there is sufficient evidence to conclude that the mean enrollment at four-year colleges is higher than at two-year colleges.

67. Subscripts: 1: mechanical engineering; 2: electrical engineering

a. $H_0: \mu_1 \geq \mu_2$

b. $H_a: \mu_1 < \mu_2$

c. $\bar{X}_1 - \bar{X}_2$ is the difference between the mean entry level salaries of mechanical engineers and electrical engineers.

d. t_{108}

e. test statistic: $t = -0.82$

f. *p*-value: 0.2061

g. Check student's solution.

h.

i. Alpha: 0.05

ii. Decision: Cannot reject the null hypothesis.

iii. Reason for Decision: *p*-value > alpha

iv. Conclusion: At the 5% significance level, there is insufficient evidence to conclude that the mean entry-level salaries of mechanical engineers is lower than that of electrical engineers.

69. a. $H_0: \mu_1 = \mu_2$

b. $H_a: \mu_1 \neq \mu_2$

c. $\bar{X}_1 - \bar{X}_2$ is the difference between the mean times for completing a lap in races and in practices.

d. $t_{20.32}$

e. test statistic: −4.70

f. *p*-value: 0.0001

g. Check student's solution.

h.

i. Alpha: 0.05

ii. Decision: Cannot accept the null hypothesis.

iii. Reason for Decision: *p*-value < alpha

iv. Conclusion: At the 5% significance level, there is sufficient evidence to conclude that the mean time for completing a lap in races is different from that in practices.

71. a. $H_0: \mu_1 = \mu_2$

b. $H_a: \mu_1 \neq \mu_2$

c. is the difference between the mean times for completing a lap in races and in practices.

d. $t_{40.94}$

e. test statistic: –5.08
f. p-value: zero
g. Check student's solution.
h.
   i. Alpha: 0.05
   ii. Decision: Cannot accept the null hypothesis.
   iii. Reason for Decision: p-value < alpha
   iv. Conclusion: At the 5% significance level, there is sufficient evidence to conclude that the mean time for completing a lap in races is different from that in practices.

74. c

76. Test: two independent sample means, population standard deviations unknown. Random variable: $\bar{X}_1 - \bar{X}_2$ Distribution:

$H_0: \mu_1 = \mu_2 H_a: \mu_1 < \mu_2$ H_0: $\mu_1 = \mu_2$ H_a: $\mu_1 < \mu_2$ The mean age of entering prostitution in Canada is lower than the mean age in the United States. Graph: left-tailed p-value : 0.0151 Decision: Cannot reject $H0$. Conclusion: At the 1% level of significance, from the sample data, there is not sufficient evidence to conclude that the mean age of entering prostitution in Canada is lower than the mean age in the United States.

78. d

80. a. H_0: $P_W = P_B$
b. H_a: $P_W \neq P_B$
c. The random variable is the difference in the proportions of White and Black suicide victims, aged 15 to 24.
d. normal for two proportions
e. test statistic: –0.1944
f. p-value: 0.8458
g. Check student's solution.
h.
   i. Alpha: 0.05
   ii. Decision: Cannot accept the null hypothesis.
   iii. Reason for decision: p-value > alpha
   iv. Conclusion: At the 5% significance level, there is insufficient evidence to conclude that the proportions of White and Black female suicide victims, aged 15 to 24, are different.

82. Subscripts: 1 = Cabrillo College, 2 = Lake Tahoe College

a. H_0:p_1=p_2
b. H_a:p_1≠p_2

c. The random variable is the difference between the proportions of Hispanic students at Cabrillo College and Lake Tahoe College.
d. normal for two proportions
e. test statistic: 4.29
f. *p*-value: 0.00002
g. Check student's solution.
h.
   i. Alpha: 0.05
   ii. Decision: Cannot accept the null hypothesis.
   iii. Reason for decision: *p*-value < alpha
   iv. Conclusion: There is sufficient evidence to conclude that the proportions of Hispanic students at Cabrillo College and Lake Tahoe College are different.

84. a

85. Test: two independent sample proportions.Random variable: $p'_1 - p'_2$ Distribution:
H_0:p_1=p_2
H_a:p_1≠p_2 The proportion of eReader users is different for the 16- to 29-year-old users from that of the 30 and older users. Graph: two-tailed

87. Test: two independent sample proportions Random variable: $p'_1 - p'_2$ Distribution:
H_0:p_1=p_2
H_a:p_1>p_2 A higher proportion of tablet owners are aged 16 to 29 years old than are 30 years old and older. Graph: right-tailed Do not reject the H_0. Conclusion: At the 1% level of significance, from the sample data, there is not sufficient evidence to conclude that a higher proportion of tablet owners are aged 16 to 29 years old than are 30 years old and older.

89. Subscripts: 1: men; 2: women

a. H_0:p_1≤p_2
b. H_a:p_1>p_2
c. P'_1–P'_2 is the difference between the proportions of men and women who enjoy shopping for electronic equipment.
d. normal for two proportions
e. test statistic: 0.22
f. *p*-value: 0.4133
g. Check student's solution.

h.
   i. Alpha: 0.05
   ii. Decision: Cannot reject the null hypothesis.
   iii. Reason for Decision: p-value > alpha
   iv. Conclusion: At the 5% significance level, there is insufficient evidence to conclude that the proportion of men who enjoy shopping for electronic equipment is more than the proportion of women.

91. a. $H_0{:}p_1=p_2$
b. $H_a{:}p_1\neq p_2$
c. $P'_1-P'_2$ is the difference between the proportions of men and women that have at least one pierced ear.
d. normal for two proportions
e. test statistic: –4.82
f. p-value: zero
g. Check student's solution.
h.
   i. Alpha: 0.05
   ii. Decision: Cannot accept the null hypothesis.
   iii. Reason for Decision: p-value < alpha
   iv. Conclusion: At the 5% significance level, there is sufficient evidence to conclude that the proportions of males and females with at least one pierced ear is different.

92. *a.* $H_0{:}\ \mu_d = 0$
b. $H_a{:}\ \mu_d > 0$
c. The random variable X_d is the mean difference in work times on days when eating breakfast and on days when not eating breakfast.
d. t_9
e. test statistic: 4.8963
f. p-value: 0.0004
g. Check student's solution.
h.
   i. Alpha: 0.05
   ii. Decision: Cannot accept the null hypothesis.
   iii. Reason for Decision: p-value < alpha
   iv. Conclusion: At the 5% level of significance, there is sufficient evidence to conclude that the mean difference in work times on days when eating breakfast and on days when not eating breakfast has increased.

94. Subscripts: 1 = boys, 2 = girls

a. $H_0: \mu_1 \leq \mu_2$
b. $H_a: \mu_1 > \mu_2$
c. The random variable is the difference in the mean auto insurance costs for boys and girls.
d. normal
e. test statistic: $z = 2.50$
f. p-value: 0.0062
g. Check student's solution.
h.
   i. Alpha: 0.05
   ii. Decision: Cannot accept the null hypothesis.
   iii. Reason for Decision: p-value < alpha
   iv. Conclusion: At the 5% significance level, there is sufficient evidence to conclude that the mean cost of auto insurance for teenage boys is greater than that for girls.

96. Subscripts: 1 = non-hybrid sedans, 2 = hybrid sedans

a. $H_0: \mu_1 \geq \mu_2$
b. $H_a: \mu_1 < \mu_2$
c. The random variable is the difference in the mean miles per gallon of non-hybrid sedans and hybrid sedans.
d. normal
e. test statistic: 6.36
f. p-value: 0
g. Check student's solution.
h.
   i. Alpha: 0.05
   ii. Decision: Cannot accept the null hypothesis.
   iii. Reason for decision: p-value < alpha
   iv. Conclusion: At the 5% significance level, there is sufficient evidence to conclude that the mean miles per gallon of non-hybrid sedans is less than that of hybrid sedans.

98. a. $H_0: \mu_d = 0$
b. $H_a: \mu_d < 0$
c. The random variable X_d is the average difference between husband's and wife's satisfaction level.
d. t_9
e. test statistic: $t = -1.86$
f. p-value: 0.0479

g. Check student's solution
h.
   i. Alpha: 0.05
   ii. Decision: Cannot accept the null hypothesis, but run another test.
   iii. Reason for Decision: p-value < alpha
   iv. Conclusion: This is a weak test because alpha and the p-value are close. However, there is insufficient evidence to conclude that the mean difference is negative.

99. p-value = 0.1494 At the 5% significance level, there is insufficient evidence to conclude that the medication lowered cholesterol levels after 12 weeks.

103. Test: two matched pairs or paired samples (t-test) Random variable: $\bar{X}_d$ Distribution: t_{12} H_0: $\mu_d = 0$ H_a: $\mu_d > 0$ The mean of the differences of new female breast cancer cases in the south between 2013 and 2012 is greater than zero. The estimate for new female breast cancer cases in the south is higher in 2013 than in 2012.Graph: right-tailed p-value: 0.0004 Decision: Cannot accept H_0 Conclusion: At the 5% level of significance, from the sample data, there is sufficient evidence to conclude that there was a higher estimate of new female breast cancer cases in 2013 than in 2012.

105. Test: matched or paired samples (t-test) Difference data: {–0.9, –3.7. –3.2, –0.5, 0.6, –1.9, –0.5, 0.2, 0.6, 0.4, 1.7, –2.4, 1.8} Random Variable: $\bar{X}_d$ Distribution: H_0: $\mu_d = 0$ H_a: $\mu_d < 0$ The mean of the differences of the rate of underemployment in the northeastern states between 2012 and 2011 is less than zero. The underemployment rate went down from 2011 to 2012. Graph: left-tailed. Decision: Cannot reject H_0. Conclusion: At the 5% level of significance, from the sample data, there is not sufficient evidence to conclude that there was a decrease in the underemployment rates of the northeastern states from 2011 to 2012.

107. e

109. d

111. f

113. e

115. f

117. a

11 Chapter THE CHI-SQUARE DISTRIBUTION AND ITS APPLICATIONS

Figure 11.1 The chi-square distribution can be used to find relationships between two things, like grocery prices at different stores. (credit: Pete/flickr)

INTRODUCTION: AN OVERVIEW

Have you ever contemplated if lottery winning numbers are uniformly distributed or if certain numbers appear with increased regularity? What if the preferred genres of films varied among different age demographics? What if a coffee machine dispensed a consistent quantity of coffee each time? These questions can be addressed by the implementation of a hypothesis test.You will now study a new distribution, one that is used to determine the answers to such questions. This distribution is called the chi-square distribution.

In this chapter, you will learn the three major applications of the chi-square distribution:

1. the goodness-of-fit test, which determines if data fit a particular distribution, such as in the lottery example
2. the test of independence, which determines if events are independent, such as in the movie example
3. the test of a single variance, which tests variability, such as in the coffee example

11.1 FACTS ABOUT THE CHI-SQUARE DISTRIBUTION

The notation for the **chi-square distribution** is:

$$\chi \sim \chi^2_{df}$$

where df = degrees of freedom which depends on how chi-square is being used. (If you want to practice calculating chi-square probabilities then use $df = n - 1$. The degrees of freedom for the three major uses are each calculated differently.)

For the χ^2 distribution, the population mean is $\mu = df$ and the population standard deviation is $\sigma = \sqrt{2(df)}$.

The random variable is shown as χ^2.

The random variable for a chi-square distribution with k degrees of freedom is the sum of k independent, squared standard normal variables.

$$\chi^2 = (Z_1)^2 + (Z_2)^2 + \ldots + (Z_k)^2$$

1. The curve is nonsymmetrical and skewed to the right.
2. There is a different chi-square curve for each *df*.

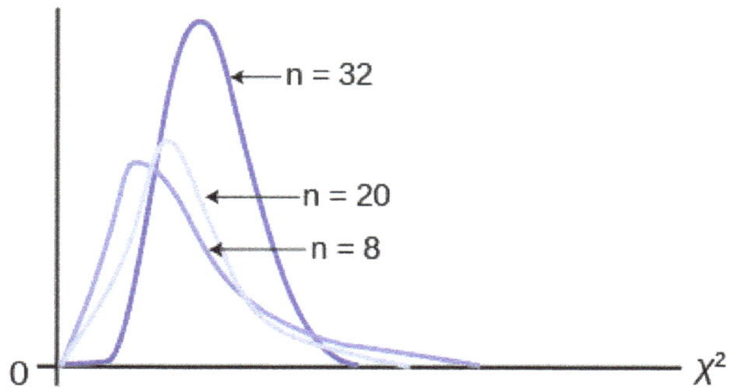

Figure 11.2

3. The test statistic for any test is always greater than or equal to zero.
4. When $df > 90$, the chi-square curve approximates the normal distribution. For $X \sim \chi^2_{1,000}$ the mean, $\mu = df = 1,000$ and the standard deviation, $\sigma = \sqrt{2(1,000)} = 44.7$. Therefore, $X \sim N(1,000, 44.7)$, approximately.

The mean, μ, is located just to the right of the peak.

11.2 TEST OF A SINGLE VARIANCE

Thus far our interest has been exclusively on the population parameter μ or it's counterpart in the binomial, p. Surely the mean of a population is the most critical piece of information to have, but in some cases we are interested in the variability of the outcomes of some distribution. In almost all production processes quality is measured not only by how closely the machine matches the target, but also the variability of the process. If one were filling bags with potato chips not only would there be interest in the average weight of the bag, but also how much variation there was in the weights. No one wants to be assured that the average weight is accurate when their bag has no chips. Electricity voltage may meet some average level, but great variability, spikes, can cause serious damage to electrical machines, especially computers. I would not only like to have a high mean grade in my classes, but also low variation about this mean. In short, statistical tests concerning the variance of a distribution have great value and many applications.

A **test of a single variance** assumes that the underlying distribution is **normal.** The null and alternative hypotheses are stated in terms of the **population variance.** The test statistic is:

$$\chi_c^2 = \frac{(n-1)s^2}{\sigma_0^2}$$

where:

- n = the total number of observations in the sample data
- s^2 = sample variance
- σ_0^2 = hypothesized value of the population variance
- $H_0: \sigma^2 = \sigma_0^2$
- $H_a: \sigma^2 \neq \sigma_0^2$

You may think of s as the random variable in this test. The number of degrees of freedom is $df = n - 1$. A test of a single variance may be right-tailed, left-tailed, or two-tailed. Example 11.1 will show you how to set up the null and alternative hypotheses. The null and alternative hypotheses contain statements about the population variance.

EXAMPLE 11.1

Problem

Math instructors are not only interested in how their students do on exams, on average, but how the exam scores vary. To many instructors, the variance (or standard deviation) may be more important than the average.

Suppose a math instructor believes that the standard deviation for his final exam is five points. One of his best students thinks otherwise. The student claims that the standard deviation is more than five points. If the student were to conduct a hypothesis test, what would the null and alternative hypotheses be?

Solution 11.1

Even though we are given the population standard deviation, we can set up the test using the population variance as follows..

- H_0: $\sigma^2 \leq 5^2$
- H_a: $\sigma^2 > 5^2$

TRY IT 11.1

A SCUBA instructor wants to record the collective depths each of his students' dives during their checkout. He is interested in how the depths vary, even though everyone should have been at the same depth. He believes the standard deviation is three feet. His assistant thinks the standard deviation is less than three feet. If the instructor were to conduct a test, what would the null and alternative hypotheses be?

EXAMPLE 11.2

With individual lines at its various windows, a post office finds that the standard deviation for waiting times for customers on Friday afternoon is 7.2 minutes. The post office experiments with a single, main waiting line and finds that for a random sample of 25 customers, the waiting times for customers have a standard deviation of 3.5 minutes on a Friday afternoon.

With a significance level of 5%, test the claim that **a single line causes lower variation among waiting times for customers.**

Solution 11.2

Since the claim is that a single line causes less variation, this is a test of a single variance. The parameter is the population variance, σ^2.

Random Variable: The sample standard deviation, s, is the random variable. Let s = standard deviation for the waiting times.

- $H0$: $\sigma^2 \geq 7.22$
- Ha: $\sigma^2 < 7.22$

The word **"less"** tells you this is a left-tailed test.

Distribution for the test χ^2_{24}, where:

- n = the number of customers sampled
- $df = n - 1 = 25 - 1 = 24$

Calculate the test statistic:

$$\chi_c^2 = \frac{(n - 1)s^2}{\sigma^2} = \frac{(25 - 1)(3.5)^2}{7.2^2} = 5.67$$

where $n = 25$, $s = 3.5$, and $\sigma = 7.2$.

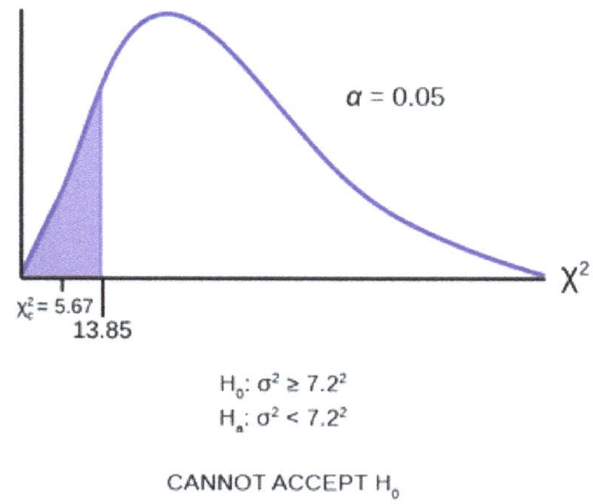

Figure 11.3

The graph of the Chi-square shows the distribution and marks the critical value with 24 degrees of freedom at 95% level of confidence, $\alpha = 0.05$, 13.85. The critical value of 13.85 came from the Chi squared table which is read very much like the students t table. The difference is that the students t distribution is symmetrical and the Chi squared distribution is not. At the top of the Chi squared table we see not only the familiar 0.05, 0.10, etc. but also 0.95, 0.975, etc. These are the columns used to find the left hand critical value. The graph also marks the calculated χ^2 test statistic of 5.67. Comparing the test statistic with the critical value, as we have done with all other hypothesis tests, we reach the conclusion.

Make a decision: Because the calculated test statistic is in the tail we cannot accept *H0*. This means that you reject $\sigma^2 \geq 7.22$. In other words, you do not think the variation in waiting times is 7.2 minutes or more; you think the variation in waiting times is less.

Conclusion: At a 5% level of significance, from the data, there is sufficient evidence to conclude that a single line causes a lower variation among the waiting times **or** with a single line, the customer waiting times vary less than 7.2 minutes.

EXAMPLE 11.3

Professor Hadley has a weakness for cream filled donuts, but he believes that some bakeries are not properly filling the donuts. A sample of 24 donuts reveals a mean amount of filling equal to 0.04 cups, and the sample standard deviation is 0.11 cups. Professor Hadley has an interest in the average quantity of filling, of course, but he is particularly distressed if one donut is radically different from another. Professor Hadley does not like surprises.

Test at 95% the null hypothesis that the population variance of donut filling is significantly different from the average amount of filling.

Solution 11.3

This is clearly a problem dealing with variances. In this case we are testing a single sample rather than comparing two samples from different populations. The null and alternative hypotheses are thus:

$$H_0 : \sigma^2 = 0.04$$

$$H_0 : \sigma^2 \neq 0.04$$

The test is set up as a two-tailed test because Professor Hadley has shown concern with too much variation in filling as well as too little: his dislike of a surprise is any level of filling outside the expected average of 0.04 cups. The test statistic is calculated to be:

$$\chi_c^2 = \frac{(n-1)s^2}{\sigma_o^2} = \frac{(24-1)0.11^2}{0.04^2} = 6.9575$$

The calculated $\chi 2$ test statistic, 6.96, is in the tail therefore at a 0.05 level of significance, we cannot accept the null hypothesis that the variance in the donut filling is equal to 0.04 cups. It seems that Professor Hadley is destined to meet disappointment with each bit.

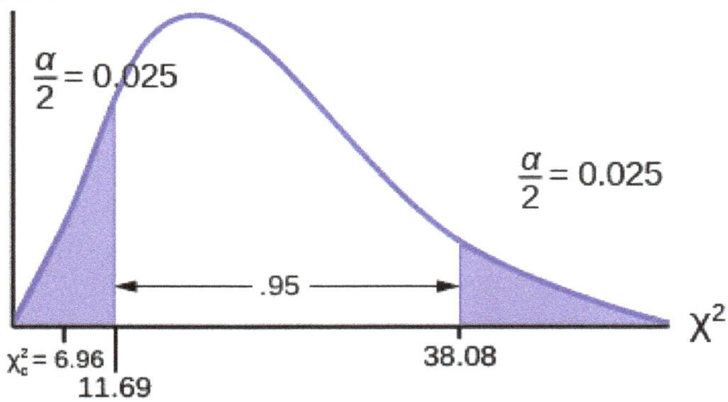

Figure 11.4

TRY IT 11.3

The FCC conducts broadband speed tests to measure how much data per second passes between a consumer's computer and the internet. As of August of 2012, the standard deviation of Internet speeds across Internet Service Providers (ISPs) was

12.2 percent. Suppose a sample of 15 ISPs is taken, and the standard deviation is 13.2. An analyst claims that the standard deviation of speeds is more than what was reported. State the null and alternative hypotheses, compute the degrees of freedom, the test statistic, sketch the graph of the distribution and mark the area associated with the level of confidence, and draw a conclusion. Test at the 1% significance level.

11.3 GOODNESS-OF-FIT TEST

In this type of hypothesis test, you determine whether the data **"fit"** a particular distribution or not. For example, you may suspect your unknown data fit a binomial distribution. You use a chi-square test (meaning the distribution for the hypothesis test is chi-square) to determine if there is a fit or not. **The null and the alternative hypotheses for this test may be written in sentences or may be stated as equations or inequalities.**

The test statistic for a goodness-of-fit test is:

$$\sum_k \frac{(O-E)^2}{E}$$

where:

- O = **observed values** (data)
- E = **expected values** (from theory)
- k = the number of different data cells or categories

The observed values are the data values and the expected values are the values you would expect to get if the null hypothesis were true. There are n terms of the form $\frac{(O-E)^2}{E}$.

The number of degrees of freedom is df = (number of categories – 1).

The goodness-of-fit test is almost always right-tailed. If the observed values and the corresponding expected values are not close to each other, then the test statistic can get very large and will be way out in the right tail of the chi-square curve.

NOTE

The number of expected values inside each cell needs to be at least five in order to use this test.

EXAMPLE 11.4

Absenteeism of college students from math classes is a major concern to math instructors because missing class appears to increase the drop rate. Suppose that a study was done to determine if the actual student absenteeism rate follows faculty perception. The faculty expected that a group of 100 students would miss class according to Table 11.1.

Table 11.1

Number of absences per term	Expected number of students
0–2	50
3–5	30
6–8	12
9–11	6
12+	2

A random survey across all mathematics courses was then done to determine the actual number **(observed)** of absences in a course. The chart in Table 11.2 displays the results of that survey.

Table 11.2

Number of absences per term	Actual number of students
0–2	35
3–5	40
6–8	20
9–11	1
12+	4

Determine the null and alternative hypotheses needed to conduct a goodness-of-fit test.

***H_0*: Student absenteeism **fits** faculty perception.

The alternative hypothesis is the opposite of the null hypothesis.

***H_a*: Student absenteeism **does not fit** faculty perception.

a. Can you use the information as it appears in the charts to conduct the goodness-of-fit test?

Solution 11.4

a. **No.** Notice that the expected number of absences for the "12+" entry is less than five (it is two). Combine that group with the "9–11" group to create new tables where the number of students for each entry are at least five. The new results are in **Table 11.2** and **Table 11.3**.

Solution 11.4

a. **No.** Notice that the expected number of absences for the "12+" entry is less than five (it is two). Combine that group with the "9–11" group to create new tables where the number of students for each entry are at least five. The new results are in Table 11.3 and Table 11.4.

Table 11.3

Number of absences per term	Expected number of students
0–2	50
3–5	30
6–8	12
9+	8

Table 11.4

Number of absences per term	Actual number of students
0–2	35
3–5	40
6–8	20
9+	5

b. What is the number of degrees of freedom (*df*)?

Solution 11.4

b. There are four "cells" or categories in each of the new tables.

df = number of cells – 1 = 4 – 1 = 3

TRY IT 11.4

A factory manager needs to understand how many products are defective versus how many are produced. The number of expected defects is listed in Table 11.5.

Table 11.5

Number produced	Number defective
0–100	5
101–200	6
201–300	7
301–400	8
401–500	10

A random sample was taken to determine the actual number of defects. Table 11.6 shows the results of the survey.

Table 11.6

Number produced	Number defective
0–100	5
101–200	7
201–300	8
301–400	9
401–500	11

State the null and alternative hypotheses needed to conduct a goodness-of-fit test, and state the degrees of freedom.

EXAMPLE 11.5

Employers want to know which days of the week employees are absent in a five-day work week. Most employers would like to believe that employees are absent equally during the week. Suppose a random sample of 60 managers were asked on which day of the week they had the highest number of employee absences. The results were distributed as in Table 11.7. For the population of employees, do the days for the highest number of absences occur with equal frequencies during a five-day work week? Test at a 5% significance level.

Table 11.7 Day of the Week Employees were Most Absent

	Monday	Tuesday	Wednesday	Thursday	Friday
Number of absences	15	12	9	9	15

Solution 11.5

The null and alternative hypotheses are:

- *H0*: The absent days occur with equal frequencies, that is, they fit a uniform distribution.
- *Ha*: The absent days occur with unequal frequencies, that is, they do not fit a uniform distribution.

If the absent days occur with equal frequencies, then, out of 60 absent days (the total in the sample: 15 + 12 + 9 + 9 + 15 = 60), there would be 12 absences on Monday, 12 on Tuesday, 12 on Wednesday, 12 on Thursday, and 12 on Friday. These numbers are the **expected** (E) values. The values in the table are the **observed** (O) values or data.

This time, calculate the $\chi 2$ test statistic by hand. Make a chart with the following headings and fill in the columns:

- Expected (E) values (12, 12, 12, 12, 12)
- Observed (O) values (15, 12, 9, 9, 15)
- $(O - E)$
- $(O - E)^2$
- $(O - E)^2$
- $\frac{(O-E)^2}{E}$

Now add (sum) the last column. The sum is three. This is the χ^2 test statistic.

The calculated test statistics is 3 and the critical value of the χ^2 distribution at 4 degrees of freedom the 0.05 level of confidence is 9.48. This value is found in the $\chi 2$ table at the 0.05 column on the degrees of freedom row 4.

The degrees of freedom are the number of cells – 1 = 5 – 1 = 4

Next, complete a graph like the following one with the proper labeling and shading. (You should shade the right tail.)

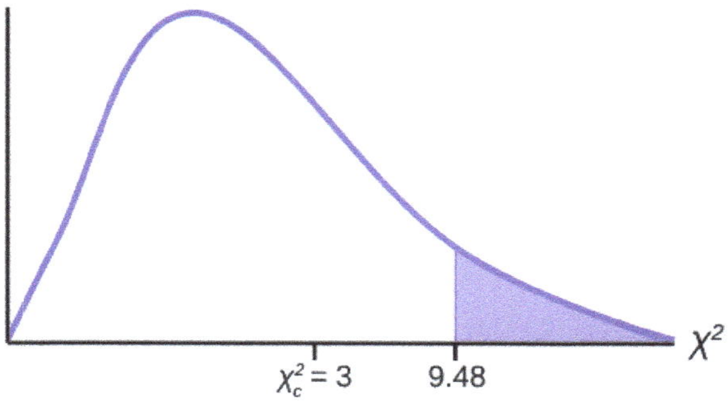

Figure 11.5

$$\chi^2_c = \sum_k \frac{(O-E)^2}{E} = 3$$

The decision is not to reject the null hypothesis because the calculated value of the test statistic is not in the tail of the distribution.

Conclusion: At a 5% level of significance, from the sample data, there is not sufficient evidence to conclude that the absent days do not occur with equal frequencies.

TRY IT 11.5

Teachers want to know which night each week their students are doing most of their homework. Most teachers think that students do homework equally throughout the week. Suppose a random sample of 56 students were asked on which night of the week they did the most homework. The results were distributed as in Table 11.8.

Table 11.8

	Sunday	Monday	Tuesday	Wednesday	Thursday	Friday	Saturday
Number of students	11	8	10	7	10	5	5

From the population of students, do the nights for the highest number of students doing the majority of their homework occur with equal frequencies during a week? What type of hypothesis test should you use?

EXAMPLE 11.6

One study indicates that the number of televisions that American families have is distributed (this is the **given** distribution for the American population) as in Table 11.9.

Table 11.9

Number of Televisions	Percent
0	10
1	16
2	55
3	11
4+	8

The table contains expected (E) percents.

A random sample of 600 families in the far western United States resulted in the data in Table 11.10.

Table 11.10

Number of Televisions	Frequency
0	66
1	119
2	340
3	60
4+	15
	Total = 600

The table contains observed (O) frequency values.

At the 1% significance level, does it appear that the distribution "number of televisions" of far western United States families is different from the distribution for the American population as a whole?

Solution 11.6

This problem asks you to test whether the far western United States families distribution fits the distribution of the American families. This test is always right-tailed.

The first table contains expected percentages. To get expected (*E*) frequencies, multiply the percentage by 600. The expected frequencies are shown in Table 11.11.

Table 11.11

Number of televisions	Percent	Expected frequency
0	10	(0.10)(600) = 60
1	16	(0.16)(600) = 96
2	55	(0.55)(600) = 330
3	11	(0.11)(600) = 66
over 3	8	(0.08)(600) = 48

Therefore, the expected frequencies are 60, 96, 330, 66, and 48.

H_0: The "number of televisions" distribution of far western United States families is the same as the "number of televisions" distribution of the American population.

H_a: The "number of televisions" distribution of far western United States families is different from the "number of televisions" distribution of the American population.

Distribution for the test: $\chi^2 4$ where df = (the number of cells) – 1 = 5 – 1 = 4.

Calculate the test statistic: $\chi^2 = 29.65$

Graph:

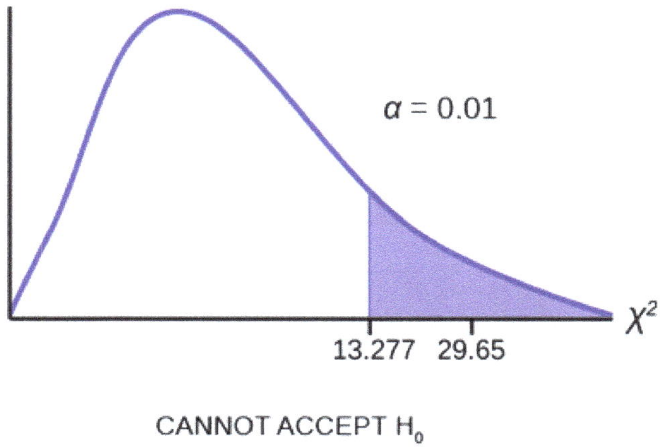

Figure 11.6

The graph of the Chi-square shows the distribution and marks the critical value with four degrees of freedom at 99% level of confidence, α = .01, 13.277. The graph also marks the calculated chi squared test statistic of 29.65. Comparing the test statistic with the critical value, as we have done with all other hypothesis tests, we reach the conclusion.

Make a decision: Because the test statistic is in the tail of the distribution we cannot accept the null hypothesis.

This means you reject the belief that the distribution for the far western states is the same as that of the American population as a whole.

Conclusion: At the 1% significance level, from the data, there is sufficient evidence to conclude that the "number of televisions" distribution for the far western United States is different from the "number of televisions" distribution for the American population as a whole.

TRY IT11.6

The expected percentage of the number of pets students have in their homes is distributed (this is the given distribution for the student population of the United States) as in Table 11.12.

Table 11.12

Number of pets	Percent
0	18
1	25
2	30
3	18
4+	9

A random sample of 1,000 students from the Eastern United States resulted in the data in Table 11.13.

Table 11.13

Number of pets	Frequency
0	210
1	240
2	320
3	140
4+	90

At the 1% significance level, does it appear that the distribution "number of pets" of students in the Eastern United States is different from the distribution for the United States student population as a whole?

EXAMPLE11.7

Suppose you flip two coins 100 times. The results are 20*HH*, 27*HT*, 30*TH*, and 23*TT*. Are the coins fair? Test at a 5% significance level.

Solution 11.7

This problem can be set up as a goodness-of-fit problem. The sample space for flipping two fair coins is {*HH*,*HT*,*TH*,*TT*}. Out of 100 flips, you would expect 25*HH*, 25*HT*, 25*TH*, and 25*TT*. This is the expected distribution from the binomial probability distribution. The question, "Are the coins fair?" is the same as saying, "Does the distribution of the coins (20*HH*, 27*HT*, 30*TH*, 23*TT*) fit the expected distribution?"

Random Variable : Let*X*= the number of heads in one flip of the two coins.*X*takes on the values 0, 1, 2. (There are 0, 1, or 2 heads in the flip of two coins.) Therefore, the**number of cells is three.** Since*X*= the number of heads, the observed frequencies are 20 (for two heads), 57 (for one head), and 23 (for zero heads or both tails). The expected frequencies are 25 (for two heads), 50 (for one head), and 25 (for zero heads or both tails). This test is right-tailed.

H_0: The coins are fair.

H_a: The coins are not fair.

Distribution for the test:$\chi^2$2where*df*= 3 – 1 = 2.

Calculate the test statistic:χ^2= 2.14

Graph:

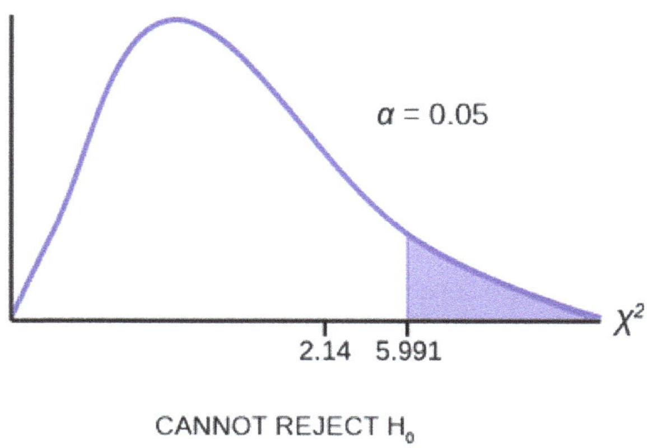

Figure 11.7

The graph of the Chi-square shows the distribution and marks the critical value with two degrees of freedom at 95% level of confidence, α = 0.05, 5.991. The graph also marks the calculated χ^2 test statistic of 2.14. Comparing the test statistic with the critical value, as we have done with all other hypothesis tests, we reach the conclusion.

Conclusion: There is insufficient evidence to conclude that the coins are not fair: we cannot reject the null hypothesis that the coins are fair.

11.4 TEST OF INDEPENDENCE

Tests of independence involve using a contingency table of observed (data) values.

The test statistic for a test of independence is similar to that of a goodness-of-fit test:

$$\sum_{(i \cdot j)} \frac{(O-E)^2}{E}$$

where:

- O = observed values
- E = expected values
- i = the number of rows in the table
- j = the number of columns in the table

There are i·ji·j terms of the form $\frac{(O-E)^2}{E}$.

A test of independence determines whether two factors are independent or not. You first encountered the term independence in 3.2 Independent and Mutually Exclusive Events earlier. As a review, consider the following example.

NOTE

The expected value inside each cell needs to be at least five in order for you to use this test.

EXAMPLE 11.8

Suppose A = a speeding violation in the last year and B = a cell phone user while driving. If A and B are independent then $P(A$ ∩∩ $B) = P(A)P(B)$. A ∩∩ B is the event that a driver received a speeding violation last year and also used a cell phone while driving. Suppose, in a study of drivers who received speeding violations in the last year, and who used cell phone while driving, that 755 people were surveyed. Out of the 755, 70 had a speeding violation and 685 did not; 305 used cell phones while driving and 450 did not.

Let y = expected number of drivers who used a cell phone while driving and received speeding violations.

If A and B are independent, then $P(A$ ∩∩ $B) = P(A)P(B)$. By substitution,

$$\frac{y}{755} = \left(\frac{70}{755}\right)\left(\frac{305}{755}\right)$$

Solve for *y*: $y = \frac{(70)(305)}{755} = 28.3$

About 28 people from the sample are expected to use cell phones while driving and to receive speeding violations.

In a test of independence, we state the null and alternative hypotheses in words. Since the contingency table consists of two factors, the null hypothesis states that the factors are independent and the alternative hypothesis states that they are not independent (dependent). If we do a test of independence using the example, then the null hypothesis is:

H0*H*0: Being a cell phone user while driving and receiving a speeding violation are independent events; in other words, they have no effect on each other.

If the null hypothesis were true, we would expect about 28 people to use cell phones while driving and to receive a speeding violation.

The test of independence is always right-tailed because of the calculation of the test statistic. If the expected and observed values are not close together, then the test statistic is very large and way out in the right tail of the chi-square curve, as it is in a goodness-of-fit.

The number of degrees of freedom for the test of independence is:

df = (number of columns - 1)(number of rows - 1)

The following formula calculates the expected number (*E*):

$$E = \frac{\text{(row total)(column total)}}{\text{total number surveyed}}$$

TRY IT 11.8

A sample of 300 students is taken. Of the students surveyed, 50 were music students, while 250 were not. Ninety-seven of the 300 surveyed were on the honor roll, while 203 were not. If we assume being a music student and being on the honor roll are independent events, what is the expected number of music students who are also on the honor roll?

EXAMPLE 11.9

A volunteer group, provides from one to nine hours each week with disabled senior citizens. The program recruits among community college students, four-year college students, and non students. In Table 11.14 is a sample of the adult volunteers and the number of hours they volunteer per week.

Table 11.14 Number of Hours Worked Per Week by Volunteer Type (Observed) The table contains observed (O) values (data).

Type of volunteer	1–3 Hours	4–6 Hours	7–9 Hours	Row total
Community college students	111	96	48	255
Four-year college students	96	133	61	290
Nonstudents	91	150	53	294
Column total	298	379	162	839

Is the number of hours volunteered independent of the type of volunteer?

Solution 11.9

The **observed table** and the question at the end of the problem, "Is the number of hours volunteered independent of the type of volunteer?" tell you this is a test of independence. The two factors are number of hours volunteered and type of volunteer. This test is always right-tailed.

H_0: The number of hours volunteered is independent of the type of volunteer.

Ha: The number of hours volunteered is dependent on the type of volunteer.

The expected results are in Table 11.14.

Table 11.15 Number of Hours Worked Per Week by Volunteer Type (Expected) The table contains expected (*E*) values (data).

Type of volunteer	1-3 Hours	4-6 Hours	7-9 Hours
Community college students	90.57	115.19	49.24
Four-year college students	103.00	131.00	56.00
Nonstudents	104.42	132.81	56.77

For example, the calculation for the expected frequency for the top left cell is

$$E = \frac{\text{(row total)(column total)}}{\text{total number surveyed}} = \frac{(255)(298)}{839} = 90.57$$

Calculate the test statistic: $\chi^2 = 12.99$ (calculator or computer)

Distribution for the test: $\chi^2 4$

df = (3 columns – 1)(3 rows – 1) = (2)(2) = 4

Graph:

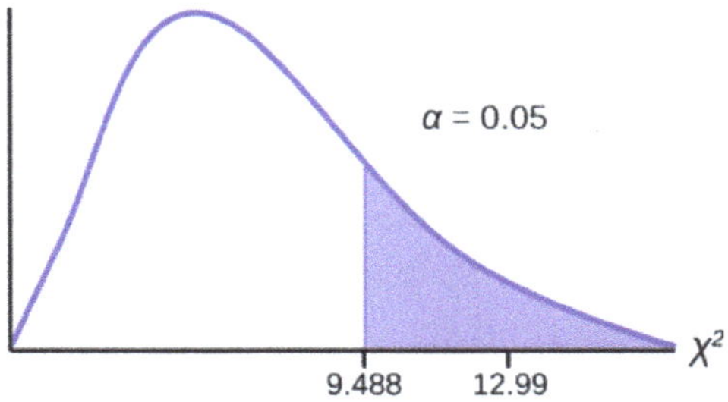

Figure 11.8

The graph of the Chi-square shows the distribution and marks the critical value with four degrees of freedom at 95% level of confidence, α = 0.05, 9.488. The graph also marks the calculated χ2cχc2 test statistic of 12.99. Comparing the test statistic with the critical value, as we have done with all other hypothesis tests, we reach the conclusion.

Make a decision: Because the calculated test statistic is in the tail we cannot accept H_0. This means that the factors are not independent.

Conclusion: At a 5% level of significance, from the data, there is sufficient evidence to conclude that the number of hours volunteered and the type of volunteer are dependent on one another.

For the example in Table 11.15, if there had been another type of volunteer, teenagers, what would the degrees of freedom be?

TRY IT 11.9

The Bureau of Labor Statistics gathers data about employment in the United States. A sample is taken to calculate the number of U.S. citizens working in one of several industry sectors over time. Table 11.16 shows the results:

Table 11.16

Industry sector	2000	2010	2020	Total
Nonagriculture wage and salary	13,243	13,044	15,018	41,305
Goods-producing, excluding agriculture	2,457	1,771	1,950	6,178
Services-providing	10,786	11,273	13,068	35,127
Agriculture, forestry, fishing, and hunting	240	214	201	655
Nonagriculture self-employed and unpaid family worker	931	894	972	2,797
Secondary wage and salary jobs in agriculture and private household industries	14	11	11	36
Secondary jobs as a self-employed or unpaid family worker	196	144	152	492
Total	27,867	27,351	31,372	86,590

We want to know if the change in the number of jobs is independent of the change in years. State the null and alternative hypotheses and the degrees of freedom.

EXAMPLE 11.10

De Anza College is interested in the relationship between anxiety level and the need to succeed in school. A random sample of 400 students took a test that measured anxiety level and need to succeed in school. Table 11.17 shows the results. De Anza College wants to know if anxiety level and need to succeed in school are independent events.

Table 11.17 Need to Succeed in School vs. Anxiety Level

Need to succeed in school	High anxiety	Med-high anxiety	Medium anxiety	Med-low anxiety	Low anxiety	Row total
High need	35	42	53	15	10	155
Medium need	18	48	63	33	31	193
Low need	4	5	11	15	17	52
Column total	57	95	127	63	58	400

a. How many high anxiety level students are expected to have a high need to succeed in school?

Solution 11.10

a. The column total for a high anxiety level is 57. The row total for high need to succeed in school is 155. The sample size or total surveyed is 400.

$$E = \frac{\text{(row total)(column total)}}{\text{total surveyed}} = \frac{155 \cdot 57}{400} = 22.09$$

The expected number of students who have a high anxiety level and a high need to succeed in school is about 22.

b. If the two variables are independent, how many students do you expect to have a low need to succeed in school and a med-low level of anxiety?

Solution 11.10

b. The column total for a med-low anxiety level is 63. The row total for a low need to succeed in school is 52. The sample size or total surveyed is 400.

c. $E = \frac{\text{(row total)(column total)}}{\text{total surveyed}} =$ ________

Solution 11.10

c. $E = \frac{\text{(row total)(column total)}}{\text{total surveyed}} = 8.19$

d. The expected number of students who have a med-low anxiety level and a low need to succeed in school is about ________.

Solution 11.10

d. 8

11.5 TEST FOR HOMOGENEITY

The goodness–of–fit test can be used to decide whether a population fits a given distribution, but it will not suffice to decide whether two populations follow the same unknown distribution. A different test, called the **test for homogeneity**, can be used to draw a conclusion about whether two populations have the same distribution. To calculate the test statistic for a test for homogeneity, follow the same procedure as with the test of independence.

NOTE

The expected value inside each cell needs to be at least five in order for you to use this test.

Hypotheses

H_0: The distributions of the two populations are the same.

H_a: The distributions of the two populations are not the same.

Test Statistic Use a χ^2 test statistic. It is computed in the same way as the test for independence.

Degrees of Freedom (*df*)*df* = number of columns - 1

Requirements

All values in the table must be greater than or equal to five.

Common Uses

Comparing two populations. For example: men vs. women, before vs. after, east vs. west. The variable is categorical with more than two possible response values.

EXAMPLE 11.11

Do male and female college students have the same distribution of living arrangements? Use a level of significance of 0.05. Suppose that 250 randomly selected male college students and 300 randomly selected female college students were asked about their living arrangements: dormitory, apartment, with parents, other. The results are shown in Table 11.18. Do male and female college students have the same distribution of living arrangements?

Table 11.18 Distribution of living arrangements for college males and college females

	Dormitory	Apartment	With Parents	Other
Males	72	84	49	45
Females	91	86	88	35

Solution 11.1

H_0: The distribution of living arrangements for male college students is the same as the distribution of living arrangements for female college students.

H_a: The distribution of living arrangements for male college students is not the same as the distribution of living arrangements for female college students.

Degrees of Freedom (*df*):

df = number of columns – 1 = 4 – 1 = 3

Distribution for the test:$\chi^2 3$

Calculate the test statistic: χ2c = 10.129

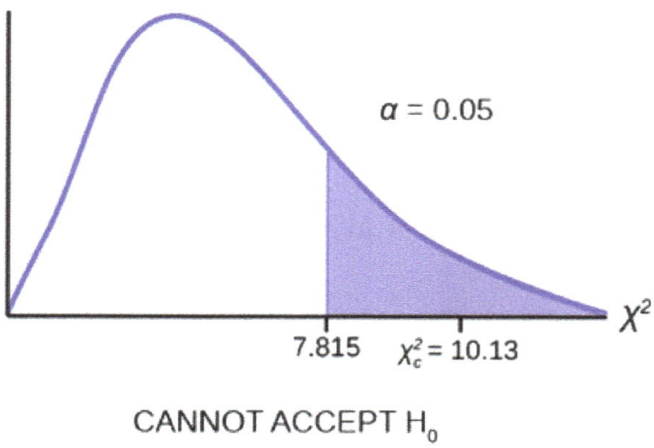

Figure 11.9

The graph of the Chi-square shows the distribution and marks the critical value with three degrees of freedom at 95% level of confidence, α = 0.05, 7.815. The graph also marks the calculated χ^2 test statistic of 10.129. Comparing the test statistic with the critical value, as we have done with all other hypothesis tests, we reach the conclusion.

Make a decision: Because the calculated test statistic is in the tail we cannot accept H_0. This means that the distributions are not the same.

Conclusion: At a 5% level of significance, from the data, there is sufficient evidence to conclude that the distributions of living arrangements for male and female college students are not the same.

Notice that the conclusion is only that the distributions are not the same. We cannot use the test for homogeneity to draw any conclusions about how they differ.

TRY IT 11.11

Do families and singles have the same distribution of cars? Use a level of significance of 0.05. Suppose that 100 randomly selected families and 200 randomly selected singles were asked what type of car they drove: sport, sedan, hatchback, truck, van/SUV. The results are shown in Table 11.19. Do families and singles have the same distribution of cars? Test at a level of significance of 0.05.

Table 11.19

	Sport	Sedan	Hatchback	Truck	Van/SUV
Family	5	15	35	17	28
Single	45	65	37	46	7

TRY IT 11.11

Ivy League schools receive many applications, but only some can be accepted. At the schools listed in Table 11.20, two types of applications are accepted: regular and early decision.

Table 11.20

Application type accepted	Brown	Columbia	Cornell	Dartmouth	Penn	Yale
Regular	2,115	1,792	5,306	1,734	2,685	1,245
Early decision	577	627	1,228	444	1,195	761

We want to know if the number of regular applications accepted follows the same distribution as the number of early applications accepted. State the null and alternative hypotheses, the degrees of freedom and the test statistic, sketch the graph of the χ^2 distribution and show the critical value and the calculated value of the test statistic, and draw a conclusion about the test of homogeneity.

11.6 COMPARISON OF THE CHI-SQUARE TESTS

Above the χ^2 test statistic was used in three different circumstances. The following bulleted list is a summary of which χ^2 test is the appropriate one to use in different circumstances.

- **Goodness-of-Fit:** Use the goodness-of-fit test to decide whether a population with an unknown distribution "fits" a known distribution. In this case there will be a single qualitative survey question or a single outcome of an experiment from a single population. Goodness-of-Fit is typically used to see if the population is uniform (all outcomes occur with equal frequency), the population is normal, or the population is the same as another population with a known distribution. The null and alternative hypotheses are:

- H_0: The population fits the given distribution.H_a: The population does not fit the given distribution.
- **Independence:** Use the test for independence to decide whether two variables (factors) are independent or dependent. In this case there will be two qualitative survey questions or experiments and a contingency table will be constructed. The goal is to see if the two variables are unrelated (independent) or related (dependent). The null and alternative hypotheses are:
- H_0: The two variables (factors) are independent.
- H_a: The two variables (factors) are dependent.
- **Homogeneity:** Use the test for homogeneity to decide if two populations with unknown distributions have the same distribution as each other. In this case there will be a single qualitative survey question or experiment given to two different populations. The null and alternative hypotheses are:
- H_0: The two populations follow the same distribution.
- H_a: The two populations have different distributions.

Key Terms

Contingency Table a table that displays sample values for two different factors that may be dependent or contingent on one another; it facilitates determining conditional probabilities.

Goodness-of-Fit a hypothesis test that compares expected and observed values in order to look for significant differences within one non-parametric variable. The degrees of freedom used equals the (number of categories – 1).

Test for Homogeneity a test used to draw a conclusion about whether two populations have the same distribution. The degrees of freedom used equals the (number of columns – 1).

Test of Independence a hypothesis test that compares expected and observed values for contingency tables in order to test for independence between two variables. The degrees of freedom used equals the (number of columns – 1) multiplied by the (number of rows – 1).

CHAPTER REVIEW

11.1 Facts About the Chi-Square Distribution

The chi-square distribution is a useful tool for assessment in a series of problem categories. These problem categories include primarily (i) whether a data set fits a particular distribution, (ii) whether the distributions of two populations are the same, (iii) whether two events might be independent, and (iv) whether there is a different variability than expected within a population.

An important parameter in a chi-square distribution is the degrees of freedom *df* in a given problem. The random variable in the chi-square distribution is the sum of squares of *df* standard normal variables, which must be independent. The key characteristics of the chi-square distribution also depend directly on the degrees of freedom.

The chi-square distribution curve is skewed to the right, and its shape depends on the degrees of freedom *df*. For $df > 90$, the curve approximates the normal distribution. Test statistics based on the chi-square distribution are always greater than or equal to zero. Such application tests are almost always right-tailed tests.

11.2 Test of a Single Variance

To test variability, use the chi-square test of a single variance. The test may be left-, right-, or two-tailed, and its hypotheses are always expressed in terms of the variance (or standard deviation).

11.3 Goodness-of-Fit Test

To assess whether a data set fits a specific distribution, you can apply the goodness-of-fit hypothesis test that uses the chi-square distribution. The null hypothesis for this test states that the data come from the assumed distribution. The test compares observed values against the values you would expect to have if your data followed the assumed distribution. The test is almost always right-tailed. Each observation or cell category must have an expected value of at least five.

11.4 Test of Independence

To assess whether two factors are independent or not, you can apply the test of independence that uses the chi-square distribution. The null hypothesis for this test states that the two factors are independent. The test compares observed values to expected values. The test is right-tailed. Each observation or cell category must have an expected value of at least 5.

11.5 Test for Homogeneity

To assess whether two data sets are derived from the same distribution—which need not be known, you can apply the test for homogeneity that uses the chi-square distribution. The null hypothesis for this test states that the populations of the two data sets come from the same distribution. The test compares the observed values against the expected values if the two populations followed the same distribution. The test is right-tailed. Each observation or cell category must have an expected value of at least five.

11.6 Comparison of the Chi-Square Tests

The goodness-of-fit test is typically used to determine if data fits a particular distribution. The test of independence makes use of a contingency table to determine the independence of two factors. The test for homogeneity determines whether two populations come from the same distribution, even if this distribution is unknown.

11.1 Facts About the Chi-Square Distribution

$\chi^2 = (Z_1)^2 + (Z_2)^2 + \ldots (Z_{df})^2$ chi-square distribution random variable

$\mu_{\chi^2} = df$ chi-square distribution population mean

$\sqrt{\sigma\chi 2=2(df)}$ Chi-Square distribution population standard deviation

11.2 Test of a Single Variance

$\chi^2 = \frac{(n-1)s^2}{\sigma_0^2}$ Test of a single variance statistic where: n: sample size

s: sample standard deviation

σ0σ0: hypothesized value of the population standard deviation

$df = n - 1$ Degrees of freedom

Test of a Single Variance

- Use the test to determine variation.
- The degrees of freedom is the number of samples – 1.
- The test statistic is $\frac{(n-1)s^2}{\sigma_0^2}$, where n = sample size, s^2 = sample variance, and σ^2 = population variance.
- The test may be left-, right-, or two-tailed.

11.3 Goodness-of-Fit Test

$\sum_k \frac{(O-E)^2}{E}$ goodness-of-fit test statistic where:

O: observed values

E: expected values

k: number of different data cells or categories

$df = k - 1$ degrees of freedom

11.4 Test of Independence

Test of Independence

- The number of degrees of freedom is equal to (number of columns - 1)(number of rows - 1).
- The test statistic is $\sum_{i \cdot j} \frac{(O-E)^2}{E}$ where O = observed values, E = expected values, i = the number of rows in the table, and j = the number of columns in the table.
- If the null hypothesis is true, the expected number E=(row total)(column total)total surveyed$E$=(row total)(column total)total surveyed.

11.5 Test for Homogeneity

$\sum_{i \cdot j} \frac{(O-E)^2}{E}$ Homogeneity test statistic where: O = observed values

E = expected values

i = number of rows in data contingency table

j = number of columns in data contingency table

$df = (i - 1)(j - 1)$ Degrees of freedom

PRACTICE

11.1 Facts About the Chi-Square Distribution

1. If the number of degrees of freedom for a chi-square distribution is 25, what is the population mean and standard deviation?
2. If $df > 90$, the distribution is _____________. If $df = 15$, the distribution is ________________.
3. When does the chi-square curve approximate a normal distribution?
4. Where is μ located on a chi-square curve?
5. Is it more likely the *df* is 90, 20, or two in the graph?

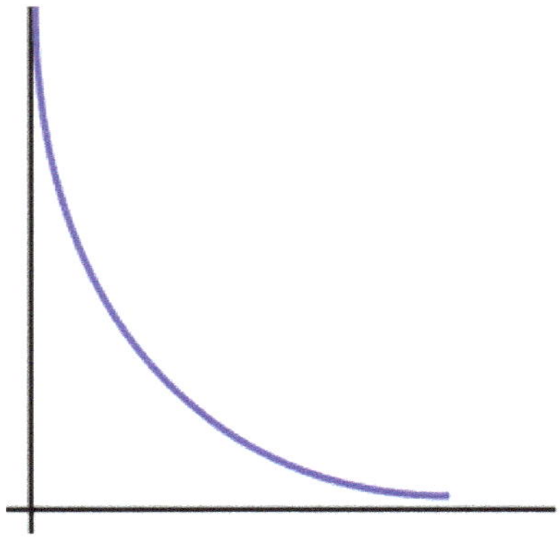

Figure 11.10

11.2 Test of a Single Variance

Use the following information to answer the next three exercises: An archer's standard deviation for his hits is six (data is measured in distance from the center of the target). An observer claims the standard deviation is less.

6. What type of test should be used?

7. State the null and alternative hypotheses.

8. Is this a right-tailed, left-tailed, or two-tailed test?

Use the following information to answer the next three exercises: The standard deviation of heights for students in a school is 0.81. A random sample of 50 students is taken, and the standard deviation of heights of the sample is 0.96. A researcher in charge of the study believes the standard deviation of heights for the school is greater than 0.81.

9. What type of test should be used?

10. State the null and alternative hypotheses.

11. df = ________

Use the following information to answer the next four exercises: The average waiting time in a doctor's office varies. The standard deviation of waiting times in a doctor's office is 3.4 minutes. A random sample of 30 patients in the doctor's office has a standard deviation of waiting times of 4.1 minutes. One doctor believes the variance of waiting times is greater than originally thought.

12. What type of test should be used?

13. What is the test statistic?

14. What can you conclude at the 5% significance level?

11.3 Goodness-of-Fit Test

Determine the appropriate test to be used in the next three exercises.

15. An archaeologist is calculating the distribution of the frequency of the number of artifacts she finds in a dig site. Based on previous digs, the archaeologist creates an expected distribution broken down by grid sections in the dig site. Once the site has been fully excavated, she compares the actual number of artifacts found in each grid section to see if her expectation was accurate.

16. An economist is deriving a model to predict outcomes on the stock market. He creates a list of expected points on the stock market index for the next two weeks. At the close of each day's trading, he records the actual points on the index. He wants to see how well his model matched what actually happened.

17. A personal trainer is putting together a weight-lifting program for her clients. For a 90-day program, she expects each client to lift a specific maximum weight each week. As she goes along, she records the actual maximum weights her clients lifted. She wants to know how well her expectations met with what was observed.

Use the following information to answer the next five exercises: A teacher predicts that the distribution of grades on the final exam will be and they are recorded in Table 11.21.

Table 11.21

Grade	Proportion
A	0.25
B	0.30
C	0.35
D	0.10

The actual distribution for a class of 20 is in Table 11.22.

Table 11.22

Grade	Frequency
A	7
B	7
C	5
D	1

18. df=df= ______

19. State the null and alternative hypotheses.

20. χ^2 test statistic = ______

21. At the 5% significance level, what can you conclude?

Use the following information to answer the next nine exercises: The following data are real. The cumulative number of AIDS cases reported for Santa Clara County is broken down by ethnicity as in Table 11.23.

Table 11.23

Ethnicity	Number of cases
White	2,229
Hispanic	1,157
Black/African-American	457
Asian, Pacific Islander	232
	Total = 4,075

The percentage of each ethnic group in Santa Clara County is as in Table 11.24.

Table 11.24

Ethnicity	Percentage of total county population	Number expected (round to two decimal places)
White	42.9%	1748.18
Hispanic	26.7%	
Black/African-American	2.6%	
Asian, Pacific Islander	27.8%	
	Total = 100%	

22. If the ethnicities of AIDS victims followed the ethnicities of the total county population, fill in the expected number of cases per ethnic group. *Perform a goodness-of-fit test to determine whether the occurrence of AIDS cases follows the ethnicities of the general population of Santa Clara County.*

23. H_0: _______

24. H_a: _______

25. Is this a right-tailed, left-tailed, or two-tailed test?

26. degrees of freedom = _______

27. χ^2 test statistic = _______

28. Graph the situation. Label and scale the horizontal axis. Mark the mean and test statistic. Shade in the region corresponding to the confidence level.

Figure 11.11

Let $\alpha = 0.05$

Decision: ________________

Reason for the Decision: ________________

Conclusion (write out in complete sentences): ________________

29. Does it appear that the pattern of AIDS cases in Santa Clara County corresponds to the distribution of ethnic groups in this county? Why or why not?

11.4 Test of Independence

Determine the appropriate test to be used in the next three exercises.

30. A pharmaceutical company is interested in the relationship between age and presentation of symptoms for a common viral infection. A random sample is taken of 500 people with the infection across different age groups.

31. The owner of a baseball team is interested in the relationship between player salaries and team winning percentage. He takes a random sample of 100 players from different organizations.

32. A marathon runner is interested in the relationship between the brand of shoes runners wear and their run times. She takes a random sample of 50 runners and records their run times as well as the brand of shoes they were wearing.

Use the following information to answer the next seven exercises: Transit Railroads is interested in the relationship between travel distance and the ticket class purchased. A random sample of 200 passengers is taken. Table 11.25 shows the results. The railroad wants to know if a passenger's choice in ticket class is independent of the distance they must travel.

Table 11.25

Traveling distance	Third class	Second class	First class	Total
1–100 miles	21	14	6	41
101–200 miles	18	16	8	42
201–300 miles	16	17	15	48
301–400 miles	12	14	21	47
401–500 miles	6	6	10	22
Total	73	67	60	200

33. State the hypotheses.

H_0: _______

H_a: _______

34. df = _______

35. How many passengers are expected to travel between 201 and 300 miles and purchase second-class tickets?

36. How many passengers are expected to travel between 401 and 500 miles and purchase first-class tickets?

37. What is the test statistic?

38. What can you conclude at the 5% level of significance?

Use the following information to answer the next eight exercises: An article in the New England Journal of Medicine, discussed a study on smokers in California and Hawaii. In one part of the report, the self-reported ethnicity and smoking levels per day were given. Of the people smoking at most ten cigarettes per day, there were 9,886 African American people, 2,745 Native Hawaiian people, 12,831 Latino people, 8,378 Japanese American people and 7,650 White people. Of the people smoking 11 to 20 cigarettes per day, there were 6,514 African American people, 3,062 Native Hawaiian people, 4,932 Latino people, 10,680 Japanese American people, and 9,877 White people. Of the people smoking 21 to 30 cigarettes per day, there were 1,671 African American people, 1,419 Native Hawaiian people, 1,406 Latino people, 4,715 Japanese American people, and 6,062 White people. Of the people smoking at least 31 cigarettes per day, there were 759 African American people, 788 Native Hawaiian people, 800 Latino people, 2,305 Japanese American people, and 3,970 White people.

39. Complete the table.

Table 11.26 Smoking Levels by Ethnicity (Observed)

Smoking level per day	African American	Native Hawaiian	Latino	Japanese American	White	Totals
1-10						
11-20						
21-30						
31+						
Totals						

39. State the hypotheses.

H_0: _______ H_a: _______

41. Enter expected values in Table 11.26. Round to two decimal places.

Calculate the following values:

42. df = _______

43. χ^2 test statistic = ______

44. Is this a right-tailed, left-tailed, or two-tailed test? Explain why.

45. Graph the situation. Label and scale the horizontal axis. Mark the mean and test statistic. Shade in the region corresponding to the confidence level.

Figure 11.12

State the decision and conclusion (in a complete sentence) for the following preconceived levels of α.

46. $\alpha = 0.05$

a. Decision: ____________________
b. Reason for the decision: ____________________
c. Conclusion (write out in a complete sentence): ____________________

47. $\alpha = 0.01$

a. Decision: ____________________

b. Reason for the decision: ____________________
c. Conclusion (write out in a complete sentence): ____________________

11.5 Test for Homogeneity

48. A math teacher wants to see if two of her classes have the same distribution of test scores. What test should she use?

49. What are the null and alternative hypotheses for Exercise 11.48?

50. A market researcher wants to see if two different stores have the same distribution of sales throughout the year. What type of test should he use?

51. A meteorologist wants to know if East and West Australia have the same distribution of storms. What type of test should she use?

52. What condition must be met to use the test for homogeneity?

Use the following information to answer the next five exercises: Do private practice doctors and hospital doctors have the same distribution of working hours? Suppose that a sample of 100 private practice doctors and 150 hospital doctors are selected at random and asked about the number of hours a week they work. The results are shown in Table 11.27.

Table 11.27

	20–30	30–40	40–50	50–60
Private practice	16	40	38	6
Hospital	8	44	59	39

53. State the null and alternative hypotheses.

54. df = _______

55. What is the test statistic?

56. What can you conclude at the 5% significance level?

11.6 Comparison of the Chi-Square Tests

57. Which test do you use to decide whether an observed distribution is the same as an expected distribution?

58. What is the null hypothesis for the type of test from Exercise 11.57?

59. Which test would you use to decide whether two factors have a relationship?

60. Which test would you use to decide if two populations have the same distribution?

61. How are tests of independence similar to tests for homogeneity?

62. How are tests of independence different from tests for homogeneity?

11.1 Facts About the Chi-Square Distribution

Decide whether the following statements are true or false.

63. As the number of degrees of freedom increases, the graph of the chi-square distribution looks more and more symmetrical.

64. The standard deviation of the chi-square distribution is twice the mean.

65. The mean and the median of the chi-square distribution are the same if $df = 24$.

11.2 Test of a Single Variance

Use the following information to answer the next twelve exercises: Suppose an airline claims that its flights are consistently on time with an average delay of at most 15 minutes. It claims that the average delay is so consistent that the variance is no more than 150 minutes. Doubting the consistency part of the claim, a disgruntled traveler calculates the delays for his next 25 flights. The average delay for those 25 flights is 22 minutes with a standard deviation of 15 minutes.

66. Is the traveler disputing the claim about the average or about the variance?

67. A sample standard deviation of 15 minutes is the same as a sample variance of __________ minutes.

68. Is this a right-tailed, left-tailed, or two-tailed test?

69. H_0: __________

70. df = ________

71. chi-square test statistic = ________

72. Graph the situation. Label and scale the horizontal axis. Mark the mean and test statistic. Shade the area associated with the level of confidence.

73. Let $\alpha = 0.05$

Decision: ________

Conclusion (write out in a complete sentence.): ________

74. How did you know to test the variance instead of the mean?

75. If an additional test were done on the claim of the average delay, which distribution would you use?

76. If an additional test were done on the claim of the average delay, but 45 flights were surveyed, which distribution would you use?

77. A plant manager is concerned her equipment may need recalibrating. It seems that the actual weight of the 15 oz. cereal boxes it fills has been fluctuating. The standard deviation should be at most 0.5 oz. In order to determine if the machine needs to be recalibrated, 84 randomly selected boxes of cereal from the next day's production were weighed. The standard deviation of the 84 boxes was 0.54. Does the machine need to be recalibrated?

78. Consumers may be interested in whether the cost of a particular calculator varies from store to store. Based on surveying 43 stores, which yielded a sample mean of $84 and a sample standard deviation of $12, test the claim that the standard deviation is greater than $15.

79. Isabella, an accomplished Bay to Breakers runner, claims that the standard deviation for her time to run the 7.5 mile race is at most three minutes. To test her claim, Rupinder looks up five of her race times. They are 55 minutes, 61 minutes, 58 minutes, 63 minutes, and 57 minutes.

80. Airline companies are interested in the consistency of the number of babies on each flight, so that they have adequate safety equipment. They are also interested in the variation of the number of babies. Suppose that an airline executive believes the average number of babies on flights is six with a variance of nine at most. The airline conducts a survey. The results of the 18 flights surveyed give a sample average of 6.4 with a sample standard deviation of 3.9. Conduct a hypothesis test of the airline executive's belief.

81. The number of births per woman in China is 1.6 down from 5.91 in 1966. This fertility rate has been attributed to the law passed in 1979 restricting births to one per woman. Suppose that a group of students studied whether or not the standard deviation of births per woman was greater than 0.75. They asked 50 women across China the number of births they had had. The results are shown in **Table 11.28.** Does the students' survey indicate that the standard deviation is greater than 0.75?

Table 11.28

# of births	Frequency
0	5
1	30
2	10
3	5

82. According to an avid aquarist, the average number of fish in a 20-gallon tank is 10, with a standard deviation of two. His friend, also an aquarist, does not believe that the standard deviation is two. She counts the number of fish in 15 other 20-gallon tanks. Based on the results that follow, do you think that the standard deviation is different from two? Data: 11; 10; 9; 10; 10; 11; 11; 10; 12; 9; 7; 9; 11; 10; 11

83. The manager of "Frenchies" is concerned that patrons are not consistently receiving the same amount of French fries with each order. The chef claims that the standard deviation for a ten-ounce order of fries is at most 1.5 oz., but the manager thinks that it may be higher. He randomly weighs 49 orders of fries, which yields a mean of 11 oz. and a standard deviation of two oz.

84. You want to buy a specific computer. A sales representative of the manufacturer claims that retail stores sell this computer at an average price of $1,249 with a very narrow standard deviation of $25. You find a website that has a price comparison for the same computer at a series of stores as follows: $1,299; $1,229.99; $1,193.08; $1,279; $1,224.95; $1,229.99; $1,269.95; $1,249. Can you argue that pricing has a larger standard deviation than claimed by the manufacturer? Use the 5% significance level. As a potential buyer, what would be the practical conclusion from your analysis?

85. A company packages apples by weight. One of the weight grades is Class A apples. Class A apples have a mean weight of 150 g, and there is a maximum allowed weight tolerance of 5% above or below the mean for apples in the same consumer package. A batch of apples is selected to be included in a Class A apple package. Given the following apple weights of the batch, does the fruit comply with the Class A grade weight tolerance requirements. Conduct an appropriate hypothesis test.

(a) at the 5% significance level

(b) at the 1% significance level

Weights in selected apple batch (in grams): 158; 167; 149; 169; 164; 139; 154; 150; 157; 171; 152; 161; 141; 166; 172;

11.3 Goodness-of-Fit Test

86. A six-sided die is rolled 120 times. Fill in the expected frequency column. Then, conduct a hypothesis test to determine if the die is fair. The data in **Table 11.29** are the result of the 120 rolls.

Table 11.29

Face value	Frequency	Expected frequency
1	15	
2	29	
3	16	
4	15	
5	30	
6	15	

87. The marital status distribution of the U.S. male population, ages 15 and older, is as shown in Table 11.30.

Table 11.30

Marital status	Percent	Expected frequency
Never married	31.3	
Married	56.1	
Widowed	2.5	
Divorced/Separated	10.1	

Suppose that a random sample of 400 U.S. young adult males, 18 to 24 years old, yielded the following frequency distribution. We are interested in whether this age group of males fits the distribution of the U.S. adult population. Calculate the frequency one would expect when surveying 400 people. Fill in Table 11.30, rounding to two decimal places.

Table 11.31

Marital status	Frequency
Never married	140
Married	238
Widowed	2
Divorced/Separated	20

Use the following information to answer the next two exercises: The columns in Table 11.32 contain the Race/Ethnicity of U.S. Public Schools for a recent year, the percentages for the Advanced Placement Examinee Population for that class, and the Overall Student Population. Suppose the right column contains the result of a survey of 1,000 local students from that year who took an AP Exam.

Table 11.32

Race/Ethnicity	AP examinee population	Overall student population	Survey frequency
Asian, Asian American, or Pacific Islander	10.2%	5.4%	113
Black or African-American	8.2%	14.5%	94
Hispanic or Latino	15.5%	15.9%	136
American Indian or Alaska Native	0.6%	1.2%	10
White	59.4%	61.6%	604
Not reported/other	6.1%	1.4%	43

88. Perform a goodness-of-fit test to determine whether the local results follow the distribution of the U.S. overall student population based on ethnicity.

89. Perform a goodness-of-fit test to determine whether the local results follow the distribution of U.S. AP examinee population, based on ethnicity.

90. The City of South Lake Tahoe, CA, has an Asian population of 1,419 people, out of a total population of 23,609. Suppose that a survey of 1,419 self-reported Asians in the Manhattan, NY, area yielded the data in Table 11.33. Conduct a goodness-of-fit test to determine if the self-reported sub-groups of Asians in the Manhattan area fit that of the Lake Tahoe area.

Table 11.33

Race	Lake Tahoe frequency	Manhattan frequency
Asian Indian	131	174
Chinese	118	557
Filipino	1,045	518
Japanese	80	54
Korean	12	29
Vietnamese	9	21
Other	24	66

Use the following information to answer the next two exercises: UCLA conducted a survey of more than 263,000 college freshmen from 385 colleges in fall 2005. The results of students' expected majors by gender were reported in *The Chronicle of Higher Education (2/2/2006)*. Suppose a survey of 5,000 graduating females and 5,000 graduating males was done as a follow-up last year to determine what their actual majors were. The results are shown in the tables for Exercise 11.91 and Exercise 11.92. The second column in each table does not add to 100% because of rounding.

91. Conduct a goodness-of-fit test to determine if the actual college majors of graduating females fit the distribution of their expected majors.

Table 11.34

Major	Women - expected major	Women - actual major
Arts & Humanities	14.0%	670
Biological Sciences	8.4%	410
Business	13.1%	685
Education	13.0%	650
Engineering	2.6%	145
Physical Sciences	2.6%	125

Professional	18.9%	975
Social Sciences	13.0%	605
Technical	0.4%	15
Other	5.8%	300
Undecided	8.0%	420

92. Conduct a goodness-of-fit test to determine if the actual college majors of graduating males fit the distribution of their expected majors.

Table 11.35

Major	Men - expected major	Men - actual major
Arts & Humanities	11.0%	600
Biological Sciences	6.7%	330
Business	22.7%	1130
Education	5.8%	305
Engineering	15.6%	800
Physical Sciences	3.6%	175
Professional	9.3%	460
Social Sciences	7.6%	370
Technical	1.8%	90
Other	8.2%	400
Undecided	6.6%	340

Read the statement and decide whether it is true or false.

93. In general, if the observed values and expected values of a goodness-of-fit test are not close together, then the test statistic can get very large and on a graph will be way out in the right tail.

94. Use a goodness-of-fit test to determine if high school principals believe that students are absent equally during the week or not.

95. The test to use to determine if a six-sided die is fair is a goodness-of-fit test.

96. In a goodness-of fit test, if the p-value is 0.0113, in general, do not reject the null hypothesis.

97. A sample of 212 commercial businesses was surveyed for recycling one commodity; a commodity here means any one type of recyclable material such as plastic or aluminum. Table 11.36 shows the business categories in the survey, the sample size of each category, and the number of businesses in each category that recycle one commodity. Based on the study, on average half of the businesses were expected to be recycling one commodity. As a result, the last column shows the expected number of businesses in each category that recycle one commodity. At the 5% significance level, perform a hypothesis test to determine if the observed number of businesses that recycle one commodity follows the uniform distribution of the expected values.

Table 11.36

Business type	Number in class	Observed number that recycle one commodity	Expected number that recycle one commodity
Office	35	19	17.5
Retail/Wholesale	48	27	24
Food/Restaurants	53	35	26.5
Manufacturing/Medical	52	21	26
Hotel/Mixed	24	9	12

98. **Table 11.37** contains information from a survey among 499 participants classified according to their age groups. The second column shows the percentage of obese people per age class among the study participants. The last column comes from a different study at the national level that shows the corresponding percentages of obese people in the same age classes in the USA. Perform a hypothesis test at the 5% significance level to determine whether the survey participants are a representative sample of the USA obese population.

Table 11.37

Age class (years)	Obese (percentage)	Expected USA average (percentage)
20–30	15.0	32.6
31–40	26.5	32.6
41–50	13.6	36.6
51–60	21.9	36.6
61–70	21.0	39.7

11.4 Test of Independence

99. A recent debate about where in the United States skiers believe the skiing is best prompted the following survey. Test to see if the best ski area is independent of the level of the skier.

Table 11.38

U.S. ski area	Beginner	Intermediate	Advanced
Tahoe	20	30	40
Utah	10	30	60
Colorado	10	40	50

100. Car manufacturers are interested in whether there is a relationship between the size of car an individual drives and the number of people in the driver's family (that is, whether car size and family size are independent). To test this, suppose that 800 car owners were randomly surveyed with the results in **Table 11.39**. Conduct a test of independence.

Table 11.39

Family Size	Sub & Compact	Mid-size	Full-size	Van & Truck
1	20	35	40	35
2	20	50	70	80
3–4	20	50	100	90
5+	20	30	70	70

101. College students may be interested in whether or not their majors have any effect on starting salaries after graduation. Suppose that 300 recent graduates were surveyed as to their majors in college and their starting salaries after graduation. Table 11.40 shows the data. Conduct a test of independence.

Table 11.40

Major	< \$50,000	\$50,000 – \$68,999	\$69,000 +
English	5	20	5
Engineering	10	30	60
Nursing	10	15	15
Business	10	20	30
Psychology	20	30	20

102. Some travel agents claim that honeymoon hot spots vary according to age of the bride. Suppose that 280 recent brides were interviewed as to where they spent their honeymoons. The information is given in Table 11.41. Conduct a test of independence.

Table 11.41

Location	20–29	30–39	40–49	50 and over
Niagara Falls	15	25	25	20
Poconos	15	25	25	10
Europe	10	25	15	5
Virgin Islands	20	25	15	5

103. A manager of a sports club keeps information concerning the main sport in which members participate and their ages. To test whether there is a relationship between the age of a member and his or her choice of sport, 643 members of the sports club are randomly selected. Conduct a test of independence.

Table 11.42

Sport	18 - 25	26 - 30	31 - 40	41 and over
Racquetball	42	58	30	46
Tennis	58	76	38	65
Swimming	72	60	65	33

104. A major food manufacturer is concerned that the sales for its skinny french fries have been decreasing. As a part of a feasibility study, the company conducts research into the types of fries sold across the country to determine if the type of fries sold is independent of the area of the country. The results of the study are shown in **Table 11.43**. Conduct a test of independence.

Table 11.43

Type of Fries	Northeast	South	Central	West
Skinny fries	70	50	20	25
Curly fries	100	60	15	30
Steak fries	20	40	10	10

105. According to Dan Lenard, an independent insurance agent in the Buffalo, N.Y. area, the following is a breakdown of the amount of life insurance purchased by males in the following age groups. He is interested in whether the age of the male and the amount of life insurance purchased are independent events. Conduct a test for independence.

Table 11.44

Age of males	None	< $200,000	$200,000–$400,000	$401,001–$1,000,000	$1,000,001+
20–29	40	15	40	0	5
30–39	35	5	20	20	10
40–49	20	0	30	0	30
50+	40	30	15	15	10

106. Suppose that 600 thirty-year-olds were surveyed to determine whether or not there is a relationship between the level of education an individual has and salary. Conduct a test of independence.

Table 11.45

Annual salary	Not a high school graduate	High school graduate	College graduate	Masters or doctorate
< $30,000	15	25	10	5
$30,000–$40,000	20	40	70	30
$40,000–$50,000	10	20	40	55
$50,000–$60,000	5	10	20	60
$60,000+	0	5	10	150

Read the statement and decide whether it is true or false.

107. The number of degrees of freedom for a test of independence is equal to the sample size minus one.

108. The test for independence uses tables of observed and expected data values.

109. The test to use when determining if the college or university a student chooses to attend is related to his or her socioeconomic status is a test for independence.

110. In a test of independence, the expected number is equal to the row total multiplied by the column total divided by the total surveyed.

111. An ice cream maker performs a nationwide survey about favorite flavors of ice cream in different geographic areas of the U.S. Based on Table 11.46, do the numbers suggest that geographic location is independent of favorite ice cream flavors? Test at the 5% significance level.

Table 11.46

U.S. region/ Flavor	Strawberry	Chocolate	Vanilla	Rocky road	Mint chocolate chip	Pistachio	Row total
West	12	21	22	19	15	8	97
Midwest	10	32	22	11	15	6	96
East	8	31	27	8	15	7	96
South	15	28	30	8	15	6	102
Column total	45	112	101	46	60	27	391

112. Table 11.47 provides a recent survey of the youngest online entrepreneurs whose net worth is estimated at one million dollars or more. Their ages range from 17 to 30. Each cell in the table illustrates the number of entrepreneurs who correspond to the specific age group and their net worth. Are the ages and net worth independent? Perform a test of independence at the 5% significance level.

Table 11.47

Age group\ Net worth value (in millions of US dollars)	1–5	6–24	≥25	Row total
17–25	8	7	5	20
26–30	6	5	9	20
Column total	14	12	14	40

113. A 2013 poll in California surveyed people about taxing sugar-sweetened beverages. The results are presented in Table 11.48, and are classified by ethnic group and response type. Are the poll responses independent of the participants' ethnic group? Conduct a test of independence at the 5% significance level.

Table 11.48

Opinion/ Ethnicity	Asian-American	White/Non-Hispanic	African-American	Latino	Row total
Against tax	48	433	41	160	682
In favor of tax	54	234	24	147	459
No opinion	16	43	16	19	94
Column total	118	710	81	326	1235

11.5 Test for Homogeneity

114. A psychologist is interested in testing whether there is a difference in the distribution of personality types for business majors and social science majors. The results of the study are shown in Table 11.49. Conduct a test of homogeneity. Test at a 5% level of significance.

Table 11.49

	Open	Conscientious	Extrovert	Agreeable	Neurotic
Business	41	52	46	61	58
Social Science	72	75	63	80	65

115. Do men and women select different breakfasts? The breakfasts ordered by randomly selected men and women at a popular breakfast place is shown in **Table 11.50**. Conduct a test for homogeneity at a 5% level of significance.

Table 11.50

	French toast	Pancakes	Waffles	Omelettes
Men	47	35	28	53
Women	65	59	55	60

116. A fisherman is interested in whether the distribution of fish caught in Green Valley Lake is the same as the distribution of fish caught in Echo Lake. Of the 191 randomly selected fish caught in Green Valley Lake, 105 were rainbow trout, 27 were other trout, 35 were bass, and 24 were catfish. Of the 293 randomly selected fish caught in Echo Lake, 115 were rainbow trout, 58 were other trout, 67 were bass, and 53 were catfish. Perform a test for homogeneity at a 5% level of significance.

117. In 2007, the United States had 1.5 million homeschooled students, according to the U.S. National Center for Education Statistics. In **Table 11.51** you can see that parents decide to homeschool their children for different reasons, and some reasons are ranked by parents as more important than others. According to the survey results shown in the table, is the distribution of applicable reasons the same as the distribution of the most important reason? Provide your assessment at the 5% significance level. Did you expect the result you obtained?

Table 11.51

Reasons for Homeschooling	Applicable reason (in thousands of respondents)	Most important reason (in thousands of respondents)	Row total
Concern about the environment of other schools	1,321	309	1,630
Dissatisfaction with academic instruction at other schools	1,096	258	1,354
To provide religious or moral instruction	1,257	540	1,797
Child has special needs, other than physical or mental	315	55	370
Nontraditional approach to child's education	984	99	1,083
Other reasons (e.g., finances, travel, family time, etc.)	485	216	701
Column total	5,458	1,477	6,935

118. When looking at energy consumption, we are often interested in detecting trends over time and how they correlate among different countries. The information in Table 11.52 shows the average energy use (in units of kg of oil equivalent per capita) in the USA and the joint European Union countries (EU) for the six-year period 2005 to 2010. Do the energy use values in these two areas come from the same distribution? Perform the analysis at the 5% significance level.

Table 11.52

Year	European Union	United States	Row total
2010	3,413	7,164	10,557
2009	3,302	7,057	10,359
2008	3,505	7,488	10,993
2007	3,537	7,758	11,295
2006	3,595	7,697	11,292
2005	3,613	7,847	11,460
Column total	20,965	45,011	65,976

119. The Insurance Institute for Highway Safety collects safety information about all types of cars every year, and publishes a report of Top Safety Picks among all cars, makes, and models. Table 11.53 presents the number of Top Safety Picks in six car categories for the two years 2009 and 2013. Analyze the table data to conclude whether the distribution of cars that earned the Top Safety Picks safety award has remained the same between 2009 and 2013. Derive your results at the 5% significance level.

Table 11.53

Year \ Car type	Small	Mid-size	Large	Small SUV	Mid-size SUV	Large SUV	Row total
2009	12	22	10	10	27	6	87
2013	31	30	19	11	29	4	124
Column total	43	52	29	21	56	10	211

11.6 Comparison of the Chi-Square Tests

120. Is there a difference between the distribution of community college statistics students and the distribution of university statistics students in what technology they use on their homework? Of some randomly selected community college students, 43 used a computer, 102 used a calculator with built in statistics functions, and 65 used a table from the textbook. Of some randomly selected university students, 28 used a computer, 33 used a calculator with built in statistics functions, and 40 used a table from the textbook. Conduct an appropriate hypothesis test using a 0.05 level of significance.

Read the statement and decide whether it is true or false.

121. If $df = 2$, the chi-square distribution has a shape that reminds us of the exponential.

Bringing It Together: Homework

122. a. Explain why a goodness-of-fit test and a test of independence are generally right-tailed tests.

b. If you did a left-tailed test, what would you be testing?

REFERENCES

11.1 Facts About the Chi-Square Distribution

Data from *Parade Magazine.*

"HIV/AIDS Epidemiology Santa Clara County."Santa Clara County Public Health Department, May 2011.

11.2 Test of a Single Variance

"AppleInsider Price Guides." Apple Insider, 2013. Available online at http://appleinsider.com/mac_price_guide (accessed May 14, 2013).

Data from the World Bank, June 5, 2012.

11.3 Goodness-of-Fit Test

Data from the U.S. Census Bureau

Data from the College Board. Available online at http://www.collegeboard.com.

Data from the U.S. Census Bureau, Current Population Reports.

Ma, Y., E.R. Bertone, E.J. Stanek III, G.W. Reed, J.R. Hebert, N.L. Cohen, P.A. Merriam, I.S. Ockene, "Association between Eating Patterns and Obesity in a Free-living US Adult Population." *American Journal of Epidemiology* volume 158, no. 1, pages 85-92.

Ogden, Cynthia L., Margaret D. Carroll, Brian K. Kit, Katherine M. Flegal, "Prevalence of Obesity in the United States, 2009–2010." NCHS Data Brief no. 82, January 2012. Available online at http://www.cdc.gov/nchs/data/databriefs/db82.pdf (accessed May 24, 2013).

Stevens, Barbara J., "Multi-family and Commercial Solid Waste and Recycling Survey." Arlington Count, VA. Available online at http://www.arlingtonva.us/departments/EnvironmentalServices/SW/file84429.pdf (accessed May 24,2013).

11.4 Test of Independence

DiCamilo, Mark, Mervin Field, "Most Californians See a Direct Linkage between Obesity and Sugary Sodas. Two in Three Voters Support Taxing Sugar-Sweetened Beverages If Proceeds are Tied to Improving School Nutrition and Physical Activity Programs." The Field Poll, released Feb. 14, 2013. Available online at http://field.com/fieldpollonline/subscribers/Rls2436.pdf (accessed May 24, 2013).

Harris Interactive, "Favorite Flavor of Ice Cream." Available online at http://www.statisticbrain.com/favorite-flavor-of-ice-cream (accessed May 24, 2013)

"Youngest Online Entrepreneurs List." Available online at http://www.statisticbrain.com/youngest-online-entrepreneur-list (accessed May 24, 2013).

11.5 Test for Homogeneity

Data from the Insurance Institute for Highway Safety, 2013. Available online at www.iihs.org/iihs/ratings (accessed May 24, 2013).

"Energy use (kg of oil equivalent per capita)." The World Bank, 2013. Available online at http://data.worldbank.org/indicator/EG.USE.PCAP.KG.OE/countries (accessed May 24, 2013).

"Parent and Family Involvement Survey of 2007 National Household Education Survey Program (NHES)," U.S. Department of Education, National Center for Education Statistics. Available online at http://nces.ed.gov/pubsearch/pubsinfo.asp?pubid=2009030 (accessed May 24, 2013).

"Parent and Family Involvement Survey of 2007 National Household Education Survey Program (NHES)," U.S. Department of Education, National Center for Education Statistics. Available online at http://nces.ed.gov/pubs2009/2009030_sup.pdf (accessed May 24, 2013).

SOLUTIONS

1. mean = 25 and standard deviation = 7.0711

3. when the number of degrees of freedom is greater than 90

5. $df = 2$

6. a test of a single variance

8. a left-tailed test

10 $H_0: \sigma^2 = 0.81^2$;

$H_a: \sigma^2 > 0.81^2$

12. a test of a single variance

16. a goodness-of-fit test

18. 3

20. 2.04

21. We decline to reject the null hypothesis. There is not enough evidence to suggest that the observed test scores are significantly different from the expected test scores.

23. H_0: the distribution of AIDS cases follows the ethnicities of the general population of Santa Clara County.

25. right-tailed

27. 2016.136

28. Graph: Check student's solution. Decision: Cannot accept the null hypothesis. Reason for the Decision: Calculated value of test statistics is either in or out of the tail of the distribution.

Conclusion (write out in complete sentences): The make-up of AIDS cases does not fit the ethnicities of the general population of Santa Clara County.

30. a test of independence

32. a test of independence

34. 8

36. 6.6

39.

Table 11.54

Smoking level per day	African American	Native Hawaiian	Latino	Japanese Americans	White	Totals
1-10	9,886	2,745	12,831	8,378	7,650	41,490
11-20	6,514	3,062	4,932	10,680	9,877	35,065
21-30	1,671	1,419	1,406	4,715	6,062	15,273
31+	759	788	800	2,305	3,970	8,622
Totals	18,830	8,014	19,969	26,078	27,559	10,0450

41.

Table 11.55

Smoking level per day	African American	Native Hawaiian	Latino	Japanese Americans	White
1-10	7777.57	3310.11	8248.02	10771.29	11383.01
11-20	6573.16	2797.52	6970.76	9103.29	9620.27
21-30	2863.02	1218.49	3036.20	3965.05	4190.23
31+	1616.25	687.87	1714.01	2238.37	2365.49

43. 10,301.8

44. right

46. a. Cannot accept the null hypothesis.

b. Calculated value of test statistics is either in or out of the tail of the distribution.

c. There is sufficient evidence to conclude that smoking level is dependent on ethnic group.

48. test for homogeneity

50. test for homogeneity

52. All values in the table must be greater than or equal to five.

54. 3

57. a goodness-of-fit test

59. a test for independence

61. Answers will vary. Sample answer: Tests of independence and tests for homogeneity both calculate the test statistic the same way $\sum_{(ij)} \frac{(O-E)^2}{E}$. In addition, all values must be greater than or equal to five.

63. true

65. false

67. 225

69. H_0: $\sigma^2 \leq 150$

71. 36

72. Check student's solution.

74. The claim is that the variance is no more than 150 minutes.

76. a Student's *t*- or normal distribution

78.
a. H_0: $\sigma = 15$
b. H_a: $\sigma > 15$
c. $df = 42$
d. chi-square with $df = 42$
e. test statistic = 26.88
f. Check student's solution.
g.
  i. Alpha = 0.05
  ii. Decision: Cannot reject null hypothesis.
  iii. Reason for decision: Calculated value of test statistics is either in or out of the tail of the distribution.
  iv. Conclusion: There is insufficient evidence to conclude that the standard deviation is greater than 15.

80.
a. H_0: $\sigma \leq 3$
b. H_a: $\sigma > 3$
c. $df = 17$
d. chi-square distribution with $df = 17$
e. test statistic = 28.73
f. Check student's solution.
g.

i. Alpha: 0.05
ii. Decision: Cannot accept the null hypothesis.
iii. Reason for decision: Calculated value of test statistics is either in or out of the tail of the distribution.
iv. Conclusion: There is sufficient evidence to conclude that the standard deviation is greater than three.

82. a. H_0: $\sigma = 2$

b. H_a: $\sigma \neq 2$

c. $df = 14$

d. chi-square distribution with $df = 14$

e. chi-square test statistic = 5.2094

f. Check student's solution.

g.

i. Alpha = 0.05
ii. Decision: Cannot accept the null hypothesis
iii. Reason for decision: Calculated value of test statistics is either in or out of the tail of the distribution.
iv. Conclusion: There is sufficient evidence to conclude that the standard deviation is different than 2.

84. The sample standard deviation is $34.29.

$H_0 : \sigma^2 = 25^2$

$H_a : \sigma^2 > 25^2$

$df = n - 1 = 7.$

test statistic: $x^2 = x_7^2 = \frac{(n-1)s^2}{25^2} = \frac{(8-1)(34.29)^2}{25^2} = 13.169$;

Alpha: 0.05

Decision: Cannot reject the null hypothesis.

Reason for decision: Calculated value of test statistics is either in or out of the tail of the distribution.

Conclusion: At the 5% level, there is insufficient evidence to conclude that the variance is more than 625.

87. Table

11.56

Marital status	Percent	Expected frequency
Never married	31.3	125.2
Married	56.1	224.4

Marital status	Percent	Expected frequency
Widowed	2.5	10
Divorced/Separated	10.1	40.4

a. The data fits the distribution.
b. The data does not fit the distribution.
c. 3
d. chi-square distribution with $df = 3$
e. 19.27
f. 0.0002
g. Check student's solution.
h.
   i. Alpha = 0.05
   ii. Decision: Cannot accept null hypothesis at the 5% level of significance
   iii. Reason for decision: Calculated value of test statistics is either in or out of the tail of the distribution.
   iv. Conclusion: Data does not fit the distribution.

89. a. H_0: The local results follow the distribution of the U.S. AP examinee population
b. H_a: The local results do not follow the distribution of the U.S. AP examinee population
c. $df = 5$
d. chi-square distribution with $df = 5$
e. chi-square test statistic = 13.4
f. Check student's solution.
g.
   i. Alpha = 0.05
   ii. Decision: Cannot accept null when $a = 0.05$
   iii. Reason for Decision: Calculated value of test statistics is either in or out of the tail of the distribution.
   iv. Conclusion: Local data do not fit the AP Examinee Distribution.
   v. Decision: Do not reject null when $a = 0.01$
   vi. Conclusion: There is insufficient evidence to conclude that local data do not follow the distribution of the U.S. AP examinee distribution.

91. *a.* H_0: The actual college majors of graduating females fit the distribution of their expected majors
b. H_a: The actual college majors of graduating females do not fit the distribution of their expected majors

c. $df = 10$
d. chi-square distribution with $df = 10$
e. test statistic = 11.48
f. Check student's solution.
g.
   i. Alpha = 0.05
   ii. Decision: Cannot reject null when $a = 0.05$ and $a = 0.01$
   iii. Reason for decision: Calculated value of test statistics is either in or out of the tail of the distribution.
   iv. Conclusion: There is insufficient evidence to conclude that the distribution of actual college majors of graduating females fits the distribution of their expected majors.

94. true

96. false

98. The hypotheses for the goodness-of-fit test are:

a. H_0: Surveyed obese fit the distribution of expected obese
b. H_a: Surveyed obese do not fit the distribution of expected obese
   Use a chi-square distribution with $df = 4$ to evaluate the data.
   The test statistic is $X^2 = 9.85$
   The P-value = 0.0431

At 5% significance level, $\alpha = 0.05$. For this data, $P < \alpha$. Reject the null hypothesis.

At the 5% level of significance, from the data, there is sufficient evidence to conclude that the surveyed obese do not fit the distribution of expected obese.

100. a. H_0: Car size is independent of family size.
b. H_a: Car size is dependent on family size.
c. $df = 9$
d. chi-square distribution with $df = 9$
f. test statistic = 15.8284
g. Check student's solution.
h.
   i. Alpha: 0.05
   ii. Decision: Cannot reject the null hypothesis.
   iii. Reason for decision: Calculated value of test statistics is either in or out of the tail of the distribution.
   iv. Conclusion: At the 5% significance level, there is insufficient evidence to conclude that car size and family size are dependent.

102. a. H_0: Honeymoon locations are independent of bride's age.
b. H_a: Honeymoon locations are dependent on bride's age.
c. $df = 9$
d. chi-square distribution with $df = 9$
e. test statistic = 15.7027
f. Check student's solution.
g.
   i. Alpha: 0.05
   ii. Decision: Cannot reject the null hypothesis.
   iii. Reason for decision: Calculated value of test statistics is either in or out of the tail of the distribution.
   iv. Conclusion: At the 5% significance level, there is insufficient evidence to conclude that honeymoon location and bride age are dependent.

104. *a.* H_0: The types of fries sold are independent of the location.
b. H_a: The types of fries sold are dependent on the location.
c. $df = 6$
d. chi-square distribution with $df = 6$
e. test statistic =18.8369
f. Check student's solution.
g.
   i. Alpha: 0.05
   ii. Decision: Cannot accept the null hypothesis.
   iii. Reason for decision: Calculated value of test statistics is either in or out of the tail of the distribution.
   iv. Conclusion: At the 5% significance level, There is sufficient evidence that types of fries and location are dependent.

106. *a.* H_0: Salary is independent of level of education.
b. H_a: Salary is dependent on level of education.
c $df = 12$
d. chi-square distribution with $df = 12$
e. test statistic = 255.7704
f. Check student's solution.
g. Alpha: 0.05
Decision: Cannot accept the null hypothesis.
Reason for decision: Calculated value of test statistics is either in or out of the tail of the distribution.

Conclusion: At the 5% significance level, there is sufficient evidence to conclude that salary and level of education are dependent.

108. true

110. true

112. H_0: Age is independent of the youngest online entrepreneurs' net worth.

a. H_a: Age is dependent on the net worth of the youngest online entrepreneurs.

b. $df = 2$

c. chi-square distribution with $df = 2$

d. test statistic = 1.76

e. Check student's solution.

f.

i. Alpha: 0.05

ii. Decision: Cannot reject the null hypothesis.

iii. Reason for decision: Calculated value of test statistics is either in or out of the tail of the distribution.

iv. Conclusion: At the 5% significance level, there is insufficient evidence to conclude that age and net worth for the youngest online entrepreneurs are dependent.

114. *a.* H_0: The distribution for personality types is the same for both majors

b. H_a: The distribution for personality types is not the same for both majors

c. $df = 4$

d. chi-square with $df = 4$

e. test statistic = 3.01

f. Check student's solution.

g.

i. Alpha: 0.05

ii. Decision: Cannot reject the null hypothesis.

iii. Reason for decision: Calculated value of test statistics is either in or out of the tail of the distribution.

iv Conclusion: There is insufficient evidence to conclude that the distribution of personality types is different for business and social science majors.

116. *a.* H_0: The distribution for fish caught is the same in Green Valley Lake and in Echo Lake.

b. H_a: The distribution for fish caught is not the same in Green Valley Lake and in Echo Lake.

c. 3

d. chi-square with *df* = 3

e. 11.75

f. Check student's solution.

g.

  i. Alpha: 0.05
  ii. Decision: Cannot accept the null hypothesis.
  iii. Reason for decision: Calculated value of test statistics is either in or out of the tail of the distribution.
  iv. Conclusion: There is evidence to conclude that the distribution of fish caught is different in Green Valley Lake and in Echo Lake

118. *a.* H_0: The distribution of average energy use in the USA is the same as in Europe between 2005 and 2010.

b. H_a: The distribution of average energy use in the USA is not the same as in Europe between 2005 and 2010.

c. *df* = 4

d. chi-square with *df* = 4

e. test statistic = 2.7434

f. Check student's solution.

g.

  i. Alpha: 0.05
  ii. Decision: Cannot reject the null hypothesis.
  iii. Reason for decision: Calculated value of test statistics is either in or out of the tail of the distribution.
  iv. Conclusion: At the 5% significance level, there is insufficient evidence to conclude that the average energy use values in the US and EU are not derived from different distributions for the period from 2005 to 2010.

120. *a.* H_0: The distribution for technology use is the same for community college students and university students.

b. H_a: The distribution for technology use is not the same for community college students and university students.

c. 2

d. chi-square with *df* = 2

e. 7.05

f. *p*-value = 0.0294

g. Check student's solution.

i. Alpha: 0.05
ii. Decision: Cannot accept the null hypothesis.
iii. Reason for decision: p-value < alpha
iv. Conclusion: There is sufficient evidence to conclude that the distribution of technology use for statistics homework is not the same for statistics students at community colleges and at universities.

122. a. The test statistic is always positive and if the expected and observed values are not close together, the test statistic is large and the null hypothesis will be rejected.

b. Testing to see if the data fits the distribution "too well" or is too perfect.

12 Chapter
F DISTRIBUTION AND ONE-WAY ANOVA METHODS

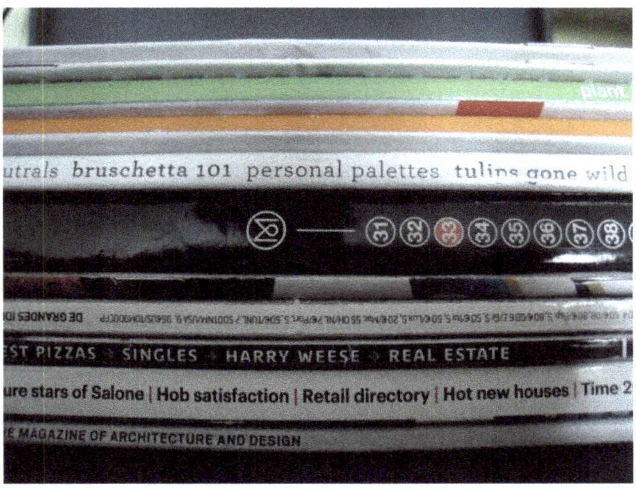

Figure 12.1 One-way ANOVA is used to measure information from several groups.

INTRODUCTION: AN OVERVIEW

Numerous statistical applications in psychology, social sciences, business management, and natural sciences encompass multiple groups. An environmentalist seeks to determine whether the mean level of contamination differs among several bodies of water. A sociologist seeks to determine whether an individual's income is influenced by their upbringing. A consumer seeking a new automobile may evaluate the average fuel efficiency of various models. Statisticians have devised a method known as "Analysis of Variance" (abbreviated ANOVA) for hypothesis testing that compare means across many groups. This chapter will cover the most basic type of ANOVA, known as single factor or one-way ANOVA. You will also examine the F distribution, utilized for one-way ANOVA, and the test for variance comparisons between two groups. This is a concise summary of one-way ANOVA.

One-Way ANOVA, as provided herein, is predominantly dependent on a calculator or computer.

12.1 TEST OF TWO VARIANCES

This chapter introduces a new probability density function, the F distribution. This distribution is used for many applications including ANOVA and for testing equality across multiple means. We begin with the F distribution and the test of hypothesis of differences in variances. It is often desirable to compare two variances rather than two averages. For instance, college administrators would like two college professors grading exams to have the same variation in their grading. In order for a lid to fit a container, the variation in the lid and the container should be approximately the same. A supermarket might be interested in the variability of check-out times for two checkers. In finance, the variance is a measure of risk and thus an interesting question would be to test the hypothesis that two different investment portfolios have the same variance, the volatility.

In order to perform a *F* test of two variances, it is important that the following are true:

1. The populations from which the two samples are drawn are approximately normally distributed.
2. The two populations are independent of each other.

Unlike most other hypothesis tests in this book, the *F* test for equality of two variances is very sensitive to deviations from normality. If the two distributions are not normal, or close, the test can give a biased result for the test statistic.

Suppose we sample randomly from two independent normal populations. Let σ21σ12 and σ22σ22 be the unknown population variances and s21s12 and s22s22 be the sample variances. Let the sample sizes be n_1 and n_2. Since we are interested in comparing the two sample variances, we use the *F* ratio:

$$F = \frac{\left[\frac{s_1^2}{\sigma_1^2}\right]}{\left[\frac{s_2^2}{\sigma_2^2}\right]}$$

F has the distribution $F \sim F(n_1 - 1, n_2 - 1)$

where $n_1 - 1$ are the degrees of freedom for the numerator and $n_2 - 1$ are the degrees of freedom for the denominator.

If the null hypothesis is $\sigma_1^2 = \sigma_2^2$ then the *F* Ratio, test statistic, becomes

$$F_c = \frac{\left[\frac{s_1^2}{\sigma_1^2}\right]}{\left[\frac{s_2^2}{\sigma_2^2}\right]} = \frac{s_1^2}{s_2^2}$$

The various forms of the hypotheses tested are:

Table 12.1

Two-Tailed Test	One-Tailed Test	One-Tailed Test
$H_0: \sigma_1^2 = \sigma_2^2$	$H_0: \sigma_1^2 \leq \sigma_2^2$	$H_0: \sigma_1^2 \geq \sigma_2^2$
$H_1: \sigma_1^2 \neq \sigma_2^2$	$H_1: \sigma_1^2 > \sigma_2^2$	$H_1: \sigma_1^2 < \sigma_2^2$

A more general form of the null and alternative hypothesis for a two tailed test would be :

$$H_0 : \frac{\sigma_1^2}{\sigma_2^2} = \delta_0$$

$$H_a : \frac{\sigma_1^2}{\sigma_2^2} \neq \delta_0$$

Where if $\delta_0 = 1$ it is a simple test of the hypothesis that the two variances are equal. This form of the hypothesis does have the benefit of allowing for tests that are more than for simple differences and can accommodate tests for specific differences as we did for differences in means and differences in proportions. This form of the hypothesis also shows the relationship between the F distribution and the χ^2 : the F is a ratio of two chi squared distributions a distribution we saw in the last chapter. This is helpful in determining the degrees of freedom of the resultant F distribution.

If the two populations have equal variances, then s_1^2 and s_2^2 are close in value and the test statistic $F_c = \frac{s_1^2}{s_2^2}$ is close to one. But if the two population variances are very different, s_1^2 and s_2^2 tend to be very different, too. Choosing s_1^2 as the larger sample variance causes the ratio $\frac{s_1^2}{s_2^2}$ to be greater than one. If s_1^2 and s_2^2 are far apart, then $F_c = \frac{s_1^2}{s_2^2}$ is a large number.

Therefore, if *F* is close to one, the evidence favors the null hypothesis (the two population variances are equal). But if *F* is much larger than one, then the evidence is against the null hypothesis. In essence, we are asking if the calculated F statistic, test statistic, is significantly different from one.

To determine the critical points we have to find $F_{\alpha, df1, df2}$. See Appendix A for the F table. This F table has values for various levels of significance from 0.1 to 0.001 designated as "p" in the first column. To find the critical value choose the desired significance level and follow down and across to find the critical value at the intersection of the two different degrees of freedom. The F distribution has two different degrees of freedom, one associated with the numerator, $_{df1}$, and one associated with the denominator, $_{df2}$ and to complicate matters the F distribution is not symmetrical and changes the degree of skewness as the degrees of freedom change. The degrees of freedom in the numerator is n_1-1, where n_1 is the sample size for group 1, and the degrees of freedom in the denominator is n_2-1, where n_2 is the sample size for group 2. $F_{\alpha, df1, df2}$ will give the critical value on the upper end of the F distribution.

To find the critical value for the lower end of the distribution, reverse the degrees of freedom and divide the F-value from the table into one.

- Upper tail critical value : $F_{\alpha, df1, df2}$
- Lower tail critical value : $1/F_{\alpha, df2, df1}$

When the calculated value of F is between the critical values, not in the tail, we cannot reject the null hypothesis that the two variances came from a population with the same variance. If the calculated F-value is in either tail we cannot accept the null hypothesis just as we have been doing for all of the previous tests of hypothesis.

An alternative way of finding the critical values of the F distribution makes the use of the F-table easier. We note in the F-table that all the values of F are greater than one therefore the critical F value for the left hand tail will always be less than one because to find the critical value on the left tail we divide an F value into the number one as shown above. We also note that if the sample variance in the numerator of the test statistic is larger than the sample variance in the denominator, the resulting F value will be greater than one. The shorthand method for this test is thus to be sure that the larger of the two sample variances is placed in the numerator to calculate the test statistic. This will mean that only the right hand tail critical value will have to be found in the F-table.

EXAMPLE 12.1

Two college instructors are interested in whether or not there is any variation in the way they grade math exams. They each grade the same set of 10 exams. The first instructor's grades have a variance of 52.3. The second instructor's grades have a variance of 89.9. Test the claim that the first instructor's variance is smaller. (In most colleges, it is desirable for the variances of exam grades to be nearly the same among instructors.) The level of significance is 10%.

Solution 12.1

Let 1 and 2 be the subscripts that indicate the first and second instructor, respectively.

$n_1 = n_2 = 10$.

H_0: σ21≥σ22σ12≥σ22 and H_a: σ21 < σ22σ12 < σ22

Calculate the test statistic: By the null hypothesis (σ21 ≥ σ22)(σ12 ≥ σ22), the F

$$F_c = \frac{s_2{}^2}{s_1{}^2} = \frac{89.9}{52.3} = 1.719$$

Critical value for the test: $F_{9,9} = 5.35$ where $n_1 - 1 = 9$ and $n_2 - 1 = 9$.

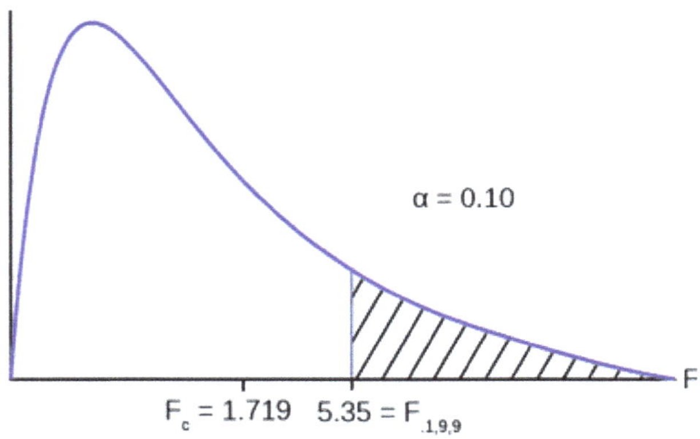

Figure 12.2

Make a decision: Since the calculated F value is not in the tail we cannot reject H_0.

Conclusion: With a 10% level of significance, from the data, there is insufficient evidence to conclude that the variance in grades for the first instructor is smaller.

TRY IT 12.1

The New York Choral Society divides male singers up into four categories from highest voices to lowest: Tenor1, Tenor2, Bass1, Bass2. In the table are heights of the men in the Tenor1 and Bass2 groups. One suspects that taller men will have lower voices, and that the variance of height may go up with the lower voices as well. Do we have good evidence that the variance of the heights of singers in each of these two groups (Tenor1 and Bass2) are different?

Table 12.2

Tenor1	Bass 2	Tenor 1	Bass 2	Tenor 1	Bass 2
69	72	67	72	68	67
72	75	70	74	67	70
71	67	65	70	64	70
66	75	72	66		69
76	74	70	68		72
74	72	68	75		71
71	72	64	68		74
66	74	73	70		75
68	72	66	72		

12.2 ONE-WAY ANOVA

The purpose of a one-way ANOVA test is to determine the existence of a statistically significant difference among several group means. The test actually uses **variances** to help determine if the means are equal or not. In order to perform a one-way ANOVA test, there are five basic **assumptions** to be fulfilled:

1. Each population from which a sample is taken is assumed to be normal.
2. All samples are randomly selected and independent.
3. The populations are assumed to have equal standard deviations (or variances).
4. The factor is a categorical variable.
5. The response is a numerical variable.

The Null and Alternative Hypotheses

The null hypothesis is simply that all the group population means are the same. The alternative hypothesis is that at least one pair of means is different. For example, if there are *k* groups:

H0:μ1=μ2=μ3=. . .μk$H0:\mu1=\mu2=\mu3=...\mu k$

HaHa: At least two of the group means μ1,μ2,μ3,. . . ,μk$\mu1,\mu2,\mu3,...,\mu k$ are not equal. That is, $\mu i \neq \mu j$ for some $i \neq j$.

The graphs, a set of box plots representing the distribution of values with the group means indicated by a horizontal line through the box, help in the understanding of the hypothesis test. In the first graph (red box plots), $H_0: \mu_1 = \mu_2 = \mu_3$ and the three populations have the same distribution if the null hypothesis is true. The variance of the combined data is approximately the same as the variance of each of the populations.

If the null hypothesis is false, then the variance of the combined data is larger which is caused by the different means as shown in the second graph (green box plots).

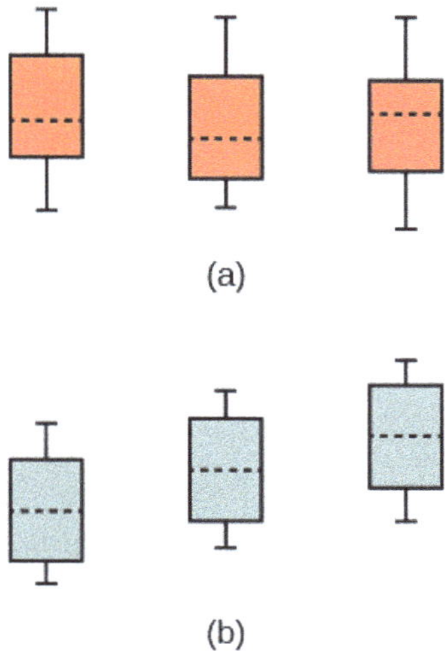

Figure 12.3 (a) H_0 is true. All means are the same; the differences are due to random variation. (b) H_0 is not true. All means are not the same; the differences are too large to be due to random variation.

12.3 THE F DISTRIBUTION AND THE F-RATIO

The distribution used for the hypothesis test is a new one. It is called the ***F* distribution**, invented by George Snedecor but named in honor of Sir Ronald Fisher, an English statistician. The *F* statistic is a ratio (a fraction). There are two sets of degrees of freedom; one for the numerator and one for the denominator.

For example, if *F* follows an *F* distribution and the number of degrees of freedom for the numerator is four, and the number of degrees of freedom for the denominator is ten, then $F \sim F_{4,10}$.

To calculate the ***F* ratio**, two estimates of the variance are made.

- **Variance between samples:** An estimate of σ^2 that is the variance of the sample means multiplied by *n* (when the sample sizes are the same.). If the samples are different sizes, the variance between samples is weighted to account for the different sample sizes. The variance is also called variation due to treatment or explained variation.
- **Variance within samples:** An estimate of σ^2 that is the average of the sample variances (also known as a pooled variance). When the sample sizes are different, the variance within samples is weighted. The variance is also called the variation due to error or unexplained variation.

1. $SS_{between}$ = the **sum of squares** that represents the variation among the different samples
2. SS_{within} = the sum of squares that represents the variation within samples that is due to chance.

To find a "sum of squares" means to add together squared quantities that, in some cases, may be weighted. We used sum of squares to calculate the sample variance and the sample standard deviation in Chapter 2 Descriptive Statistics.

MS means "mean square." $MS_{between}$ is the variance between groups, and MS_{within} is the variance within groups.

Calculation of Sum of Squares and Mean Square

- k = the number of different groups
- n_j = the size of the jth group
- s_j = the sum of the values in the jth group
- n = total number of all the values combined (total sample size: Σn_j)
- x = one value: $\Sigma x = \Sigma s_j$
- Sum of squares of all values from every group combined: Σx^2
- Between group variability: $SS_{total} = \Sigma x^2 - \frac{\left(\sum x^2\right)}{n}$
- Total sum of squares: $\sum x^2 - \frac{\left(\sum x\right)^2}{n}$
- Explained variation: sum of squares representing variation among the different samples:

$$SS_{between} = \sum\left[\frac{(s_j)^2}{n_j}\right] - \frac{\left(\sum s_j\right)^2}{n}$$

- Unexplained variation: sum of squares representing variation within samples due to chance: $SS_{within} = SS_{total} - SS_{between}$
- df's for different groups (df's for the numerator): $df = k - 1$
- Equation for errors within samples (df's for the denominator): $df_{within} = n - k$
- Mean square (variance estimate) explained by the different groups:

$$MS_{within} = \frac{SS_{within}}{df_{within}}$$

- Mean square (variance estimate) that is due to chance (unexplained):

$$MS_{between} = \frac{SS_{between}}{df_{between}}$$

- $MS_{between}$ and MS_{within} can be written as follows:
- $MS_{between} = \frac{SS_{between}}{df_{between}} = \frac{SS_{between}}{k-1}$

- $MS_{within} = \frac{SS_{within}}{df_{within}} = \frac{SS_{within}}{n - k}$

The one-way ANOVA test depends on the fact that $MS_{between}$ can be influenced by population differences among means of the several groups. Since MS_{within} compares values of each group to its own group mean, the fact that group means might be different does not affect MS_{within}.

The null hypothesis says that all groups are samples from populations having the same normal distribution. The alternate hypothesis says that at least two of the sample groups come from populations with different normal distributions. If the null hypothesis is true, $MS_{between}$ and MS_{within} should both estimate the same value.

NOTE

The null hypothesis says that all the group population means are equal. The hypothesis of equal means implies that the populations have the same normal distribution, because it is assumed that the populations are normal and that they have equal variances.

F-Ratio or *F* Statistic

$$F = \frac{MS_{\text{between}}}{MS_{\text{within}}}$$

If $MS_{between}$ and MS_{within} estimate the same value (following the belief that H_0 is true), then the *F*-ratio should be approximately equal to one. Mostly, just sampling errors would contribute to variations away from one. As it turns out, $MS_{between}$ consists of the population variance plus a variance produced from the differences between the samples. MS_{within} is an estimate of the population variance. Since variances are always positive, if the null hypothesis is false, $MS_{between}$ will generally be larger than MS_{within}.Then the *F*-ratio will be larger than one. However, if the population effect is small, it is not unlikely that MS_{within} will be larger in a given sample.

The foregoing calculations were done with groups of different sizes. If the groups are the same size, the calculations simplify somewhat and the *F*-ratio can be written as:

_F_-Ratio Formula when the groups are the same size

$$F = \frac{n \cdot s_{\overline{x}}^{\ 2}}{s^2_{\ \text{pooled}}}$$

where ...

- n = the sample size
- $df_{numerator} = k - 1$
- $df_{denominator} = n - k$
- s^2 pooled = the mean of the sample variances (pooled variance)
- sx–2sx–2 = the variance of the sample means

Data are typically put into a table for easy viewing. One-Way ANOVA results are often displayed in this manner by computer software.

Table 12.3

Source of variation	Sum of squares (SS)	Degrees of freedom (df)	Mean square (MS)	F
Factor (Between)	SS(Factor)	k – 1	MS(Factor) = SS(Factor)/(k – 1)	F = MS(Factor)/MS(Error)
Error (Within)	SS(Error)	n – k	MS(Error) = SS(Error)/(n – k)	
Total	SS(Total)	n – 1		

EXAMPLE 12.2

Three different diet plans are to be tested for mean weight loss. The entries in the table are the weight losses for the different plans. The one-way ANOVA results are shown in Table 12.4.

Table 12.4

Plan 1: n1 = 4	Plan 2: n2 = 3	Plan 3: n3 = 3
5	3.5	8
4.5	7	4
4		3.5
3	4.5	

$s_1 = 16.5$, $s_2 = 15$, $s_3 = 15.5$

Following are the calculations needed to fill in the one-way ANOVA table. The table is used to conduct a hypothesis test.

$$SS(between) = \sum\left[\frac{(s_j)^2}{n_j}\right] - \frac{\left(\sum s_j\right)^2}{n}$$

$$= \frac{s_1^2}{4} + \frac{s_2^2}{3} + \frac{s_3^2}{3} - \frac{(s_1 + s_2 + s_3)^2}{10}$$

where $n_1 = 4, n_2 = 3, n_3 = 3$ and $n = n_1 + n_2 + n_3 = 10$

$$= \frac{(16.5)^2}{4} + \frac{(15)^2}{3} + \frac{(15.5)^2}{3} - \frac{(16.5 + 15 + 15.5)^2}{10}$$

$$SS(between) = 2.2458$$

$$S(total) = \sum x^2 - \frac{(\sum x)^2}{n}$$

$$= \left(5^2 + 4.5^2 + 4^2 + 3^2 + 3.5^2 + 7^2 + 4.5^2 + 8^2 + 4^2 + 3.5^2\right)$$

$$- \frac{(5 + 4.5 + 4 + 3 + 3.5 + 7 + 4.5 + 8 + 4 + 3.5)^2}{10}$$

$$= 244 - \frac{47^2}{10} = 244 - 220.9$$

$$SS(total) = 23.1$$

$$SS(within) = SS(total) - SS(between)$$

$$= 23.1 - 2.2458$$

$$SS(within) = 20.8542$$

Table 12.5

Source of variation	Sum of squares (SS)	Degrees of freedom (df)	Mean square (MS)	F
Factor (Between)	SS(Factor) = SS(Between) = 2.2458	k – 1 = 3 groups – 1 = 2	MS(Factor) = SS(Factor)/ (k – 1) = 2.2458/2 = 1.1229	F = MS(Factor)/ MS(Error) = 1.1229/2.9792 = 0.3769
Error (Within)	SS(Error) = SS(Within) = 20.8542	n – k = 10 total data – 3 groups = 7	MS(Error) = SS(Error)/ (n – k) = 20.8542/7 = 2.9792	
Total	SS(Total) = 2.2458 + 20.8542 = 23.1	n – 1 = 10 total data – 1 = 9		

TRY IT 12.2

As part of an experiment to see how different types of soil cover would affect slicing tomato production, Marist College students grew tomato plants under different soil cover conditions. Groups of three plants each had one of the following treatments

- bare soil
- a commercial ground cover
- black plastic
- straw
- compost

All plants grew under the same conditions and were the same variety. Students recorded the weight (in grams) of tomatoes produced by each of the n = 15 plants:

Table 12.6

Bare: n1 = 3	Ground Cover: n2 = 3	Plastic: n3 = 3	Straw: n4 = 3	Compost: n5 = 3
2,625	5,348	6,583	7,285	6,277
2,997	5,682	8,560	6,897	7,818
4,915	5,482	3,830	9,230	8,677

Create the one-way ANOVA table.

The one-way ANOVA hypothesis test is always right-tailed because larger F-values are way out in the right tail of the F-distribution curve and tend to make us reject H_0.

EXAMPLE 12.3

Let's return to the slicing tomato exercise in Try It 12.2. The means of the tomato yields under the five mulching conditions are represented by $\mu_1, \mu_2, \mu_3, \mu_4, \mu_5$. We will conduct a hypothesis test to determine if all means are the same or at least one is different. Using a significance level of 5%, test the null hypothesis that there is no difference in mean yields among the five groups against the alternative hypothesis that at least one mean is different from the rest.

Solution 12.3

The null and alternative hypotheses are:

$H_0: \mu_1 = \mu_2 = \mu_3 = \mu_4 = \mu_5$

$H_a: \mu_i \neq \mu_j$ some $i \neq j$

The one-way ANOVA results are shown in Table 12.7

Table 12.7

Source of variation	Sum of squares (SS)	Degrees of freedom (df)	Mean square (MS)	F
Factor (Between)	36,648,561	5 − 1 = 4	$\frac{36,648,561}{4} = 9,162,140$	$\frac{9,162,140}{2,044,672.6} = 4.4810$
Error (Within)	20,446,726	15 − 5 = 10	$\frac{20,446,726}{10} = 2,044,672.6$	
Total	57,095,287	15 − 1 = 14		

Distribution for the test: $F_{4,10}$

$df(num) = 5 - 1 = 4$

$df(denom) = 15 - 5 = 10$

Test statistic: $F = 4.4810$

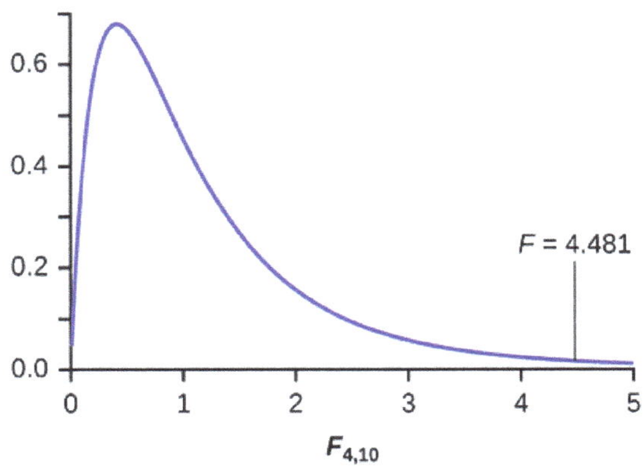

Figure 12.4

Probability Statement: p-value = $P(F > 4.481) = 0.0248$.

Compare α and the p-value: $\alpha = 0.05$, p-value = 0.0248

Make a decision: Since $\alpha > p$-value, we cannot accept H_0.

Conclusion: At the 5% significance level, we have reasonably strong evidence that differences in mean yields for slicing tomato plants grown under different mulching conditions are unlikely to be due to chance alone. We may conclude that at least some of mulches led to different mean yields.

TRY IT 12.3

MRSA, or *Staphylococcus aureus*, can cause a serious bacterial infections in hospital patients. Table 12.8 shows various colony counts from different patients who may or may not have MRSA. The data from the table is plotted in Figure 12.5.

Table 12.8

Conc = 0.6	Conc = 0.8	Conc = 1.0	Conc = 1.2	Conc = 1.4
9	16	22	30	27
66	93	147	199	168
98	82	120	148	132

Plot of the data for the different concentrations:

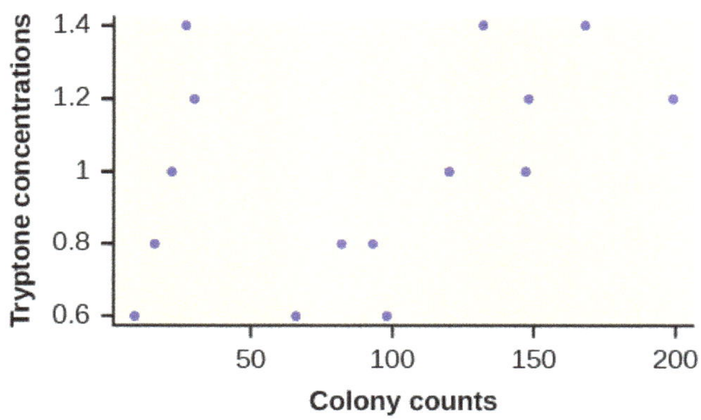

Figure 12.5

Test whether the mean number of colonies are the same or are different. Construct the ANOVA table, find the *p*-value, and state your conclusion. Use a 5% significance level.

EXAMPLE 12.4

Four sororities took a random sample of sisters regarding their grade means for the past term. The results are shown in Table 12.9.

Table 12.9 Mean grades for four sororities

Sorority 1	Sorority 2	Sorority 3	Sorority 4
2.17	2.63	2.63	3.79
1.85	1.77	3.78	3.45
2.83	3.25	4.00	3.08
1.69	1.86	2.55	2.26
3.33	2.21	2.45	3.18

Using a significance level of 1%, is there a difference in mean grades among the sororities?

Solution 12.4

Let $\mu1$, $\mu2$, $\mu3$, $\mu4$ be the population means of the sororities. Remember that the null hypothesis claims that the sorority groups are from the same normal distribution. The alternate hypothesis says that at least two of the sorority groups come from populations with different normal distributions. Notice that the four sample sizes are each five.

NOTE

This is an example of a balanced design, because each factor (i.e., sorority) has the same number of observations.

$H0$: $\mu1 = \mu2 = \mu3 = \mu4$

Ha: Not all of the means $\mu1$, $\mu2$, $\mu3$, $\mu4$ are equal.

Distribution for the test: $F3,16$

where $k = 4$ groups and $n = 20$ samples in total

$df(num) = k - 1 = 4 - 1 = 3$

$df(denom) = n - k = 20 - 4 = 16$

Calculate the test statistic: $F = 2.23$

Graph:

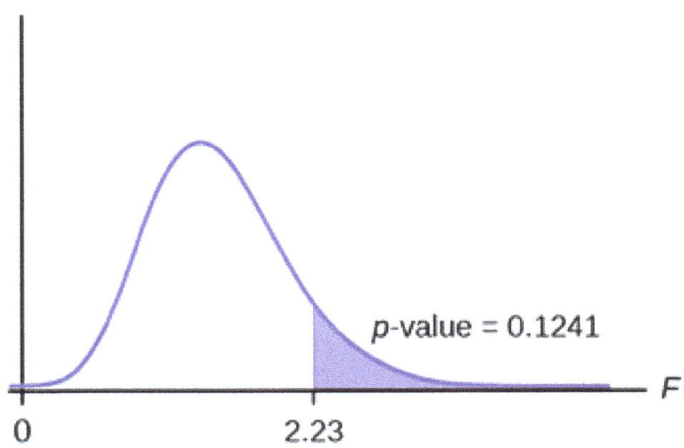

Figure 12.6

Probability statement: p-value = $P(F > 2.23) = 0.1241$

Compare α and the p-value: $\alpha = 0.01$

p-value = 0.1241

$\alpha < p$-value

Make a decision: Since $\alpha < p$-value, you cannot reject *H0*.

Conclusion: There is not sufficient evidence to conclude that there is a difference among the mean grades for the sororities.

TRY IT 12.4

Four sports teams took a random sample of players regarding their GPAs for the last year. The results are shown in Table 12.10.

Table 12.10 GPAs for four sports teams

Basketball	Baseball	Hockey	Lacrosse
3.6	2.1	4.0	2.0
2.9	2.6	2.0	3.6
2.5	3.9	2.6	3.9
3.3	3.1	3.2	2.7
3.8	3.4	3.2	2.5

Use a significance level of 5%, and determine if there is a difference in GPA among the teams.

EXAMPLE 12.5

A fourth grade class is studying the environment. One of the assignments is to grow bean plants in different soils. Tommy chose to grow his bean plants in soil found outside his classroom mixed with dryer lint. Tara chose to grow her bean plants in potting soil bought at the local nursery. Nick chose to grow his bean plants in soil from his mother's garden. No chemicals were used on the plants, only water. They were grown inside the classroom next to a large window. Each child grew five plants. At the end of the growing period, each plant was measured, producing the data (in inches) in Table 12.11.

Table 12.11

Tommy's plants	Tara's plants	Nick's plants
24	25	23
21	31	27
23	23	22
30	20	30
23	28	20

Does it appear that the three media in which the bean plants were grown produce the same mean height? Test at a 3% level of significance.

Solution 12.5

This time, we will perform the calculations that lead to the F' statistic. Notice that each group has the same number of plants, so we will use the formula $F' = \frac{n \cdot s_{\bar{x}}^{2}}{s^{2}_{pooled}}$.

First, calculate the sample mean and sample variance of each group.

Table 12.12

	Tommy's plants	Tara's plants	Nick's plants
Sample mean	24.2	25.4	24.4
Sample variance	11.7	18.3	16.3

Next, calculate the variance of the three group means (Calculate the variance of 24.2, 25.4, and 24.4). Variance of the group means = 0.413 = sx−2sx−2

Then $MS_{between} = ns_{\bar{x}}^{2} = (5)(0.413)$ where n = 5 is the sample size (number of plants each child grew).

Calculate the mean of the three sample variances (Calculate the mean of 11.7, 18.3, and 16.3). Mean of the sample variances = 15.433 = s^2 *pooled*

Then $MS_{within} = s^2_{pooled} = 15.433$.

The F statistic (or F ratio) is $F = \frac{MS_{\text{between}}}{MS_{\text{within}}} = \frac{ns_{\bar{x}}^{2}}{s^{2}_{pooled}} = \frac{(5)(0.413)}{15.433} = 0.134$

The *dfs* for the numerator = the number of groups – 1 = 3 – 1 = 2.

The *dfs* for the denominator = the total number of samples – the number of groups = 15 – 3 = 12

The distribution for the test is $F_{2,12}$ and the F statistic is $F = 0.134$

The p-value is $P(F > 0.134) = 0.8759$.

Decision: Since $\alpha = 0.03$ and the p-value = 0.8759, then you cannot reject H_0. (Why?)

Conclusion: With a 3% level of significance, from the sample data, the evidence is not sufficient to conclude that the mean heights of the bean plants are different.

Notation

The notation for the F distribution is $F \sim F_{df(num),df(denom)}$

where $df(num) = df_{\text{between}}$ and $df(denom) = df_{\text{within}}$

The mean for the F distribution is $\mu = \frac{df(num)}{df(denom) - 2}$

12.4 FACTS ABOUT THE F DISTRIBUTION

Here are some facts about the *F* distribution.

1. The curve is not symmetrical but skewed to the right.
2. There is a different curve for each set of degrees of freedom.
3. The *F* statistic is greater than or equal to zero.
4. As the degrees of freedom for the numerator and for the denominator get larger, the curve approximates the normal as can be seen in the two figures below. Figure (b) with more degrees of freedom is more closely approaching the normal distribution, but remember that the *F* cannot ever be less than zero so the distribution does not have a tail that goes to infinity on the left as the normal distribution does.
5. Other uses for the *F* distribution include comparing two variances and two-way Analysis of Variance. Two-Way Analysis is beyond the scope of this chapter.

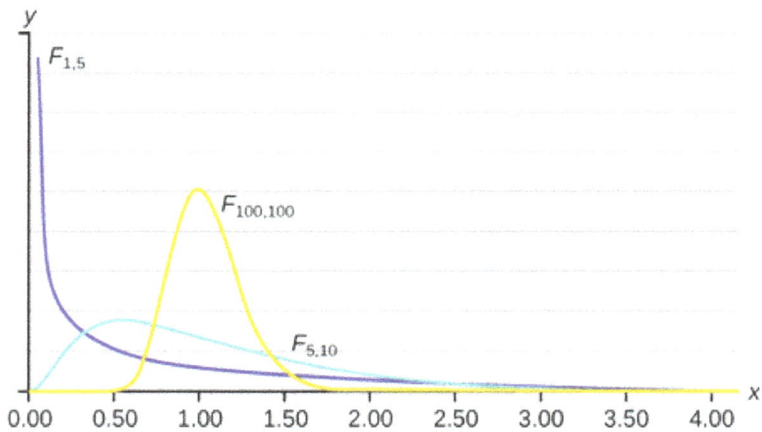

Figure 12.7

Key Terms

Analysis of Variance also referred to as ANOVA, is a method of testing whether or not the means of three or more populations are equal. The method is applicable if:

- all populations of interest are normally distributed.
- the populations have equal standard deviations.
- samples (not necessarily of the same size) are randomly and independently selected from each population.
- there is one independent variable and one dependent variable.

The test statistic for analysis of variance is the *F*-ratio.

One-Way ANOVA a method of testing whether or not the means of three or more populations are equal; the method is applicable if:

- all populations of interest are normally distributed.
- the populations have equal standard deviations.
- samples (not necessarily of the same size) are randomly and independently selected from each population.

The test statistic for analysis of variance is the *F*-ratio.

Variance mean of the squared deviations from the mean; the square of the standard deviation. For a set of data, a deviation can be represented as $x - \overline{x}$ where *x* is a value of the data and $\overline{x}$ is the sample mean. The sample variance is equal to the sum of the squares of the deviations divided by the difference of the sample size and one.

CHAPTER REVIEW

12.1 Test of Two Variances

The *F* test for the equality of two variances rests heavily on the assumption of normal distributions. The test is unreliable if this assumption is not met. If both distributions are normal, then the ratio of the two sample variances is distributed as an *F* statistic, with numerator and denominator degrees of freedom that are one less than the samples sizes of the corresponding two groups. A **test of two variances** hypothesis test determines if two variances are the same. The distribution for the hypothesis test is the *F* distribution with two different degrees of freedom.

Assumptions:

1. The populations from which the two samples are drawn are normally distributed.
2. The two populations are independent of each other.

12.2 One-Way ANOVA

Analysis of variance extends the comparison of two groups to several, each a level of a categorical variable (factor). Samples from each group are independent, and must be randomly selected from normal populations with equal variances. We test the null hypothesis of equal means of the response in every group versus the alternative hypothesis of one or more group means being different from the others. A one-way ANOVA hypothesis test determines if several population means are equal. The distribution for the test is the *F* distribution with two different degrees of freedom.

Assumptions:

1. Each population from which a sample is taken is assumed to be normal.
2. All samples are randomly selected and independent.
3. The populations are assumed to have equal standard deviations (or variances).

12.3 The F Distribution and the F-Ratio

Analysis of variance compares the means of a response variable for several groups. ANOVA compares the variation within each group to the variation of the mean of each group. The ratio of these two is the *F* statistic from an *F* distribution with (number of groups – 1) as the numerator degrees of freedom and (number of observations – number of groups) as the denominator degrees of freedom. These statistics are summarized in the ANOVA table.

12.4 Facts About the F Distribution

The graph of the *F* distribution is always positive and skewed right, though the shape can be mounded or exponential depending on the combination of numerator and denominator degrees of freedom. The *F* statistic is the ratio of a measure of the variation in the group means to a similar measure of the variation within the groups. If the null hypothesis is correct, then the numerator should be small compared to the denominator. A small *F* statistic will result, and the area under the *F* curve to the right will be large, representing a large *p*-value. When the null hypothesis of equal group means is incorrect, then the numerator should be large compared to the denominator, giving a large *F* statistic and a small area (small *p*-value) to the right of the statistic under the *F* curve.

When the data have unequal group sizes (unbalanced data), then techniques from 12.3 The F Distribution and the F-Ratio need to be used for hand calculations. In the case of balanced data (the groups are the same size) however, simplified calculations based on group means and variances may be used. In practice, of course, software is usually employed in the analysis. As in any analysis, graphs of various sorts should be used in conjunction with numerical techniques. Always look at your data!

FORMULA REVIEW

12.1 Test of Two Variances

$$H_0: \frac{\sigma_1^2}{\sigma_2^2} = \delta_0$$

$$H_a: \frac{\sigma_1^2}{\sigma_2^2} \neq \delta_0$$

if δ0=1 then

$$H_0 : \sigma_1^2 = \sigma_2^2$$
$$H_a : \sigma_1^2 \neq \sigma_2$$

Test statistic is :

$$F_c = \frac{S_1^2}{S_2^2}$$

12.3 The F Distribution and the F-Ratio

$$SS_{\text{between}} = \sum \left[\frac{(s_j)^2}{n_j} \right] - \frac{\left(\sum s_j \right)^2}{n}$$

$$SS_{\text{total}} = \sum x^2 - \frac{\left(\sum x \right)^2}{n}$$

$$SS_{\text{within}} = SS_{\text{total}} - SS_{\text{between}}$$

$$df_{\text{between}} = df(num) = k - 1$$

$$df_{\text{within}} = df(denom) = n - k$$

$$MS_{\text{between}} = \frac{SS_{\text{between}}}{df_{\text{between}}}$$

$$MS_{\text{within}} = \frac{SS_{\text{within}}}{df_{\text{within}}}$$

$$F = \frac{MS_{\text{between}}}{MS_{\text{within}}}$$

- k = the number of groups
- n_j = the size of the jth group
- s_j = the sum of the values in the jth group
- n = the total number of all values (observations) combined
- x = one value (one observation) from the data
- sx–² = the variance of the sample means
- s²pooled$s2pooled$ = the mean of the sample variances (pooled variance)

PRACTICE

12.1 Test of Two Variances

Use the following information to answer the next two exercises. There are two assumptions that must be true in order to perform an *F* test of two variances.

1. Name one assumption that must be true.

2. What is the other assumption that must be true?

Use the following information to answer the next five exercises. Two coworkers commute from the same building. They are interested in whether or not there is any variation in the time it takes them to drive to work. They each record their times for 20 commutes. The first worker's times have a variance of 12.1. The second worker's times have a variance of 16.9. The first worker thinks that he is more consistent with his commute times. Test the claim at the 10% level. Assume that commute times are normally distributed.

3. State the null and alternative hypotheses.

4. What is s_1 in this problem?

5. What is s_2 in this problem?

6. What is n?

7. What is the *F* statistic?

8. What is the critical value?

9. Is the claim accurate?

Use the following information to answer the next four exercises. Two students are interested in whether or not there is variation in their test scores for math class. There are 15 total math tests they have taken so far. The first student's grades have a standard deviation of 38.1. The second student's grades have a standard deviation of 22.5. The second student thinks his scores are more consistent.

10. State the null and alternative hypotheses.

11. What is the *F* Statistic?

12. What is the critical value?

13. At the 5% significance level, do we reject the null hypothesis?

Use the following information to answer the next three exercises. Two cyclists are comparing the variances of their overall paces going uphill. Each cyclist records his or her speeds going up 35 hills. The first cyclist has a variance of 23.8 and the second cyclist has a variance of 32.1. The cyclists want to see if their variances are the same or different. Assume that commute times are normally distributed.

14. State the null and alternative hypotheses.

15. What is the *F* Statistic?

16. At the 5% significance level, what can we say about the cyclists' variances?

12.2 One-Way ANOVA

Use the following information to answer the next five exercises. There are five basic assumptions that must be fulfilled in order to perform a one-way ANOVA test. What are they?

17. Write one assumption.

18. Write another assumption.

19. Write a third assumption.

20. Write a fourth assumption.

12.3 The F Distribution and the F-Ratio

Use the following information to answer the next eight exercises. Groups of men from three different areas of the country are to be tested for mean weight. The entries in Table 12.13 are the weights for the different groups.

Table 12.13

Group 1	Group 2	Group 3
216	202	170
198	213	165
240	284	182
187	228	197
176	210	201

21. What is the Sum of Squares Factor?

22. What is the Sum of Squares Error?

23. What is the *df* for the numerator?

24. What is the *df* for the denominator?

25. What is the Mean Square Factor?

26. What is the Mean Square Error?

27. What is the *F* statistic?

Use the following information to answer the next eight exercises. Girls from four different soccer teams are to be tested for mean goals scored per game. The entries in Table 12.14 are the goals per game for the different teams.

Table 12.14

Team 1	Team 2	Team 3	Team 4
1	2	0	3
2	3	1	4
0	2	1	4
3	4	0	3
2	4	0	2

28. What is $SS_{between}$?

29. What is the *df* for the numerator?

30. What is $MS_{between}$?

31. What is SS_{within}?

32. What is the *df* for the denominator?

33. What is MS_{within}?

34. What is the *F* statistic?

35. Judging by the *F* statistic, do you think it is likely or unlikely that you will reject the null hypothesis?

12.4 Facts About the F Distribution

36. An *F* statistic can have what values?

37. What happens to the curves as the degrees of freedom for the numerator and the denominator get larger?

Use the following information to answer the next seven exercise. Four basketball teams took a random sample of players regarding how high each player can jump (in inches). The results are shown in Table 12.15.

Table 12.15

Team 1	Team 2	Team 3	Team 4	Team 5
36	32	48	38	41
42	35	50	44	39
51	38	39	46	40

38. What is the *df(num)*?

39. What is the *df(denom)*?

40. What are the Sum of Squares and Mean Squares Factors?

41. What are the Sum of Squares and Mean Squares Errors?

42. What is the *F* statistic?

43. What is the *p*-value?

44. At the 5% significance level, is there a difference in the mean jump heights among the teams?

Use the following information to answer the next seven exercises. A video game developer is testing a new game on three different groups. Each group represents a different target market for the game. The developer collects scores from a random sample from each group. The results are shown in Table 12.16

Table 12.16

Group A	Group B	Group C
101	151	101
108	149	109
98	160	198
107	112	186
111	126	160

45. What is the *df(num)*?

46. What is the *df(denom)*?

47. What are the $SS_{between}$ and $MS_{between}$?

48. What are the SS_{within} and MS_{within}?

49. What is the *F* Statistic?

50. What is the *p*-value?

51. At the 10% significance level, are the scores among the different groups different?

Use the following information to answer the next three exercises. Suppose a group is interested in determining whether teenagers obtain their drivers licenses at approximately the same average age across the country. Suppose that the following data are randomly collected from five teenagers in each region of the country. The numbers represent the age at which teenagers obtained their drivers licenses.

Table 12.17

	Northeast	South	West	Central	East
	16.3	16.9	16.4	16.2	17.1
	16.1	16.5	16.5	16.6	17.2
	16.4	16.4	16.6	16.5	16.6
	16.5	16.2	16.1	16.4	16.8
$\bar{x}$ =	________	________	________	________	________
s^2=	________	________	________	________	________

Enter the data into your calculator or computer.

52. p-value = ______

State the decisions and conclusions (in complete sentences) for the following preconceived levels of α.

53. $\alpha = 0.05$

a. Decision: ________________________________

b. Conclusion: ______________________________

54. $\alpha = 0.01$

a. Decision: ________________________________

b. Conclusion: ______________________________

Homework

12.1 Test of Two Variances

55. Three students, Linda, Tuan, and Javier, are given five laboratory rats each for a nutritional experiment. Each rat's weight is recorded in grams. Linda feeds her rats Formula A, Tuan feeds his rats Formula B, and Javier feeds his rats Formula C. At the end of a specified time period, each rat is weighed again and the net gain in grams is recorded.+

Table 12.18

Linda's rats	Tuan's rats	Javier's rats
43.5	47.0	51.2
39.4	40.5	40.9
41.3	38.9	37.9
46.0	46.3	45.0
38.2	44.2	48.6

Determine whether or not the variance in weight gain is statistically the same among Javier's and Linda's rats. Test at a significance level of 10%.

56. A grassroots group opposed to a proposed increase in the gas tax claimed that the increase would hurt working-class people the most, since they commute the farthest to work. Suppose that the group randomly surveyed 24 individuals and asked them their daily one-way commuting mileage. The results are as follows.

Table 12.19

Working-class	Professional (middle incomes)	Professional (wealthy)
17.8	16.5	8.5
26.7	17.4	6.3
49.4	22.0	4.6

Working-class	Professional (middle incomes)	Professional (wealthy)
9.4	7.4	12.6
65.4	9.4	11.0
47.1	2.1	28.6
19.5	6.4	15.4
51.2	13.9	9.3

Determine whether or not the variance in mileage driven is statistically the same among the working class and professional (middle income) groups. Use a 5% significance level.

Use the following information to answer the next two exercises. The following table lists the number of pages in four different types of magazines.

Table 12.20

Home decorating	News	Health	Computer
172	87	82	104
286	94	153	136
163	123	87	98
205	106	103	207
197	101	96	146

57. Which two magazine types do you think have the same variance in length?

58. Which two magazine types do you think have different variances in length?

59. Is the variance for the amount of money, in dollars, that shoppers spend on Saturdays at the mall the same as the variance for the amount of money that shoppers spend on Sundays at the mall? Suppose that the Table 12.21 shows the results of a study.

Table 12.21

Saturday	Sunday	Saturday	Sunday
75	44	62	137
18	58	0	82
150	61	124	39
94	19	50	127
62	99	31	141
73	60	118	73
	89		

60. Are the variances for incomes on the East Coast and the West Coast the same? Suppose that Table 12.22 shows the results of a study. Income is shown in thousands of dollars. Assume that both distributions are normal. Use a level of significance of 0.05.

Table 12.22

East	West
38	71
47	126
30	42
82	51
75	44
52	90
115	88
67	

61. Thirty men in college were taught a method of finger tapping. They were randomly assigned to three groups of ten, with each receiving one of three doses of caffeine: 0 mg, 100 mg, 200 mg. This is approximately the amount in no, one, or two cups of coffee. Two hours after ingesting the caffeine, the men had the rate of finger tapping per minute recorded. The experiment was double blind, so neither the recorders nor the students knew which group they were in. Does caffeine affect the rate of tapping, and if so how?

Table 12.23

Here are the data:

0 mg	100 mg	200 mg	0 mg	100 mg	200 mg
242	248	246	245	246	248
244	245	250	248	247	252
247	248	248	248	250	250
242	247	246	244	246	248
246	243	245	242	244	250

62. King Manuel I, Komnenus ruled the Byzantine Empire from Constantinople (Istanbul) during the years 1145 to 1180 A.D. The empire was very powerful during his reign, but declined significantly afterwards. Coins minted during his era were found in Cyprus, an island in the eastern Mediterranean Sea. Nine coins were from his first coinage, seven from the second, four from the third, and seven from a fourth. These spanned most of his reign. We have data on the silver content of the coins:

Table 12.24

First coinage	Second coinage	Third coinage	Fourth coinage
5.9	6.9	4.9	5.3
6.8	9.0	5.5	5.6
6.4	6.6	4.6	5.5
7.0	8.1	4.5	5.1

First coinage	Second coinage	Third coinage	Fourth coinage
6.6	9.3		6.2
7.7	9.2		5.8
7.2	8.6		5.8
6.9			
6.2			

Did the silver content of the coins change over the course of Manuel's reign?

Here are the means and variances of each coinage. The data are unbalanced.

Table 12.25

	First	Second	Third	Fourth
Mean	6.7444	8.2429	4.875	5.6143
Variance	0.2953	1.2095	0.2025	0.1314

63. The American League and the National League of Major League Baseball are each divided into three divisions: East, Central, and West. Many years, fans talk about some divisions being stronger (having better teams) than other divisions. This may have consequences for the postseason. For instance, in 2012 Tampa Bay won 90 games and did not play in the postseason, while Detroit won only 88 and did play in the postseason. This may have been an oddity, but is there good evidence that in the 2012 season, the American League divisions were significantly different in overall records? Use the following data to test whether the mean number of wins per team in the three American League divisions were the same or not. Note that the data are not balanced, as two divisions had five teams, while one had only four.

Table 12.26

Division	Team	Wins
East	NY Yankees	95
East	Baltimore	93
East	Tampa Bay	90
East	Toronto	73
East	Boston	69

Table 12.27

Division	Team	Wins
Central	Detroit	88
Central	Chicago Sox	85
Central	Kansas City	72
Central	Cleveland	68
Central	Minnesota	66

Table 12.28

Division	Team	Wins
West	Oakland	94
West	Texas	93
West	LA Angels	89
West	Seattle	75

12.2 One-Way ANOVA

64. Three different traffic routes are tested for mean driving time. The entries in the **Table 12.29** are the driving times in minutes on the three different routes.

Table 12.29

Route 1	Route 2	Route 3
30	27	16
32	29	41
27	28	22
35	36	31

State $SS_{between}$, SS_{within}, and the F statistic.

65. Suppose a group is interested in determining whether teenagers obtain their drivers licenses at approximately the same average age across the country. Suppose that the following data are randomly collected from five teenagers in each region of the country. The numbers represent the age at which teenagers obtained their drivers licenses.

Table 12.30

	Northeast	South	West	Central	East
	16.3	16.9	16.4	16.2	17.1
	16.1	16.5	16.5	16.6	17.2
	16.4	16.4	16.6	16.5	16.6
	16.5	16.2	16.1	16.4	16.8
$\bar{x}$ =	________	________	________	________	________
s^2=	________	________	________	________	________

State the hypotheses.

H_0: ____________

H_a: ____________

12.3 The F Distribution and the F-Ratio

Use the following information to answer the next three exercises. Suppose a group is interested in determining whether teenagers obtain their drivers licenses at approximately the same average age across the country. Suppose that the following data are randomly collected from five teenagers in each region of the country. The numbers represent the age at which teenagers obtained their drivers licenses.

Table 12.31

	Northeast	South	West	Central	East
	16.3	16.9	16.4	16.2	17.1
	16.1	16.5	16.5	16.6	17.2
	16.4	16.4	16.6	16.5	16.6
	16.5	16.2	16.1	16.4	16.8
$\bar{x}$ =	________	________	________	________	________
s^2=	________	________	________	________	________

H_0: $\mu_1 = \mu_2 = \mu_3 = \mu_4 = \mu_5$

$H\alpha$: At least any two of the group means $\mu_1, \mu_2, ..., \mu_5$ are not equal.

66. degrees of freedom – numerator: *df*(*num*) = _________

67. degrees of freedom – denominator: *df*(*denom*) = ________

68. *F* statistic = ________

12.4 Facts About the F Distribution

69. Three students, Linda, Tuan, and Javier, are given five laboratory rats each for a nutritional experiment. Each rat's weight is recorded in grams. Linda feeds her rats Formula A, Tuan feeds his rats Formula B, and Javier feeds his rats Formula C. At the end of a specified time period, each rat is weighed again, and the net gain in grams is recorded. Using a significance level of 10%, test the hypothesis that the three formulas produce the same mean weight gain.

Table 12.32 Weights of Student Lab Rats

Linda's rats	Tuan's rats	Javier's rats
43.5	47.0	51.2
39.4	40.5	40.9
41.3	38.9	37.9
46.0	46.3	45.0
38.2	44.2	48.6

70. A grassroots group opposed to a proposed increase in the gas tax claimed that the increase would hurt working-class people the most, since they commute the farthest to work. Suppose that the group randomly surveyed 24 individuals and asked them their daily one-way commuting mileage. The results are in **Table 12.33.** Using a 5% significance level, test the hypothesis that the three mean commuting mileages are the same.

Table 12.33

Working-class	Professional (middle incomes)	Professional (wealthy)
17.8	16.5	8.5
26.7	17.4	6.3
49.4	22.0	4.6
9.4	7.4	12.6
65.4	9.4	11.0
47.1	2.1	28.6
19.5	6.4	15.4
51.2	13.9	9.3

Use the following information to answer the next two exercises. Table 12.34 lists the number of pages in four different types of magazines.

Table 12.34

Home decorating	News	Health	Computer
172	87	82	104
286	94	153	136
163	123	87	98
205	106	103	207
197	101	96	146

71. Using a significance level of 5%, test the hypothesis that the four magazine types have the same mean length.

72. Eliminate one magazine type that you now feel has a mean length different from the others. Redo the hypothesis test, testing that the remaining three means are statistically the same. Use a new solution sheet. Based on this test, are the mean lengths for the remaining three magazines statistically the same?

73. A researcher wants to know if the mean times (in minutes) that people watch their favorite news station are the same. Suppose that **Table 12.35** shows the results of a study.

Table 12.35

CNN	FOX	Local
45	15	72
12	43	37
18	68	56
38	50	60
23	31	51
35	22	

Assume that all distributions are normal, the four population standard deviations are approximately the same, and the data were collected independently and randomly. Use a level of significance of 0.05.

74. Are the means for the final exams the same for all statistics class delivery types? **Table 12.36** shows the scores on final exams from several randomly selected classes that used the different delivery types.

Table 12.36

Online	Hybrid	Face-to-Face
72	83	80
84	73	78
77	84	84
80	81	81
81		86
		79
		82

Assume that all distributions are normal, the four population standard deviations are approximately the same, and the data were collected independently and randomly. Use a level of significance of 0.05.

75. Are the mean number of times a month a person eats out the same for White, Black, Hispanic and Asian people? Suppose that **Table 12.37** shows the results of a study.

Table 12.37

White	Black	Hispanic	Asian
6	4	7	8
8	1	3	3
2	5	5	5
4	2	4	1
6		6	7

Assume that all distributions are normal, the four population standard deviations are approximately the same, and the data were collected independently and randomly. Use a level of significance of 0.05.

76. Are the mean numbers of daily visitors to a ski resort the same for the three types of snow conditions? Suppose that **Table 12.38** shows the results of a study.

Table 12.38

Powder	Machine Made	Hard Packed
1,210	2,107	2,846
1,080	1,149	1,638
1,537	862	2,019
941	1,870	1,178
	1,528	2,233
	1,382	

Assume that all distributions are normal, the four population standard deviations are approximately the same, and the data were collected independently and randomly. Use a level of significance of 0.05.

77. Sanjay made identical paper airplanes out of three different weights of paper, light, medium and heavy. He made four airplanes from each of the weights, and launched them himself across the room. Here are the distances (in meters) that his planes flew.

Table 12.39

Paper type/Trial	Trial 1	Trial 2	Trial 3	Trial 4
Heavy	5.1 meters	3.1 meters	4.7 meters	5.3 meters
Medium	4 meters	3.5 meters	4.5 meters	6.1 meters
Light	3.1 meters	3.3 meters	2.1 meters	1.9 meters

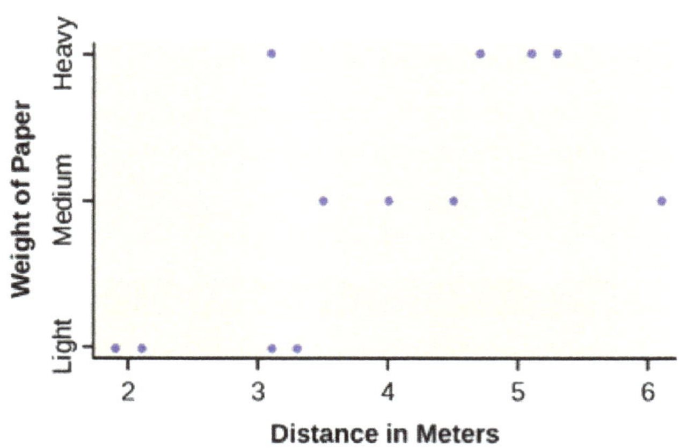

Figure 12.8

a. Take a look at the data in the graph. Look at the spread of data for each group (light, medium, heavy). Does it seem reasonable to assume a normal distribution with the same variance for each group? Yes or No.
b. Why is this a balanced design?
c. Calculate the sample mean and sample standard deviation for each group.
d. Does the weight of the paper have an effect on how far the plane will travel? Use a 1% level of significance. Complete the test using the method shown in the bean plant example in Figure 12.8.
   - variance of the group means __________
   - $MS_{between}$ = ___________
   - mean of the three sample variances ___________
   - MS_{within} = _____________
   - *F* statistic = ____________
   - *df(num)* = __________, *df(denom)* = ___________
   - number of groups _______
   - number of observations _______
   - *p*-value = __________ (*P*(*F* > _______) = __________)
   - Graph the *p*-value.
   - decision: _______________________
   - conclusion: ____ ___________

78. DDT is a pesticide that has been banned from use in the United States and most other areas of the world. It is quite effective, but persisted in the environment and over time became seen as harmful to higher-level organisms. Famously, egg shells of eagles and other raptors were believed to be thinner and prone to breakage in the nest because of ingestion of DDT in the food chain of the birds.

An experiment was conducted on the number of eggs (fecundity) laid by female fruit flies. There are three groups of flies. One group was bred to be resistant to DDT (the RS group). Another was bred to be especially susceptible to DDT (SS). Finally there was a control line of non-selected or typical fruitflies (NS). Here are the data:

Table 12.40

RS	SS	NS	RS	SS	NS
12.8	38.4	35.4	22.4	23.1	22.6
21.6	32.9	27.4	27.5	29.4	40.4
14.8	48.5	19.3	20.3	16	34.4

RS	SS	NS	RS	SS	NS
23.1	20.9	41.8	38.7	20.1	30.4
34.6	11.6	20.3	26.4	23.3	14.9
19.7	22.3	37.6	23.7	22.9	51.8
22.6	30.2	36.9	26.1	22.5	33.8
29.6	33.4	37.3	29.5	15.1	37.9
16.4	26.7	28.2	38.6	31	29.5
20.3	39	23.4	44.4	16.9	42.4
29.3	12.8	33.7	23.2	16.1	36.6
14.9	14.6	29.2	23.6	10.8	47.4
27.3	12.2	41.7			

The values are the average number of eggs laid daily for each of 75 flies (25 in each group) over the first 14 days of their lives. Using a 1% level of significance, are the mean rates of egg selection for the three strains of fruitfly different? If so, in what way? Specifically, the researchers were interested in whether or not the selectively bred strains were different from the nonselected line, and whether the two selected lines were different from each other.

Here is a chart of the three groups:

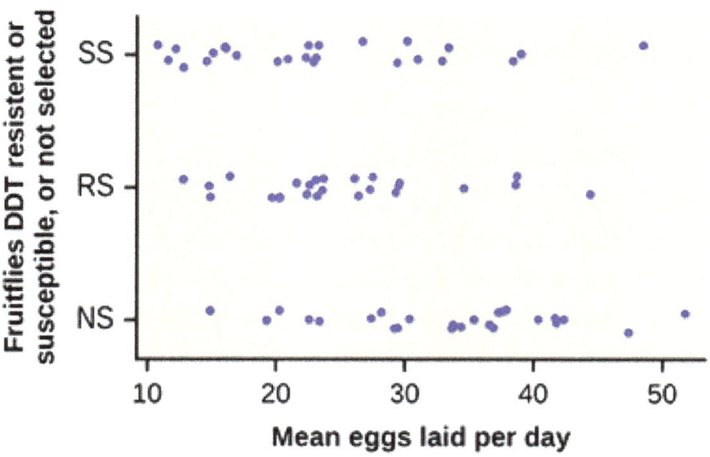

Figure 12.9

79. The data shown is the recorded body temperatures of 130 subjects as estimated from available histograms.

Traditionally we are taught that the normal human body temperature is 98.6 F. This is not quite correct for everyone. Are the mean temperatures among the four groups different?

Calculate 95% confidence intervals for the mean body temperature in each group and comment about the confidence intervals.

Table 12.41

FL	FH	ML	MH	FL	FH	ML	MH
96.4	96.8	96.3	96.9	98.4	98.6	98.1	98.6
96.7	97.7	96.7	97	98.7	98.6	98.1	98.6
97.2	97.8	97.1	97.1	98.7	98.6	98.2	98.7
97.2	97.9	97.2	97.1	98.7	98.7	98.2	98.8
97.4	98	97.3	97.4	98.7	98.7	98.2	98.8
97.6	98	97.4	97.5	98.8	98.8	98.2	98.8
97.7	98	97.4	97.6	98.8	98.8	98.3	98.9
97.8	98	97.4	97.7	98.8	98.8	98.4	99
97.8	98.1	97.5	97.8	98.8	98.9	98.4	99
97.9	98.3	97.6	97.9	99.2	99	98.5	99
97.9	98.3	97.6	98	99.3	99	98.5	99.2
98	98.3	97.8	98		99.1	98.6	99.5
98.2	98.4	97.8	98		99.1	98.6	
98.2	98.4	97.8	98.3		99.2	98.7	
98.2	98.4	97.9	98.4		99.4	99.1	
98.2	98.4	98	98.4		99.9	99.3	
98.2	98.5	98	98.6		100	99.4	
98.2	98.6	98	98.6		100.8		

REFERENCES

12.1 Test of Two Variances

"MLB Vs. Division Standings – 2012." Available online at http://espn.go.com/mlb/standings/_/year/2012/type/vs-division/order/true.

12.3 The F Distribution and the F-Ratio

Tomato Data, Marist College School of Science (unpublished student research)

12.4 Facts About the F Distribution

Data from a fourth grade classroom in 1994 in a private K – 12 school in San Jose, CA.

Hand, D.J., F. Daly, A.D. Lunn, K.J. McConway, and E. Ostrowski. *A Handbook of Small Datasets: Data for Fruitfly Fecundity.* London: Chapman & Hall, 1994.

Hand, D.J., F. Daly, A.D. Lunn, K.J. McConway, and E. Ostrowski. *A Handbook of Small Datasets.* London: Chapman & Hall, 1994, pg. 50.

Hand, D.J., F. Daly, A.D. Lunn, K.J. McConway, and E. Ostrowski. A Handbook of Small Datasets. London: Chapman & Hall, 1994, pg. 118.

"MLB Standings – 2012." Available online at http://espn.go.com/mlb/standings/_/year/2012.

Mackowiak, P. A., Wasserman, S. S., and Levine, M. M. (1992), "A Critical Appraisal of 98.6 Degrees F, the Upper Limit of the Normal Body Temperature, and Other Legacies of Carl Reinhold August Wunderlich," *Journal of the American Medical Association*, 268, 1578-1580.

SOLUTIONS

1. The populations from which the two samples are drawn are normally distributed.

3. $H_0: \sigma_1 = \sigma_2$ $H_a: \sigma_1 < \sigma_2$ or H_0: $\sigma_1^2 = \sigma_2^2$ H_a: $\sigma_1^2 < \sigma_2^2$

5. 4.11

7. 0.7159

9. No, at the 10% level of significance, we cannot reject the null hypothesis and state that the data do not show that the variation in drive times for the first worker is less than the variation in drive times for the second worker.

11. 2.8674

13. Cannot accept the null hypothesis. There is enough evidence to say that the variance of the grades for the first student is higher than the variance in the grades for the second student.

15. 0.7414

17. Each population from which a sample is taken is assumed to be normal.

19. The populations are assumed to have equal standard deviations (or variances).

21. 4,939.2

23. 2

25. 2,469.6

27. 3.7416

29. 3

31. 13.2

33. 0.825

35. Because a one-way ANOVA test is always right-tailed, a high *F* statistic corresponds to a low *p*-value, so it is likely that we cannot accept the null hypothesis.

37. The curves approximate the normal distribution.

39. ten

41. SS = 237.33; MS = 23.73

43. 0.1614

45. two

47. $SS = 5{,}700.4$;

$MS = 2{,}850.2$

49. 3.6101

51. Yes, there is enough evidence to show that the scores among the groups are statistically significant at the 10% level.

55. a. $H_0: \sigma_1^2 = \sigma_2^2$

b. $H_a: \sigma_1^2 \neq \sigma_1^2$

c. $df(num) = 4$; $df(denom) = 4$

d. $F_{4,4}$

e. 3.00

f. Check student's solution.

g. Decision: Cannot reject the null hypothesis; Conclusion: There is insufficient evidence to conclude that the variances are different.

58. The answers may vary. Sample answer: Home decorating magazines and news magazines have different variances.

60. a. $H_0: = \sigma_1^2 = \sigma_2^2$

b. $H_a: \sigma_1^2 \neq \sigma_1^2$

c. $df(n) = 7$, $df(d) = 6$

d. $F_{7,6}$

e. 0.8117

f. 0.7825

g. Check student's solution.

i. Alpha: 0.05

ii. Decision: Cannot reject the null hypothesis.

iii. Reason for decision: calculated test statistics is not in the tail of the distribution

iv. Conclusion: There is not sufficient evidence to conclude that the variances are different.

62. Here is a strip chart of the silver content of the coins:

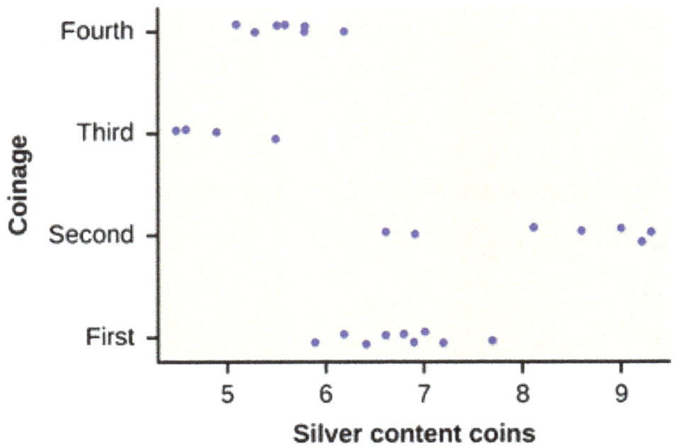

Figure 12.10

While there are differences in spread, it is not unreasonable to use ANOVA techniques. Here is the completed ANOVA table:

Table 12.42

Source of variation	Sum of squares (SS)	Degrees of freedom (df)	Mean square (MS)	F
Factor (Between)	37.748	4 – 1 = 3	12.5825	26.272
Error (Within)	11.015	27 – 4 = 23	0.4789	
Total	48.763	27 – 1 = 26		

$P(F > 26.272) = 0$;Cannot accept the null hypothesis for any alpha. There is sufficient evidence to conclude that the mean silver content among the four coinages are different. From the strip chart, it appears that the first and second coinages had higher silver contents than the third and fourth.

63. Here is a stripchart of the number of wins for the 14 teams in the AL for the 2012 season.

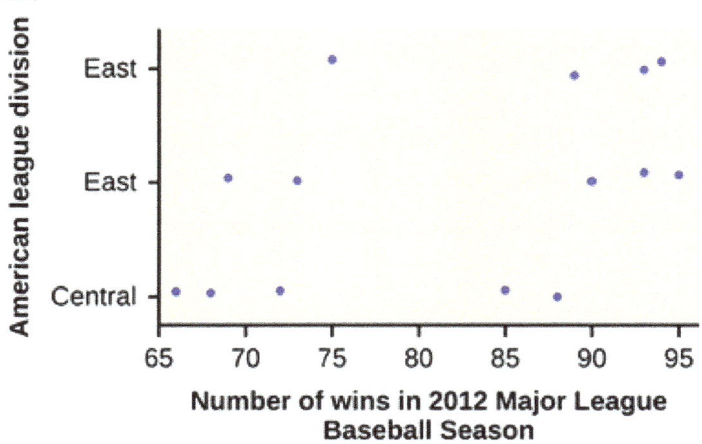

Figure 12.11

While the spread seems similar, there may be some question about the normality of the data, given the wide gaps in the middle near the 0.500 mark of 82 games (teams play 162 games each season in MLB). However, one-way ANOVA is robust. Here is the ANOVA table for the data:

Table 12.43

Source of variation	Sum of squares (SS)	Degrees of freedom (df)	Mean square (MS)	F
Factor (Between)	344.16	3 – 1 = 2	172.08	
Error (Within)	1,219.55	14 – 3 = 11	110.87	1.5521
Total	1,563.71	14 – 1 = 13		

$P(F > 1.5521) = 0.2548$

Since the *p*-value is so large, there is not good evidence against the null hypothesis of equal means. We cannot reject the null hypothesis. Thus, for 2012, there is not any have any good evidence of a significant difference in mean number of wins between the divisions of the American League.

64. $SS_{between} = 26$

$SS_{within} = 441$

$F = 0.2653$

67. $df(denom) = 15$

69. a. $H_0: \mu_L = \mu_T = \mu_J$

b. H_a: at least any two of the means are different

c. $df(num) = 2; df(denom) = 12$

d. *F* distribution

e. 0.67

f. 0.5305

g. Check student's solution.

h. Decision:Cannot reject null hypothesis; Conclusion: There is insufficient evidence to conclude that the means are different.

72. a. $H_a: \mu_c = \mu_n = \mu_h$

b. At least any two of the magazines have different mean lengths.

c. $df(num) = 2, df(denom) = 12$

d. *F* distribution

e. $F = 15.28$

f. *p*-value = 0.001

g. Check student's solution.

Alpha: 0.05
Decision: Cannot accept the null hypothesis.
Reason for decision: *p*-value < alpha
Conclusion: There is sufficient evidence to conclude that the mean lengths of the magazines are different.

74. *a.* H_0: $\mu_o = \mu_h = \mu_f$
b. At least two of the means are different.
c. $df(n) = 2$, $df(d) = 13$
d. $F_{2,13}$
e. 0.64
f. 0.5437
g. Check student's solution.
Alpha: 0.05
Decision: Cannot reject the null hypothesis.
Reason for decision: p-value > alpha
Conclusion: The mean scores of different class delivery are not different.

76. *a.* H_0: $\mu_p = \mu_m = \mu_h$
b. At least any two of the means are different.
c. $df(n) = 2$, $df(d) = 12$
d. $F_{2,12}$
e. 3.13
f. 0.0807
g. Check student's solution.
Alpha: 0.05
Decision: Cannot reject the null hypothesis.
Reason for decision: *p*-value > alpha
Conclusion: There is not sufficient evidence to conclude that the mean numbers of daily visitors are different.

78. The data appear normally distributed from the chart and of similar spread. There do not appear to be any serious outliers, so we may proceed with our ANOVA calculations, to see if we have good evidence of a difference between the three groups.

H_0:μ_1=μ_2=μ_3; H_a:μ_i≠; ≠; some i≠j Define μ_1, μ_2, μ_3, as the population mean number of eggs laid by the three groups of fruit flies. *F* statistic = 8.6657; *p*-value = 0.0004

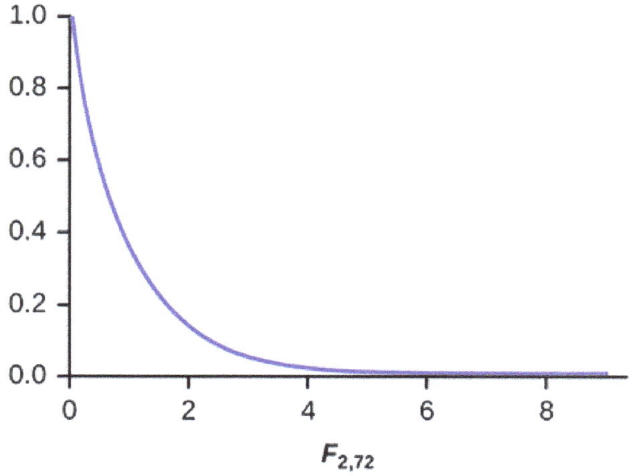

Figure 12.12

Decision: Since the *p*-value is less than the level of significance of 0.01, we reject the null hypothesis.

Conclusion: We have good evidence that the average number of eggs laid during the first 14 days of life for these three strains of fruitflies are different.

Interestingly, if you perform a two sample *t*-test to compare the RS and NS groups they are significantly different ($p = 0.0013$). Similarly, SS and NS are significantly different ($p = 0.0006$). However, the two selected groups, RS and SS are *not* significantly different ($p = 0.5176$). Thus we appear to have good evidence that selection either for resistance or for susceptibility involves a reduced rate of egg production (for these specific strains) as compared to flies that were not selected for resistance or susceptibility to DDT. Here, genetic selection has apparently involved a loss of fecundity.

13 Chapter

LINEAR REGRESSION AND CORRELATION METHODS

Figure 13.1 Linear regression and correlation can help you determine if an auto mechanic's salary is related to his work experience. (credit: Joshua Rothhaas)

INTRODUCTION: AN OVERVIEW

Professionals frequently seek to understand the relationships between two or more numerical variables. Is there a correlation between a student's grade on the second math exam and their grade on the final exam? What is the nature of the relationship and its strength? Your income may be influenced by your degree, occupation, years of experience, abilities, gender, or ethnicity. The compensation for a repair technician's labor is often established by a base fee in addition to an hourly rate. These examples may or may not be associated with a model, indicating that a theory posits the existence of a relationship. The connection between a cause and an effect, commonly termed a model, constitutes the basis of the scientific process and underpins our understanding of the functioning of the world. Commencing with a theory and creating a model of the theoretical relationship should yield a prediction, referred to earlier as a hypothesis. The hypothesis pertains to a comprehensive array of relationships. In Economics, the consumer choice model relies on assumptions about human behavior, including the desire to maximize utility, awareness of the advantages of one product over another, and personal preferences, encompassing likes and dislikes. These factors collectively produced the demand curve. Consequently, we estimate that an increase in pricing will result in a decrease in the quantity demanded. Economics includes models that examine the relationship between the prices of items and the market structure in which a firm works, such as monopoly versus competition. Models predicting the likelihood of selection for on-the-job training positions, the effects of Federal Reserve policy alterations, and economic development, among other factors. Models are not exclusive to Economics, even among the social sciences. In political science, models exist that forecast bureaucratic behavior in response to varying conditions, predicated on assumptions regarding the objectives of the bureaucrats. Models of political behavior address strategic decision-making in both foreign relations and domestic politics. The so-called hard sciences constitute the foundation of the scientific method, since they have endeavored over the centuries to elucidate the perplexing world surrounding us. Certain early models elicit amusement now, such as the concept of spontaneous production of life. These early models are regarded now as little more than fundamental myths created to impose order on perceived chaos.The foundation of all model building is the perhaps the arrogant statement that we know what caused the result we see. This is embodied in the simple mathematical statement of the functional form that $y = f(x)$. The response, Y, is caused by the stimulus, X. Every model will eventually come to this final place and it will be here that the theory will live or die. Will the data support this hypothesis? If so then fine, we shall believe this version of the world until a better theory comes to replace it. This is the process by which we moved from flat earth to round earth, from earth-center solar system to sun-center solar system, and on and on.

The scientific method does not confirm a theory for all time: it does not prove "truth". All theories are subject to review and may be overturned. These are lessons we learned as we first developed the concept of the hypothesis test earlier in this book. Here, as we begin this section, these concepts deserve review because the tool we will develop here is the cornerstone of the scientific method and the stakes are higher. Full theories will rise or fall because of this statistical tool; regression and the more advanced versions call econometrics.

This chapter will commence with correlation, the examination of correlations between variables that may or may not be based on a causal framework. The variables either move in the same direction or in opposing directions. In other words, their movement is not arbitrary. Correlation quantifies the extent to which an assertion holds true. Subsequently, we create a tool to assess causal relationships: regression analysis. We will design models and tests to assess their statistical validity. If they are determined to be so, we can utilize them for predictions: if we altered the value of this variable as a matter of policy, what would occur with this other variable? What would be the impact of a 50-cent per gallon fuel tax on carbon emissions, sales of Hummers and hybrids, and the utilization of mass transit? The capacity to address such inquiries underscores the significance of regression as a tool for comprehending our environment and informing prudent policy choices.

13.1 THE CORRELATION COEFFICIENT *R*

As we begin this section we note that the type of data we will be working with has changed. Perhaps unnoticed, all the data we have been using is for a single variable. It may be from two samples, but it is still a univariate variable. The type of data described in the examples above and for any model of cause and effect is bivariate data — "bi" for two variables. In reality, statisticians use multivariate data, meaning many variables.

For our work we can classify data into three broad categories, time series data, cross-section data, and panel data. We met the first two very early on. Time series data measures a single unit of observation; say a person, or a company or a country, as time passes. What are measured will be at least two characteristics, say the person's income, the quantity of a particular good they buy and the price they paid. This would be three pieces of information in one time period, say 1985. If we followed that person across time we would have those same pieces of information for 1985,1986, 1987, etc. This would constitute a times series data set. If we did this for 10 years we would have 30 pieces of information concerning this person's consumption habits of this good for the past decade and we would know their income and the price they paid.

A second type of data set is for cross-section data. Here the variation is not across time for a single unit of observation, but across units of observation during one point in time. For a particular period of time we would gather the price paid, amount purchased, and income of many individual people.

A third type of data set is panel data. Here a panel of units of observation is followed across time. If we take our example from above we might follow 500 people, the unit of observation, through time, ten years, and observe their income, price paid and quantity of the good purchased. If we had 500 people and data for ten years for price, income and quantity purchased we would have 15,000 pieces of information. These types of data sets are very expensive to construct and maintain. They do, however, provide a tremendous amount of information that can be used to answer very important questions. As an example, what is the effect on the labor force participation rate of women as their family of origin, mother and father, age? Or are there differential effects on health outcomes depending upon the age at which a person started smoking? Only panel data can give answers to these and related questions because we must follow multiple people across time. The work we do here however will not be fully appropriate for data sets such as these.

Beginning with a set of data with two independent variables we ask the question: are these related? One way to visually answer this question is to create a scatter plot of the data. We could not do that before when we were doing descriptive statistics because those data were univariate. Now we have bivariate data so we can plot in two dimensions. Three dimensions are possible on a flat piece of paper, but become very hard to fully conceptualize. Of course, more than three dimensions cannot be graphed although the relationships can be measured mathematically.

To provide mathematical precision to the measurement of what we see we use the correlation coefficient. The correlation tells us something about the co-movement of two variables, but nothing about why this movement occurred. Formally, correlation analysis assumes that both variables being analyzed are independent variables. This means that neither one causes the movement in the other. Further, it means that neither variable is dependent on the other, or for that matter, on any other variable. Even with these limitations, correlation analysis can yield some interesting results.

The correlation coefficient, ρ (pronounced rho), is the mathematical statistic for a population that provides us with a measurement of the strength of a linear relationship between the two variables. For a sample of data, the statistic, r, developed by Karl Pearson in the early 1900s, is an estimate of the population correlation and is defined mathematically as:

$$r = \frac{\frac{1}{n-1}\Sigma\left(X_{1i} - \bar{X}_1\right)\left(X_{2i} - \bar{X}_2\right)}{s_{x_1} s_{x_2}}$$

OR

$$r = \frac{\Sigma X_{1i} X_{2i} - n\bar{X}_1 - \bar{X}_2}{\sqrt{\left(\Sigma X_{1i}^2 - n\bar{X}_1^2\right)\left(\Sigma X_{2i}^2 - n\bar{X}_2^2\right)}}$$

where s_{x1} and s_{x2} are the standard deviations of the two independent variables X_1 and X_2, $\bar{X}_1$ and $\bar{X}_2$ are the sample means of the two variables, and X_{1i} and X_{2i} are the individual observations of X_1 and X_2. The correlation coefficient r ranges in value from

-1 to 1. The second equivalent formula is often used because it may be computationally easier. As scary as these formulas look they are really just the ratio of the covariance between the two variables and the product of their two standard deviations. That is to say, it is a measure of relative variances.

In practice all correlation and regression analysis will be provided through computer software designed for these purposes. Anything more than perhaps one-half a dozen observations creates immense computational problems. It was because of this fact that correlation, and even more so, regression, were not widely used research tools until after the advent of "computing machines". Now the computing power required to analyze data using regression packages is deemed almost trivial by comparison to just a decade ago.

To visualize any linear relationship that may exist review the plot of a scatter diagrams of the standardized data. Figure 13.2 presents several scatter diagrams and the calculated value of r. In panels (a) and (b) notice that the data generally trend together, (a) upward and (b) downward. Panel (a) is an example of a positive correlation and panel (b) is an example of a negative correlation, or relationship. The sign of the correlation coefficient tells us if the relationship is a positive or negative (inverse) one. If all the values of X_1 and X_2 are on a straight line the correlation coefficient will be either 1 or -1 depending on whether the line has a positive or negative slope and the closer to one or negative one the stronger the relationship between the two variables. BUT ALWAYS REMEMBER THAT THE CORRELATION COEFFICIENT DOES NOT TELL US THE SLOPE.

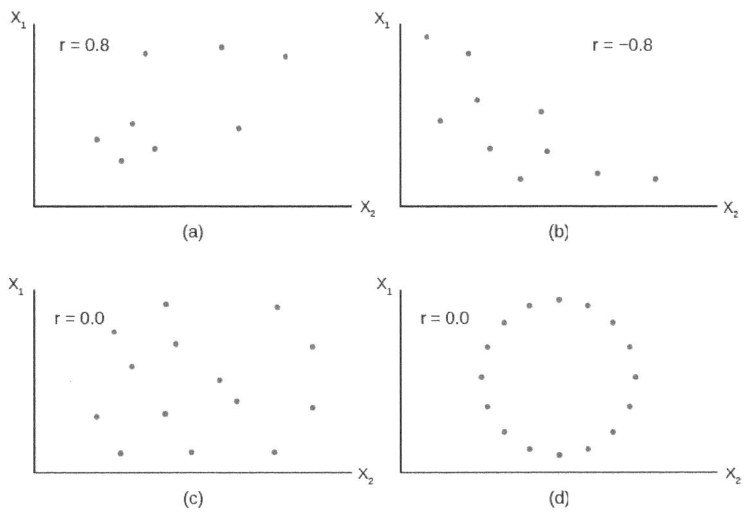

Figure 13.2

Remember, all the correlation coefficient tells us is whether or not the data are linearly related. In panel (d) the variables obviously have some type of very specific relationship to each other, but the correlation coefficient is zero, indicating no **linear** relationship exists.

If you suspect a linear relationship between X_1 and X_2 then *r* can measure how strong the linear relationship is.

What the VALUE of *r* tells us:

- The value of *r* is always between −1 and +1: $-1 \le r \le 1$.
- The size of the correlation *r* indicates the strength of the linear relationship between X_1 and X_2. Values of *r* close to −1 or to +1 indicate a stronger linear relationship between X_1 and X_2.
- If $r = 0$ there is absolutely no linear relationship between X_1 and X_2 (no linear correlation).
- If $r = 1$, there is perfect positive correlation. If $r = -1$, there is perfect negative correlation. In both these cases, all of the original data points lie on a straight line: ANY straight line no matter what the slope. Of course, in the real world, this will not generally happen.

What the SIGN of *r* tells us

- A positive value of *r* means that when X_1 increases, X_2 tends to increase and when X_1 decreases, X_2 tends to decrease (positive correlation).
- A negative value of *r* means that when X_1 increases, X_2 tends to decrease and when X_1 decreases, X_2 tends to increase (negative correlation).

NOTE

Strong correlation does not suggest that X_1 causes X_2 or X_2 causes X_1. We say "correlation does not imply causation."

13.2 TESTING THE SIGNIFICANCE OF THE CORRELATION COEFFICIENT

The correlation coefficient, *r*, tells us about the strength and direction of the linear relationship between X_1 and X_2.

The sample data are used to compute *r*, the correlation coefficient for the sample. If we had data for the entire population, we could find the population correlation coefficient. But because we have only sample data, we cannot calculate the population correlation coefficient. The sample correlation coefficient, *r*, is our estimate of the unknown population correlation coefficient.

- ρ = population correlation coefficient (unknown)

- r = sample correlation coefficient (known; calculated from sample data)

The hypothesis test lets us decide whether the value of the population correlation coefficient ρ is "close to zero" or "significantly different from zero". We decide this based on the sample correlation coefficient r and the sample size n.

If the test concludes that the correlation coefficient is significantly different from zero, we say that the correlation coefficient is "significant."

- Conclusion: There is sufficient evidence to conclude that there is a significant linear relationship between X_1 and X_2 because the correlation coefficient is significantly different from zero.
- What the conclusion means: There is a significant linear relationship X_1 and X_2. If the test concludes that the correlation coefficient is not significantly different from zero (it is close to zero), we say that correlation coefficient is "not significant".

Performing the Hypothesis Test

- **Null Hypothesis: H_0: $\rho = 0$**
- **Alternate Hypothesis: H_a: $\rho \neq 0$**

What the Hypotheses Mean in Words

- **Null Hypothesis H_0:** The population correlation coefficient IS NOT significantly different from zero. There IS NOT a significant linear relationship (correlation) between X_1 and X_2 in the population.
- **Alternate Hypothesis H_a:** The population correlation coefficient is significantly different from zero. There is a significant linear relationship (correlation) between X_1 and X_2 in the population.

Drawing a Conclusion

There are two methods of making the decision concerning the hypothesis. The test statistic to test this hypothesis is:

$$t_c = \frac{r}{\sqrt{\frac{(1-r^2)}{(n-2)}}}$$

OR

$$t_c = \frac{r\sqrt{n-2}}{\sqrt{1-r^2}}$$

Where the second formula is an equivalent form of the test statistic, n is the sample size and the degrees of freedom are n-2. This is a t-statistic and operates in the same way as other t tests. Calculate the t-value and compare that with the critical value from the t-table at the appropriate degrees of freedom and the level of confidence you wish to maintain. If the calculated value is in the tail then cannot accept the null hypothesis that there is no linear relationship between these two independent random variables. If the calculated t-value is NOT in the tailed then cannot reject the null hypothesis that there is no linear relationship between the two variables.

A quick shorthand way to test correlations is the relationship between the sample size and the correlation. If:

$$|r| \geq \frac{2}{\sqrt{n}}$$

then this implies that the correlation between the two variables demonstrates that a linear relationship exists and is statistically significant at approximately the 0.05 level of significance. As the formula indicates, there is an inverse relationship between the sample size and the required correlation for significance of a linear relationship. With only 10 observations, the required correlation for significance is 0.6325, for 30 observations the required correlation for significance decreases to 0.3651 and at 100 observations the required level is only 0.2000.

Correlations may be helpful in visualizing the data, but are not appropriately used to "explain" a relationship between two variables. Perhaps no single statistic is more misused than the correlation coefficient. Citing correlations between health conditions and everything from place of residence to eye color have the effect of implying a cause and effect relationship. This simply cannot be accomplished with a correlation coefficient. The correlation coefficient is, of course, innocent of this misinterpretation. It is the duty of the analyst to use a statistic that is designed to test for cause and effect relationships and report only those results if they are intending to make such a claim. The problem is that passing this more rigorous test is difficult so lazy and/or unscrupulous "researchers" fall back on correlations when they cannot make their case legitimately.

13.3 LINEAR EQUATIONS

Linear regression for two variables is based on a linear equation with one independent variable. The equation has the form:

$$y = a + \text{b}x$$

where *a* and *b* are constant numbers.

The variable x is the independent variable, and y is the dependent variable. Another way to think about this equation is a statement of cause and effect. The X variable is the cause and the Y variable is the hypothesized effect. Typically, you choose a value to substitute for the independent variable and then solve for the dependent variable.

EXAMPLE 13.1

The following examples are linear equations.

$$y = 3 + 2x$$
$$y = -0.01 + 1.2x$$

The graph of a linear equation of the form $y = a + bx$ is a **straight line.** Any line that is not vertical can be described by this equation.

EXAMPLE 13.2

Graph the equation $y = -1 + 2x$.

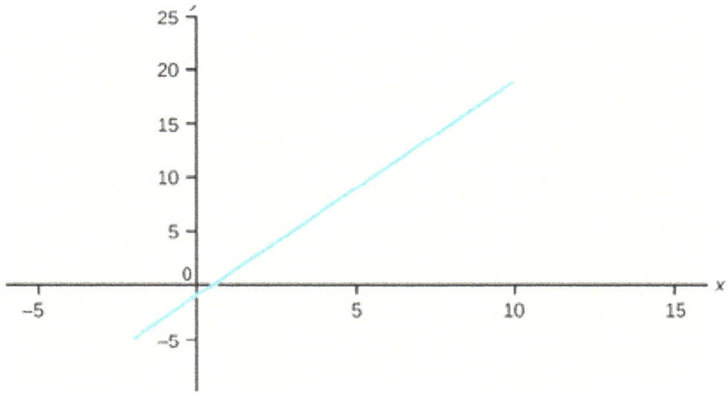

Figure 13.3

TRY IT 13.2

Is the following an example of a linear equation? Why or why not?

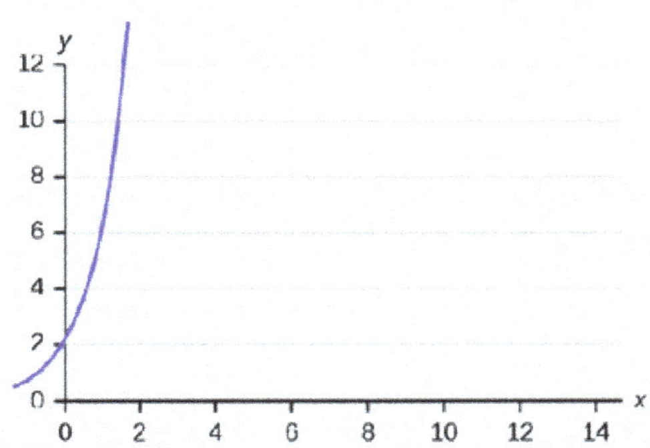

Figure 13.4

EXAMPLE 13.3

Aaron's Word Processing Service (AWPS) does word processing. The rate for services is $32 per hour plus a $31.50 one-time charge. The total cost to a customer depends on the number of hours it takes to complete the job.

Find the equation that expresses the total cost in terms of the number of hours required to complete the job.

Solution 13.3

Let x = the number of hours it takes to get the job done.

Let y = the total cost to the customer.

The $31.50 is a fixed cost. If it takes x hours to complete the job, then $(32)(x)$ is the cost of the word processing only. The total cost is: $y = 31.50 + 32x$

Slope and *Y*-Intercept of a Linear Equation

For the linear equation $y = a + bx$, b = slope and a = y-intercept. From algebra recall that the slope is a number that describes the steepness of a line, and the y-intercept is the y coordinate of the point $(0, a)$ where the line crosses the y-axis. From calculus the slope is the first derivative of the function. For a linear function the slope is $dy / dx = b$ where we can read the mathematical expression as "the change in y (dy) that results from a change in x $(dx) = b * dx$".

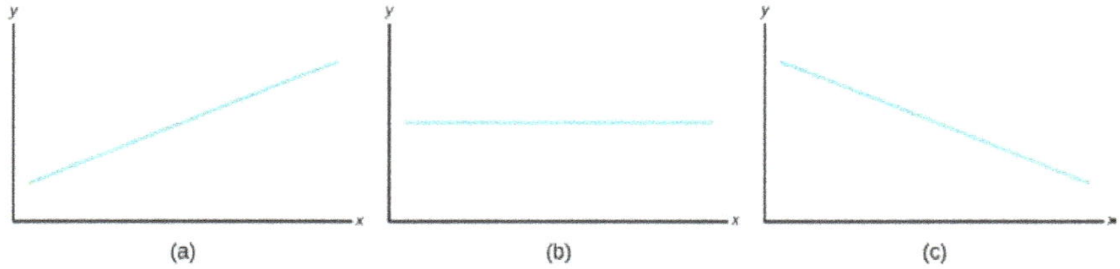

Figure 13.5 Three possible graphs of $y = a + bx$. (a) If $b > 0$, the line slopes upward to the right. (b) If $b = 0$, the line is horizontal. (c) If $b < 0$, the line slopes downward to the right.

EXAMPLE 13.4

Svetlana tutors to make extra money for college. For each tutoring session, she charges a one-time fee of $25 plus $15 per hour of tutoring. A linear equation that expresses the total amount of money Svetlana earns for each session she tutors is $y = 25 + 15x$.

What are the independent and dependent variables? What is the y-intercept and what is the slope? Interpret them using complete sentences.

Solution 13.4

The independent variable (x) is the number of hours Svetlana tutors each session. The dependent variable (y) is the amount, in dollars, Svetlana earns for each session.

The y-intercept is 25 (a = 25). At the start of the tutoring session, Svetlana charges a one-time fee of $25 (this is when x = 0). The slope is 15 (b = 15). For each session, Svetlana earns $15 for each hour she tutors.

13.4 THE REGRESSION EQUATION

Regression analysis is a statistical technique that can test the hypothesis that a variable is dependent upon one or more other variables. Further, regression analysis can provide an estimate of the magnitude of the impact of a change in one variable on another. This last feature, of course, is all important in predicting future values.

Regression analysis is based upon a functional relationship among variables and further, assumes that the relationship is linear. This linearity assumption is required because, for the most part, the theoretical statistical properties of non-linear estimation are not well worked out yet by the mathematicians and econometricians. This presents us with some difficulties in economic analysis because many of our theoretical models are nonlinear. The marginal cost curve, for example, is decidedly nonlinear as is the total cost function, if we are to believe in the effect of specialization of labor and the Law of Diminishing Marginal Product. There are techniques for overcoming some of these difficulties, exponential and logarithmic transformation of the data for example, but at the outset we must recognize that standard ordinary least squares (OLS) regression analysis will always use a linear function to estimate what might be a nonlinear relationship.

The general linear regression model can be stated by the equation:

$$y_i = \beta_0 + \beta_1 X_{1i} + \beta_2 X_{2i} + \cdots + \beta_k X_{ki} + \varepsilon_i$$

where β_0 is the intercept, β_i's are the slope between Y and the appropriate X_i, and ε (pronounced epsilon), is the error term that captures errors in measurement of Y and the effect on Y of any variables missing from the equation that would contribute to explaining variations in Y. This equation is the theoretical population equation and therefore uses Greek letters. The equation we will estimate will have the Roman equivalent symbols. This is parallel to how we kept track of the population parameters and sample parameters before. The symbol for the population mean was μ and for the sample mean X‾‾‾$\overline{X}$ and for the population standard deviation was σ and for the sample standard deviation was s. The equation that will be estimated with a sample of data for two independent variables will thus be:

$$y_i = b_0 + b_1 x_{1i} + b_2 x_{2i} + e_i$$

As with our earlier work with probability distributions, this model works only if certain assumptions hold. These are that the Y is normally distributed, the errors are also normally distributed with a mean of zero and a constant standard deviation, and that the error terms are independent of the size of X and independent of each other.

Assumptions of the Ordinary Least Squares Regression Model

Each of these assumptions needs a bit more explanation. If one of these assumptions fails to be true, then it will have an effect on the quality of the estimates. Some of the failures of these assumptions can be fixed while others result in estimates that quite simply provide no insight into the questions the model is trying to answer or worse, give biased estimates.

1. The independent variables, xixi , are all measured without error, and are fixed numbers that are independent of the error term. This assumption is saying in effect that Y is deterministic, the result of a fixed component "X" and a random error component "ϵ."
2. The error term is a random variable with a mean of zero and a constant variance. The meaning of this is that the variances of the independent variables are independent of the value of the variable. Consider the relationship between personal income and the quantity of a good purchased as an example of a case where the variance is dependent upon the value of the independent variable, income. It is plausible that as income increases the variation around the amount purchased will also increase simply because of the flexibility provided with higher levels of income. The assumption is for constant variance with respect to the magnitude of the independent variable called homoscedasticity. If the assumption fails, then it is called heteroscedasticity. Figure 13.6 shows the case of homoscedasticity where all three distributions have the same variance around the predicted value of Y regardless of the magnitude of X.
3. Error terms should be normally distributed. This can be seen in Figure 13.6 by the shape of the distributions placed on the predicted line at the expected value of the relevant value of Y.
4. The independent variables are independent of Y, but are also assumed to be independent of the other X variables. The model is designed to estimate the effects of independent variables on some dependent variable in accordance

with a proposed theory. The case where some or more of the independent variables are correlated is not unusual. There may be no cause and effect relationship among the independent variables, but nevertheless they move together. Take the case of a simple supply curve where quantity supplied is theoretically related to the price of the product and the prices of inputs. There may be multiple inputs that may over time move together from general inflationary pressure. The input prices will therefore violate this assumption of regression analysis. This condition is called multicollinearity, which will be taken up in detail later.

5. The error terms are uncorrelated with each other. This situation arises from an effect on one error term from another error term. While not exclusively a time series problem, it is here that we most often see this case. An X variable in time period one has an effect on the Y variable, but this effect then has an effect in the next time period. This effect gives rise to a relationship among the error terms. This case is called autocorrelation, "self-correlated." The error terms are now not independent of each other, but rather have their own effect on subsequent error terms.

Figure 13.6 shows the case where the assumptions of the regression model are being satisfied. The estimated line is y^=a+bx.y^=a+bx. Three values of X are shown. A normal distribution is placed at each point where X equals the estimated line and the associated error at each value of Y. Notice that the three distributions are normally distributed around the point on the line, and further, the variation, variance, around the predicted value is constant indicating homoscedasticity from assumption 2. Figure 13.6 does not show all the assumptions of the regression model, but it helps visualize these important ones.

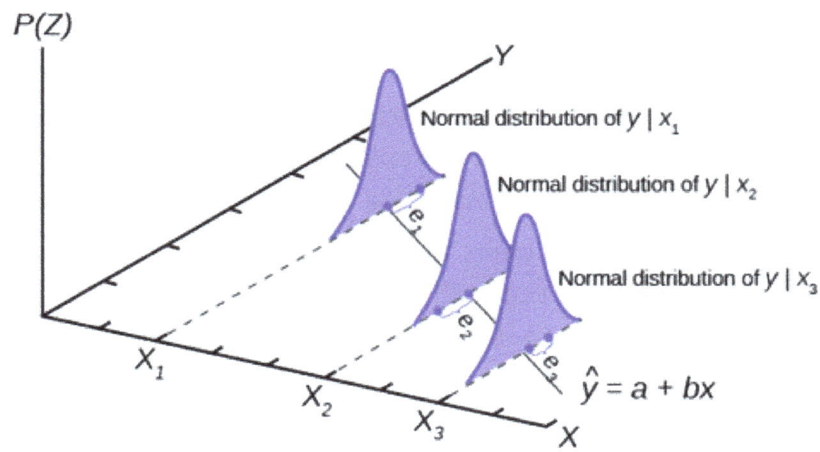

Figure 13.6

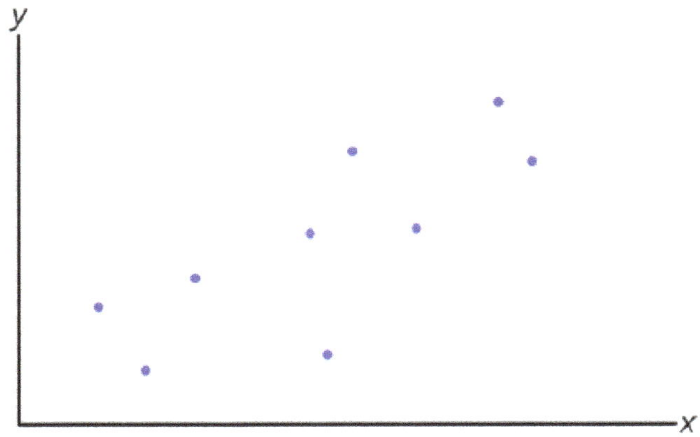

$$y = \beta_0 + \beta_1 X + \varepsilon$$

Figure 13.7

This is the general form that is most often called the multiple regression model. So-called "simple" regression analysis has only one independent (right-hand) variable rather than many independent variables. Simple regression is just a special case of multiple regression. There is some value in beginning with simple regression: it is easy to graph in two dimensions, difficult to graph in three dimensions, and impossible to graph in more than three dimensions. Consequently, our graphs will be for the simple regression case. Figure 13.7 presents the regression problem in the form of a scatter plot graph of the data set where it is hypothesized that Y is dependent upon the single independent variable X.

A basic relationship from Macroeconomic Principles is the consumption function. This theoretical relationship states that as a person's income rises, their consumption rises, but by a smaller amount than the rise in income. If Y is consumption and X is income in the equation below Figure 13.7, the regression problem is, first, to establish that this relationship exists, and second, to determine the impact of a change in income on a person's consumption. The parameter β_1 was called the Marginal Propensity to Consume in Macroeconomics Principles.

Each "dot" in Figure 13.7 represents the consumption and income of different individuals at some point in time. This was called cross-section data earlier; observations on variables at one point in time across different people or other units of measurement. This analysis is often done with time series data, which would be the consumption and income of one individual or country at different points in time. For macroeconomic problems it is common to use times series aggregated data for a whole country. For this particular theoretical concept these data are readily available in the annual report of the President's Council of Economic Advisors.

The regression problem comes down to determining which straight line would best represent the data in Figure 13.8. Regression analysis is sometimes called "least squares" analysis because the method of determining which line best "fits" the data is to minimize the sum of the squared residuals of a line put through the data.

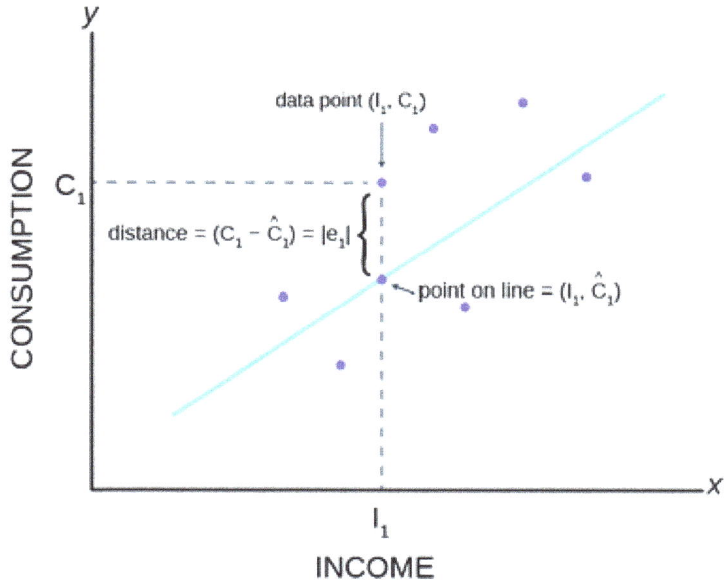

Figure 13.8

Population Equation: $C = \beta_0 + \beta_1 \text{ Income} + \varepsilon$

Estimated Equation: $C = b_0 + b_1 \text{ Income} + e$

This figure shows the assumed relationship between consumption and income from macroeconomic theory. Here the data are plotted as a scatter plot and an estimated straight line has been drawn. From this graph we can see an error term, e_1. Each data point also has an error term. Again, the error term is put into the equation to capture effects on consumption that are not caused by income changes. Such other effects might be a person's savings or wealth, or periods of unemployment. We will see how by minimizing the sum of these errors we can get an estimate for the slope and intercept of this line.

Consider the graph below. The notation has returned to that for the more general model rather than the specific case of the Macroeconomic consumption function in our example.

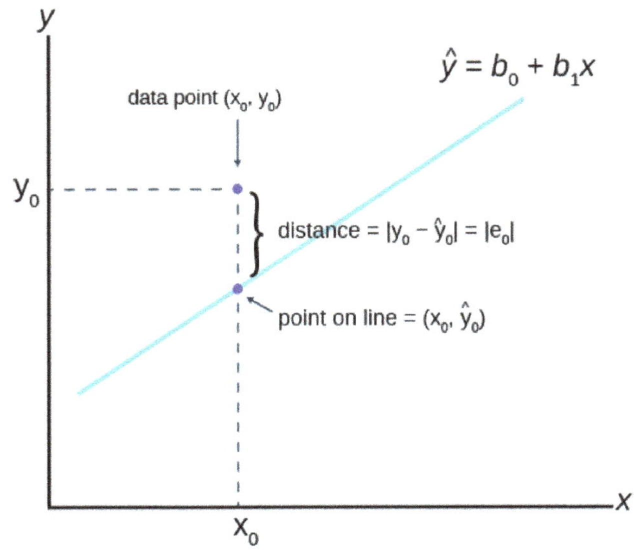

Figure 13.9

The ŷ is read **"y hat"** and is the **estimated value of *y*.** (In Figure 13.8 C^*C*^ represents the estimated value of consumption because it is on the estimated line.) It is the value of *y* obtained using the regression line. ŷ is not generally equal to *y* from the data.

The term y0-ŷ0=e0*y*0-ŷ0=*e*0 is called the "error" or residual. It is not an error in the sense of a mistake. The error term was put into the estimating equation to capture missing variables and errors in measurement that may have occurred in the dependent variables. The absolute value of a residual measures the vertical distance between the actual value of *y* and the estimated value of *y*. In other words, it measures the vertical distance between the actual data point and the predicted point on the line as can be seen on the graph at point X_0.

If the observed data point lies above the line, the residual is positive, and the line underestimates the actual data value for *y*.

If the observed data point lies below the line, the residual is negative, and the line overestimates that actual data value for *y*.

In the graph, y0-ŷ0=e0*y*0-ŷ0=*e*0 is the residual for the point shown. Here the point lies above the line and the residual is positive. For each data point the residuals, or errors, are calculated $y_i - \hat{y}_i = e_i$ for i = 1, 2, 3, ..., n where n is the sample size. Each $|e|$ is a vertical distance.

The sum of the errors squared is the term obviously called Sum of Squared Errors (SSE).

Using calculus, you can determine the straight line that has the parameter values of b_0 and b_1 that minimizes the SSE. When you make the SSE a minimum, you have determined the points that are on the line of best fit. It turns out that the line of best fit has the equation:

$$\hat{y} = b_0 + b_1 x$$

where $b_0 = \bar{y} - b_1 \bar{x}$ and $b_1 = \frac{\Sigma (x - \bar{x})(y - \bar{y})}{\Sigma (x - \bar{x})^2} = \frac{\text{cov}(x, y)}{s_x^{\ 2}}$

The sample means of the *x* values and the *y* values are x¯*x*¯ and y−*y*−, respectively. The best fit line always passes through the point (x¯*x*¯, y−*y*−) called the points of means.

The slope *b* can also be written as:

$$b_1 = r_{\text{y,x}}\left(\frac{s_y}{s_x}\right)$$

where s_y = the standard deviation of the *y* values and s_x = the standard deviation of the *x* values and *r* is the correlation coefficient between *x* and *y*.

These equations are called the Normal Equations and come from another very important mathematical finding called the Gauss-Markov Theorem without which we could not do regression analysis. The Gauss-Markov Theorem tells us that the estimates we get from using the ordinary least squares (OLS) regression method will result in estimates that have some very important properties. In the Gauss-Markov Theorem it was proved that a least squares line is BLUE, which is, **B**est, **L**inear, **U**nbiased, **E**stimator. Best is the statistical property that an estimator is the one with the minimum variance. Linear refers to the property of the type of line being estimated. An unbiased estimator is one whose estimating function has an expected mean equal to the mean of the population. (You will remember that the expected value of *μ*x¯μ*x*¯ was equal to the population mean μ in accordance with the Central Limit Theorem. This is exactly the same concept here).

Both Gauss and Markov were giants in the field of mathematics, and Gauss in physics too, in the 18th century and early 19th century. They barely overlapped chronologically and never in geography, but Markov's work on this theorem was based extensively on the earlier work of Carl Gauss. The extensive applied value of this theorem had to wait until the middle of this last century.

Using the OLS method we can now find the **estimate of the error variance** which is the variance of the squared errors, e2. This is sometimes called the standard error of the estimate. (Grammatically this is probably best said as the estimate of the error's variance) The formula for the estimate of the error variance is:

$$s_e^2 = \frac{\Sigma (y_i - \hat{y}_i)^2}{n - k} = \frac{\Sigma e_i^2}{n - k}$$

where ŷ is the predicted value of y and y is the observed value, and thus the term $(yi-\hat{y}i)^2$ is the squared errors that are to be minimized to find the estimates of the regression line parameters. This is really just the variance of the error terms and follows our regular variance formula. One important note is that here we are dividing by (n-k)(n-k), which is the degrees of freedom. The degrees of freedom of a regression equation will be the number of observations, n, reduced by the number of estimated parameters, which includes the intercept as a parameter.

The variance of the errors is fundamental in testing hypotheses for a regression. It tells us just how "tight" the dispersion is about the line. As we will see shortly, the greater the dispersion about the line, meaning the larger the variance of the errors, the less probable that the hypothesized independent variable will be found to have a significant effect on the dependent variable. In short, the theory being tested will more likely fail if the variance of the error term is high. Upon reflection this should not be a surprise. As we tested hypotheses about a mean we observed that large variances reduced the calculated test statistic and thus it failed to reach the tail of the distribution. In those cases, the null hypotheses could not be rejected. If we cannot reject the null hypothesis in a regression problem, we must conclude that the hypothesized independent variable has no effect on the dependent variable.

A way to visualize this concept is to draw two scatter plots of x and y data along a predetermined line. The first will have little variance of the errors, meaning that all the data points will move close to the line. Now do the same except the data points will have a large estimate of the error variance, meaning that the data points are scattered widely along the line. Clearly the confidence about a relationship between x and y is effected by this difference between the estimate of the error variance.

Testing the Parameters of the Line

The whole goal of the regression analysis was to test the hypothesis that the dependent variable, Y, was in fact dependent upon the values of the independent variables as asserted by some foundation theory, such as the consumption function example. Looking at the estimated equation under Figure 13.8, we see that this amounts to determining the values of b_0 and b_1. Notice that again we are using the convention of Greek letters for the population parameters and Roman letters for their estimates.

The regression analysis output provided by the computer software will produce an estimate of b_0 and b_1, and any other b's for other independent variables that were included in the estimated equation. The issue is how good are these estimates? In order to test a hypothesis concerning any estimate, we have found that we need to know the underlying sampling distribution. It should come as no surprise at his stage in the course that the answer is going to be the normal distribution. This can be seen by remembering the assumption that the error term in the population, ε, is normally distributed. If the error term is normally distributed and the variance of the estimates of the equation parameters, b_0 and b_1, are determined by the variance of the error term, it follows that the variances of the parameter estimates are also normally distributed. And indeed this is just the case.

We can see this by the creation of the test statistic for the test of hypothesis for the slope parameter, β_1 in our consumption function equation. To test whether or not Y does indeed depend upon X, or in our example, that consumption depends upon income, we need only test the hypothesis that β_1 equals zero. This hypothesis would be stated formally as:

$$H_0 : \beta_1 = 0$$
$$H_a : \beta_1 \neq 0$$

If we cannot reject the null hypothesis, we must conclude that our theory has no validity. If we cannot reject the null hypothesis that $\beta_1 = 0$ then b_1, the coefficient of Income, is zero and zero times anything is zero. Therefore the effect of Income on Consumption is zero. There is no relationship as our theory had suggested.

Notice that we have set up the presumption, the null hypothesis, as "no relationship". This puts the burden of proof on the alternative hypothesis. In other words, if we are to validate our claim of finding a relationship, we must do so with a level of significance greater than 90, 95, or 99 percent. The *status quo* is ignorance, no relationship exists, and to be able to make the claim that we have actually added to our body of knowledge we must do so with significant probability of being correct. John Maynard Keynes got it right and thus was born Keynesian economics starting with this basic concept in 1936.

The test statistic for this test comes directly from our old friend the standardizing formula:

$$t_c = \frac{b_1 - \beta_1}{S_{b_1}}$$

where b_1 is the estimated value of the slope of the regression line, β_1 is the hypothesized value of beta, in this case zero, and Sb1$Sb1$ is the standard deviation of the estimate of b_1. In this case we are asking how many standard deviations is the estimated slope away from the hypothesized slope. This is exactly the same question we asked before with respect to a hypothesis about a mean: how many standard deviations is the estimated mean, the sample mean, from the hypothesized mean?

The test statistic is written as a student's *t*-distribution, but if the sample size is larger enough so that the degrees of freedom are greater than 30 we may again use the normal distribution. To see why we can use the student's t or normal distribution we have only to look at Sb1$Sb1$,the formula for the standard deviation of the estimate of b_1:

$$S_{b_1} = \frac{S_e^2}{\sqrt{(x_i - \bar{x})^2}}$$

or

$$S_{b_1} = \frac{S_e^2}{(n-1)S_x^2}$$

Where S_e is the estimate of the error variance and S^2_x is the variance of x values of the coefficient of the independent variable being tested.

We see that S_e, the estimate of the error variance, is part of the computation. Because the estimate of the error variance is based on the assumption of normality of the error terms, we can conclude that the sampling distribution of the b's, the coefficients of our hypothesized regression line, are also normally distributed.

One last note concerns the degrees of freedom of the test statistic, ν=n-k. Previously we subtracted 1 from the sample size to determine the degrees of freedom in a student's t problem. Here we must subtract one degree of freedom for each parameter estimated in the equation. For the example of the consumption function we lose 2 degrees of freedom, one for b0$b0$, the intercept, and one for b_1, the slope of the consumption function. The degrees of freedom would be n - k - 1, where k is the number of independent variables and the extra one is lost because of the intercept. If we were estimating an equation with three independent variables, we would lose 4 degrees of freedom: three for the independent variables, k, and one more for the intercept.

The decision rule for acceptance or rejection of the null hypothesis follows exactly the same form as in all our previous test of hypothesis. Namely, if the calculated value of t (or Z) falls into the tails of the distribution, where the tails are defined by α ,the required significance level in the test, we cannot accept the null hypothesis. If on the other hand, the calculated value of the test statistic is within the critical region, we cannot reject the null hypothesis.

If we conclude that we cannot accept the null hypothesis, we are able to state with (1-α)$(1-\alpha)$ level of confidence that the slope of the line is given by b_1. This is an extremely important conclusion. Regression analysis not only allows us to test if a cause and effect relationship exists, we can also determine the magnitude of that relationship, if one is found to exist. It is this feature of regression analysis that makes it so valuable. If models can be developed that have statistical validity, we are then able to simulate the effects of changes in variables that may be under our control with some degree of probability , of course. For example, if advertising is demonstrated to effect sales, we can determine the effects of changing the advertising budget and decide if the increased sales are worth the added expense.

Multicollinearity

Our discussion earlier indicated that like all statistical models, the OLS regression model has important assumptions attached. Each assumption, if violated, has an effect on the ability of the model to provide useful and meaningful estimates. The Gauss-Markov Theorem has assured us that the OLS estimates are unbiased and minimum variance, but this is true only under the assumptions of the model. Here we will look at the effects on OLS estimates if the independent variables are correlated. The other assumptions and the methods to mitigate the difficulties they pose if they are found to be violated are examined in Econometrics courses. We take up multicollinearity because it is so often prevalent in Economic models and it often leads to frustrating results.

The OLS model assumes that all the independent variables are independent of each other. This assumption is easy to test for a particular sample of data with simple correlation coefficients. Correlation, like much in statistics, is a matter of degree: a little is not good, and a lot is terrible.

The goal of the regression technique is to tease out the independent impacts of each of a set of independent variables on some hypothesized dependent variable. If two 2 independent variables are interrelated, that is, correlated, then we cannot isolate the effects on Y of one from the other. In an extreme case where x1x1 is a linear combination of x2x2, correlation equal to one, both variables move in identical ways with Y. In this case it is impossible to determine the variable that is the true cause of the effect on Y. (If the two variables were actually perfectly correlated, then mathematically no regression results could actually be calculated.)

The normal equations for the coefficients show the effects of multicollinearity on the coefficients.

$$b_1 = \frac{s_y\left(r_{x_1 y} - r_{x_1 x_2} r_{x_2 y}\right)}{s_{x_1}\left(1 - r_{x_1 x_2}^2\right)}$$

$$b_2 = \frac{s_y\left(r_{x_2 y} - r_{x_1 x_2} r_{x_1 y}\right)}{s_{x_2}\left(1 - r_{x_1 x_2}^2\right)}$$

$$b_0 = \bar{y} - b_1 \bar{x}_1 - b_2 \bar{x}_2$$

The correlation between x_1 and x_2, $r^2_{x_1x_2}$ appears in the denominator of both the estimating formula for b1$b1$ and b2$b2$. If the assumption of independence holds, then this term is zero. This indicates that there is no effect of the correlation on the coefficient. On the other hand, as the correlation between the two independent variables increases the denominator decreases, and thus the estimate of the coefficient increases. The correlation has the same effect on both of the coefficients of these two variables. In essence, each variable is "taking" part of the effect on Y that should be attributed to the collinear variable. This results in biased estimates.

Multicollinearity has a further deleterious impact on the OLS estimates. The correlation between the two independent variables also shows up in the formulas for the estimate of the variance for the coefficients.

$$s^2_{b_1} = \frac{s^2_e}{(n-1)s^2_{x_1}\left(1 - r^2_{x_1x_2}\right)}$$

$$s^2_{b_2} = \frac{s^2_e}{(n-1)s^2_{x_2}\left(1 - r^2_{x_1x_2}\right)}$$

Here again we see the correlation between x1$x1$ and x2$x2$ in the denominator of the estimates of the variance for the coefficients for both variables. If the correlation is zero as assumed in the regression model, then the formula collapses to the familiar ratio of the variance of the errors to the variance of the relevant independent variable. If however the two independent variables are correlated, then the variance of the estimate of the coefficient increases. This results in a smaller t-value for the test of hypothesis of the coefficient. In short, multicollinearity results in failing to reject the null hypothesis that the X variable has no impact on Y when in fact X does have a statistically significant impact on Y. Said another way, the large standard errors of the estimated coefficient created by multicollinearity suggest statistical insignificance even when the hypothesized relationship is strong.

How Good is the Equation?

In the last section we concerned ourselves with testing the hypothesis that the dependent variable did indeed depend upon the hypothesized independent variable or variables. It may be that we find an independent variable that has some effect on the dependent variable, but it may not be the only one, and it may not even be the most important one. Remember that the error term was placed in the model to capture the effects of any missing independent variables. It follows that the error term may be used to give a measure of the "goodness of fit" of the equation taken as a whole in explaining the variation of the dependent variable, Y.

The multiple correlation coefficient, also called the coefficient of multiple determination or the coefficient of determination, is given by the formula:

$$R^2 = \frac{\text{SSR}}{\text{SST}}$$

where SSR is the regression sum of squares, the squared deviation of the predicted value of y from the mean value of $(\hat{y} - \bar{y})$, and SST is the total sum of squares which is the total squared deviation of the dependent variable, y, from its mean value, including the error term, SSE, the sum of squared errors. Figure 13.10 shows how the total deviation of the dependent variable, y, is partitioned into these two pieces.

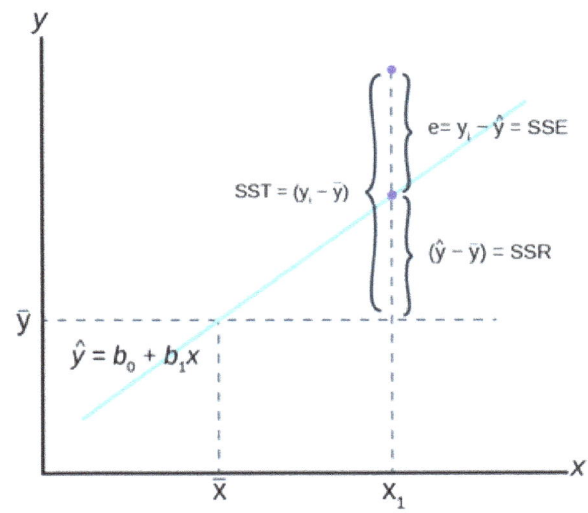

Figure 13.10

Figure 13.10 shows the estimated regression line and a single observation, x_1. Regression analysis tries to explain the variation of the data about the mean value of the dependent variable, y. The question is, why do the observations of y vary from the average level of y? The value of y at observation x_1 varies from the mean of y by the difference (yi-y–yi-y–). The sum of these differences squared is SST, the sum of squares total. The actual value of y at x_1 deviates from the estimated value, ŷ, by the difference between the estimated value and the actual value, (ŷ-ŷ). We recall that this is the error term, e, and the sum of these errors is SSE, sum of squared errors. The deviation of the predicted value of y, ŷ, from the mean value of y is $(\hat{y} - \bar{y})$,and is the SSR, sum of squares regression. It is called "regression" because it is the deviation explained by the regression. (Sometimes the SSR is called SSM for sum of squares mean because it measures the deviation from the mean value of the dependent variable, y, as shown on the graph.).

Because the SST = SSR + SSE we see that the multiple correlation coefficient is the percent of the variance, or deviation in y from its mean value, that is explained by the equation when taken as a whole. R^2 will vary between zero and 1, with zero indicating that none of the variation in y was explained by the equation and a value of 1 indicating that 100% of the variation in y was explained by the equation. For time series studies expect a high R^2 and for cross-section data expect low R^2.

While a high R^2 is desirable, remember that it is the tests of the hypothesis concerning the existence of a relationship between a set of independent variables and a particular dependent variable that was the motivating factor in using the regression model. It is validating a cause and effect relationship developed by some theory that is the true reason that we chose the regression analysis. Increasing the number of independent variables will have the effect of increasing R^2. To account for this effect the proper measure of the coefficient of determination is the R–2, adjusted for degrees of freedom, to keep down mindless addition of independent variables.

There is no statistical test for the R^2 and thus little can be said about the model using R^2 with our characteristic confidence level. Two models that have the same size of SSE, that is sum of squared errors, may have very different R^2 if the competing models have different SST, total sum of squared deviations. The goodness of fit of the two models is the same; they both have the same sum of squares unexplained, errors squared, but because of the larger total sum of squares on one of the models the R^2 differs. Again, the real value of regression as a tool is to examine hypotheses developed from a model that predicts certain relationships among the variables. These are tests of hypotheses on the coefficients of the model and not a game of maximizing R^2.

Another way to test the general quality of the overall model is to test the coefficients as a group rather than independently. Because this is multiple regression (more than one X), we use the F-test to determine if our coefficients collectively affect Y. The hypothesis is:

$$H_o : \beta_1 = \beta_2 = \ \dots \ = \beta_i = 0$$

Ha:Ha: "at least one of the βi is not equal to 0"

If the null hypothesis cannot be rejected, then we conclude that none of the independent variables contribute to explaining the variation in Y. Reviewing Figure 13.10 we see that SSR, the explained sum of squares, is a measure of just how much of the variation in Y is explained by all the variables in the model. SSE, the sum of the errors squared, measures just how much is unexplained. It follows that the ratio of these two can provide us with a statistical test of the model as a whole. Remembering that the F distribution is a ratio of Chi squared distributions and that variances are distributed according to Chi Squared, and the sum of squared errors and the sum of squares are both variances, we have the test statistic for this hypothesis as:

$$F_c = \frac{\left(\frac{SSR}{k}\right)}{\left(\frac{SSE}{n-k-1}\right)}$$

where *n* is the number of observations and *k* is the number of independent variables. It can be shown that this is equivalent to:

$$F_c = \frac{n-k-1}{k} * \frac{R^2}{1-R^2}$$

Figure 13.10 where R^2 is the coefficient of determination which is also a measure of the "goodness" of the model.

As with all our tests of hypothesis, we reach a conclusion by comparing the calculated F statistic with the critical value given our desired level of confidence. If the calculated test statistic, an F statistic in this case, is in the tail of the distribution, then we cannot accept the null hypothesis. By not being able to accept the null hypotheses we conclude that this specification of this model has validity, because at least one of the estimated coefficients is significantly different from zero.

An alternative way to reach this conclusion is to use the p-value comparison rule. The p-value is the area in the tail, given the calculated F statistic. In essence, the computer is finding the F value in the table for us. The computer regression output for the calculated F statistic is typically found in the ANOVA table section labeled "significance F". How to read the output of an Excel regression is presented below. This is the probability of NOT accepting a false null hypothesis. If this probability is less than our pre-determined alpha error, then the conclusion is that we cannot accept the null hypothesis.

Dummy Variables

Thus far the analysis of the OLS regression technique assumed that the independent variables in the models tested were continuous random variables. There are, however, no restrictions in the regression model against independent variables that are binary. This opens the regression model for testing hypotheses concerning categorical variables such as gender, race, region of the country, before a certain data, after a certain date and innumerable others. These categorical variables take on only two values, 1 and 0, success or failure, from the binomial probability distribution. The form of the equation becomes:

$$\hat{y} = b_0 + b_2x_2 + b_1x_1$$

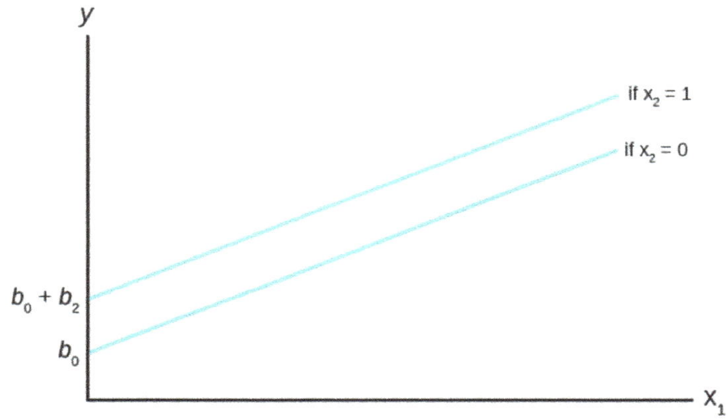

Figure 13.11

where x_2=0,1. X_2 is the dummy variable and X_1 is some continuous random variable. The constant, b_0, is the y-intercept, the value where the line crosses the y-axis. When the value of $X_2 = 0$, the estimated line crosses at b_0. When the value of $X_2 = 1$ then the estimated line crosses at $b_0 + b_2$. In effect the dummy variable causes the estimated line to shift either up or down by the size of the effect of the characteristic captured by the dummy variable. Note that this is a simple parallel shift and does not affect the impact of the other independent variable; X_1.This variable is a continuous random variable and predicts different values of y at different values of X_1 holding constant the condition of the dummy variable.

An example of the use of a dummy variable is the work estimating the impact of gender on salaries. There is a full body of literature on this topic and dummy variables are used extensively. For this example the salaries of elementary and secondary school teachers for a particular state is examined. Using a homogeneous job category, school teachers, and for a single state reduces many of the variations that naturally effect salaries such as differential physical risk, cost of living in a particular state, and other working conditions. The estimating equation in its simplest form specifies salary as a function of various teacher characteristic that economic theory would suggest could affect salary. These would include education level as a measure of potential productivity, age and/or experience to capture on-the-job training, again as a measure of productivity. Because the data are for school teachers employed in a public school districts rather than workers in a for-profit company, the school district's average revenue per average daily student attendance is included as a measure of ability to pay. The results of the regression analysis using data on 24,916 school teachers are presented below.

Table 13.1 Earnings Estimate for Elementary and Secondary School Teachers

Variable	Regression Coefficients (b)	Standard Errors of the estimates for teacher's earnings function (sb)
Intercept	4269.9	
Gender (male = 1)	632.38	13.39
Total Years of Experience	52.32	1.10
Years of Experience in Current District	29.97	1.52
Education	629.33	13.16
Total Revenue per ADA	90.24	3.76
R−2*R*−2	.725	
n	24,916	

The coefficients for all the independent variables are significantly different from zero as indicated by the standard errors. Dividing the standard errors of each coefficient results in a t-value greater than 1.96 which is the required level for 95% significance. The binary variable, our dummy variable of interest in this analysis, is gender where male is given a value of 1 and female given a value of 0. The coefficient is significantly different from zero with a dramatic t-statistic of 47 standard deviations. We thus cannot accept the null hypothesis that the coefficient is equal to zero. Therefore we conclude that there is a premium paid male teachers of $632 after holding constant experience, education and the wealth of the school district in which the teacher is employed. It is important to note that these data are from some time ago and the $632 represents a six percent salary premium at that time. A graph of this example of dummy variables is presented below.

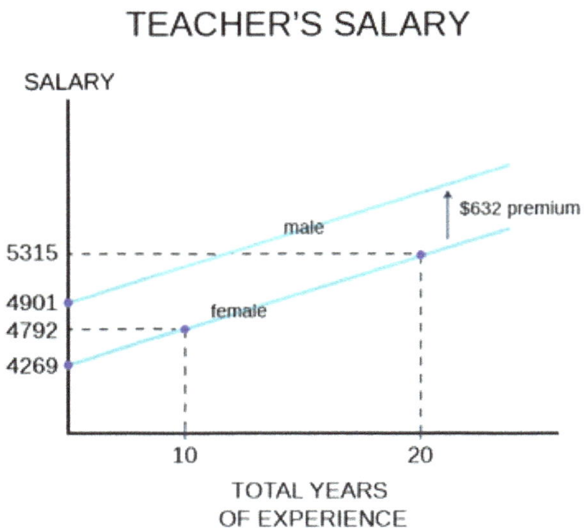

Figure 13.12

In two dimensions, salary is the dependent variable on the vertical axis and total years of experience was chosen for the continuous independent variable on horizontal axis. Any of the other independent variables could have been chosen to illustrate the effect of the dummy variable. The relationship between total years of experience has a slope of $52.32 per year of experience and the estimated line has an intercept of $4,269 if the gender variable is equal to zero, for female. If the gender variable is equal to 1, for male, the coefficient for the gender variable is added to the intercept and thus the relationship between total years of experience and salary is shifted upward parallel as indicated on the graph. Also marked on the graph are various points for reference. A female school teacher with 10 years of experience receives a salary of $4,792 on the basis of her experience only, but this is still $109 less than a male teacher with zero years of experience.

A more complex interaction between a dummy variable and the dependent variable can also be estimated. It may be that the dummy variable has more than a simple shift effect on the dependent variable, but also interacts with one or more of the other continuous independent variables. While not tested in the example above, it could be hypothesized that the impact of gender on salary was not a one-time shift, but impacted the value of additional years of experience on salary also. That is, female school teacher's salaries were discounted at the start, and further did not grow at the same rate from the effect of experience as for male school teachers. This would show up as a different slope for the relationship between total years of experience for males than for females. If this is so then females school teachers would not just start behind their male colleagues (as measured by the shift in the estimated regression line), but would fall further and further behind as time and experienced increased.

The graph below shows how this hypothesis can be tested with the use of dummy variables and an interaction variable.

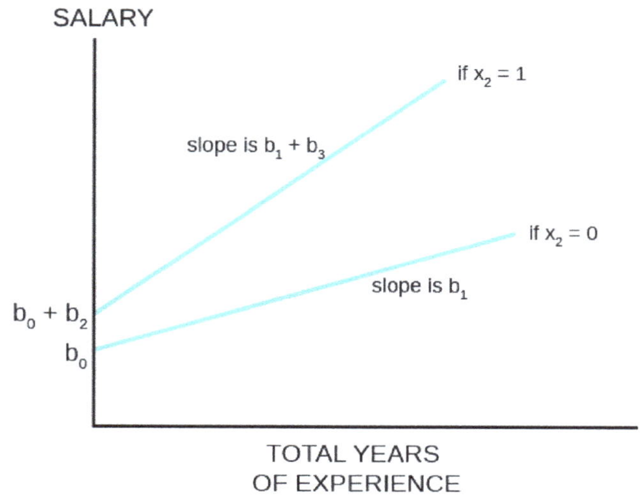

$$\hat{y} = b_0 + b_2x_2 + b_1x_1 + b_3x_2x_1$$

Figure 13.13

The estimating equation shows how the slope of X_1, the continuous random variable experience, contains two parts, b_1 and b_3. This occurs because of the new variable X_2 X_1, called the interaction variable, was created to allow for an effect on the slope of X_1 from changes in X_2, the binary dummy variable. Note that when the dummy variable, $X_2 = 0$ the interaction variable has a value of 0, but when $X_2 = 1$ the interaction variable has a value of X_1. The coefficient b_3 is an estimate of the difference in the coefficient of X_1 when $X_2 = 1$ compared to when $X_2 = 0$. In the example of teacher's salaries, if there is a premium paid to male teachers that affects the rate of increase in salaries from experience, then the rate at which male teachers' salaries rises would be $b_1 + b_3$ and the rate at which female teachers' salaries rise would be simply b_1. This hypothesis can be tested with the hypothesis:

$$H_0 : \beta_3 = 0 | \beta_1 = 0, \ \beta_2 = 0$$
$$H_a : \beta_3 \neq 0 | \beta_1 \neq 0, \ \beta_2 \neq 0$$

This is a t-test using the test statistic for the parameter β_3. If we cannot accept the null hypothesis that β_3=0 we conclude there is a difference between the rate of increase for the group for whom the value of the binary variable is set to 1, males in this example. This estimating equation can be combined with our earlier one that tested only a parallel shift in the estimated line. The earnings/experience functions in Figure 13.13 are drawn for this case with a shift in the earnings function and a difference in the slope of the function with respect to total years of experience.

EXAMPLE 13.5

A random sample of 11 statistics students produced the following data, where *x* is the third exam score out of 80, and *y* is the final exam score out of 200. Can you predict the final exam score of a randomly selected student if you know the third exam score?

Table 13.2 Table showing the scores on the final exam based on scores from the third exam.

x (third exam score)	y (final exam score)
65	175
67	133
71	185
71	163
66	126
75	198
67	153
70	163
71	159
69	151
69	159

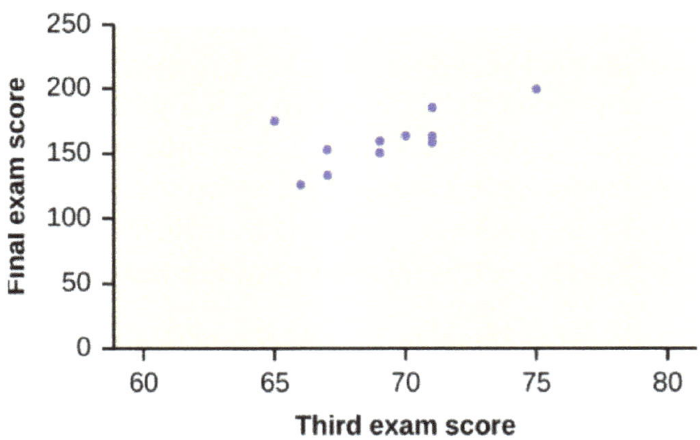

Figure 13.14 Scatter plot showing the scores on the final exam based on scores from the third exam.

13.5 INTERPRETATION OF REGRESSION COEFFICIENTS: ELASTICITY AND LOGARITHMIC TRANSFORMATION

As we have seen, the coefficient of an equation estimated using OLS regression analysis provides an estimate of the slope of a straight line that is assumed be the relationship between the dependent variable and at least one independent variable. From the calculus, the slope of the line is the first derivative and tells us the magnitude of the impact of a one unit change in the XX variable upon the value of the YY variable measured in the units of the YY variable. As we saw in the case of dummy variables, this can show up as a parallel shift in the estimated line or even a change in the slope of the line through an interactive variable. Here we wish to explore the concept of elasticity and how we can use a regression analysis to estimate the various elasticities in which economists have an interest.

The concept of elasticity is borrowed from engineering and physics where it is used to measure a material's responsiveness to a force, typically a physical force such as a stretching/pulling force. It is from here that we get the term an "elastic" band. In economics, the force in question is some market force such as a change in price or income. Elasticity is measured as a percentage change/response in both engineering applications and in economics. The value of measuring in percentage terms is that the units of measurement do not play a role in the value of the measurement and thus allows direct comparison between elasticities. As an example, if the price of gasoline increased say 50 cents from an initial price of $3.00 and generated a decline in monthly consumption for a consumer from 50 gallons to 48 gallons we calculate the elasticity to be 0.25. The price elasticity is the percentage change in quantity resulting from some percentage change in price. A 16 percent increase in price has generated only a 4 percent decrease in demand: 16% price change → 4% quantity change or .04/.16 = .25. This is called an inelastic demand meaning a small response to the price change. This comes about because there are few if any real substitutes for gasoline; perhaps public transportation, a bicycle or walking. Technically, of course, the percentage change in demand from a price increase is a decline in demand thus price elasticity is a negative number. The common convention, however, is to talk about elasticity as the absolute value of the number. Some goods have many substitutes: pears for apples for plums, for grapes, etc. etc. The elasticity for such goods is larger than one and are called elastic in demand. Here a small percentage change in price will induce a large percentage change in quantity demanded. The consumer will easily shift the demand to the close substitute.

While this discussion has been about price changes, any of the independent variables in a demand equation will have an associated elasticity. Thus, there is an income elasticity that measures the sensitivity of demand to changes in income: not much for the demand for food, but very sensitive for yachts. If the demand equation contains a term for substitute goods, say candy bars in a demand equation for cookies, then the responsiveness of demand for cookies from changes in prices of candy bars can be measured. This is called the cross-price elasticity of demand

and to an extent can be thought of as brand loyalty from a marketing view. How responsive is the demand for Coca-Cola to changes in the price of Pepsi?

Now imagine the demand for a product that is very expensive. Again, the measure of elasticity is in percentage terms thus the elasticity can be directly compared to that for gasoline: an elasticity of 0.25 for gasoline conveys the same information as an elasticity of 0.25 for $25,000 car. Both goods are considered by the consumer to have few substitutes and thus have inelastic demand curves, elasticities less than one.

The mathematical formulae for various elasticities are:

$$\text{Price elasticity:} \eta_p = \frac{(\%\Delta Q)}{(\%\Delta P)}$$

Where η is the Greek small case letter eta used to designate elasticity. Δ is read as "change".

$$\text{Income elasticity:} \eta_Y = \frac{(\%\Delta Q)}{(\%\Delta Y)}$$

Where Y is used as the symbol for income.

$$\text{Cross-Price elasticity:} \eta_{p1} = \frac{(\%\Delta Q_1)}{(\%\Delta P_2)}$$

Where P2 is the price of the substitute good.

Examining closer the price elasticity we can write the formula as:

$$\eta_p = \frac{(\%\Delta Q)}{(\%\Delta P)} = \frac{dQ}{dP}\left(\frac{P}{Q}\right) = b\left(\frac{P}{Q}\right)$$

Where bb is the estimated coefficient for price in the OLS regression.

The first form of the equation demonstrates the principle that elasticities are measured in percentage terms. Of course, the ordinary least squares coefficients provide an estimate of the impact of a unit change in the independent variable, X, on the dependent variable measured in units of Y. These coefficients are not elasticities, however, and are shown in the second way of writing the formula for elasticity as $\left(\frac{dQ}{dP}\right)$, the derivative of the estimated demand function which is simply the slope of the regression line. Multiplying the slope times $\frac{P}{Q}$ provides an elasticity measured in percentage terms.

Along a straight-line demand curve the percentage change, thus elasticity, changes continuously as the scale changes, while the slope, the estimated regression coefficient, remains constant. Going back to the demand for gasoline. A change in price from \$3.00 to \$3.50 was a 16 percent increase in price. If the beginning price were \$5.00 then the same 50¢ increase would be only a 10 percent increase generating a different elasticity. Every straight-line demand curve has a range of elasticities starting at the top left, high prices, with large elasticity numbers, elastic demand, and decreasing as one goes down the demand curve, inelastic demand.

In order to provide a meaningful estimate of the elasticity of demand the convention is to estimate the elasticity at the point of means. Remember that all OLS regression lines will go through the point of means. At this point is the greatest weight of the data used to estimate the coefficient. The formula to estimate an elasticity when an OLS demand curve has been estimated becomes:

$$\eta_p = b\left(\frac{\bar{P}}{\bar{Q}}\right)$$

Where $\bar{P}$ and $\bar{Q}$ are the mean values of these data used to estimate bb, the price coefficient.

The same method can be used to estimate the other elasticities for the demand function by using the appropriate mean values of the other variables; income and price of substitute goods for example.

Logarithmic Transformation of the Data

Ordinary least squares estimates typically assume that the population relationship among the variables is linear thus of the form presented in The Regression Equation. In this form the interpretation of the coefficients is as discussed above; quite simply the coefficient provides an estimate of the impact of a one **unit** change in X on Y measured in units of Y. It does not matter just where along the line one wishes to make the measurement because it is a straight line with a constant slope thus constant estimated level of impact per unit change. It may be, however, that the analyst wishes to estimate not the simple unit measured impact on the Y variable, but the magnitude of the percentage impact on Y of a one unit change in the X variable. Such a case might be how a unit change in experience, say one year, effects not the absolute amount of a worker's wage, but the percentage impact on the worker's wage. Alternatively, it may be that the question asked is the unit measured impact on Y of a specific percentage increase in X. An example may be "by how many dollars will sales increase if the firm spends X percent more on advertising?" The third possibility is the case of elasticity discussed above. Here we are interested in the percentage impact on quantity demanded for a given percentage change in price, or income or perhaps the price of a substitute good. All three of these cases can be estimated by transforming the data to logarithms before running the regression. The resulting coefficients will then provide a percentage change measurement of the relevant variable.

To summarize, there are four cases:

1. Unit ΔX → Unit ΔY (Standard OLS case)
2. Unit ΔX → %ΔY
3. %ΔX → Unit ΔY
4. %ΔX → %ΔY (elasticity case)

Case 1: The ordinary least squares case begins with the linear model developed above:

$$Y = a + bX$$

where the coefficient of the independent variable $b = \frac{dY}{dX}$ is the slope of a straight line and thus measures the impact of a unit change in X on Y measured in units of Y.

Case 2: The underlying estimated equation is:

$$\log(Y) = a + bX$$

The equation is estimated by converting the Y values to logarithms and using OLS techniques to estimate the coefficient of the X variable, b. This is called a semi-log estimation. Again, differentiating both sides of the equation allows us to develop the interpretation of the X coefficient b:

$$d(\log_Y) = bdX$$

$$\frac{dY}{Y} = bdX$$

Multiply by 100 to covert to percentages and rearranging terms gives:

$$100b = \frac{\%\Delta Y}{\text{Unit } \Delta X}$$

100*b* is thus the percentage change in Y resulting from a unit change in X.

Case 3: In this case the question is "what is the unit change in Y resulting from a percentage change in X?" What is the dollar loss in revenues of a five percent increase in price or what is the total dollar cost impact of a five percent increase in labor costs? The estimated equation for this case would be:

$$Y = a + B\log(X)$$

Here the calculus differential of the estimated equation is:

$$dY = bd(\log X)$$
$$dY = b\frac{dX}{X}$$

Divide by 100 to get percentage and rearranging terms gives:

$$\frac{b}{100} = \frac{dY}{100\frac{dX}{X}} = \frac{\text{Unit } \Delta Y}{\% \Delta X}$$

Therefore, $b100$ is the increase in Y measured in units from a one percent increase in X.

Case 4: This is the elasticity case where both the dependent and independent variables are converted to logs before the OLS estimation. This is known as the log-log case or double log case, and provides us with direct estimates of the elasticities of the independent variables. The estimated equation is:

$$\log Y = a + b\log X$$

Differentiating we have:

$$d(\log Y) = bd(\log X)$$
$$d(\log X) = b\frac{1}{X}dX$$

thus:

$$\frac{1}{Y}dY = b\frac{1}{X}dX \quad \text{OR} \quad \frac{dY}{Y} = b\frac{dX}{X} \quad \text{OR} \quad b = \frac{dY}{dX}\left(\frac{X}{Y}\right)$$

and $b = \frac{\% \Delta Y}{\% \Delta X}$ our definition of elasticity. We conclude that we can directly estimate the elasticity of a variable through double log transformation of the data. The estimated coefficient is the elasticity. It is common to use double log transformation of all variables in the estimation of demand functions to get estimates of all the various elasticities of the demand curve.

13.6 PREDICTING WITH A REGRESSION EQUATION

One important value of an estimated regression equation is its ability to predict the effects on Y of a change in one or more values of the independent variables. The value of this is obvious. Careful policy cannot be made without estimates of the effects that may result. Indeed, it is the desire for particular results that drive the formation of most policy. Regression models can be, and have been, invaluable aids in forming such policies.

The Gauss-Markov theorem assures us that the point estimate of the impact on the dependent variable derived by putting in the equation the hypothetical values of the independent variables one wishes to simulate will result in an estimate of the dependent variable which is minimum variance and unbiased. That is to say that from this equation comes the best unbiased point estimate of y given the values of x.

$$\hat{y} = b_0 + b, X_{1i} + \cdots + b_k X_{ki}$$

Remember that point estimates do not carry a particular level of probability, or level of confidence, because points have no "width" above which there is an area to measure. This was why we developed confidence intervals for the mean and proportion earlier. The same concern arises here also. There are actually two different approaches to the issue of developing estimates of changes in the independent variable, or variables, on the dependent variable. The first approach wishes to measure the expected mean value of y from a specific change in the value of x: this specific value implies the expected value. Here the question is: what is the mean impact on y that would result from multiple hypothetical experiments on y at this specific value of x. Remember that there is a variance around the estimated parameter of x and thus each experiment will result in a bit of a different estimate of the predicted value of y.

The second approach to estimate the effect of a specific value of x on y treats the event as a single experiment: you choose x and multiply it times the coefficient and that provides a single estimate of y. Because this approach acts as if there were a single experiment the variance that exists in the parameter estimate is larger than the variance associated with the expected value approach.

The conclusion is that we have two different ways to predict the effect of values of the independent variable(s) on the dependent variable and thus we have two different intervals. Both are correct answers to the question being asked, but there are two different questions. To avoid confusion, the first case where we are asking for the expected value of the mean of the estimated y, is called a confidence interval as we have named this concept before. The second case, where we are asking for the estimate of the impact on the dependent variable y of a single experiment using a value of x, is called the prediction interval. The test statistics for these two interval measures within which the estimated value of y will fall are:

Confidence Interval for Expected Value of Mean Value of y for x=x_p

$$\hat{y} = \pm t_{\frac{\alpha}{2}} s_e \left(\sqrt{\frac{1}{n} + \frac{(x_p - \bar{x})^2}{s_x}} \right)$$

Prediction Interval for an Individual y for x = x_p

$$\hat{y} = \pm t_{\frac{\alpha}{2}} s_e \left(\sqrt{1 + \frac{1}{n} + \frac{(x_p - \bar{x})^2}{s_x}} \right)$$

Where s_e is the standard deviation of the error term and s_x is the standard deviation of the x variable.

The mathematical computations of these two test statistics are complex. Various computer regression software packages provide programs within the regression functions to provide answers to inquires of estimated predicted values of y given various values chosen for the x variable(s). It is important to know just which interval is being tested in the computer package because the difference in the size of the standard deviations will change the size of the interval estimated. This is shown in Figure 13.15.

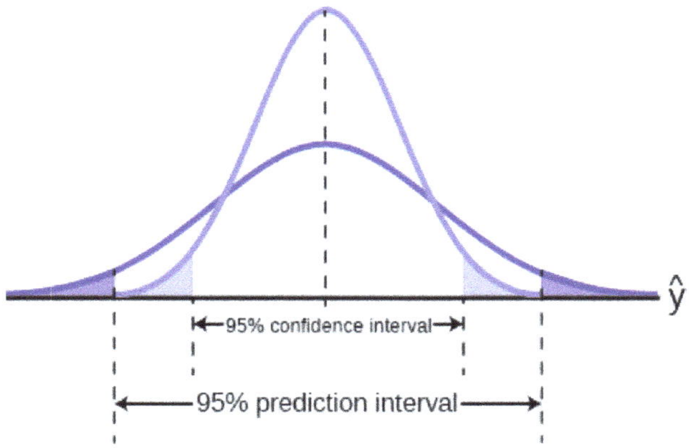

Figure 13.15 Prediction and confidence intervals for regression equation; 95% confidence level.

Figure 13.15 shows visually the difference the standard deviation makes in the size of the estimated intervals. The confidence interval, measuring the expected value of the dependent variable, is smaller than the prediction interval for the same level of confidence. The expected value method assumes that the experiment is conducted multiple times rather than just once as in the other method. The logic here is similar, although not identical, to that discussed when developing the relationship between the sample size and the confidence interval using the Central Limit Theorem. There, as the number of experiments increased, the distribution narrowed and the confidence interval became tighter around the expected value of the mean.

It is also important to note that the intervals around a point estimate are highly dependent upon the range of data used to estimate the equation regardless of which approach is being used for prediction. Remember that all regression equations go through the point of means, that is, the mean value of y and the mean values of all independent variables in the equation. As the value of x chosen to estimate the associated value of y is further from the point of means the width of the estimated interval around the point estimate increases. Choosing values of x beyond the range of the data used to estimate the equation possess even greater danger of creating estimates with little use; very large intervals, and risk of error. Figure 13.16 shows this relationship.

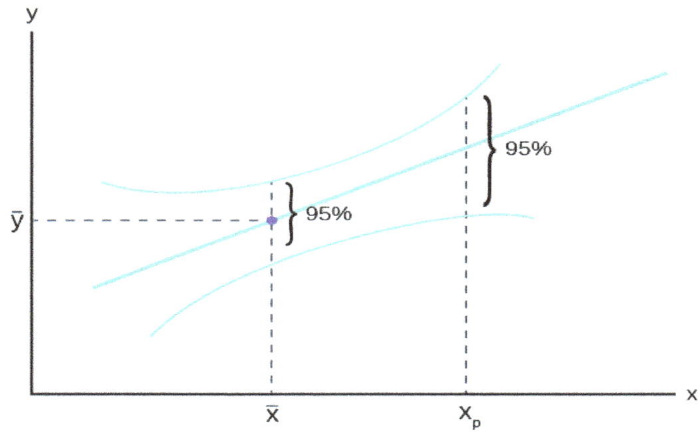

Figure 13.16 Confidence interval for an individual value of x, X_p, at 95% level of confidence

Figure 13.16 demonstrates the concern for the quality of the estimated interval whether it is a prediction interval or a confidence interval. As the value chosen to predict y, X_p in the graph, is further from the central weight of the data, X⁻⁻⁻X^-, we see the interval expand in width even while holding constant the level of confidence. This shows that the precision of any estimate will diminish as one tries to predict beyond the largest weight of the data and most certainly will degrade rapidly for predictions beyond the range of the data. Unfortunately, this is just where most predictions are desired. They can be made, but the width of the confidence interval may be so large as to render the prediction useless. Only actual calculation and the particular application can determine this, however.

EXAMPLE 13.6

Recall the third exam/final exam example .

We found the equation of the best-fit line for the final exam grade as a function of the grade on the third-exam. We can now use the least-squares regression line for prediction. Assume the coefficient for X was determined to be significantly different from zero.

Suppose you want to estimate, or predict, the mean final exam score of statistics students who received 73 on the third exam. The exam scores (x-values) range from 65 to 75. Since 73 is between the x-values 65 and 75, we feel comfortable to substitute $x = 73$ into the equation. Then:

$$\hat{y} = -173.51 + 4.83(73) = 179.08$$

We predict that statistics students who earn a grade of 73 on the third exam will earn a grade of 179.08 on the final exam, on average.

a. What would you predict the final exam score to be for a student who scored a 66 on the third exam?

Solution 13.6

a. 145.27

b. What would you predict the final exam score to be for a student who scored a 90 on the third exam?

Solution 13.6

b. The x values in the data are between 65 and 75. Ninety is outside of the domain of the observed x values in the data (independent variable), so you cannot reliably predict the final exam score for this student. (Even though it is possible to enter 90 into the equation for x and calculate a corresponding y value, the y value that you get will have a confidence interval that may not be meaningful.)

To understand really how unreliable the prediction can be outside of the observed x values observed in the data, make the substitution $x = 90$ into the equation.

$$\hat{y} = -173.51 + 4.83(90) = 261.19$$

The final-exam score is predicted to be 261.19. The largest the final-exam score can be is 200.

13.7 HOW TO USE MICROSOFT EXCELR FOR REGRESSION ANALYSIS

This section of this chapter is here in recognition that what we are now asking requires much more than a quick calculation of a ratio or a square root. Indeed, the use of regression analysis was almost non- existent before the middle of the last century and did not really become a widely used tool until perhaps the late 1960's and early 1970's. Even then the computational ability of even the largest IBM machines is laughable by today's standards. In the early days programs were developed by the researchers and shared. There was no market for something called "software" and certainly nothing called "apps", an entrant into the market only a few years old.

With the advent of the personal computer and the explosion of a vital software market we have a number of regression and statistical analysis packages to choose from. Each has their merits. We have chosen Microsoft Excel because of the wide-spread availability both on college campuses and in the post-college market place. Stata is an alternative and has features that will be important for more advanced econometrics study if you choose to follow this path. Even more advanced packages exist, but typically require the analyst to do some significant amount of programing to conduct their analysis. The goal of this section is to demonstrate how to use Excel to run a regression and then to do so with an example of a simple version of a demand curve.

The first step to doing a regression using Excel is to load the program into your computer. If you have Excel you have the Analysis ToolPak although you may not have it activated. The program calls upon a significant amount of space so is not loaded automatically.

To activate the Analysis ToolPak follow these steps:

Click "File" > "Options" > "Add-ins" to bring up a menu of the add-in "ToolPaks". Select "Analysis ToolPak" and click "GO" next to "Manage: excel add-ins" near the bottom of the window. This will open a new window where you click "Analysis ToolPak" (make sure there is a green check mark in the box) and then click "OK". Now there should be an Analysis tab under the data menu. These steps are presented in the following screen shots.

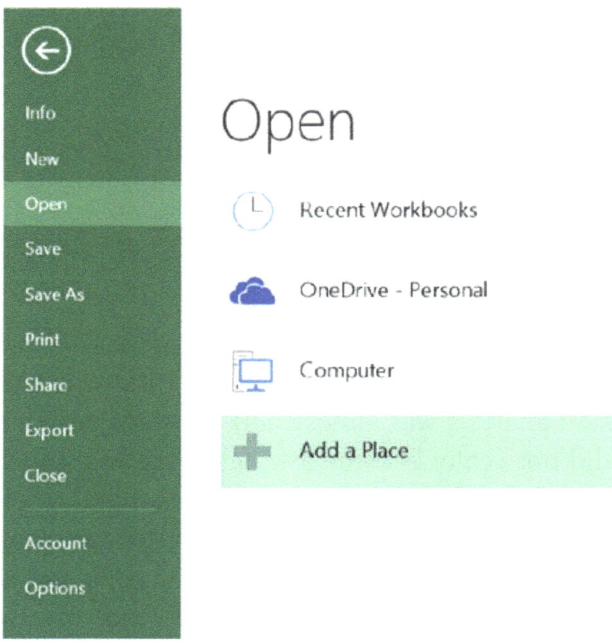

Figure 13.17

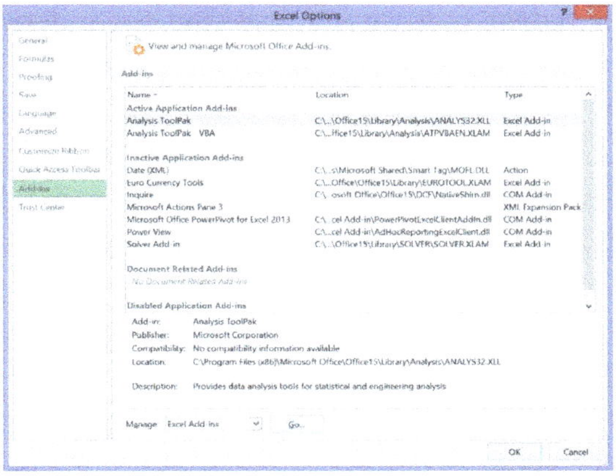

Figure 13.18

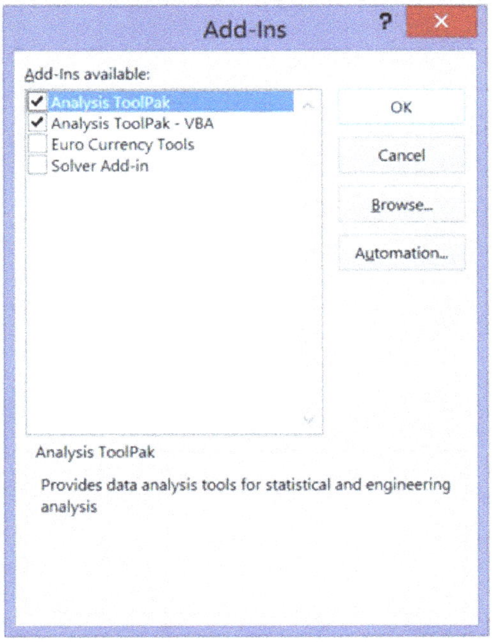

Figure 13.19

Figure 13.20

Click "Data" then "Data Analysis" and then click "Regression" and "OK". Congratulations, you have made it to the regression window. The window asks for your inputs. Clicking the box next to the Y and X ranges will allow you to use the click and drag feature of Excel to select your input ranges. Excel has one odd quirk and that is the click and drop feature requires that the independent variables, the X variables, are all together, meaning that they form a single matrix. If your data are set up with the Y variable between two columns of X variables Excel will not allow you to use click and drag. As an example, say Column A and Column C are independent variables and Column B is the Y variable, the dependent variable. Excel will not allow you to click and drop the data ranges. The solution is to move the column with the Y variable to column A and then you can click and drag. The same problem arises again if you want to run the regression with only some of the X variables. You will need to set up the matrix so all the X variables you wish to regress are in a tightly formed matrix. These steps are presented in the following scene shots.

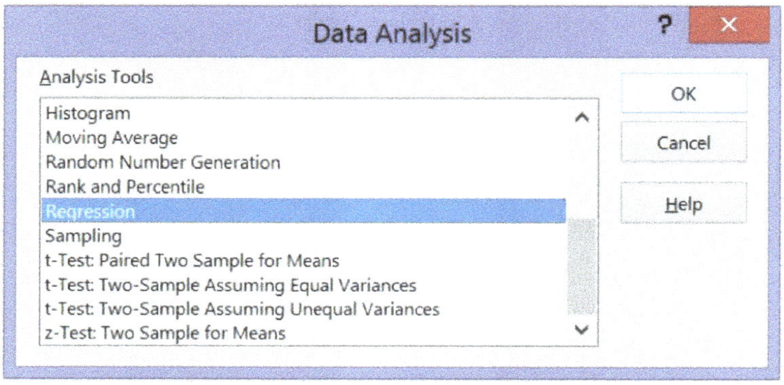

Figure 13.21

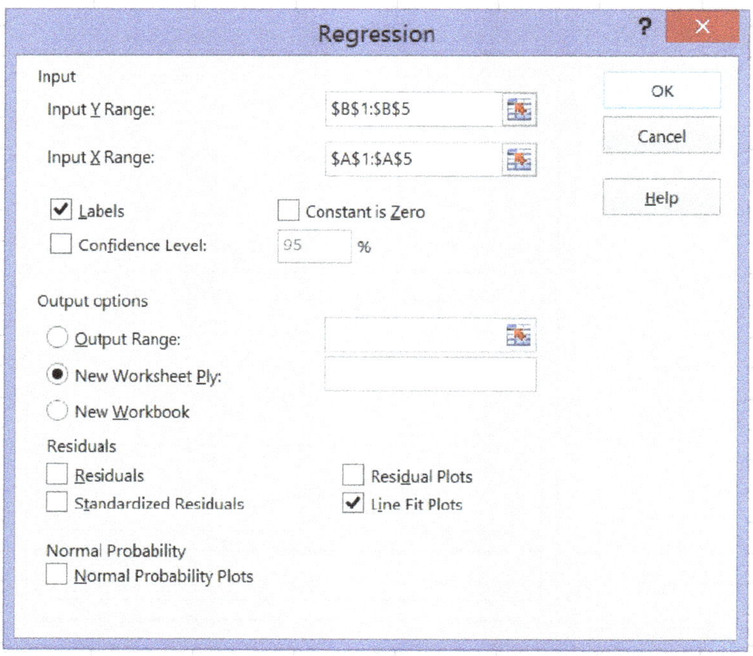

Figure 13.22

Once you have selected the data for your regression analysis and told Excel which one is the dependent variable (Y) and which ones are the independent valuables (X's), you have several choices as to the parameters and how the output will be displayed. Refer to screen shot Figure 13.22 under "Input" section. If you check the "labels" box the program will place the entry in the first column of each variable as its name in the output. You can enter an actual name, such as price or income in a demand analysis, in row one of the Excel spreadsheet for each variable and it will be displayed in the output.

The level of significance can also be set by the analyst. This will not change the calculated t statistic, called t stat, but will alter the p value for the calculated t statistic. It will also alter the boundaries of the confidence intervals for the coefficients. A 95 percent confidence interval is always presented, but with a change in this you will also get other levels of confidence for the intervals.

Excel also will allow you to suppress the intercept. This forces the regression program to minimize the residual sum of squares under the condition that the estimated line must go through the origin. This is done in cases where there is no meaning in the model at some value other than zero, zero for the start of the line. An example is an economic production function that is a relationship between the number of units of an input, say hours of labor, and output. There is no meaning of positive output with zero workers.

Once the data are entered and the choices are made click OK and the results will be sent to a separate new worksheet by default. The output from Excel is presented in a way typical of other regression package programs. The first block of information gives the overall statistics of the regression: Multiple R, R Squared, and the R squared adjusted for degrees of freedom, which is the one you want to report. You also get the Standard error (of the estimate) and the number of observations in the regression.

The second block of information is titled ANOVA which stands for Analysis of Variance. Our interest in this section is the column marked F. This is the calculated F statistics for the null hypothesis that all of the coefficients are equal to zero verse the alternative that at least one of the coefficients are not equal to zero. This hypothesis test was presented in 13.4 under "How Good is the Equation?" The next column gives the p value for this test under the title "Significance F". If the p value is less than say 0.05 (the calculated F statistic is in the tail) we can say with 90 % confidence that we cannot accept the null hypotheses that all the coefficients are equal to zero. This is a good thing: it means that at least one of the coefficients is significantly different from zero thus do have an effect on the value of Y.

The last block of information contains the hypothesis tests for the individual coefficient. The estimated coefficients, the intercept and the slopes, are first listed and then each standard error (of the estimated coefficient) followed by the t stat (calculated student's t statistic for the null hypothesis that the coefficient is equal to zero). We compare the t stat and the critical value of the student's t, dependent on the degrees of freedom, and determine if we have enough evidence to reject the null that the variable has no effect on Y. Remember that we have set up the null hypothesis as the status quo and our claim that we know what caused the Y to change is in the alternative hypothesis. We want to reject the status quo and substitute our version of the world, the alternative hypothesis. The next column contains the p values for this hypothesis test followed by the estimated upper and lower bound of the confidence interval of the estimated slope parameter for various levels of confidence set by us at the beginning.

Estimating the Demand for Roses

Here is an example of using the Excel program to run a regression for a particular specific case: estimating the demand for roses. We are trying to estimate a demand curve, which from economic theory we expect certain variables affect how much of a good we buy. The relationship between the price of a good and the quantity demanded is the demand curve. Beyond that we have the demand function that includes other relevant variables: a person's income, the price of substitute goods, and perhaps other variables such as season of the year or the price of complimentary goods. Quantity demanded will be our Y variable, and Price of roses, Price of carnations and Income will be our independent variables, the X variables.

For all of these variables theory tells us the expected relationship. For the price of the good in question, roses, theory predicts an inverse relationship, the negatively sloped demand curve. Theory also predicts the relationship between the quantity demanded of one good, here roses, and the price of a substitute, carnations in this example. Theory predicts that this should be a positive or direct relationship; as the price of the substitute falls we substitute away from roses to the cheaper substitute, carnations. A reduction in the price of the substitute generates a reduction in demand for the good being analyzed, roses here. Reduction generates reduction is a positive relationship. For normal goods, theory also predicts a positive relationship; as our incomes rise we buy more of the good, roses. We expect these results because that is what is predicted by a hundred years of economic theory and research. Essentially we are testing these century-old hypotheses. The data gathered was determined by the model that is being tested. This should always be the case. One is not doing inferential statistics by throwing a mountain of data into a computer and asking the machine for a theory. Theory first, test follows.

These data here are national average prices and income is the nation's per capita personal income. Quantity demanded is total national annual sales of roses. These are annual time series data; we are tracking the rose market for the United States from 1984-2017, 33 observations.

Because of the quirky way Excel requires how the data are entered into the regression package it is best to have the independent variables, price of roses, price of carnations and income next to each other on the spreadsheet. Once your data are entered into the spreadsheet it is always good to look at the data. Examine the range, the means and the standard deviations. Use your understanding of descriptive statistics from the very first part of this course. In large data sets you will not be able to "scan" the data. The Analysis ToolPac makes it easy to get the range, mean, standard deviations and other parameters of the distributions. You can also quickly get the correlations among the variables. Examine for outliers. Review the history. Did something happen? Was here a labor strike, change in import fees, something that makes these observations unusual? Do not take the data without question. There may have been a typo somewhere, who knows without review.

Go to the regression window, enter the data and select 95% confidence level and click "OK". You can include the labels in the input range if you have put a title at the top of each column, but be sure to click the "labels" box on the main regression page if you do.

The regression output should show up automatically on a new worksheet.

SUMMARY OUTPUT

Regression Statistics	
Multiple R	0.8560327
R Square	0.732792
Adjusted R Square	0.699391
Standard Error	3629.3427
Observations	33

ANOVA

	df	*SS*	*MS*	*F*	*Significance F*
Regression	3	577972629.2	2.89E+08	21.9392274	2.59893E-05
Residual	29	210754050.4	13172128		
Total	32	788726679.5			

	Coefficients	*Standard Error*	*t Stat*	*P-value*	*Lower 95%*	*Upper 95%*
Intercept	183475.43	16791.81835	10.92648	7.89854E-09	147878.367	219072.5
Price of Roses	-1.7607	0.2982	-5.9043	5.20E-05	-2.4049	-1.1164
Price of Carnations	1.3397	0.5273	2.5407	0.0246	0.208	2.4789
Income (per capita)	3.0338	1.2308	2.464901	0.00886322	0.621432	5.4446

Figure 13.23

The first results presented is the R-Square, a measure of the strength of the correlation between Y and X_1, X_2, and X_3 taken as a group. Our R-square here of 0.699, adjusted for degrees of freedom, means that 70% of the variation in Y, demand for roses, can be explained by variations in X_1, X_2, and X_3, Price of roses, Price of carnations and Income. There is no statistical test to determine the "significance" of an R^2. Of course a higher R^2 is preferred, but it is really the significance of the coefficients that will determine the value of the theory being tested and which will become part of any policy discussion if they are demonstrated to be significantly different from zero.

Looking at the third panel of output we can write the equation as:

$$Y = b_0 + b_1 X_1 + b_2 X_2 + b_3 X_3 + e$$

where b_0 is the intercept, b_1 is the estimated coefficient on price of roses, and b_2 is the estimated coefficient on price of carnations, b_3 is the estimated effect of income and e is the error term. The equation is written in Roman letters indicating that these are the estimated values and not the population parameters, β's.

Our estimated equation is:

Quantity of roses sold=183,475−1.76Price of roses+1.33Price of carnations+3.03Income

We first observe that the signs of the coefficients are as expected from theory. The demand curve is downward sloping with the negative sign for the price of roses. Further the signs of both the price of carnations and income coefficients are positive as would be expected from economic theory.

Interpreting the coefficients can tell us the magnitude of the impact of a change in each variable on the demand for roses. It is the ability to do this which makes regression analysis such a valuable tool. The estimated coefficients tell us that an increase the price of roses by one dollar will lead to a 1.76 reduction in the number roses purchased. The price of carnations seems to play an important role in the demand for roses as we see that increasing the price of carnations by one dollar would increase the demand for roses by 1.33 units as consumers would substitute away from the now more expensive carnations. Similarly, increasing per capita income by one dollar will lead to a 3.03 unit increase in roses purchased.

These results are in line with the predictions of economics theory with respect to all three variables included in this estimate of the demand for roses. It is important to have a theory first that predicts the significance or at least the direction of the coefficients. Without a theory to test, this research tool is not much more helpful than the correlation coefficients we learned about earlier.

We cannot stop there, however. We need to first check whether our coefficients are statistically significant from zero. We set up a hypothesis of:

$$H_0 : \beta_1 = 0$$
$$H_a : \beta_1 \neq 0$$

for all three coefficients in the regression. Recall from earlier that we will not be able to definitively say that our estimated b_1 is the actual real population of β_1, but rather only that with (1-α)% level of confidence that we cannot reject the null hypothesis that our estimated β_1 is significantly different from zero. The analyst is making a claim that the price of roses causes an impact on quantity demanded.

Indeed, that each of the included variables has an impact on the quantity of roses demanded. The claim is therefore in the alternative hypotheses. It will take a very large probability, 0.95 in this case, to overthrow the null hypothesis, the status quo, that $\beta = 0$. In all regression hypothesis tests the claim is in the alternative and the claim is that the theory has found a variable that has a significant impact on the Y variable.

The test statistic for this hypothesis follows the familiar standardizing formula which counts the number of standard deviations, t, that the estimated value of the parameter, b_1, is away from the hypothesized value, β_0, which is zero in this case:

$$t_c = \frac{b_1 - \beta_0}{S_{b_1}}$$

The computer calculates this test statistic and presents it as "t stat". You can find this value to the right of the standard error of the coefficient estimate. The standard error of the coefficient for b_1 is S_{b1} in the formula. To reach a conclusion we compare this test statistic with the critical value of the student's t at degrees of freedom n-3-1 =29, and alpha = 0.025 (5% significance level for a two-tailed test). Our t stat for b_1 is approximately 5.90 which is greater than 1.96 (the critical value we looked up in the t-table), so we cannot accept our null hypotheses of no effect. We conclude that Price has a significant effect because the calculated t value is in the tail. We conduct the same test for b_2 and b_3. For each variable, we find that we cannot accept the null hypothesis of no relationship because the calculated t-statistics are in the tail for each case, that is, greater than the critical value. All variables in this regression have been determined to have a significant effect on the demand for roses.

These tests tell us whether or not an individual coefficient is significantly different from zero, but does not address the overall quality of the model. We have seen that the R squared adjusted for degrees of freedom indicates this model with these three variables explains 70% of the variation in quantity of roses demanded. We can also conduct a second test of the model taken as a whole. This is the F test presented in section 13.4 of this chapter. Because this is a multiple regression (more than one X), we use the F-test to determine if our coefficients collectively affect Y. The hypothesis is:

$$H_0 : \beta_1 = \beta_2 = \ldots = \beta i = 0$$

$$H_a : \text{"at least one of the } \beta_i \text{ is not equal to 0"}$$

Under the ANOVA section of the output we find the calculated F statistic for this hypotheses. For this example the F statistic is 21.9. Again, comparing the calculated F statistic with the critical value given our desired level of significance and the degrees of freedom will allow us to reach a conclusion.

The best way to reach a conclusion for this statistical test is to use the p-value comparison rule. The p-value is the area in the tail, given the calculated F statistic. In essence the computer is finding the F value in the table for us and calculating the p-value. In the Summary Output under "significance F" is this probability. For this example, it is calculated to be 2.6 x 10^{-5}, or 2.6 then moving the decimal five places to the left. (.000026) This is an almost infinitesimal level of probability and is certainly less than our alpha level of .05 for a 5 percent level of significance.

By not being able to accept the null hypotheses we conclude that this specification of this model has validity because at least one of the estimated coefficients is significantly different from zero. Since F-calculated is greater than F-critical, we cannot accept H_0, meaning that X_1, X_2 and X_3 *together* has a significant effect on Y.

The advancement of computing technology and the software applicable for academic and business study has enabled the resolution of inquiries that were previously inexpressible just a few years ago. Data is accessible in electronic format and may be sent for analysis with unprecedented methods and velocities compared to a decade ago. The vast scale of available data sets for research and analysis today yields superior findings compared to previous eras. Even with merely an Excel spreadsheet, we may perform advanced research. This section provides the resources necessary to undertake this intriguing research, with the sole constraint being your creativity.

Terminolgy

a is the symbol for the Y-Intercept Sometimes written as b0*b*0, because when writing the theoretical linear model *β*0 is used to represent a coefficient for a population.

b is the symbol for Slope The word coefficient will be used regularly for the slope, because it is a number that will always be next to the letter "x." It will be written as b_1 when a sample is used, and β_1 will be used with a population or when writing the theoretical linear model.

Bivariate two variables are present in the model where one is the "cause" or independent variable and the other is the "effect" of dependent variable.

Linear a model that takes data and regresses it into a straight line equation.

Multivariate a system or model where more than one independent variable is being used to predict an outcome. There can only ever be one dependent variable, but there is no limit to the number of independent variables.

R^2 – Coefficient of Determination

This is a number between 0 and 1 that represents the percentage variation of the dependent variable that can be explained by the variation in the independent variable. Sometimes calculated by the equation $R^2 = \frac{SSR}{SST}$ where SSR is the "Sum of Squares Regression" and SST is the "Sum of Squares Total." The appropriate coefficient of determination to be reported should always be adjusted for degrees of freedom first.

Residual or "error" the value calculated from subtracting y0-y^0=e0$y0-y^\wedge 0=e0$. The absolute value of a residual measures the vertical distance between the actual value of *y* and the estimated value of *y* that appears on the best-fit line.

R - **Correlation Coefficient** A number between -1 and 1 that represents the strength and direction of the relationship between "X" and "Y." The value for "*r*" will equal 1 or -1 only if all the plotted points form a perfectly straight line.

Sum of Squared Errors (SSE) the calculated value from adding up all the squared residual terms. The hope is that this value is very small when creating a model.

X – the independent variable This will sometimes be referred to as the "predictor" variable, because these values were measured in order to determine what possible outcomes could be predicted.

Y – the dependent variable Also, using the letter "y" represents actual values while y^$y^\wedge$ represents predicted or estimated values. Predicted values will come from plugging in observed "x" values into a linear model.

CHAPTER REVIEW

13.3 Linear Equations

The most basic type of association is a linear association. This type of relationship can be defined algebraically by the equations used, numerically with actual or predicted data values, or graphically from a plotted curve. (Lines are classified as straight curves.) Algebraically, a linear equation typically takes the form $y = mx + b$, where *m* and *b* are constants, **x** is the independent variable, *y* is the dependent variable. In a statistical context, a linear equation is written in the form $y = a + bx$, where *a* and *b* are the constants. This form is used to help readers distinguish the statistical context from the algebraic context. In the equation $y = a + bx$, the constant *b*, called the coefficient, represents the slope. The constant *a* is called the y-intercept.

The slope of a line is a value that describes the rate of change between the independent and dependent variables. The slope tells us how the dependent variable (*y*) changes for every one unit increase in the independent (*x*) variable, on average. The *y*-intercept is used to describe the dependent variable when the independent variable equals zero.

13.4 The Regression Equation

It is hoped that this discussion of regression analysis has demonstrated the tremendous potential value it has as a tool for testing models and helping to better understand the world around us. The regression model has its limitations, especially the requirement that the underlying relationship be approximately linear. To the extent that the true relationship is nonlinear it may be approximated with a linear relationship or nonlinear forms of transformations that can be estimated with linear techniques. Double logarithmic transformation of the data will provide an easy way to test this particular shape of the relationship. A reasonably good quadratic form (the shape of the total cost curve from Microeconomics Principles) can be generated by the equation:

$$Y = a + b_1 X + b_2 X^2$$

where the values of X are simply squared and put into the equation as a separate variable.

There is much more in the way of econometric "tricks" that can bypass some of the more troublesome assumptions of the general regression model. This statistical technique is so valuable that further study would provide any student significant, statistically significant, dividends.

PRACTICE

13.1 The Correlation Coefficient *R*

1. In order to have a correlation coefficient between traits A and B, it is necessary to have:
   a. one group of subjects, some of whom possess characteristics of trait A, the remainder possessing those of trait B
   b. measures of trait A on one group of subjects and of trait B on another group
   c. two groups of subjects, one which could be classified as A or not A, the other as B or not B
   d. two groups of subjects, one which could be classified as A or not A, the other as B or not B
2. Define the Correlation Coefficient and give a unique example of its use.
3. If the correlation between age of an auto and money spent for repairs is +.90
   a. 81% of the variation in the money spent for repairs is explained by the age of the auto
   b. 81% of money spent for repairs is unexplained by the age of the auto
   c. 90% of the money spent for repairs is explained by the age of the auto
   d. none of the above

4. Suppose that college grade-point average and verbal portion of an IQ test had a correlation of .40. What percentage of the variance do these two have in common?

   a. 20
   b. 16
   c. 40
   d. 80

5. True or false? If false, explain why: The coefficient of determination can have values between -1 and +1.

6. True or False: Whenever r is calculated on the basis of a sample, the value which we obtain for r is only an estimate of the true correlation coefficient which we would obtain if we calculated it for the entire population.

7. Under a "scatter diagram" there is a notation that the coefficient of correlation is .10. What does this mean?

   a. plus and minus 10% from the means includes about 68% of the cases
   b. one-tenth of the variance of one variable is shared with the other variable
   c. one-tenth of one variable is caused by the other variable
   d. on a scale from -1 to +1, the degree of linear relationship between the two variables is +.10

8. The correlation coefficient for X and Y is known to be zero. We then can conclude that:

   a. X and Y have standard distributions
   b. the variances of X and Y are equal
   c. there exists no relationship between X and Y
   d. there exists no linear relationship between X and Y
   e. none of these

9. What would you guess the value of the correlation coefficient to be for the pair of variables: "number of man-hours worked" and "number of units of work completed"?

   a. Approximately 0.9
   b. Approximately 0.4
   c. Approximately 0.0
   d. Approximately -0.4
   e. Approximately -0.9

10. In a given group, the correlation between height measured in feet and weight measured in pounds is +.68. Which of the following would alter the value of r?

   a. height is expressed centimeters.
   b. weight is expressed in Kilograms.
   c. both of the above will affect r.
   d. neither of the above changes will affect r.

13.2 Testing the Significance of the Correlation Coefficient

11. Define a t Test of a Regression Coefficient, and give a unique example of its use.

12. The correlation between scores on a neuroticism test and scores on an anxiety test is high and positive; therefore

a. anxiety causes neuroticism
b. those who score low on one test tend to score high on the other.
c. those who score low on one test tend to score low on the other.
d. no prediction from one test to the other can be meaningfully made.

13.3 Linear Equations

13. True or False? If False, correct it: Suppose a 95% confidence interval for the slope *β* of the straight line regression of Y on X is given by -3.5 < *β* < -0.5. Then a two-sided test of the hypothesis $H0{:}\beta{=}{-1}$ would result in rejection of H0$H0$ at the 1% level of significance.

14. True or False: It is safer to interpret correlation coefficients as measures of association rather than causation because of the possibility of spurious correlation.

15. We are interested in finding the linear relation between the number of widgets purchased at one time and the cost per widget. The following data has been obtained:

X: Number of widgets purchased – 1, 3, 6, 10, 15

Y: Cost per widget(in dollars) – 55, 52, 46, 32, 25

Suppose the regression line is y^=–2.5x+60$y\wedge{=}{-}2.5y{+}60$. We compute the average price per widget if 30 are purchased and observe which of the following?

a. y^=15dollars; obviously, we are mistaken; the prediction y^$y\wedge$ is actually +15 dollars.
b. y^=15dollars, which seems reasonable judging by the data.
c. y^=-15dollars, which is obvious nonsense. The regression line must be incorrect.
d. y^=–15dollars, which is obvious nonsense. This reminds us that predicting Y outside the range of X values in our data is a very poor practice.

16. Discuss briefly the distinction between correlation and causality.

17. True or False: If r is close to + or -1, we shall say there is a strong correlation, with the tacit understanding that we are referring to a linear relationship and nothing else.

13.4 The Regression Equation

18. Suppose that you have at your disposal the information below for each of 30 drivers. Propose a model (including a very brief indication of symbols used to represent independent variables) to explain how miles per gallon vary from driver to driver on the basis of the factors measured.

Information:

1. miles driven per day
2. weight of car
3. number of cylinders in car
4. average speed
5. miles per gallon
6. number of passengers

19. Consider a sample least squares regression analysis between a dependent variable (Y) and an independent variable (X). A sample correlation coefficient of –1 (minus one) tells us that

a. there is no relationship between Y and X in the sample
b. there is no relationship between Y and X in the population
c. there is a perfect negative relationship between Y and X in the population
d. there is a perfect negative relationship between Y and X in the sample.

20. In correlational analysis, when the points scatter widely about the regression line, this means that the correlation is

a. negative.
b. low.
c. heterogeneous.
d. between two measures that are unreliable.

13.5 Interpretation of Regression Coefficients: Elasticity and Logarithmic Transformation

21. In a linear regression, why do we need to be concerned with the range of the independent (X) variable?

22. Suppose one collected the following information where X is diameter of tree trunk and Y is tree height.

Table 13.3

X	Y
4	8
2	4
8	18
6	22
10	30
6	8

Regression equation: $\hat{y}_i = -3.6 + 3.1 \cdot X_i$

What is your estimate of the average height of all trees having a trunk diameter of 7 inches?

23. The manufacturers of a chemical used in flea collars claim that under standard test conditions each additional unit of the chemical will bring about a reduction of 5 fleas (i.e. where Xj=amount of chemicalXj=amount of chemical and Y_J=B_0+B_1·X_J+E_J, $H0$: B_1=-5

Suppose that a test has been conducted and results from a computer include:

Intercept = 60

Slope = -4

Standard error of the regression coefficient = 1.0

Degrees of Freedom for Error = 2000

95% Confidence Interval for the slope -2.04, -5.96

Is this evidence consistent with the claim that the number of fleas is reduced at a rate of 5 fleas per unit chemical?

13.6 Predicting with a Regression Equation

24. True or False? If False, correct it: Suppose you are performing a simple linear regression of Y on X and you test the hypothesis that the slope *β* is zero against a two-sided alternative. You have n=25n=25 observations and your computed test (t) statistic is 2.6. Then your *P*-value is given by .01 < *P* < .02, which gives borderline significance (i.e. you would reject H0$H0$ at α=.02α=.02 but fail to reject H0$H0$ at α=.01α=.01).

25. An economist is interested in the possible influence of "Miracle Wheat" on the average yield of wheat in a district. To do so he fits a linear regression of average yield per year against year after introduction of "Miracle Wheat" for a ten year period.

The fitted trend line is

y^j=80+1.5·Xjy^j=80+1.5·Xj

(Yj: Average yield in j year after introduction)

(Xj:j year after introduction).

a. What is the estimated average yield for the fourth year after introduction?
b. Do you want to use this trend line to estimate yield for, say, 20 years after introduction? Why? What would your estimate be?

26. An interpretation of r=0.5 is that the following part of the Y-variation is associated with which variation in X:

a. most
b. half
c. very little
d. one quarter
e. none of these

27. Which of the following values of r indicates the most accurate prediction of one variable from another?

a. r=1.18
b. r=-.77
c. r=.68

13.7 How to Use Microsoft Excel® for Regression Analysis

28.

A computer program for multiple regression has been used to fit

$$\hat{y}_j = b_0 + b_1 \cdot X_{1j} + b_2 \cdot X_{2j} + b_3 \cdot X_{3j}.$$

Part of the computer output includes:

Table 13.4

i	bibi	SbiSbi
0	8	1.6
1	2.2	.24
2	-.72	.32
3	0.005	0.002

a. Calculation of confidence interval for b2$b2$ consists of _______ ± (a student's t value) (_______)
b. The confidence level for this interval is reflected in the value used for _______.
c. The degrees of freedom available for estimating the variance are directly concerned with the value used for _______

29. An investigator has used a multiple regression program on 20 data points to obtain a regression equation with 3 variables. Part of the computer output is:

Table 13.5

Variable	Coefficient	Standard Error of bibi
1	0.45	0.21
2	0.80	0.10
3	3.10	0.86

a. 0.80 is an estimate of ___________.

b. 0.10 is an estimate of ___________.

c. Assuming the responses satisfy the normality assumption, we can be 95% confident that the value of β2$\beta 2$ is in the interval,_______ ± [$t_{.025}$ · _______], where $t_{.025}$ is the critical value of the student's *t*-distribution with ____ degrees of freedom.

SOLUTIONS

1. d

2. A measure of the degree to which variation of one variable is related to variation in one or more other variables. The most commonly used correlation coefficient indicates the degree to which variation in one variable is described by a straight line relation with another variable.

Suppose that sample information is available on family income and Years of schooling of the head of the household. A correlation coefficient = 0 would indicate no linear association at all between these two variables. A correlation of 1 would indicate perfect linear association (where all variation in family income could be associated with schooling and vice versa).

3. a. 81% of the variation in the money spent for repairs is explained by the age of the auto

4. b. 16

5. The coefficient of determination is r⋅⋅2 with 0 ≤ r⋅⋅2 ≤ 1, since -1 ≤ r ≤ 1.

6. True

7. d. on a scale from -1 to +1, the degree of linear relationship between the two variables is +.10

8. d. there exists no linear relationship between X and Y

9. Approximately 0.9

10. d. neither of the above changes will affect r.

11. Definition: A t test is obtained by dividing a regression coefficient by its standard error and then comparing the result to critical values for Students' t with Error *df.* It provides a test of the claim that βi=0$\beta i=0$ when all other variables have been included in the relevant regression model. Example: Suppose that 4 variables are suspected of influencing some response. Suppose that the results of fitting $Yi=\beta_0+\beta_1X_1i+\beta_2X_2i+\beta_3X_3i+\beta_4X_4i+e_i$ include:

Table 13.6

Variable	Regression coefficient	Standard error of regular coefficient
.5	1	-3
.4	2	+2
.02	3	+1
.6	4	-.5

t calculated for variables 1, 2, and 3 would be 5 or larger in absolute value while that for variable 4 would be less than 1. For most significance levels, the hypothesis β_1=0 would be rejected. But, notice that this is for the case when X_2, X_3, and X_4 have been included in the regression. For most significance levels, the hypothesis β_4=0 would be continued (retained) for the case where X1X1, X2X2, and X3X3 are in the regression. Often this pattern of results will result in computing another regression involving only X1X1, X2X2, X3X3, and examination of the t ratios produced for that case.

12. c. those who score low on one test tend to score low on the other.
13. False. Since H0:β=−1$H0{:}\beta{=}{-}1$ would not be rejected at α=0.05$\alpha{=}0.05$, it would not be rejected at α=0.01$\alpha{=}0.01$.
14. True
15. d
16. Some variables seem to be related, so that knowing one variable's status allows us to predict the status of the other. This relationship can be measured and is called correlation. However, a high correlation between two variables in no way proves that a cause-and-effect relation exists between them. It is entirely possible that a third factor causes both variables to vary together.
17. True
18. $Y_j = b_0 + b_1 \cdot X_1 + b_2 \cdot X_2 + b_3 \cdot X_3 + b_4 \cdot X_4 + b_5 \cdot X_6 + e_j$
19. d. there is a perfect negative relationship between Y and X in the sample.
20. b. low
21. The precision of the estimate of the Y variable depends on the range of the independent (X) variable explored. If we explore a very small range of the X variable, we won't be able to make much use of the regression. Also, extrapolation is not recommended.
22. $\hat{y} = -3.6 + (3.1 \cdot 7) = 18.1$

23. Most simply, since -5 is included in the confidence interval for the slope, we can conclude that the evidence is consistent with the claim at the 95% confidence level.

Using a t test: H_0: B_1=-5 H_A: B_1≠-5 $t_{\text{calculated}} = \frac{-5-(-4)}{1} = -1$ $t_{\text{critical}} = -1.96$

Since $t_{\text{calc}} < t_{\text{crit}}$ we retain the null hypothesis that B_1=-5.

24. True. $t_{(\text{critical, df = 23, two-tailed, } \alpha = .02)} = \pm 2.5$ $t_{\text{critical, df = 23, two-tailed, } \alpha = .01} = \pm 2.8$

25.

a. 80+1.5·4=8680+1.5·4=86
b. No. Most business statisticians would not want to extrapolate that far. If someone did, the estimate would be 110, but some other factors probably come into play with 20 years.

26. d. one quarter

27. b. r=-.77r=-.77

28.

a. -.72, .32
b. the t value
c. the t value

29.

a. The population value for β_2, the change that occurs in Y with a unit change in X_2, when the other variables are held constant.
b. The population value for the standard error of the distribution of estimates of β_2.
c. .8, .1, 16 = 20 – 4.

APPENDIX A:

STATISTICAL TABLES

F Distribution

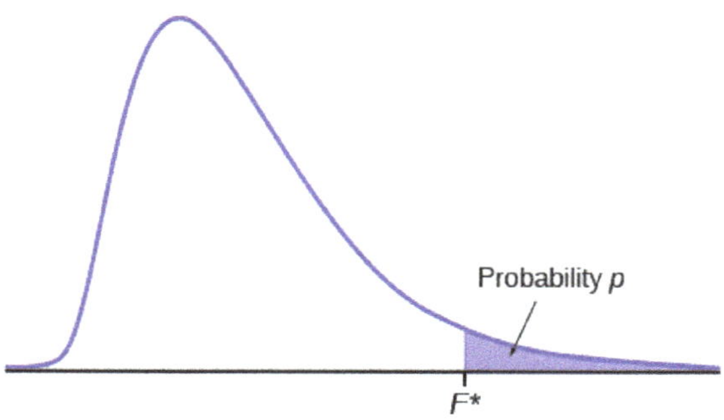

Figure A1 Table entry for *p* is the critical value *F with probability *p* lying to its right.**

Table A1 *F* critical values

Degrees of freedom in the denominator	p	Degrees of freedom in the numerator 1	2	3	4	5	6	7	8	9
1	.100	39.86	49.50	53.59	55.83	57.24	58.20	58.91	59.44	59.86
	.050	161.45	199.50	215.71	224.58	230.16	233.99	236.77	238.88	240.54
	.025	647.79	799.50	864.16	899.58	921.85	937.11	948.22	956.66	963.28
	.010	4052.2	4999.5	5403.4	5624.6	5763.6	5859.0	5928.4	5981.1	6022.5
	.001	405284	500000	540379	562500	576405	585937	592873	598144	602284
2	.100	8.53	9.00	9.16	9.24	9.29	9.33	9.35	9.37	9.38
	.050	18.51	19.00	19.16	19.25	19.30	19.33	19.35	19.37	19.38
	.025	38.51	39.00	39.17	39.25	39.30	39.33	39.36	39.37	39.39
	.010	98.50	99.00	99.17	99.25	99.30	99.33	99.36	99.37	99.39
	.001	998.50	999.00	999.17	999.25	999.30	999.33	999.36	999.37	999.39
3	.100	5.54	5.46	5.39	5.34	5.31	5.28	5.27	5.25	5.24
	.050	10.13	9.55	9.28	9.12	9.01	8.94	8.89	8.85	8.81
	.025	17.44	16.04	15.44	15.10	14.88	14.73	14.62	14.54	14.47
	.010	34.12	30.82	29.46	28.71	28.24	27.91	27.67	27.49	27.35
	.001	167.03	148.50	141.11	137.10	134.58	132.85	131.58	130.62	129.86
4	.100	4.54	4.32	4.19	4.11	4.05	4.01	3.98	3.95	3.94
	.050	7.71	6.94	6.59	6.39	6.26	6.16	6.09	6.04	6.00
	.025	12.22	10.65	9.98	9.60	9.36	9.20	9.07	8.98	8.90
	.010	21.20	18.00	16.69	15.98	15.52	15.21	14.98	14.80	14.66
	.001	74.14	61.25	56.18	53.44	51.71	50.53	49.66	49.00	48.47
5	.100	4.06	3.78	3.62	3.52	3.45	3.40	3.37	3.34	3.32
	.050	6.61	5.79	5.41	5.19	5.05	4.95	4.88	4.82	4.77
	.025	10.01	8.43	7.76	7.39	7.15	6.98	6.85	6.76	6.68
	.010	16.26	13.27	12.06	11.39	10.97	10.67	10.46	10.29	10.16
	.001	47.18	37.12	33.20	31.09	29.75	28.83	28.16	27.65	27.24
6	.100	3.78	3.46	3.29	3.18	3.11	3.05	3.01	2.98	2.96
	.050	5.99	5.14	4.76	4.53	4.39	4.28	4.21	4.15	4.10
	.025	8.81	7.26	6.60	6.23	5.99	5.82	5.70	5.60	5.52
	.010	13.75	10.92	9.78	9.15	8.75	8.47	8.26	8.10	7.98
	.001	35.51	27.00	23.70	21.92	20.80	20.03	19.46	19.03	18.69
7	.100	3.59	3.26	3.07	2.96	2.88	2.83	2.78	2.75	2.72
	.050	5.59	4.74	4.35	4.12	3.97	3.87	3.79	3.73	3.68
	.025	8.07	6.54	5.89	5.52	5.29	5.12	4.99	4.90	4.82
	.010	12.25	9.55	8.45	7.85	7.46	7.19	6.99	6.84	6.72
	.001	29.25	21.69	18.77	17.20	16.21	15.52	15.02	14.63	14.33

Table A2 *F* critical values (continued)

		Degrees of freedom in the numerator										
Degrees of freedom in the denominator	p	10	12	15	20	25	30	40	50	60	120	1000
1	.100	60.19	60.71	61.22	61.74	62.05	62.26	62.53	62.69	62.79	63.06	63.30
	.050	241.88	243.91	245.95	248.01	249.26	250.10	251.14	251.77	252.20	253.25	254.19
	.025	968.63	976.71	984.87	993.10	998.08	1001.4	1005.6	1008.1	1009.8	1014.0	1017.7
	.010	6055.8	6106.3	6157.3	6208.7	6239.8	6260.6	6286.8	6302.5	6313.0	6339.4	6362.7
	.001	605621	610668	615764	620908	624017	626099	628712	630285	631337	633972	636301
2	.100	9.39	9.41	9.42	9.44	9.45	9.46	9.47	9.47	9.47	9.48	9.49
	.050	19.40	19.41	19.43	19.45	19.46	19.46	19.47	19.48	19.48	19.49	19.49
	.025	39.40	39.41	39.43	39.45	39.46	39.46	39.47	39.48	39.48	39.49	39.50
	.010	99.40	99.42	99.43	99.45	99.46	99.47	99.47	99.48	99.48	99.49	99.50
	.001	999.40	999.42	999.43	999.45	999.46	999.47	999.47	999.48	999.48	999.49	999.50
3	.100	5.23	5.22	5.20	5.18	5.17	5.17	5.16	5.15	5.15	5.14	5.13
	.050	8.79	8.74	8.70	8.66	8.63	8.62	8.59	8.58	8.57	8.55	8.53
	.025	14.42	14.34	14.25	14.17	14.12	14.08	14.04	14.01	13.99	13.95	13.91
	.010	27.23	27.05	26.87	26.69	26.58	26.50	26.41	26.35	26.32	26.22	26.14
	.001	129.25	128.32	127.37	126.42	125.84	125.45	124.96	124.66	124.47	123.97	123.53
4	.100	3.92	3.90	3.87	3.84	3.83	3.82	3.80	3.80	3.79	3.78	3.76
	.050	5.96	5.91	5.86	5.80	5.77	5.75	5.72	5.70	5.69	5.66	5.63
	.025	8.84	8.75	8.66	8.56	8.50	8.46	8.41	8.38	8.36	8.31	8.26
	.010	14.55	14.37	14.20	14.02	13.91	13.84	13.75	13.69	13.65	13.56	13.47
	.001	48.05	47.41	46.76	46.10	45.70	45.43	45.09	44.88	44.75	44.40	44.09
5	.100	3.30	3.27	3.24	3.21	3.19	3.17	3.16	3.15	3.14	3.12	3.11
	.050	4.74	4.68	4.62	4.56	4.52	4.50	4.46	4.44	4.43	4.40	4.37
	.025	6.62	6.52	6.43	6.33	6.27	6.23	6.18	6.14	6.12	6.07	6.02
	.010	10.05	9.89	9.72	9.55	9.45	9.38	9.29	9.24	9.20	9.11	9.03
	.001	26.92	26.42	25.91	25.39	25.08	24.87	24.60	24.44	24.33	24.06	23.82
6	.100	2.94	2.90	2.87	2.84	2.81	2.80	2.78	2.77	2.76	2.74	2.72
	.050	4.06	4.00	3.94	3.87	3.83	3.81	3.77	3.75	3.74	3.70	3.67
	.025	5.46	5.37	5.27	5.17	5.11	5.07	5.01	4.98	4.96	4.90	4.86
	.010	7.87	7.72	7.56	7.40	7.30	7.23	7.14	7.09	7.06	6.97	6.89
	.001	18.41	17.99	17.56	17.12	16.85	16.67	16.44	16.31	16.21	15.98	15.77
7	.100	2.70	2.67	2.63	2.59	2.57	2.56	2.54	2.52	2.51	2.49	2.47
	.050	3.64	3.57	3.51	3.44	3.40	3.38	3.34	3.32	3.30	3.27	3.23
	.025	4.76	4.67	4.57	4.47	4.40	4.36	4.31	4.28	4.25	4.20	4.15
	.010	6.62	6.47	6.31	6.16	6.06	5.99	5.91	5.86	5.82	5.74	5.66
	.001	14.08	13.71	13.32	12.93	12.69	12.53	12.33	12.20	12.12	11.91	11.72

Table A3 *F* critical values (continued)

Degrees of freedom in the denominator	p	Degrees of freedom in the numerator 1	2	3	4	5	6	7	8	9
8	.100	3.46	3.11	2.92	2.81	2.73	2.67	2.62	2.59	2.56
	.050	5.32	4.46	4.07	3.84	3.69	3.58	3.50	3.44	3.39
	.025	7.57	6.06	5.42	5.05	4.82	4.65	4.53	4.43	4.36
	.010	11.26	8.65	7.59	7.01	6.63	6.37	6.18	6.03	5.91
	.001	25.41	18.49	15.83	14.39	13.48	12.86	12.40	12.05	11.77
9	.100	3.36	3.01	2.81	2.69	2.61	2.55	2.51	2.47	2.44
	.050	5.12	4.26	3.86	3.63	3.48	3.37	3.29	3.23	3.18
	.025	7.21	5.71	5.08	4.72	4.48	4.32	4.20	4.10	4.03
	.010	10.56	8.02	6.99	6.42	6.06	5.80	5.61	5.47	5.35
	.001	22.86	16.39	13.90	12.56	11.71	11.13	10.70	10.37	10.11
10	.100	3.29	2.92	2.73	2.61	2.52	2.46	2.41	2.38	2.35
	.050	4.96	4.10	3.71	3.48	3.33	3.22	3.14	3.07	3.02
	.025	6.94	5.46	4.83	4.47	4.24	4.07	3.95	3.85	3.78
	.010	10.04	7.56	6.55	5.99	5.64	5.39	5.20	5.06	4.94
	.001	21.04	14.91	12.55	11.28	10.48	9.93	9.52	9.20	8.96
11	.100	3.23	2.86	2.66	2.54	2.45	2.39	2.34	2.30	2.27
	.050	4.84	3.98	3.59	3.36	3.20	3.09	3.01	2.95	2.90
	.025	6.72	5.26	4.63	4.28	4.04	3.88	3.76	3.66	3.59
	.010	9.65	7.21	6.22	5.67	5.32	5.07	4.89	4.74	4.63
	.001	19.69	13.81	11.56	10.35	9.58	9.05	8.66	8.35	8.12
12	.100	3.18	2.81	2.61	2.48	2.39	2.33	2.28	2.24	2.21
	.050	4.75	3.89	3.49	3.26	3.11	3.00	2.91	2.85	2.80
	.025	6.55	5.10	4.47	4.12	3.89	3.73	3.61	3.51	3.44
	.010	9.33	6.93	5.95	5.41	5.06	4.82	4.64	4.50	4.39
	.001	18.64	12.97	10.80	9.63	8.89	8.38	8.00	7.71	7.48
13	.100	3.14	2.76	2.56	2.43	2.35	2.28	2.23	2.20	2.16
	.050	4.67	3.81	3.41	3.18	3.03	2.92	2.83	2.77	2.71
	.025	6.41	4.97	4.35	4.00	3.77	3.60	3.48	3.39	3.31
	.010	9.07	6.70	5.74	5.21	4.86	4.62	4.44	4.30	4.19
	.001	17.82	12.31	10.21	9.07	8.35	7.86	7.49	7.21	6.98
14	.100	3.10	2.73	2.52	2.39	2.31	2.24	2.19	2.15	2.12
	.050	4.60	3.74	3.34	3.11	2.96	2.85	2.76	2.70	2.65
	.025	6.30	4.86	4.24	3.89	3.66	3.50	3.38	3.29	3.21
	.010	8.86	6.51	5.56	5.04	4.69	4.46	4.28	4.14	4.03
	.001	17.14	11.78	9.73	8.62	7.92	7.44	7.08	6.80	6.58
15	.100	3.07	2.70	2.49	2.36	2.27	2.21	2.16	2.12	2.09
	.050	4.54	3.68	3.29	3.06	2.90	2.79	2.71	2.64	2.59
	.025	6.20	4.77	4.15	3.80	3.58	3.41	3.29	3.20	3.12
	.010	8.68	6.36	5.42	4.89	4.56	4.32	4.14	4.00	3.89
	.001	16.59	11.34	9.34	8.25	7.57	7.09	6.74	6.47	6.26

Table A4 *F* critical values (continued)

		Degrees of freedom in the numerator										
Degrees of freedom in the denominator	p	10	12	15	20	25	30	40	50	60	120	1000
8	.100	2.54	2.50	2.46	2.42	2.40	2.38	2.36	2.35	2.34	2.32	2.30
	.050	3.35	3.28	3.22	3.15	3.11	3.08	3.04	3.02	3.01	2.97	2.93
	.025	4.30	4.20	4.10	4.00	3.94	3.89	3.84	3.81	3.78	3.73	3.68
	.010	5.81	5.67	5.52	5.36	5.26	5.20	5.12	5.07	5.03	4.95	4.87
	.001	11.54	11.19	10.84	10.48	10.26	10.11	9.92	9.80	9.73	9.53	9.36
9	.100	2.42	2.38	2.34	2.30	2.27	2.25	2.23	2.22	2.21	2.18	2.16
	.050	3.14	3.07	3.01	2.94	2.89	2.86	2.83	2.80	2.79	2.75	2.71
	.025	3.96	3.87	3.77	3.67	3.60	3.56	3.51	3.47	3.45	3.39	3.34
	.010	5.26	5.11	4.96	4.81	4.71	4.65	4.57	4.52	4.48	4.40	4.32
	.001	9.89	9.57	9.24	8.90	8.69	8.55	8.37	8.26	8.19	8.00	7.84
10	.100	2.32	2.28	2.24	2.20	2.17	2.16	2.13	2.12	2.11	2.08	2.06
	.050	2.98	2.91	2.85	2.77	2.73	2.70	2.66	2.64	2.62	2.58	2.54
	.025	3.72	3.62	3.52	3.42	3.35	3.31	3.26	3.22	3.20	3.14	3.09
	.010	4.85	4.71	4.56	4.41	4.31	4.25	4.17	4.12	4.08	4.00	3.92
	.001	8.75	8.45	8.13	7.80	7.60	7.47	7.30	7.19	7.12	6.94	6.78
11	.100	2.25	2.21	2.17	2.12	2.10	2.08	2.05	2.04	2.03	2.00	1.98
	.050	2.85	2.79	2.72	2.65	2.60	2.57	2.53	2.51	2.49	2.45	2.41
	.025	3.53	3.43	3.33	3.23	3.16	3.12	3.06	3.03	3.00	2.94	2.89
	.010	4.54	4.40	4.25	4.10	4.01	3.94	3.86	3.81	3.78	3.69	3.61
	.001	7.92	7.63	7.32	7.01	6.81	6.68	6.52	6.42	6.35	6.18	6.02
12	.100	2.19	2.15	2.10	2.06	2.03	2.01	1.99	1.97	1.96	1.93	1.91
	.050	2.75	2.69	2.62	2.54	2.50	2.47	2.43	2.40	2.38	2.34	2.30
	.025	3.37	3.28	3.18	3.07	3.01	2.96	2.91	2.87	2.85	2.79	2.73
	.010	4.30	4.16	4.01	3.86	3.76	3.70	3.62	3.57	3.54	3.45	3.37
	.001	7.29	7.00	6.71	6.40	6.22	6.09	5.93	5.83	5.76	5.59	5.44
13	.100	2.14	2.10	2.05	2.01	1.98	1.96	1.93	1.92	1.90	1.88	1.85
	.050	2.67	2.60	2.53	2.46	2.41	2.38	2.34	2.31	2.30	2.25	2.21
	.025	3.25	3.15	3.05	2.95	2.88	2.84	2.78	2.74	2.72	2.66	2.60
	.010	4.10	3.96	3.82	3.66	3.57	3.51	3.43	3.38	3.34	3.25	3.18
	.001	6.80	6.52	6.23	5.93	5.75	5.63	5.47	5.37	5.30	5.14	4.99
14	.100	2.10	2.05	2.01	1.96	1.93	1.91	1.89	1.87	1.86	1.83	1.80
	.050	2.60	2.53	2.46	2.39	2.34	2.31	2.27	2.24	2.22	2.18	2.14
	.025	3.15	3.05	2.95	2.84	2.78	2.73	2.67	2.64	2.61	2.55	2.50
	.010	3.94	3.80	3.66	3.51	3.41	3.35	3.27	3.22	3.18	3.09	3.02
	.001	6.40	6.13	5.85	5.56	5.38	5.25	5.10	5.00	4.94	4.77	4.62
15	.100	2.06	2.02	1.97	1.92	1.89	1.87	1.85	1.83	1.82	1.79	1.76
	.050	2.54	2.48	2.40	2.33	2.28	2.25	2.20	2.18	2.16	2.11	2.07
	.025	3.06	2.96	2.86	2.76	2.69	2.64	2.59	2.55	2.52	2.46	2.40
	.010	3.80	3.67	3.52	3.37	3.28	3.21	3.13	3.08	3.05	2.96	2.88
	.001	6.08	5.81	5.54	5.25	5.07	4.95	4.80	4.70	4.64	4.47	4.33

Table A5 *F* critical values (continued)

Degrees of freedom in the denominator	p	Degrees of freedom in the numerator 1	2	3	4	5	6	7	8	9
16	.100	3.05	2.67	2.46	2.33	2.24	2.18	2.13	2.09	2.06
	.050	4.49	3.63	3.24	3.01	2.85	2.74	2.66	2.59	2.54
	.025	6.12	4.69	4.08	3.73	3.50	3.34	3.22	3.12	3.05
	.010	8.53	6.23	5.29	4.77	4.44	4.20	4.03	3.89	3.78
	.001	16.12	10.97	9.01	7.94	7.27	6.80	6.46	6.19	5.98
17	.100	3.03	2.64	2.44	2.31	2.22	2.15	2.10	2.06	2.03
	.050	4.45	3.59	3.20	2.96	2.81	2.70	2.61	2.55	2.49
	.025	6.04	4.62	4.01	3.66	3.44	3.28	3.16	3.06	2.98
	.010	8.40	6.11	5.19	4.67	4.34	4.10	3.93	3.79	3.68
	.001	15.72	10.66	8.73	7.68	7.02	6.56	6.22	5.96	5.75
18	.100	3.01	2.62	2.42	2.29	2.20	2.13	2.08	2.04	2.00
	.050	4.41	3.55	3.16	2.93	2.77	2.66	2.58	2.51	2.46
	.025	5.98	4.56	3.95	3.61	3.38	3.22	3.10	3.01	2.93
	.010	8.29	6.01	5.09	4.58	4.25	4.01	3.84	3.71	3.60
	.001	15.38	10.39	8.49	7.46	6.81	6.35	6.02	5.76	5.56
19	.100	3.36	3.01	2.81	2.69	2.61	2.55	2.51	2.47	2.44
	.050	5.12	4.26	3.86	3.63	3.48	3.37	3.29	3.23	3.18
	.025	7.21	5.71	5.08	4.72	4.48	4.32	4.20	4.10	4.03
	.010	10.56	8.02	6.99	6.42	6.06	5.80	5.61	5.47	5.35
	.001	22.86	16.39	13.90	12.56	11.71	11.13	10.70	10.37	10.11
20	.100	2.97	2.59	2.38	2.25	2.16	2.09	2.04	2.00	1.96
	.050	4.35	3.49	3.10	2.87	2.71	2.60	2.51	2.45	2.39
	.025	5.87	4.46	3.86	3.51	3.29	3.13	3.01	2.91	2.84
	.010	8.10	5.85	4.94	4.43	4.10	3.87	3.70	3.56	3.46
	.001	14.82	9.95	8.10	7.10	6.46	6.02	5.69	5.44	5.24
21	.100	2.96	2.57	2.36	2.23	2.14	2.08	2.02	1.98	1.95
	.050	4.32	3.47	3.07	2.84	2.68	2.57	2.49	2.42	2.37
	.025	5.83	4.42	3.82	3.48	3.25	3.09	2.97	2.87	2.80
	.010	8.02	5.78	4.87	4.37	4.04	3.81	3.64	3.51	3.40
	.001	14.59	9.77	7.94	6.95	6.32	5.88	5.56	5.31	5.11
22	.100	2.95	2.56	2.35	2.22	2.13	2.06	2.01	1.97	1.93
	.050	4.30	3.44	3.05	2.82	2.66	2.55	2.46	2.40	2.34
	.025	5.79	4.38	3.78	3.44	3.22	3.05	2.93	2.84	2.76
	.010	7.95	5.72	4.82	4.31	3.99	3.76	3.59	3.45	3.35
	.001	14.38	9.61	7.80	6.81	6.19	5.76	5.44	5.19	4.99
23	.100	2.94	2.55	2.34	2.21	2.11	2.05	1.99	1.95	1.92
	.050	4.28	3.42	3.03	2.80	2.64	2.53	2.44	2.37	2.32
	.025	5.75	4.35	3.75	3.41	3.18	3.02	2.90	2.81	2.73
	.010	7.88	5.66	4.76	4.26	3.94	3.71	3.54	3.41	3.30
	.001	14.20	9.47	7.67	6.70	6.08	5.65	5.33	5.09	4.89

Table A6 *F* critical values (continued)

		Degrees of freedom in the numerator										
Degrees of freedom in the denominator	p	10	12	15	20	25	30	40	50	60	120	1000
16	.100	2.03	1.99	1.94	1.89	1.86	1.84	1.81	1.79	1.78	1.75	1.72
	.050	2.49	2.42	2.35	2.28	2.23	2.19	2.15	2.12	2.11	2.06	2.02
	.025	2.99	2.89	2.79	2.68	2.61	2.57	2.51	2.47	2.45	2.38	2.32
	.010	3.69	3.55	3.41	3.26	3.16	3.10	3.02	2.97	2.93	2.84	2.76
	.001	5.81	5.55	5.27	4.99	4.82	4.70	4.54	4.45	4.39	4.23	4.08
17	.100	2.00	1.96	1.91	1.86	1.83	1.81	1.78	1.76	1.75	1.72	1.69
	.050	2.45	2.38	2.31	2.23	2.18	2.15	2.10	2.08	2.06	2.01	1.97
	.025	2.92	2.82	2.72	2.62	2.55	2.50	2.44	2.41	2.38	2.32	2.26
	.010	3.59	3.46	3.31	3.16	3.07	3.00	2.92	2.87	2.83	2.75	2.66
	.001	5.58	5.32	5.05	4.78	4.60	4.48	4.33	4.24	4.18	4.02	3.87
18	.100	1.98	1.93	1.89	1.84	1.80	1.78	1.75	1.74	1.72	1.69	1.66
	.050	2.41	2.34	2.27	2.19	2.14	2.11	2.06	2.04	2.02	1.97	1.92
	.025	2.87	2.77	2.67	2.56	2.49	2.44	2.38	2.35	2.32	2.26	2.20
	.010	3.51	3.37	3.23	3.08	2.98	2.92	2.84	2.78	2.75	2.66	2.58
	.001	5.39	5.13	4.87	4.59	4.42	4.30	4.15	4.06	4.00	3.84	3.69
19	.100	1.96	1.91	1.86	1.81	1.78	1.76	1.73	1.71	1.70	1.67	1.64
	.050	2.38	2.31	2.23	2.16	2.11	2.07	2.03	2.00	1.98	1.93	1.88
	.025	2.82	2.72	2.62	2.51	2.44	2.39	2.33	2.30	2.27	2.20	2.14
	.010	3.43	3.30	3.15	3.00	2.91	2.84	2.76	2.71	2.67	2.58	2.50
	.001	5.22	4.97	4.70	4.43	4.26	4.14	3.99	3.90	3.84	3.68	3.53
20	.100	1.94	1.89	1.84	1.79	1.76	1.74	1.71	1.69	1.68	1.64	1.61
	.050	2.35	2.28	2.20	2.12	2.07	2.04	1.99	1.97	1.95	1.90	1.85
	.025	2.77	2.68	2.57	2.46	2.40	2.35	2.29	2.25	2.22	2.16	2.09
	.010	3.37	3.23	3.09	2.94	2.84	2.78	2.69	2.64	2.61	2.52	2.43
	.001	5.08	4.82	4.56	4.29	4.12	4.00	3.86	3.77	3.70	3.54	3.40
21	.100	1.92	1.87	1.83	1.78	1.74	1.72	1.69	1.67	1.66	1.62	1.59
	.050	2.32	2.25	2.18	2.10	2.05	2.01	1.96	1.94	1.92	1.87	1.82
	.025	2.73	2.64	2.53	2.42	2.36	2.31	2.25	2.21	2.18	2.11	2.05
	.010	3.31	3.17	3.03	2.88	2.79	2.72	2.64	2.58	2.55	2.46	2.37
	.001	4.95	4.70	4.44	4.17	4.00	3.88	3.74	3.64	3.58	3.42	3.28
22	.100	1.90	1.86	1.81	1.76	1.73	1.70	1.67	1.65	1.64	1.60	1.57
	.050	2.30	2.23	2.15	2.07	2.02	1.98	1.94	1.91	1.89	1.84	1.79
	.025	2.70	2.60	2.50	2.39	2.32	2.27	2.21	2.17	2.14	2.08	2.01
	.010	3.26	3.12	2.98	2.83	2.73	2.67	2.58	2.53	2.50	2.40	2.32
	.001	4.83	4.58	4.33	4.06	3.89	3.78	3.63	3.54	3.48	3.32	3.17
23	.100	1.89	1.84	1.80	1.74	1.71	1.69	1.66	1.64	1.62	1.59	1.55
	.050	2.27	2.20	2.13	2.05	2.00	1.96	1.91	1.88	1.86	1.81	1.76
	.025	2.67	2.57	2.47	2.36	2.29	2.24	2.18	2.14	2.11	2.04	1.98
	.010	3.21	3.07	2.93	2.78	2.69	2.62	2.54	2.48	2.45	2.35	2.27
	.001	4.73	4.48	4.23	3.96	3.79	3.68	3.53	3.44	3.38	3.22	3.08

Table A7 *F* critical values (continued)

Degrees of freedom in the denominator	p	Degrees of freedom in the numerator 1	2	3	4	5	6	7	8	9
24	.100	2.93	2.54	2.33	2.19	2.10	2.04	1.98	1.94	1.91
	.050	4.26	3.40	3.01	2.78	2.62	2.51	2.42	2.36	2.30
	.025	5.72	4.32	3.72	3.38	3.15	2.99	2.87	2.78	2.70
	.010	7.82	5.61	4.72	4.22	3.90	3.67	3.50	3.36	3.26
	.001	14.03	9.34	7.55	6.59	5.98	5.55	5.23	4.99	4.80
25	.100	2.92	2.53	2.32	2.18	2.09	2.02	1.97	1.93	1.89
	.050	4.24	3.39	2.99	2.76	2.60	2.49	2.40	2.34	2.28
	.025	5.69	4.29	3.69	3.35	3.13	2.97	2.85	2.75	2.68
	.010	7.77	5.57	4.68	4.18	3.85	3.63	3.46	3.32	3.22
	.001	13.88	9.22	7.45	6.49	5.89	5.46	5.15	4.91	4.71
26	.100	2.91	2.52	2.31	2.17	2.08	2.01	1.96	1.92	1.88
	.050	4.23	3.37	2.98	2.74	2.59	2.47	2.39	2.32	2.27
	.025	5.66	4.27	3.67	3.33	3.10	2.94	2.82	2.73	2.65
	.010	7.72	5.53	4.64	4.14	3.82	3.59	3.42	3.29	3.18
	.001	13.74	9.12	7.36	6.41	5.80	5.38	5.07	4.83	4.64
27	.100	2.90	2.51	2.30	2.17	2.07	2.00	1.95	1.91	1.87
	.050	4.21	3.35	2.96	2.73	2.57	2.46	2.37	2.31	2.25
	.025	5.63	4.24	3.65	3.31	3.08	2.92	2.80	2.71	2.63
	.010	7.68	5.49	4.60	4.11	3.78	3.56	3.39	3.26	3.15
	.001	13.61	9.02	7.27	6.33	5.73	5.31	5.00	4.76	4.57
28	.100	2.89	2.50	2.29	2.16	2.06	2.00	1.94	1.90	1.87
	.050	4.20	3.34	2.95	2.71	2.56	2.45	2.36	2.29	2.24
	.025	5.61	4.22	3.63	3.29	3.06	2.90	2.78	2.69	2.61
	.010	7.64	5.45	4.57	4.07	3.75	3.53	3.36	3.23	3.12
	.001	13.50	8.93	7.19	6.25	5.66	5.24	4.93	4.69	4.50
29	.100	2.89	2.50	2.28	2.15	2.06	1.99	1.93	1.89	1.86
	.050	4.18	3.33	2.93	2.70	2.55	2.43	2.35	2.28	2.22
	.025	5.59	4.20	3.61	3.27	3.04	2.88	2.76	2.67	2.59
	.010	7.60	5.42	4.54	4.04	3.73	3.50	3.33	3.20	3.09
	.001	13.39	8.85	7.12	6.19	5.59	5.18	4.87	4.64	4.45
30	.100	2.88	2.49	2.28	2.14	2.05	1.98	1.93	1.88	1.85
	.050	4.17	3.32	2.92	2.69	2.53	2.42	2.33	2.27	2.21
	.025	5.57	4.18	3.59	3.25	3.03	2.87	2.75	2.65	2.57
	.010	7.56	5.39	4.51	4.02	3.70	3.47	3.30	3.17	3.07
	.001	13.29	8.77	7.05	6.12	5.53	5.12	4.82	4.58	4.39
40	.100	2.84	2.44	2.23	2.09	2.00	1.93	1.87	1.83	1.79
	.050	4.08	3.23	2.84	2.61	2.45	2.34	2.25	2.18	2.12
	.025	5.42	4.05	3.46	3.13	2.90	2.74	2.62	2.53	2.45
	.010	7.31	5.18	4.31	3.83	3.51	3.29	3.12	2.99	2.89
	.001	12.61	8.25	6.59	5.70	5.13	4.73	4.44	4.21	4.02

Table A8 *F* critical values (continued)

Degrees of freedom in the denominator	p	Degrees of freedom in the numerator 10	12	15	20	25	30	40	50	60	120	1000
24	.100	1.88	1.83	1.78	1.73	1.70	1.67	1.64	1.62	1.61	1.57	1.54
	.050	2.25	2.18	2.11	2.03	1.97	1.94	1.89	1.86	1.84	1.79	1.74
	.025	2.64	2.54	2.44	2.33	2.26	2.21	2.15	2.11	2.08	2.01	1.94
	.010	3.17	3.03	2.89	2.74	2.64	2.58	2.49	2.44	2.40	2.31	2.22
	.001	4.64	4.39	4.14	3.87	3.71	3.59	3.45	3.36	3.29	3.14	2.99
25	.100	1.87	1.82	1.77	1.72	1.68	1.66	1.63	1.61	1.59	1.56	1.52
	.050	2.24	2.16	2.09	2.01	1.96	1.92	1.87	1.84	1.82	1.77	1.72
	.025	2.61	2.51	2.41	2.30	2.23	2.18	2.12	2.08	2.05	1.98	1.91
	.010	3.13	2.99	2.85	2.70	2.60	2.54	2.45	2.40	2.36	2.27	2.18
	.001	4.56	4.31	4.06	3.79	3.63	3.52	3.37	3.28	3.22	3.06	2.91
26	.100	1.86	1.81	1.76	1.71	1.67	1.65	1.61	1.59	1.58	1.54	1.51
	.050	2.22	2.15	2.07	1.99	1.94	1.90	1.85	1.82	1.80	1.75	1.70
	.025	2.59	2.49	2.39	2.28	2.21	2.16	2.09	2.05	2.03	1.95	1.89
	.010	3.09	2.96	2.81	2.66	2.57	2.50	2.42	2.36	2.33	2.23	2.14
	.001	4.48	4.24	3.99	3.72	3.56	3.44	3.30	3.21	3.15	2.99	2.84
27	.100	1.85	1.80	1.75	1.70	1.66	1.64	1.60	1.58	1.57	1.53	1.50
	.050	2.20	2.13	2.06	1.97	1.92	1.88	1.84	1.81	1.79	1.73	1.68
	.025	2.57	2.47	2.36	2.25	2.18	2.13	2.07	2.03	2.00	1.93	1.86
	.010	3.06	2.93	2.78	2.63	2.54	2.47	2.38	2.33	2.29	2.20	2.11
	.001	4.41	4.17	3.92	3.66	3.49	3.38	3.23	3.14	3.08	2.92	2.78
28	.100	1.84	1.79	1.74	1.69	1.65	1.63	1.59	1.57	1.56	1.52	1.48
	.050	2.19	2.12	2.04	1.96	1.91	1.87	1.82	1.79	1.77	1.71	1.66
	.025	2.55	2.45	2.34	2.23	2.16	2.11	2.05	2.01	1.98	1.91	1.84
	.010	3.03	2.90	2.75	2.60	2.51	2.44	2.35	2.30	2.26	2.17	2.08
	.001	4.35	4.11	3.86	3.60	3.43	3.32	3.18	3.09	3.02	2.86	2.72
29	.100	1.83	1.78	1.73	1.68	1.64	1.62	1.58	1.56	1.55	1.51	1.47
	.050	2.18	2.10	2.03	1.94	1.89	1.85	1.81	1.77	1.75	1.70	1.65
	.025	2.53	2.43	2.32	2.21	2.14	2.09	2.03	1.99	1.96	1.89	1.82
	.010	3.00	2.87	2.73	2.57	2.48	2.41	2.33	2.27	2.23	2.14	2.05
	.001	4.29	4.05	3.80	3.54	3.38	3.27	3.12	3.03	2.97	2.81	2.66
30	.100	1.82	1.77	1.72	1.67	1.63	1.61	1.57	1.55	1.54	1.50	1.46
	.050	2.16	2.09	2.01	1.93	1.88	1.84	1.79	1.76	1.74	1.68	1.63
	.025	2.51	2.41	2.31	2.20	2.12	2.07	2.01	1.97	1.94	1.87	1.80
	.010	2.98	2.84	2.70	2.55	2.45	2.39	2.30	2.25	2.21	2.11	2.02
	.001	4.24	4.00	3.75	3.49	3.33	3.22	3.07	2.98	2.92	2.76	2.61
40	.100	1.76	1.71	1.66	1.61	1.57	1.54	1.51	1.48	1.47	1.42	1.38
	.050	2.08	2.00	1.92	1.84	1.78	1.74	1.69	1.66	1.64	1.58	1.52
	.025	2.39	2.29	2.18	2.07	1.99	1.94	1.88	1.83	1.80	1.72	1.65
	.010	2.80	2.66	2.52	2.37	2.27	2.20	2.11	2.06	2.02	1.92	1.82
	.001	3.87	3.64	3.40	3.14	2.98	2.87	2.73	2.64	2.57	2.41	2.25

Table A9 *F* critical values (continued)

Degrees of freedom in the denominator	p	1	2	3	4	5	6	7	8	9
		Degrees of freedom in the numerator								
50	.100	2.81	2.41	2.20	2.06	1.97	1.90	1.84	1.80	1.76
	.050	4.03	3.18	2.79	2.56	2.40	2.29	2.20	2.13	2.07
	.025	5.34	3.97	3.39	3.05	2.83	2.67	2.55	2.46	2.38
	.010	7.17	5.06	4.20	3.72	3.41	3.19	3.02	2.89	2.78
	.001	12.22	7.96	6.34	5.46	4.90	4.51	4.22	4.00	3.82
60	.100	2.79	2.39	2.18	2.04	1.95	1.87	1.82	1.77	1.74
	.050	4.00	3.15	2.76	2.53	2.37	2.25	2.17	2.10	2.04
	.025	5.29	3.93	3.34	3.01	2.79	2.63	2.51	2.41	2.33
	.010	7.08	4.98	4.13	3.65	3.34	3.12	2.95	2.82	2.72
	.001	11.97	7.77	6.17	5.31	4.76	4.37	4.09	3.86	3.69
100	.100	2.76	2.36	2.14	2.00	1.91	1.83	1.78	1.73	1.69
	.050	3.94	3.09	2.70	2.46	2.31	2.19	2.10	2.03	1.97
	.025	5.18	3.83	3.25	2.92	2.70	2.54	2.42	2.32	2.24
	.010	6.90	4.82	3.98	3.51	3.21	2.99	2.82	2.69	2.59
	.001	11.50	7.41	5.86	5.02	4.48	4.11	3.83	3.61	3.44
200	.100	2.73	2.33	2.11	1.97	1.88	1.80	1.75	1.70	1.66
	.050	3.89	3.04	2.65	2.42	2.26	2.14	2.06	1.98	1.93
	.025	5.10	3.76	3.18	2.85	2.63	2.47	2.35	2.26	2.18
	.010	6.76	4.71	3.88	3.41	3.11	2.89	2.73	2.60	2.50
	.001	11.15	7.15	5.63	4.81	4.29	3.92	3.65	3.43	3.26
1000	.100	2.71	2.31	2.09	1.95	1.85	1.78	1.72	1.68	1.64
	.050	3.85	3.00	2.61	2.38	2.22	2.11	2.02	1.95	1.89
	.025	5.04	3.70	3.13	2.80	2.58	2.42	2.30	2.20	2.13
	.010	6.66	4.63	3.80	3.34	3.04	2.82	2.66	2.53	2.43
	.001	10.89	6.96	5.46	4.65	4.14	3.78	3.51	3.30	3.13

Table A10 *F* critical values (continued)

		Degrees of freedom in the numerator										
Degrees of freedom in the denominator	**p**	**10**	**12**	**15**	**20**	**25**	**30**	**40**	**50**	**60**	**120**	**1000**
50	.100	1.73	1.68	1.63	1.57	1.53	1.50	1.46	1.44	1.42	1.38	1.33
	.050	2.03	1.95	1.87	1.78	1.73	1.69	1.63	1.60	1.58	1.51	1.45
	.025	2.32	2.22	2.11	1.99	1.92	1.87	1.80	1.75	1.72	1.64	1.56
	.010	2.70	2.56	2.42	2.27	2.17	2.10	2.01	1.95	1.91	1.80	1.70
	.001	3.67	3.44	3.20	2.95	2.79	2.68	2.53	2.44	2.38	2.21	2.05
60	.100	1.71	1.66	1.60	1.54	1.50	1.48	1.44	1.41	1.40	1.35	1.30
	.050	1.99	1.92	1.84	1.75	1.69	1.65	1.59	1.56	1.53	1.47	1.40
	.025	2.27	2.17	2.06	1.94	1.87	1.82	1.74	1.70	1.67	1.58	1.49
	.010	2.63	2.50	2.35	2.20	2.10	2.03	1.94	1.88	1.84	1.73	1.62
	.001	3.54	3.32	3.08	2.83	2.67	2.55	2.41	2.32	2.25	2.08	1.92
100	.100	1.66	1.61	1.56	1.49	1.45	1.42	1.38	1.35	1.34	1.28	1.22
	.050	1.93	1.85	1.77	1.68	1.62	1.57	1.52	1.48	1.45	1.38	1.30
	.025	2.18	2.08	1.97	1.85	1.77	1.71	1.64	1.59	1.56	1.46	1.36
	.010	2.50	2.37	2.22	2.07	1.97	1.89	1.80	1.74	1.69	1.57	1.45
	.001	3.30	3.07	2.84	2.59	2.43	2.32	2.17	2.08	2.01	1.83	1.64
200	.100	1.63	1.58	1.52	1.46	1.41	1.38	1.34	1.31	1.29	1.23	1.16
	.050	1.88	1.80	1.72	1.62	1.56	1.52	1.46	1.41	1.39	1.30	1.21
	.025	2.11	2.01	1.90	1.78	1.70	1.64	1.56	1.51	1.47	1.37	1.25
	.010	2.41	2.27	2.13	1.97	1.87	1.79	1.69	1.63	1.58	1.45	1.30
	.001	3.12	2.90	2.67	2.42	2.26	2.15	2.00	1.90	1.83	1.64	1.43
1000	.100	1.61	1.55	1.49	1.43	1.38	1.35	1.30	1.27	1.25	1.18	1.08
	.050	1.84	1.76	1.68	1.58	1.52	1.47	1.41	1.36	1.33	1.24	1.11
	.025	2.06	1.96	1.85	1.72	1.64	1.58	1.50	1.45	1.41	1.29	1.13
	.010	2.34	2.20	2.06	1.90	1.79	1.72	1.61	1.54	1.50	1.35	1.16
	.001	2.99	2.77	2.54	2.30	2.14	2.02	1.87	1.77	1.69	1.49	1.22

Numerical entries represent the probability that a standard normal random variable is between 0 and *z* where $z = \frac{x - \mu}{\sigma}$.

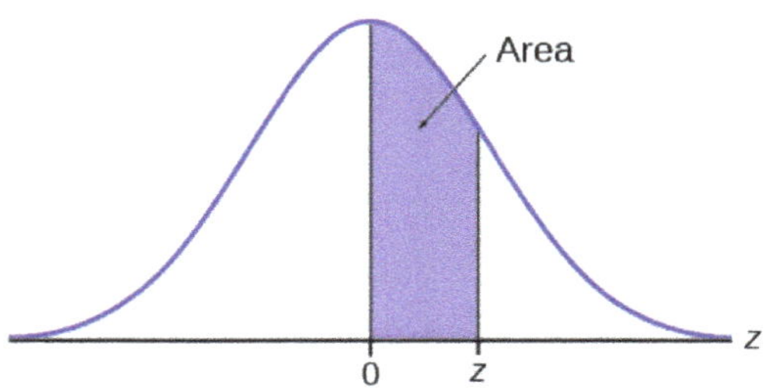

Figure A2

Standard Normal Probability Distribution: *Z* Table

Table A11 Standard Normal Distribution

z	0.00	0.01	0.02	0.03	0.04	0.05	0.06	0.07	0.08	0.09
0.0	0.0000	0.0040	0.0080	0.0120	0.0160	0.0199	0.0239	0.0279	0.0319	0.0359
0.1	0.0398	0.0438	0.0478	0.0517	0.0557	0.0596	0.0636	0.0675	0.0714	0.0753
0.2	0.0793	0.0832	0.0871	0.0910	0.0948	0.0987	0.1026	0.1064	0.1103	0.1141
0.3	0.1179	0.1217	0.1255	0.1293	0.1331	0.1368	0.1406	0.1443	0.1480	0.1517
0.4	0.1554	0.1591	0.1628	0.1664	0.1700	0.1736	0.1772	0.1808	0.1844	0.1879
0.5	0.1915	0.1950	0.1985	0.2019	0.2054	0.2088	0.2123	0.2157	0.2190	0.2224
0.6	0.2257	0.2291	0.2324	0.2357	0.2389	0.2422	0.2454	0.2486	0.2517	0.2549
0.7	0.2580	0.2611	0.2642	0.2673	0.2704	0.2734	0.2764	0.2794	0.2823	0.2852
0.8	0.2881	0.2910	0.2939	0.2967	0.2995	0.3023	0.3051	0.3078	0.3106	0.3133
0.9	0.3159	0.3186	0.3212	0.3238	0.3264	0.3289	0.3315	0.3340	0.3365	0.3389
1.0	0.3413	0.3438	0.3461	0.3485	0.3508	0.3531	0.3554	0.3577	0.3599	0.3621
1.1	0.3643	0.3665	0.3686	0.3708	0.3729	0.3749	0.3770	0.3790	0.3810	0.3830
1.2	0.3849	0.3869	0.3888	0.3907	0.3925	0.3944	0.3962	0.3980	0.3997	0.4015
1.3	0.4032	0.4049	0.4066	0.4082	0.4099	0.4115	0.4131	0.4147	0.4162	0.4177
1.4	0.4192	0.4207	0.4222	0.4236	0.4251	0.4265	0.4279	0.4292	0.4306	0.4319
1.5	0.4332	0.4345	0.4357	0.4370	0.4382	0.4394	0.4406	0.4418	0.4429	0.4441
1.6	0.4452	0.4463	0.4474	0.4484	0.4495	0.4505	0.4515	0.4525	0.4535	0.4545
1.7	0.4554	0.4564	0.4573	0.4582	0.4591	0.4599	0.4608	0.4616	0.4625	0.4633
1.8	0.4641	0.4649	0.4656	0.4664	0.4671	0.4678	0.4686	0.4693	0.4699	0.4706
1.9	0.4713	0.4719	0.4726	0.4732	0.4738	0.4744	0.4750	0.4756	0.4761	0.4767
2.0	0.4772	0.4778	0.4783	0.4788	0.4793	0.4798	0.4803	0.4808	0.4812	0.4817
2.1	0.4821	0.4826	0.4830	0.4834	0.4838	0.4842	0.4846	0.4850	0.4854	0.4857
2.2	0.4861	0.4864	0.4868	0.4871	0.4875	0.4878	0.4881	0.4884	0.4887	0.4890
2.3	0.4893	0.4896	0.4898	0.4901	0.4904	0.4906	0.4909	0.4911	0.4913	0.4916
2.4	0.4918	0.4920	0.4922	0.4925	0.4927	0.4929	0.4931	0.4932	0.4934	0.4936
2.5	0.4938	0.4940	0.4941	0.4943	0.4945	0.4946	0.4948	0.4949	0.4951	0.4952
2.6	0.4953	0.4955	0.4956	0.4957	0.4959	0.4960	0.4961	0.4962	0.4963	0.4964
2.7	0.4965	0.4966	0.4967	0.4968	0.4969	0.4970	0.4971	0.4972	0.4973	0.4974
2.8	0.4974	0.4975	0.4976	0.4977	0.4977	0.4978	0.4979	0.4979	0.4980	0.4981
2.9	0.4981	0.4982	0.4982	0.4983	0.4984	0.4984	0.4985	0.4985	0.4986	0.4986
3.0	0.4987	0.4987	0.4987	0.4988	0.4988	0.4989	0.4989	0.4989	0.4990	0.4990
3.1	0.4990	0.4991	0.4991	0.4991	0.4992	0.4992	0.4992	0.4992	0.4993	0.4993
3.2	0.4993	0.4993	0.4994	0.4994	0.4994	0.4994	0.4994	0.4995	0.4995	0.4995
3.3	0.4995	0.4995	0.4995	0.4996	0.4996	0.4996	0.4996	0.4996	0.4996	0.4997
3.4	0.4997	0.4997	0.4997	0.4997	0.4997	0.4997	0.4997	0.4997	0.4997	0.4998

Student's *t* Distribution

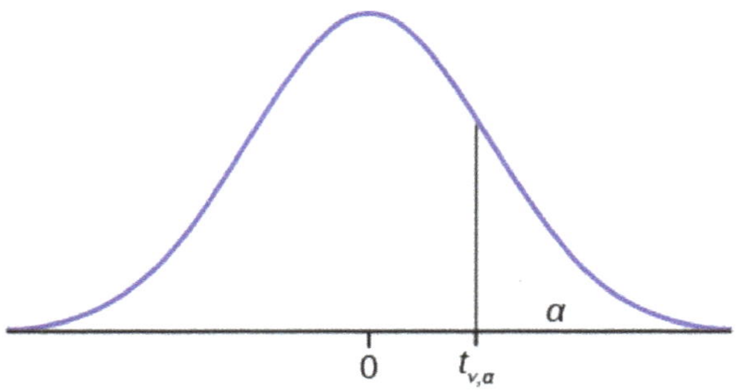

Figure A3 Upper critical values of Student's *t* Distribution with *v* Degrees of Freedom

For selected probabilities, *a*, the table shows the values $t_{v,a}$ such that $P(t_v > t_{v,a}) = a$, where t_v is a Student's *t* random variable with *v* degrees of freedom. For example, the probability is .10 that a Student's *t* random variable with 10 degrees of freedom exceeds 1.372.

Table A12 Probability of Exceeding the Critical Value NIST/SEMATECH e-Handbook of Statistical Methods, http://www.itl.nist.gov/div898/handbook/, September 2011.

v	0.10	0.05	0.025	0.01	0.005	0.001
1	3.078	6.314	12.706	31.821	63.657	318.313
2	1.886	2.920	4.303	6.965	9.925	22.327
3	1.638	2.353	3.182	4.541	5.841	10.215
4	1.533	2.132	2.776	3.747	4.604	7.173
5	1.476	2.015	2.571	3.365	4.032	5.893
6	1.440	1.943	2.447	3.143	3.707	5.208
7	1.415	1.895	2.365	2.998	3.499	4.782
8	1.397	1.860	2.306	2.896	3.355	4.499
9	1.383	1.833	2.262	2.821	3.250	4.296
10	1.372	1.812	2.228	2.764	3.169	4.143
11	1.363	1.796	2.201	2.718	3.106	4.024
12	1.356	1.782	2.179	2.681	3.055	3.929
13	1.350	1.771	2.160	2.650	3.012	3.852
14	1.345	1.761	2.145	2.624	2.977	3.787
15	1.341	1.753	2.131	2.602	2.947	3.733
16	1.337	1.746	2.120	2.583	2.921	3.686
17	1.333	1.740	2.110	2.567	2.898	3.646
18	1.330	1.734	2.101	2.552	2.878	3.610
19	1.328	1.729	2.093	2.539	2.861	3.579
20	1.325	1.725	2.086	2.528	2.845	3.552
21	1.323	1.721	2.080	2.518	2.831	3.527
22	1.321	1.717	2.074	2.508	2.819	3.505
23	1.319	1.714	2.069	2.500	2.807	3.485
24	1.318	1.711	2.064	2.492	2.797	3.467

v	0.10	0.05	0.025	0.01	0.005	0.001
25	1.316	1.708	2.060	2.485	2.787	3.450
26	1.315	1.706*	2.056	2.479	2.779	3.435
27	1.314	1.703	2.052	2.473	2.771	3.421
28	1.313	1.701	2.048	2.467	2.763	3.408
29	1.311	1.699	2.045	2.462	2.756	3.396
30	1.310	1.697	2.042	2.457	2.750	3.385
40	1.303	1.684	2.021	2.423	2.704	3.307
60	1.296	1.671	2.000	2.390	2.660	3.232
100	1.290	1.660	1.984	2.364	2.626	3.174
∞	1.282	1.645	1.960	2.326	2.576	3.090

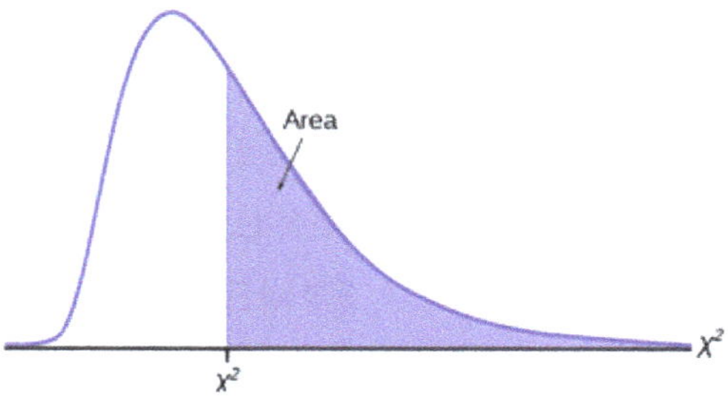

FigureA4

χ^2 Probability Distribution

Table A13 Area to the Right of the Critical Value of χ^2

df	0.995	0.990	0.975	0.950	0.900	0.100	0.050	0.025	0.010	0.005
1	0.000	0.000	0.001	0.004	0.016	2.706	3.841	5.024	6.635	7.879
2	0.010	0.020	0.051	0.103	0.211	4.605	5.991	7.378	9.210	10.597
3	0.072	0.115	0.216	0.352	0.584	6.251	7.815	9.348	11.345	12.838
4	0.207	0.297	0.484	0.711	1.064	7.779	9.488	11.143	13.277	14.860
5	0.412	0.554	0.831	1.145	1.610	9.236	11.070	12.833	15.086	16.750
6	0.676	0.872	1.237	1.635	2.204	10.645	12.592	14.449	16.812	18.548
7	0.989	1.239	1.690	2.167	2.833	12.017	14.067	16.013	18.475	20.278
8	1.344	1.646	2.180	2.733	3.490	13.362	15.507	17.535	20.090	21.955
9	1.735	2.088	2.700	3.325	4.168	14.684	16.919	19.023	21.666	23.589
10	2.156	2.558	3.247	3.940	4.865	15.987	18.307	20.483	23.209	25.188
11	2.603	3.053	3.816	4.575	5.578	17.275	19.675	21.920	24.725	26.757
12	3.074	3.571	4.404	5.226	6.304	18.549	21.026	23.337	26.217	28.300
13	3.565	4.107	5.009	5.892	7.042	19.812	22.362	24.736	27.688	29.819
14	4.075	4.660	5.629	6.571	7.790	21.064	23.685	26.119	29.141	31.319
15	4.601	5.229	6.262	7.261	8.547	22.307	24.996	27.488	30.578	32.801
16	5.142	5.812	6.908	7.962	9.312	23.542	26.296	28.845	32.000	34.267
17	5.697	6.408	7.564	8.672	10.085	24.769	27.587	30.191	33.409	35.718
18	6.265	7.015	8.231	9.390	10.865	25.989	28.869	31.526	34.805	37.156
19	6.844	7.633	8.907	10.117	11.651	27.204	30.144	32.852	36.191	38.582
20	7.434	8.260	9.591	10.851	12.443	28.412	31.410	34.170	37.566	39.997
21	8.034	8.897	10.283	11.591	13.240	29.615	32.671	35.479	38.932	41.401

df	0.995	0.990	0.975	0.950	0.900	0.100	0.050	0.025	0.010	0.005
22	8.643	9.542	10.982	12.338	14.041	30.813	33.924	36.781	40.289	42.796
23	9.260	10.196	11.689	13.091	14.848	32.007	35.172	38.076	41.638	44.181
24	9.886	10.856	12.401	13.848	15.659	33.196	36.415	39.364	42.980	45.559
25	10.520	11.524	13.120	14.611	16.473	34.382	37.652	40.646	44.314	46.928
26	11.160	12.198	13.844	15.379	17.292	35.563	38.885	41.923	45.642	48.290
27	11.808	12.879	14.573	16.151	18.114	36.741	40.113	43.195	46.963	49.645
28	12.461	13.565	15.308	16.928	18.939	37.916	41.337	44.461	48.278	50.993
29	13.121	14.256	16.047	17.708	19.768	39.087	42.557	45.722	49.588	52.336
30	13.787	14.953	16.791	18.493	20.599	40.256	43.773	46.979	50.892	53.672
40	20.707	22.164	24.433	26.509	29.051	51.805	55.758	59.342	63.691	66.766
50	27.991	29.707	32.357	34.764	37.689	63.167	67.505	71.420	76.154	79.490
60	35.534	37.485	40.482	43.188	46.459	74.397	79.082	83.298	88.379	91.952
70	43.275	45.442	48.758	51.739	55.329	85.527	90.531	95.023	100.425	104.215
80	51.172	53.540	57.153	60.391	64.278	96.578	101.879	106.629	112.329	116.321
90	59.196	61.754	65.647	69.126	73.291	107.565	113.145	118.136	124.116	128.299
100	67.328	70.065	74.222	77.929	82.358	118.498	124.342	129.561	135.807	140.169

APPENDIX B:
MATHEMATICAL PHRASES, SYMBOLS, AND FORMULAS

English Phrases Written Mathematically

Table B1

When the English says:	Interpret this as:
X is at least 4.	$X \geq 4$
The minimum of X is 4.	$X \geq 4$
X is no less than 4.	$X \geq 4$
X is greater than or equal to 4.	$X \geq 4$
X is at most 4.	$X \leq 4$
The maximum of X is 4.	$X \leq 4$
X is no more than 4.	$X \leq 4$
X is less than or equal to 4.	$X \leq 4$
X does not exceed 4.	$X \leq 4$
X is greater than 4.	$X > 4$
X is more than 4.	$X > 4$
X exceeds 4.	$X > 4$
X is less than 4.	$X < 4$
There are fewer X than 4.	$X < 4$
X is 4.	$X = 4$
X is equal to 4.	$X = 4$
X is the same as 4.	$X = 4$
X is not 4.	$X \neq 4$

When the English says:	Interpret this as:
X is not equal to 4.	$X \neq 4$
X is not the same as 4.	$X \neq 4$
X is different than 4.	$X \neq 4$

Symbols and Their Meanings

Table B2 Symbols and their Meanings

Chapter (1st used)	Symbol	Spoken	Meaning
Sampling and Data	√	The square root of	same
Sampling and Data	Π	Pi	3.14159... (a specific number)
Descriptive Statistics	Q1	Quartile one	the first quartile
Descriptive Statistics	Q2	Quartile two	the second quartile
Descriptive Statistics	Q3	Quartile three	the third quartile
Descriptive Statistics	IQR	interquartile range	Q3 – Q1 = IQR
Descriptive Statistics	x-x-	x-bar	sample mean
Descriptive Statistics	μμ	mu	population mean
Descriptive Statistics	s	s	sample standard deviation
Descriptive Statistics	s2	s squared	sample variance
Descriptive Statistics	σσ	sigma	population standard deviation
Descriptive Statistics	σ2σ2	sigma squared	population variance
Descriptive Statistics	ΣΣ	capital sigma	sum
Probability Topics	{}	brackets	set notation
Probability Topics	*S*	S	sample space
Probability Topics	*A*	Event A	event A
Probability Topics	P(A)	probability of A	probability of A occurring
Probability Topics	P(A|B)	probability of A given B	prob. of A occurring given B has occurred
Probability Topics	P(A∪B)	prob. of A or B	prob. of A or B or both occurring
Probability Topics	P(A∩B)	prob. of A and B	prob. of both A and B occurring (same time)
Probability Topics	A'	A-prime, complement of A	complement of A, not A
Probability Topics	P(A')	prob. of complement of A	same
Probability Topics	G1	green on first pick	same
Probability Topics	P(G1)	prob. of green on first pick	same
Discrete Random Variables	PDF	prob. density function	same
Discrete Random Variables	X	X	the random variable X
Discrete Random Variables	X ~	the distribution of X	same

Chapter (1st used)	Symbol	Spoken	Meaning
Discrete Random Variables	≥	greater than or equal to	same
Discrete Random Variables	≤	less than or equal to	same
Discrete Random Variables	=	equal to	same
Discrete Random Variables	≠	not equal to	same
Continuous Random Variables	*f*(*x*)	f of x	function of x
Continuous Random Variables	pdf	prob. density function	same
Continuous Random Variables	*U*	uniform distribution	same
Continuous Random Variables	*Exp*	exponential distribution	same
Continuous Random Variables	*f*(*x*) =	f of x equals	same
Continuous Random Variables	*m*	m	decay rate (for exp. dist.)
The Normal Distribution	*N*	normal distribution	same
The Normal Distribution	*z*	z-score	same
The Normal Distribution	*Z*	standard normal dist.	same
The Central Limit Theorem	X–X–	X-bar	the random variable X-bar
The Central Limit Theorem	μx–μx–	mean of X-bars	the average of X-bars
The Central Limit Theorem	σx–σx–	standard deviation of X-bars	same
Confidence Intervals	*CL*	confidence level	same
Confidence Intervals	*CI*	confidence interval	same
Confidence Intervals	*EBM*	error bound for a mean	same
Confidence Intervals	*EBP*	error bound for a proportion	same
Confidence Intervals	*t*	Student's t-distribution	same
Confidence Intervals	*df*	degrees of freedom	same
Confidence Intervals	tα2tα2	student t with $\alpha/2$ area in right tail	same
Confidence Intervals	p′p′	p-prime	sample proportion of success
Confidence Intervals	q′q′	q-prime	sample proportion of failure
Hypothesis Testing	H0H0	H-naught, H-sub 0	null hypothesis
Hypothesis Testing	HaHa	H-a, H-sub a	alternate hypothesis
Hypothesis Testing	H1H1	H-1, H-sub 1	alternate hypothesis
Hypothesis Testing	αα	alpha	probability of Type I error
Hypothesis Testing	ββ	beta	probability of Type II error
Hypothesis Testing	X2X2	X1-bar minus X2-bar	difference in sample means

Chapter (1st used)	Symbol	Spoken	Meaning
Hypothesis Testing	$\mu 1-\mu 2$	mu-1 minus mu-2	difference in population means
Hypothesis Testing	$P'1-P'2$	P1-prime minus P2-prime	difference in sample proportions
Hypothesis Testing	$p1-p2$	p1 minus p2	difference in population proportions
Chi-Square Distribution	X2$X2$	Ky-square	Chi-square
Chi-Square Distribution	OO	Observed	Observed frequency
Chi-Square Distribution	EE	Expected	Expected frequency
Linear Regression and Correlation	$y = a + bx$	y equals a plus b-x	equation of a straight line
Linear Regression and Correlation	y^y^	y-hat	estimated value of y
Linear Regression and Correlation	rr	sample correlation coefficient	same
Linear Regression and Correlation	εε	error term for a regression line	same
Linear Regression and Correlation	SSE	Sum of Squared Errors	same
F-Distribution and ANOVA	F	F-ratio	F-ratio

Formulas
Table B3

Symbols you must know Population		Sample
NN	Size	nn
μμ	Mean	x—x_
σ2$\sigma 2$	Variance	s2$s2$
σσ	Standard deviation	ss
pp	Proportion	p'p'
Single data set formulae **Population**		**Sample**
$\mu = E(x) = \frac{1}{N}\sum_{i=1}^{N}(x_i)$	Arithmetic mean	$\bar{x} = \frac{1}{n}\sum_{i=1}^{n}(x_i)$
	Geometric mean	$\tilde{x} = \left(\prod_{i=1}^{n} X_i\right)^{\frac{1}{n}}$

$Q_3 = \frac{3(n+1)}{4}$, $Q_1 = \frac{(n+1)}{4}$	Inter-quartile range IQR=Q3-Q1	$Q_3 = \frac{3(n+1)}{4}$, $Q_1 = \frac{(n+1)}{4}$
$\sigma^2 = \frac{1}{N}\sum_{i=1}^{N}(x_i-\mu)^2$	Variance	$s^2 = \frac{1}{n}\sum_{i=1}^{n}(x_i-\bar{x})^2$
Single data set formulae		
Population		**Sample**
$\mu = E(x) = \frac{1}{N}\sum_{i=1}^{N}(m_i * f_i)$	Arithmetic mean	$\bar{x} = \frac{1}{n}\sum_{i=1}^{n}(m_i * f_i)$
	Geometric mean	$\tilde{x} = \left(\prod_{i=1}^{n} X_i\right)^{\frac{1}{n}}$
$\sigma^2 = \frac{1}{N}\sum_{i=1}^{N}(m_i-\mu)^2 * f_i$	Variance	$s^2 = \frac{1}{n}\sum_{i=1}^{n}(m_i-\bar{x})^2 * f_i$
$CV = \frac{\sigma}{\mu} * 100$	Coefficient of variation	$CV = \frac{s}{\bar{x}} * 100$

Table B4

Basic probability rules	
$P(A \cap B)=P(A\mid B)\cdot P(B)$	Multiplication rule
$P(A \cup B)=P(A)+P(B)-P(A \cap B)$	Addition rule
$\cdot P(B)$ or $P(A\mid B)=P(A)P(A\mid B)=P(A)$	Independence test
Hypergeometric distribution formulae	
$nCx = \binom{n}{x} = \frac{n!}{x!(n-x)!}$	Combinatorial equation
$P(x) = \frac{\binom{A}{x}\binom{N-A}{n-x}}{\binom{N}{n}}$	Probability equation
$E(X)=\mu=np$	Mean
$\sigma^2 = \left(\frac{N-n}{N-1}\right)np(q)$	Variance
Binomial distribution formulae	
$P(x) = \frac{n!}{x!(n-x)!}p^x(q)^{n-x}$	Probability density function

$E(X) = \mu = np$	Arithmetic mean
$\sigma^2 = np(q)$	Variance

Geometric distribution formulae

$P(X = x) = (1-p)^{x-1}(p)$	Probability when xx is the first success.	Probability when xx is the number of failures before first success	$P(X = x) = (1-p)^x(p)$
$\mu = \frac{1}{p}$	Mean	Mean	$\mu = \frac{1-p}{p}$
$\sigma^2 = \frac{(1-p)}{p^2}$	Variance	Variance	$\sigma^2 = \frac{(1-p)}{p^2}$

Poisson distribution formulae

$P(x) = \frac{e^{-\mu}\mu^x}{x!}$	Probability equation
E(X)=μ$E(X)=\mu$	Mean
σ2=μ	Variance

Uniform distribution formulae

$f(x) = \frac{1}{b-a}$ for $a \leq x \leq b$	PDF
$E(X) = \mu = \frac{a+b}{2}$	Mean
$\sigma^2 = \frac{(b-a)^2}{12}$	Variance

Exponential distribution formulae

$P(X \leq x) = 1 - e^{-mx}$	Cumulative probability
$E(X) = \mu = \frac{1}{m}$ or $m = \frac{1}{\mu}$	Mean and decay factor
$\sigma^2 = \frac{1}{m^2} = \mu^2$	Variance

Table B5

The following page of formulae requires the use of the "Z", "t", "χ^2" or "F" tables.	
$Z = \frac{x-\mu}{\sigma}$	Z-transformation for normal distribution
$Z = \frac{x-np}{\sqrt{np'(q')}}$	Normal approximation to the binomial
Probability (ignores subscripts) Hypothesis testing	Confidence intervals [bracketed symbols equal margin of error] (subscripts denote locations on respective distribution tables)

$Z_c = \frac{\bar{x} - \mu_0}{\frac{\sigma}{\sqrt{n}}}$	Interval for the population mean when sigma is known $\bar{x} \pm \left[Z_{(\alpha/2)} \frac{\sigma}{\sqrt{n}}\right]$
$Z_c = \frac{\bar{x} - \mu_0}{\frac{s}{\sqrt{n}}}$	Interval for the population mean when sigma is unknown but n> $\bar{x} \pm \left[Z_{(\alpha/2)} \frac{s}{\sqrt{n}}\right]$
$t_c = \frac{\bar{x} - \mu_0}{\frac{s}{\sqrt{n}}}$	Interval for the population mean when sigma is unknown but n< $\bar{x} \pm \left[t_{(n-1),(\alpha/2)} \frac{s}{\sqrt{n}}\right]$
$Z_c = \frac{p' - p_0}{\sqrt{\frac{p_0 q_0}{n}}}$	Interval for the population proportion $p' \pm \left[Z_{(\alpha/2)} \sqrt{\frac{p'q'}{n}}\right]$
$t_c = \frac{\bar{d} - \delta_0}{s_d}$	Interval for difference between two means with matched pairs $\bar{d} \pm \left[t_{(n-1),(\alpha/2)} \frac{s_d}{\sqrt{n}}\right]$ where *sd* is the deviation of the differences
$Z_c = \frac{(\bar{x}_1 - \bar{x}_2) - \delta_0}{\sqrt{\frac{\sigma_1^2}{n_1} + \frac{\sigma_2^2}{n_2}}}$	Interval for difference between two means when sigmas are known $(\bar{x}_1 - \bar{x}_2) \pm \left[Z_{(\alpha/2)} \sqrt{\frac{\sigma_1^2}{n_1} + \frac{\sigma_2^2}{n_2}}\right]$
$t_c = \frac{(\bar{x}_1 - \bar{x}_2) - \delta_0}{\sqrt{\left(\frac{(s_1)^2}{n_1} + \frac{(s_2)^2}{n_2}\right)}}$	Interval for difference between two means with equal variances when sigmas are unknown $(\bar{x}_1 - \bar{x}_2) \pm \left[t_{df,(\alpha/2)} \sqrt{\left(\frac{(s_1)^2}{n_1} + \frac{(s_2)^2}{n_2}\right)}\right]$ where $df = \frac{\left(\frac{(s_1)^2}{n_1} + \frac{(s_2)^2}{n_2}\right)^2}{\left(\frac{1}{n_1 - 1}\right)\left(\frac{(s_1)^2}{n_1}\right)^2 + \left(\frac{1}{n_2 - 1}\right)\left(\frac{(s_2)^2}{n_2}\right)^2}$
$Z_c = \frac{(p'_1 - p'_2) - \delta_0}{\sqrt{\frac{p'_1(q'_1)}{n_1} + \frac{p'_2(q'_2)}{n_2}}}$	Interval for difference between two population proportions $(p'_1 - p'_2) \pm \left[Z_{(\alpha/2)} \sqrt{\frac{p'_1(q'_1)}{n_1} + \frac{p'_2(q'_2)}{n_2}}\right]$
$\chi^2_c = \frac{(n-1)s^2}{\sigma_0^2}$	Tests for GOF, Independence, and Homogeneity $\chi^2_c = \Sigma \frac{(O-E)^2}{E}$ Ewhere O = observed values and E = expected values
$F_c = \frac{s_1^2}{s_2^2}$	Where s21 is the sample variance which is the larger of the two sample variances

The next 3 formulae are for determining sample size with confidence intervals. (note: E represents the margin of error)		
$n = \frac{Z^2_{\left(\frac{a}{2}\right)}\sigma^2}{E^2}$ Use when sigma is known $E=x^{-}-\mu$	$n = \frac{Z^2_{\left(\frac{a}{2}\right)}(0.25)}{E^2}$ Use when p′p′ is unknown $E=p'-p$	$n = \frac{Z^2_{\left(\frac{a}{2}\right)}[p'(q')]}{E^2}$ Use when p′p′ is unknown $E=p'-p$

Table B6

Simple linear regression formulae for y=a+b(x)$y=a+b(x)$	
$r = \frac{\Sigma\left[\left(x-\bar{x}\right)\left(y-\bar{y}\right)\right]}{\sqrt{\Sigma\left(x-\bar{x}\right)^2 * \Sigma\left(y-\bar{y}\right)^2}} = \frac{S_{xy}}{S_x S_y} = \sqrt{\frac{SSR}{SST}}$	Correlation coefficient
$b = \frac{\Sigma\left[\left(x-\bar{x}\right)\left(y-\bar{y}\right)\right]}{\Sigma\left(x-\bar{x}\right)^2} = \frac{S_{xy}}{SS_x} = r_{y,x}\left(\frac{s_y}{s_x}\right)$	Coefficient b (slope)
$a = \bar{y} - b\left(\bar{x}\right)$	y-intercept
$s_e^2 = \frac{\Sigma\left(y_i - \hat{y}_i\right)^2}{n-k} = \frac{\sum_{i=1}^{n} e_i^2}{n-k}$	Estimate of the error variance
$S_b = \frac{s_e^2}{\sqrt{\left(x_i-\bar{x}\right)^2}} = \frac{s_e^2}{\left(n-1\right)s_x^2}$	Standard error for coefficient *b*
$t_c = \frac{b-\beta_0}{s_b}$	Hypothesis test for coefficient *β*
$b \pm \left[t_{n-2,\, a/2} S_b\right]$	Interval for coefficient *β*
$\hat{y} \pm \left[t_{a/2} * s_e\left(\sqrt{\frac{1}{n} + \frac{\left(x_p-\bar{x}\right)^2}{s_x}}\right)\right]$	Interval for expected value of y
$\hat{y} \pm \left[t_{a/2} * s_e\left(\sqrt{1 + \frac{1}{n} + \frac{\left(x_p-\bar{x}\right)^2}{s_x}}\right)\right]$	Prediction interval for an individual y

ANOVA formulae	
$SSR = \sum_{i=1}^{n}(\hat{y}_i - \bar{y})^2$	Sum of squares regression
$SSE = \sum_{i=1}^{n}(\hat{y}_i - \bar{y}_i)^2$	Sum of squares error
$SST = \sum_{i=1}^{n}(y_i - \bar{y})^2$	Sum of squares total
$R^2 = \frac{SSR}{SST}$	Coefficient of determination

Table B7

The following is the breakdown of a one-way ANOVA table for linear regression.				
Source of variation	**Sum of squares**	**Degrees of freedom**	**Mean squares**	**F-ratio**
Regression	SSR	1 or$k$-1	$MSR = \frac{SSR}{df_R}$	$F = \frac{MSR}{MSE}$
Error	SSE	n-k	$MSE = \frac{SSE}{df_E}$	
Total	SST	n-1		

INDEX

D

F

G